A MOST STIRRING AND SIGNIFICANT EPISODE

A MOST STIRRING <u>AND</u> SIGNIFICANT EPISODE

RELIGION AND THE RISE AND FALL OF PROHIBITION IN BLACK ATLANTA, 1865–1887

H. PAUL THOMPSON, JR.

NIU
PRESS
DeKalb, IL

© 2013 by Northern Illinois University Press
Published by the Northern Illinois University Press, DeKalb, Illinois   60115
Manufactured in the United States using acid-free paper.
All Rights Reserved
Design by Shaun Allshouse

Library of Congress Cataloging-in-Publication Data

Thompson, H. Paul.
A most stirring and significant episode : religion and the rise and fall of prohibition in Black
Atlanta, 1865–1887 / H. Paul Thompson Jr.
p. cm.
Includes bibliographical references and index.
ISBN 978-0-87580-458-3 (cloth) — ISBN 978-1-60909-073-9 (electronic)
1. Prohibition—Georgia—Atlanta—History—19th century. 2. Temperance—Georgia—
Atlanta—History—19th century. 3. Temperance and religion—Georgia—Atlanta—History—
19th century. 4. African Americans—Alcohol use—Georgia—Atlanta—History—19th
century. 5. African Americans—Religion—History—19th century. 6. African Americans—
Social conditions—19th century. I. Title.
HV5090.G4T46 2012
363.4'1089960730758231—dc23
2012030682

To God be the Glory

Harold Thompson, in memoriam

For all you have given—
Mary Thompson
Martha Bagley
Robin Rutan-Thompson

Contents

Illustrations   ix

Acknowledgments   xi

Timeline   xiii

Frequently Used Abbreviations   xv

Introduction   3

Part I—Messengers from the North

1—"Our Enterprise Flows from the Gospel of Christ"
*The Evangelical Reform Nexus Roots of Nineteenth-Century Temperance,
1785–1865*   15

2—The Message Trickles South
Introducing the Freed People to Temperance, 1865–1876   45

3—The Trickle Becomes a Flood
Northern Temperance Targets Southern Blacks, 1877–1890   85

Part II—Reformers in the South

4—Taking Ownership
Black Atlanta's Efforts to Institutionalize a Temperance-Based Moral Community   119

5—"The Most Enthusiastic Election Ever Held in This Country"
Atlanta's 1885 Local Option Election   155

6—The "Dry" Years, 1885–1887   196

7—Prohibition Revisited
Atlanta's 1887 Local Option Election   215

Afterword   241

Appendix I: Biographical Sketches of Key Personalities   249

Appendix II: Regulating Atlanta's Liquor Industry, 1865–1907   253

Notes   257

Works Cited   299

Index   317

Illustrations

Figures

Figure 1. Evangelist Charles Finney   23
Figure 2. Brown & Dwyer's Saloon and Hagan & Co.   46
Figure 3. Shermantown   49
Figure 4. Black Settlements, 1870   51
Figure 5. Black Settlements, 1880   52
Figure 6. Storrs School   74
Figure 7. First Congregational Church   77
Figure 8. Friendship Baptist Church   89
Figure 9. William E. Dodge   97
Figure 10. Antoine Graves   103
Figure 11. Reverend J. C. Price   104
Figure 12. Atlanta University Chapel   114
Figure 13. AME Bishop Henry McNeal Turner   138
Figure 14. AME Bishop Wesley J. Gaines   139
Figure 15. Reverend E. R. Carter   140
Figure 16. William A. Pledger   143
Figure 17. Good Samaritan Hall   148
Figure 18. Spelman High School Class of 1888   165
Figure 19. Clark College Class of 1889   166
Figure 20. Jackson McHenry   167
Figure 21. Honorable Jefferson Franklin Long   174
Figure 22. Dr. Roderick Dhu Badger   175
Figure 23. City Brewery (c. 1890)   200
Figure 24. City Brewery's Interracial Workforce (c. 1890)   201
Figure 25. Cartoonist's Perspective on Atlanta's 1887 Local Option Election   225
Figure 26. Anti-Prohibition Handbill, 1887   232

Tables

Table 1. Black Population in Atlanta, 1860–1900   48
Table 2. Atlanta Saloon Ownership   179
Table 3. Atlanta Saloon Employees   180
Table 4. Atlanta Registration for 1884 Municipal Election and 1885 Local Option Election   184

Table 5. Comparison of Atlanta and Fulton County Registration and Voting, 1885   186

Table 6. Local Option Election Results, 1885   187

Table 7. Local Option Registration Compared, 1885 and 1887   233

Table 8. Local Option Election Results, 1887   235

Table II.1. Number of Saloons in Atlanta   254

Table II.2. Average Annual Retail Liquor License Revenue by Decade   255

Graphs

Graph 1. Number of Persons Charged in Atlanta Police Court, July 1886–March 1887   205

Graph 2. Drunkenness as a Percentage of all Charges, July 1886–March 1887   205

Graph 3. Drunkenness as a Percentage of all Charges by Race, July 1886–March 1887   206

Acknowledgments

This book began over ten years ago in the mind of an anxious graduate student, and as in all such endeavors, over the years I have incurred innumerable debts to many wonderful people. While the ideas and arguments within these pages are largely mine, the strength of their articulation draws on untold hours of conversation with friends and mentors and innumerable instances of editing based on their comments.

I first want to honor James Roark, the man who taught me, by example, the meaning of the phrase "a gentleman and a scholar." I will always be grateful for his consummate professionalism, his wise and gentle spirit, and the liberty he granted me to explore my interests wherever they led. I will forever cherish our many conversations about my research and academia in general. Much of the credit for any clarity of writing I achieve must be attributed to E. Brooks Holifield. Dr. Holifield taught me almost everything I know about good academic writing and how to teach it. I thank Leroy Davis for suggesting I visit the Rockefeller Archives Center. It turned out to be an unexpectedly profitable lead in more ways than one.

To my mentors from afar, Jack Blocker, Jr. and David Fahey, I thank you for graciously taking me under your wing, when you did not have to, and molding me into a temperance scholar. Your generous and selfless investment in my scholarship and career truly represents the best academia has to offer.

To those who have read all (Jack Blocker, Jr., Allison Dorsey, Jack Shuler) or parts (Jacqueline Jones, David Fahey, Paul Yandle, Joseph Moore, John Thabiti Willis) of this work in one form or another and provided much generous feedback, a great big thank you! Also, thanks to the anonymous NIU Press reviewers who both praised and challenged me. I really struggled with some of your advice, but I needed it.

One of the unexpected pleasures encountered while writing this book has been to make the acquaintance of Linda Bryan, who, like myself, is a former secondary school teacher. Your enthusiasm for research, great memory, generous spirit, and incredible editing skills are truly amazing and greatly appreciated.

The number of librarians and archivists I've worked with for over a decade now is staggering. Archivists are truly a historian's best friend. Their consistent attentiveness to my ever evolving—and sometimes revolving—research was indispensable.

Thank you Mark, Susan, and the whole NIU Press team for your patience and kindness as I bombarded you with tons of questions. Your timely email responses made the process manageable.

A major part of writing this book has been a seemingly endless series of research trips that almost invariably ended too soon. I have traveled to over 20 archives and research libraries in over half a dozen states to pursue what was supposed to be a "local" research project. On most of these trips, old friends and new have graciously housed me for days—and on occasion, weeks—to defray my research expenses. I owe you all many thanks for putting up with what I am sure were excessively loquacious answers to little-more-than-courteous and perfunctory inquiries about my research. My sincerest gratitude goes to Stacy and Lily Boyd, Dan and Donna Cassidy, Ken and Lori Hoogstra, Jim and Danalee Littel, Bishop David and Rose Karaya, Frank and Jenae McKnight, Rabbi George and Debbie Stern, and Georgia Williams.

I am also thankful for those organizations who believed in me enough to support financially my research: the Rockefeller Archives Center, the Emory University History Department, the Gilder Lehrman Institute for American History, the American Congregational Association/Boston Athenæum Fellowship program, and North Greenville University.

In the spring of 2011 I taught an upper level seminar called "Religion and Reform in Nineteenth-Century America." I had a small group of dedicated, passionate students who made the three-hour class "fly by" every Tuesday evening. They read through every chapter of my manuscript and bravely interrogated my thinking and the articulation of my ideas, ultimately making for a better book. You all were awesome: Sam Andrews, Kimberly Friedrichs, Anna Hoxie, Emily Hoffman, Dianna Murray, and Sarah Scott.

But most of all, I thank my parents, my Aunt Martha, and my wife, Robin, for your prayers and support. I love you all very much. I couldn't have written this book without you.

Timeline

1808—First temperance society formed by Dr. Billy J. Clark and Rev. Lebbeus Armstrong in Moreau, NY

1814—The American Tract Society founded as the New England Tract Society

1816—African Methodist Episcopal Church's first General Conference

1825—Reverend Lyman Beecher preaches *Six Sermons on the Nature, Occasions, Signs, Evil, and Remedy of Intemperance*

1826—American Temperance Society founded

1830–1831—Charles Finney's Rochester, NY, revival

1832—American Baptist Home Mission Society founded

1836—American Temperance Union organized on the teetotal principle

1846—American Missionary Association founded

1851—Maine passes first statewide prohibition law

1865—National Temperance Society and Publication House founded
AME missionary William Gaines arrives in Atlanta and organizes Bethel AME
The first AMA missionary, Frederick Ayer, arrives in Atlanta

1866—Storrs School opened by the American Missionary Association

1867—Frederick Ayer organizes first temperance society in Black Atlanta in the Storrs School

1869—Atlanta University opened by the American Missionary Association
National Prohibition Party founded

1870—First Odd Fellows Lodge organized in Black Atlanta

1871—First Prince Hall Masonic Lodge organized in Black Atlanta

1873—First True Reformer Fountain organized in Black Atlanta

1874—Woman's Christian Temperance Union founded

1875—First Good Samaritans lodge organized in Black Atlanta

1877—Clark University opened by the Methodist Freedmen's Aid Society

1879—Atlanta Baptist Seminary opens

1880—The South's first Colored WCTU chapter established in Atlanta

1881—Spelman Seminary opened by the Women's American Baptist Home Mission Society Missions organizations meet to plan a freed-people-focused temperance campaign
    Frances E. Willard's Southern tour
    Georgia Temperance Convention held in Atlanta

1885—Georgia Temperance Convention held in Atlanta
    Passage of Georgia's General Local Option Law
    Morris Brown College opened by the AME Church
    Fulton County's first local option election, prohibition approved (November 25)

1887—Fulton County's second local option election, prohibition overturned (November 26)

1888—Consultation Convention of Leading Colored Men of Georgia held in Macon, GA

1906—Atlanta Race Riot

1908—State prohibition begins in Georgia (January 1)

Frequently Used Abbreviations

ABHMS—American Baptist Home Mission Society

AMA—American Missionary Association

AME Church—African Methodist Episcopal Church

ATrS—American Tract Society

ATrS-Boston—American Tract Society, Boston Branch

ATrS-NY—American Tract Society, New York Branch

ATS—American Temperance Society

ATU—American Temperance Union

AU—Atlanta University

IOGT—Independent Order of Good Templars

NTS—National Temperance Society and Publication House

STI—Scientific Temperance Instruction

WABHMS—Woman's American Baptist Home Mission Society

WCTU—Woman's Christian Temperance Union

A MOST STIRRING AND SIGNIFICANT EPISODE

Introduction

The decade of the 1880s was both the high-water mark of America's nine-teenth-century temperance and prohibition movement and a uniquely fluid polit-ical space between Reconstruction and the rise of Jim Crow. As such, it produced many dramatic prohibition elections, especially in the South. Among the most prominent were those held in Atlanta, Georgia, in 1885 and 1887. Atlanta is the largest U.S. city to establish prohibition by plebiscite, and African American senti-ment played a pivotal role in both elections. National prohibition's long shadow has unfortunately caused historians and the general public to largely ignore these exciting years of the temperance movement. While this book seeks to close this gap in the scholarship, it is much more than that, for it explores both the processes by which temperance values entered Black Atlanta as well as the community's re-sponse to the politicization of those values. As such, it ambitiously seeks to be a study in the social history of ideas, the limitations of grassroots reform, and the ability of the political process to expose otherwise obscured social and cultural boundaries. But this is also a religious story, for it was evangelical Christian orga-nizations that conveyed the temperance message across chronological, geographic-ic, and cultural boundaries to the freed people. This work lies at the intersection of the study of race, religion, and reform and seeks to engage students of alcohol studies as well as students of American religious history, African American his-tory, Southern history, social history, intellectual history, and urban history.

Like all historical research, this book is crafted from the answers to an intercon-nected set of questions. I initially wanted to know why Atlanta's freed people de-veloped an interest in temperance, given the plethora of other issues with which they had to contend. I learned that schools and churches overseen or operated by Northern evangelicals were constantly promoting temperance, but then I wanted to know if they did so in response to a genuine problem with alcohol abuse or if they were acting out of some preconceived notions about intemperance and/or black people. When some of the freed people adopted this new value orientation, how did their approach to reform compare with that of antebellum whites and blacks? Finally, my questioning climaxed with Atlanta's 1885 and 1887 prohibi-tion votes. The best extant evidence suggests that the majority of blacks voted dry in 1885 and the majority voted wet in 1887, but why did black voters switch sides? My answers offer a structural-functional analysis of the processes by which temperance values entered the lives of black Atlantans and of the rhetoric used during the local option campaigns. Focusing largely on the social contexts of temperance discourse, this book only hints at the impact this new value orientation had on Black Atlanta's internal social relations and institutions and on its relations with white Atlantans.

Temperance was the longest-lasting reform movement of the nineteenth century. Political scientist Thomas R. Rochon argues that the first element of any reform movement is a "critical community" of people who are "united by an overriding concern about a particular issue" but maybe little else. They "think intensively about a particular problem and . . . develop over time a shared understanding of how to view that problem." One movement may have several critical communities. While the "critical community is interested primarily in the development of new values; the movement is interested in winning social and political acceptance for those values" through collective action. Leaders of collective action choose among the ideas generated by the critical communities, reshape and repackage them, and work for cultural change through both social and political venues.

The culture is considered changed when the movement's values are no longer deemed "highly controversial." This is what nineteenth-century temperance reformers hoped to accomplish. The temperance movement began among antebellum whites and spread to African Americans. It experienced its greatest degree of both social and political success in the North. Following the war, Northerners introduced this movement and its values to the freed people. In the antebellum period, evangelical clergy and physicians comprised the first critical community on temperance, and over time theologians, educators, and others formed critical communities. Throughout the antebellum period evangelical thought infused much of the thinking of the critical communities. The social and political manifestations of the movement were seen in the thousands of local temperance societies, the development of a popular temperance culture of public speakers, fiction writers, and popular theater, and the many campaigns for local and state prohibition.[1]

In post-emancipation Black Atlanta, since the clergy were the closest thing to an intelligentsia before 1890, they alone comprised the critical community that defined the problem of intemperance among African Americans. Because 1880s Black Atlanta was so resource-poor, the clergy also had to direct collective social and political action in their community, with some help from non-clerical alumni of the various schools founded by Northerners. At its core, this book is a study of the three components of Black Atlanta's temperance movement: its religio-cultural heritage, the discourse of its critical community, and its collective social and political actions.

During my research I discovered a paucity of historical scholarship on African Americans, alcohol, and temperance prior to the rise of Jim Crow. Most scholars mention these topics as sub-points within studies examining other issues, and only a few have published works focused exclusively on African Americans and alcohol in this period. Donald Yacovone, Denise Herd, Kenneth Christmon, and Shelley Block are among the exceptions. They have identified historical patterns of how African Americans used alcohol and interacted with the temperance movement, and John Hammond Moore, Gregg Cantrell, and James Ivy have published important case studies of 1880s prohibition campaigns.[2]

We do know some important things about blacks, alcohol, and temperance in the nineteenth century. Cantrell has produced the most sophisticated analysis to date of nineteenth-century black prohibition politics, arguing that well-meaning leaders seeking the greatest good for their race could reasonably assume one of three different positions: prohibitionist, anti-prohibitionist, or aloof. One of Herd's most important contributions has been to demonstrate from a study of cirrhosis of the liver that blacks consumed less alcohol than whites in the 1800s. Other writers have identified African Americans' attitudes toward and use of alcohol, but we still lack the scholarly confidence and nuanced understanding that only a large body of monographic literature grounded in specific times and places provides. Hopefully this book will be the first of many such works on blacks, alcohol, and temperance. My goal is to build on the current scholarship by producing a work that places the intimacy of a community study in conversation with the century-long arc of the temperance movement, North and South, black and white.

This work is in conversation with the major schools of temperance scholarship produced by historians and social scientists. It was common through the 1940s for scholars to emphasize the religious roots of temperance. The first professional historians of temperance and prohibition—John Allen Krout, Gilbert Barnes, and Alice Felt Tyler—comprised this school. From the fifties through the seventies, religious explanations for temperance bowed first to sociological explanations rooted in theories about class and status and then to empirical research demonstrating the extensive use of alcohol in the early republic. In the seventies, scholars often explored temperance through the lens of class, and since the eighties gender has become a popular vehicle for teasing out its cultural meaning.[3]

Since the early 1990s scholars have once again reexamined the religious claims of nineteenth-century temperance reformers. This neo-religious school includes, among others, James Rohrer, Robert Abzug, Douglas Carlson, and Michael P. Young.[4] They argue that temperance reformers' biblical and religious discourse, worldview, and organizations must be understood on their own terms and not as a cover for sublimated class, status, or political anxieties or as ruses for cynical attempts at cultural dominance. My work contributes to this neo-religious school in several important ways. First, it argues that temperance's connection to revivalism was more than rhetorical, it was functional. Because many believed abstinence increased the likelihood of an individual's conversion, it became a pragmatic concern among evangelicals to gain converts to temperance as a prelude to gaining converts to Christianity. Second, it demonstrates how the language of temperance flowed directly from Northern pro-revival theology, and the reform became an inalienable tenet of the antebellum evangelical worldview that infused Northerners' work among the freed people. Third, this work shows why it is likely that the religious roots of temperance facilitated its acceptance among the freed people. It argues that intersections between antebellum pro-revival theology and the African elements of the African American worldview facilitated the diffusion of temperance values across racial and cultural boundaries.

Perhaps most importantly, however, I depict the evangelical missionary organizations founded early in the century as influential temperance organizations by showing that even though they were not temperance organizations per se, they effectively promoted the reform as an integral component of their larger spiritual and cultural mission in the antebellum West and the postbellum South. Compared to temperance-specific organizations like the American Temperance Society, American Temperance Union, or even the Woman's Christian Temperance Union, these societies brought far more resources to the movement for a longer period of time and often did so in a winsome manner. I will focus on the American Tract Society, the American Missionary Association, the American Baptist Home Mission Society, and the African Methodist Episcopal Church. Until now, temperance scholars have given scant attention to these groups, yet they distributed free literature, sponsored revivals where abstinence was preached, taught and mandated temperance in their schools and churches, supported efforts to get out the vote during local prohibition plebiscites, and sponsored an untold number of local temperance societies. When their activities are considered alongside the little-known yet important postbellum work of the National Temperance Society and Publication House, which is highlighted in these pages, one sees how the coordinated efforts of these previously invisible "temperance societies" created powerful synergies for the movement.

Another contribution this work seeks to make is to argue that nineteenth-century temperance was not understood by contemporaries as strictly a matter of personal morality but, rather, as an individual moral reform inseparable from its communal implications. Temperance leaders genuinely believed that individual decisions to abstain from alcohol would fundamentally alter local and national community dynamics in ways that could only benefit the entire body politic. Individual pledges to abstain were seen as a means to greater corporate good. Such thinking seemed natural to nineteenth-century Northern white evangelicals and

African Americans, to an extent that is difficult for twenty-first century Americans to fully grasp. This merger of the individual and the communal was a direct outgrowth of pro-revival theology shared by both whites and blacks as well as of the African American worldview.

Early twentieth-century American Protestants jettisoned much of this theology and its practical applications in what Martin Marty has called the "public-private split." Because private ("conservative") Protestants prioritize little more than individual conversion and public ("liberal") ones little more than communal efforts to make the world a better place, it is sometimes difficult for contemporary scholars to appreciate the integrated thinking of nineteenth-century evangelical reformers. I go to great lengths to explicate the theology and ideology of temperance reformers (both white and black) to help the reader discern the foundations, and appreciate the implications, of temperance thought as a cross-cultural value system.[5]

This book has two parts divided into seven chapters. Part I, "Messengers from the North," includes three chapters. I begin by describing what I dub the antebellum "evangelical reform nexus," which was the unique historical convergence of the practices and theology of revivalism and certain elements of republican ideology. In chapter one I describe how temperance and the organizations that brought it to Black Atlanta emerged from this nexus. The reader is introduced to the American Tract Society, American Missionary Association, African Methodist Episcopal Church, American Baptist Home Mission Society, and National Temperance Society and Publication House. In chapters two and three I examine the processes by which these organizations brought the temperance message to Atlanta's freed people. Some attention is also paid to two postbellum organizations: the Woman's Christian Temperance Union and the Woman's American Baptist Home Mission Society.

In part II, "Reformers in the South," I examine Black Atlanta's temperance movement itself, beginning with the critical community of clergy in chapter four and their collective social action. In the last three chapters I explore the efforts of reformers to bring prohibition to Fulton County, including the nature of their overwhelming obstacles.

A Word about Words

Although my narrative begins in New England, the geographic and demographic starting point for my questioning was post-emancipation Black Atlanta. "Black Atlanta" is a term used by academics at least as far back as Jerry J. Thornbery's 1977 dissertation "The Development of Black Atlanta, 1865–1885." It refers to Atlanta's black community: its individuals, institutions, and physical neighborhoods. Allison Dorsey has published the most thorough study of institutional development in nineteenth-century Black Atlanta, and my work builds on her story by showing how those institutions supported the temperance movement and were impacted by it.

Three similar words occur throughout the text: postbellum, post-emancipation, and Reconstruction. Each suggests a slightly different emphasis. I use "postbellum" to refer broadly to the city of Atlanta or the state of Georgia following the Civil War. The term encompasses the experiences of both whites and blacks. "Post-emancipation" specifies the black experience following slavery, and "Reconstruction" refers to the regional or national political period traditionally agreed to have existed from 1865 to 1877. In terms of experiencing a "reconstruction government," Georgia's was one of the shortest in duration, effectively ending in 1871.

Language is one of the most powerful tools historians have to transport readers back in time. I believe the historical actors and my readers are best served if I use the actual language of the period being studied as much as possible, because it preserves the authentic sound of the era. Following emancipation, "freedmen" was generally used to apply to all former slaves, regardless of their gender or age, although the term "freed people" also appeared in print. I will use "freedmen" in the following situations: (1) when it appears in direct quotes, (2) when I am referring only to adult males, and (3) when "freedmen" appears in the proper names of organizations or publications. I also use the generic "freedmen's aid societies," referencing groups that provided relief and assistance to the newly freed slaves, which was also a common phrase from the period.

Another period term that falls uneasily on modern ears is the term "better class" or "better classes." While modern readers might prefer "black elite," or "black middle class," these terms are historically problematic. I concur with Janette Thomas Greenwood that "better classes" is preferable for describing black leaders during the years of this study for several reasons.[6] In the 1870s and 1880s there was a mass of working-class blacks but only a tiny group of black teachers, ministers, and small business owners. During these years, status markers such as being slave or free before the Civil War, level of education, skin color, occupation, acceptance of white-middle-class values, and family connections were more important in black social life than income. Since "middle class" implies a lower and upper class, it is inaccurate to use this term for Black Atlanta during these years; unlike New Orleans or Charleston, Atlanta had no elite "class" of blacks who had been freed before the war. Higher-status blacks were not a "middle class" of workers existing between the proletariat and owners of capital, for in Atlanta industrial employers rarely hired blacks for anything other than custodial duties. Finally, and most importantly, higher-status blacks during these years referred to themselves as the "better class" or "better classes."

"Colored" is one more term from this era currently out of fashion, but like "freedmen," I will use "colored" when it appears within the proper name of an organization or publication or in a direct quote. In the nineteenth century, "colored" was also used as an adjective before the name of black chapters of the Woman's Christian Temperance Union (WCTU). Black men issued calls for "colored" temperance conventions, and during the 1885 and 1887 campaigns "colored" ward clubs were designed to get out the vote. This is the language of the period, and to call them "black WCTUs" or "African American temperance conventions" would inappropriately sanitize the past for contemporary sensibilities. Because such terminology did not exist in the nineteenth century, it will not exist in this book.

The distinction between temperance and prohibition may be lost on those drawn to this book for its African American or religious emphases. "Temperance" is frequently used to refer to the entire movement to restrict the use of intoxicating beverages, which began in the late eighteenth century and lasted into the twentieth century. Used this way, the term incorporates *attitudes*, ranging from belief in the moderate use of intoxicating beverages to total abstinence from all that intoxicates (known as "teetotalism"). "Temperance" also includes all *tactics* ranging from persuasive efforts to get individuals to stop drinking (known as "moral suasion") to support for national constitutional prohibition of the liquor traffic. My references to the "temperance movement," "temperance reform," or "temperance reformers" are occasionally meant in this general sense, but usually I am referring only to the moral suasion approach. "Legal suasion" refers to any use of local, state, or federal laws to restrict the sale or use of liquor. Amending the federal constitution was the most extreme form of legal suasion.

This book climaxes with a study of two local option elections in Fulton County, Georgia, in 1885 and 1887. Local option votes were county or municipality plebiscites in which the only issue before the public was whether to allow the retail sale of liquor by the drink. These were usually framed as votes for or against saloons and were common throughout the South in the 1870s and 1880s. Atlanta was the largest municipality within Fulton County, comprising by far its largest voter block, and its voters would determine the outcome of the plebiscite, so media attention focused there. During the contests the press referred to prohibition supporters as "prohis" or "drys," and those who opposed prohibition (anti-prohibitionists) as "antis" or "wets." To capture the flavor of the local press during these elections, I will use these terms also.

Another important word that appears frequently in this book is "evangelical." Its nineteenth-century usage differs somewhat from that of the twenty-first century. For my purposes, "evangelical" refers to those who believed one needed to undergo an individual conversion experience in order to become a Christian and therefore embraced some form of revivalism to facilitate conversions. In the twentieth century, the National Association of Evangelicals issued a doctrinal statement delineating a list of beliefs where conversion was just one of many items addressed. While many nineteenth-century evangelicals would have agreed with this whole list, others would not have, so belief in the necessity of a conversion experience is a more meaningful indicator for the period of this study. Although nineteenth-century evangelicals could not agree on what revivals were supposed to look like or the theology behind them, they never doubted that they were a fundamentally desirable phenomenon.

Finally, readers may want to know the reasons I studied freed people *in Atlanta* to understand how temperance reached former slaves. Atlanta was one of the most exciting cities in the postbellum South. Its many boosters made great claims about the city's success in rising phoenix-like from the ashes of war. Because it was a city almost completely devoid of antebellum free blacks, Atlanta is a convenient place to study the diffusion of a reform movement that arose simultaneously with the formation of an African American community. In addition, Atlanta was a veritable hotbed of temperance activism; no other Southern city could match its temperance credentials.

Several white temperance lodges sprang into existence soon after the war and were active for many years: the Knights of Jericho, Cold Water Templars, and Knights of Temperance. White Atlantans organized the first Georgia chapters of the Independent Order of Good Templars (1867), the Woman's Christian Temperance Union (1880), and the Anti-Saloon League (1905). Frances E. Willard, John B. Gough, and evangelist Sam Jones, the most popular temperance speakers of the day, visited Atlanta in the 1880s and 1890s. The Georgia Prohibition Association (1884) was organized in Atlanta, as well as the state WCTU (1883). Atlanta hosted the national WCTU convention in 1890. White Atlantans also hosted a convention of Southern Good Templars, state temperance conventions in 1881 and 1885, and an unsuccessful meeting in 1904 to launch a state Anti-Saloon League. The city's Protestant clergy distinguished themselves as outspoken advocates not only of personal temperance but also of prohibition. Self-proclaimed "New South" businessmen seeking to remake Atlanta along the lines of Northern economic principles provided a complementary secular rationale for prohibition and brought their own resources to the cause. White Atlantans also published three temperance serials between 1880 and 1900: *The Temperance Advocate, The Conflict,* and *The Southern Temperance Magazine.*

Atlanta's black temperance reformers were hardly one whit behind the activism of the city's white citizens. They built their own separate, parallel movement. Several black temperance societies existed before 1870, and Atlanta's blacks organized the state's first True Reformer lodge (1873) and first Good Samaritan lodge (1875), and the South's first Colored WCTU (1879). Its missionary schools pioneered Scientific Temperance Instruction. In 1891 Black Atlanta hosted the national convention of the Independent Order of Good Samaritans. Black Atlantans edited two temperance newspapers in the 1880s: *The Southern Recorder* and the *Herald of United Churches*. One is hard-pressed to find an urban population more at the forefront of this reform movement than Atlanta, but Northerners ignited much of this excitement, so our story begins in the North.

Part I

Messengers from the North

Drunkard, alas! I dread thy fate:
Thou art indeed a slave;
Thyself thou cannot save
From the sad bondage of thy state—
A bondage fraught with deeper wo
Than that 'neath which poor negroes bow.
—A. B. (untitled poem, 1835)

An essential condition of permanent prosperity and success for
Republican Government in America, on the part of both its colored
and white constituents, is sobriety as well as freedom.
—*National Temperance Advocate* (January 1873)

CHAPTER 1

"Our Enterprise Flows from the Gospel of Christ"

The Evangelical Reform Nexus Roots of Nineteenth-Century Temperance, 1785–1865

Nothing short of the general renewal of society ought

to satisfy any soldier of Christ.

—William Arthur, *The Tongue of Fire*

On the eastern bank of the Shepaug River in western Connecticut lies the quintessential New England town of Washington, named for the nation's "founding father." It was the first Connecticut town incorporated after the 13 colonies issued their Declaration of Independence. Homes and farming plots spread out in all directions from the village green and its adjacent white clapboard Congregational meetinghouse. Originally settled in 1735, Washington's citizens organized the First Congregational Church in 1741 and subsequently, as in other New England churches, experienced their share of conflicts over the pastor's salary and the Half-Way Covenant. Future war hero Ethan Allen was married in the church in 1762. Ebenezer Porter became pastor in September 1796. The town's exuberance over the young preacher is suggested by the decision to sponsor three ordination balls. Porter did not disappoint; he was a tour de force in Washington, a breath of fresh air for the little town whose previous pastor had served for 44 years. Porter quickly placed his mark on every religious and cultural institution within his reach. He taught in Washington's high school, operated his own mini-seminary, organized a parish home missionary society, authored petitions against Sunday mail delivery, became Washington's first superintendent of schools, led the church's first revival, and preached America's first recorded "temperance sermon" in 1805. Seeking to reproduce this passion in others, Porter held regular Monday evening meetings in his study for interested parishioners "for the purpose of promoting their own growth in piety, and their usefulness to others." It is in this last, obscure practice that we find the origins of America's organized national temperance movement.

When Ebenezer Porter left Washington in 1812 to become a professor at Andover Seminary, he continued hosting those Monday evening meetings, and although the participants were probably more spiritually mature, this meeting was similarly designed for the "purpose of devising ways and means of doing good." Regular attendees included some fellow professors; Justin Edwards, pastor of Andover's South Church; and some members of Edwards's church. Porter's friend William Hallock later recalled that these Andover meetings were "befitting the rising spirit of missions and other departments of benevolence which the great work of God at the beginning of the century had awakened." Porter's meetings were anything but academic bantering over abstruse theological issues; on the contrary, they were the womb in which the "Andover Circle" incubated various practical applications of contemporary Christian thinking. From this womb emerged such benevolent organizations as the Andover South Parish Society for the Reformation of Morals, the New England Tract Society (later renamed the American Tract Society), and the American Temperance Society. This Bible study was arguably the first "critical community" to define intemperance as an American problem.[1]

Ebenezer Porter's meetings illustrate how the temperance movement was birthed by what I call the "evangelical reform nexus," that unique intersection of religious practice, theology, and ideology which coalesced during the Second Great Awakening. Changes in evangelical Protestantism were at the root of the awakening, and key elements of the temperance movement that both reflected and fueled these changes remained prominent even in the postbellum South. This nexus produced the culture of the people who brought the temperance message to Black Atlanta; indeed, it produced the people themselves and the organizations that sent them. The organizations that emerged from this cultural intersection codified and perpetuated its values and practices, by carrying them to western settlers, non-Protestant immigrants in eastern cities, and the freed people after the Civil War.

This chapter explores the elements of theology, ideology, and religious practice that characterized temperance in both the antebellum era and in post-emancipation Atlanta. It concludes by introducing the major nexus organizations that brought temperance to Black Atlanta and showing how their reason for being and their temperance values were mutually reinforcing, thus making temperance virtually inseparable from each organization's mission in the South. This is the historical backdrop against which temperance in Black Atlanta must be understood.

Religion and the Rise of Organized Temperance

Organized antebellum temperance was rooted in evangelical, revivalistic Christianity, and gender, class, racial, and nativist prejudices notwithstanding, both contemporaneous commentary and professional scholarship abundantly attest to this fact. Temperance reformers viewed themselves as advancing a "peculiarly Christian" reform, according to Thomas Grimke, president of the Charleston, South Carolina Temperance Society; and the American Temperance Union announced, "our enterprise flows from the Gospel of Christ." But it was an 1845 sermon by Reverend Lebbeus Armstrong that most vividly juxtaposed the temperance movement and the organized church. Drawing on the allegorical language of the twelfth chapter of the Book of Revelation, Armstrong argued that distilled liquors were the "flood" from the dragon's mouth meant to destroy the woman (a type of the church), and that the "earth" helping the woman referred to the fact that a physician initiated the first temperance society. Invoking Isaiah 59:19 he argued that the temperance movement was the "standard" God raised up against the "flood" of the enemy attacking the church. According to Armstrong, temperance was the "cause of God" from the beginning, and temperance societies were God's way to "show forth his power and glory by the choice of weak things of the world to confound the mighty" and in the end to "redeem the church from the curse of intemperance, and make this earth a sober world, preparatory to an entrance upon the enjoyments of the foreordained blessings of Millennial glory." Contemporary evangelicals viewed such grandiose claims as anything but preposterous. During the antebellum years, and even into the postbellum period, it was normative for clergy and other temperance spokesmen to articulate the movement's mission and vision in theological language.[2]

Nineteenth-century reformers credited Benjamin Rush, a Philadelphia physician and signer of the Declaration of Independence, with giving birth to the American temperance movement. In 1784 Rush published *An Inquiry into the Effects of Spirituous Liquors on the Human Body and Mind,* in which he outlined the negative physical, mental, social, and moral effects of drinking "ardent spirits." Rush urged his readers to drink beer, wine, cider, and other drinks, which he labeled as "wholesome . . . compared with spirits." While this was not the total abstinence message that eventually came to define the temperance movement, Rush was ahead of his time as one of the first to cite the deleterious effects of America's rapidly increasing consumption of whiskey and rum. It took more than 20 years before people began rallying around Rush's message. Perhaps the first person to be meaningfully inspired by Rush was his physician acquaintance Billy J. Clark. Clark had been practicing in the upstate New York town of Moreau for almost a decade when he decided to address the excessive drinking he regularly witnessed. In April 1808, Dr. Clark approached his Congregational pastor, the Reverend Lebbeus Armstrong, and within a few weeks they organized the nation's first recorded temperance society, the Temperate Society of Moreau and Northumberland. Its 43 male charter members pledged themselves to drink neither distilled beverages nor wine, although wine drinking was permitted at public dinners and weddings, and as part of Holy Communion. The society met quarterly to hear speeches on temperance, with Reverend Armstrong giving the first such address on August 25. In subsequent years, thousands of societies founded on this model sprang up all across America, and they usually had some connection with a local church or clergyman.[3]

Temperance societies sought to mold public sentiment through the literature they distributed. Besides Rush's *Inquiry,* which went through numerous editions, the main genre of temperance literature through the 1820s was the printed sermon. Nearly all the clergy incorporated Rush's ideas because of his intellectual stature, but they were also deeply moved by their own personal encounters with drunkenness. Two of the earliest clergy to publish temperance sermons were Ebenezer Porter and Lyman Beecher. Finding a dead man with a whiskey bottle in the snow near his church inspired Porter to preach a temperance sermon in 1805. It was published in 1812. But Beecher, a protégé of Timothy Dwight, president of Yale University, was an even more influential temperance preacher. Like Porter, Beecher was also influenced by issues close to home. In his first parish, East Hampton, New York, Beecher witnessed merchants purposely making local American Indians drunk so they could take advantage of them in business transactions. Shortly after taking a pastorate at Litchfield, Connecticut, in 1810, just up the road from Ebenezer Porter's church, he attended two ordination celebrations where he was disgusted by the extent of inebriation he witnessed among the clergy. Soon afterward he requested and chaired a clergy committee that called for, among other things, the circulation of Porter's sermon and Rush's pamphlet, and he urged church members to "cease to consider the production of ardent spirits a part of hospitable entertainment in social visits." One thousand copies of this committee report were printed and circulated, but probably even more influential were the sermons he published after one of his early Litchfield converts became a drunkard. This so disturbed Beecher that he finally completed an unfinished sermon outline he had been neglecting, and it yielded six temperance sermons. Initially preached in the fall of 1825 and published in Boston in the spring of 1827, the *Six Sermons on the Nature, Occasions, Signs, Evils, and Remedy of Intemperance* quickly became a temperance best seller alongside Rush's *Inquiry.* One writer has equated the influence of Beecher's *Six Sermons* on the temperance movement with the influence his daughter Harriet's *Uncle Tom's Cabin* had on abolitionism. Although Rush clearly influenced Beecher, he said much more than Rush, for through these sermons he established himself as the prophet of the American temperance movement by calling for total abstinence from all intoxicating beverages (not just distilled drinks), national coordination of the temperance movement, and the creation of a public sentiment which would demand that ardent spirits cease to be a legal article of commerce. These elements became hallmarks of the movement for decades to come. Unbeknown to Beecher, the first national temperance organization formed only weeks after he preached his sixth sermon.[4]

In January 1826 Porter's Andover Circle called a meeting in Boston's Park Street Church to discuss the temperance reform. This meeting issued a call for "more systematic and more vigorous efforts" by the "Christian public to restrain and prevent the intemperate use of intoxicating liquors." In February the men approved the constitution of the American Society for the Promotion of Temperance, more commonly known as the American Temperance Society (ATS), and quickly set about producing and disseminating literature (at first printed by the American Tract Society), serving as a clearinghouse for the latest temperance news, and sending out agents to build sentiment by organizing local temperance societies. In 1829 the ATS launched the weekly *Journal of Humanity and Herald of the American Temperance Society*. The Reverends Nathaniel Hewitt and Justin Edwards, traveling agents for the Society, frequently discovered preexisting local temperance societies unknown to the Andover Circle, revealing the movement's grassroots nature. Although by 1835 there were more than eight thousand ATS-affiliated societies, even that number does not represent all such societies in the nation at the time.

The ATS worked to strengthen temperance sentiment not to fight intemperance, and in many ways it simply codified what local societies had already been doing by drafting a pledge requiring total abstinence from distilled drinks, endorsing the moral suasion approach, and focusing on keeping the temperate "dry." Justin Edwards once callously informed a friend that the organization did not seek to help inebriates, "but to induce all temperate people to continue temperate by practicing total abstinence; the drunkards, if not reformed, will die, and the land be free." Such uncharitable attitudes did not go unnoticed, and the ATS proper never grew beyond a small umbrella organization, with just a few men in the Boston area, and never actually "directed" a "national" temperance movement.[5]

The ATS and its sequel, the American Temperance Union (ATU), organized in the 1830s, considered themselves and the movement unashamedly Christian. The masthead of the *Journal of Humanity* read, "Righteousness exalteth a nation; but sin is a reproach to any people," a direct quote from Proverbs 14:34. The executive committee of the ATU asserted that God Himself was the "supporter and director" of the movement, and that temperance was a "mighty moral and religious movement, going forth from hearts imbued with the spirit of the Gospel." In fact, the clergy's involvement was so prominent that some opponents considered the movement nothing but pushy clergymen trying to control how individuals lived Monday through Saturday.[6]

The 1840s witnessed the rise of fraternal temperance lodges and juvenile temperance societies, most of which perpetuated the movement's Christian emphasis.

There were three main fraternal lodges: Sons of Temperance (est. 1843), the Independent Order of Good Samaritans (est. 1847), and the Independent Order of Good Templars (est. 1852). These groups, which operated like secret societies with formal rituals and regalia, required their members to sign abstinence pledges, held regular meetings to provide accountability and camaraderie, and sometimes offered the insurance benefits of a mutual aid or benevolent society. The Good Samaritans particularly focused on reforming drunkards. Because pledgers who had testified about their past life were known to break their pledge, shaming themselves and embarrassing the movement, the Sons of Temperance purposely kept any failures a secret and sought to gently restore backslidden brothers. These societies grew rapidly throughout the 1840s and 1850s and although their popularity fluctuated over the years, some experienced long-term success, existing until the early twentieth century. Some spread to the South, some incorporated African Americans, and some became international.[7]

Bands of Hope were temperance societies for children that originated in England and spread to the United States. A Baptist minister organized the first Band of Hope in 1847 in Leeds, when over two hundred children pledged to abstain from intoxicating beverages. Local bands sprung up around the country and eventually organized the United Kingdom Band of Hope Union in 1864. The Union published a variety of materials to support juvenile temperance work. Local bands were organized with one or more adult overseers. Children as young as seven were admitted, and sometimes teenagers comprised a "senior" group. Membership required pledging total abstinence, and some bands also pledged never to smoke or use profanity. Each band had its own constitution and elected officers. Band meetings were well organized, sometimes bordering on the liturgical. Meetings included a mixture of praying, singing, an opportunity for visitors to sign the pledge, and some sort of exhortation to abstinence. Sometimes adult "superintendents" or older students would teach the younger ones from the *Band of Hope Catechism,* which indoctrinated students in all aspects of temperance thought using the traditional catechetical question-and-answer format. Teachers taught one question a week until students understood the answer. Logbooks listed all pledge signers, and sometimes a "Roll of Honor" poster graced the wall as a public witness. Those who broke their pledge could be removed. Members were constantly encouraged to invite their friends to attend meetings and to pledge, as well as to try to convince their parents to become abstainers. Band of Hope eventually became the generic term for children's temperance societies in the U.S. and England, and several were formed among the freed people following the Civil War.[8]

These temperance organizations were not the result of legions of narrowly focused, one-issue activists. On the contrary, evangelical temperance reformers were almost invariably committed to a panoply of reforms directly or indirectly connected to their drive to win "souls" for Christ and advance the Kingdom of God. Central to this drive was the promotion of revivals, with which temperance workers were frequently involved. As revivalism and its supporting theology evolved, they developed practices and a discourse that melded naturally with the evolving temperance movement.

The Evangelical Reform Nexus Origins of the Temperance Movement

Alice Felt Tyler, one of the earliest professional historians of antebellum temperance, argues that temperance was "inseparable from the religious motif of the first half of the century." The single most important element within that motif was the "reformist revivalism," which was quickly becoming the "center of a national religious and political discourse." Another scholar has not insignificantly observed that the only Protestant churches that opposed temperance also opposed revivalism. These observations are not meant to suggest anything near unanimity of temperance opinion in the pews of evangelical churches. In fact, the first targets of temperance reformers were their fellow pew occupants. But the fact that nearly all temperance reformers were part of the pro-revival evangelical tradition is significant. Revivals were periods when conspicuously large numbers of people expressed a deep concern for their spiritual state, professed a personal faith in Jesus Christ, and subsequently joined a local church. By the early nineteenth century these revival "seasons" were often purposefully worked up by preaching designed to produce conversions by directly challenging listeners to repent of their sins and turn to Christ. Revivalism and its related theology combined with a Christian version of republicanism to undergird and project the practices, language, and rationale of temperance reform into post-emancipation Black Atlanta.[9]

"The Revivalist and the Temperance Lecturer Were Often the Same Person"

From the 1810s onward, revivals and temperance were closely related.[10] First of all, the connection was methodological in that the structure of temperance meetings mirrored that of a revival service. Like revival services, temperance meetings were designed to inform the mind, arouse sentiment, and climax with a challenge for individuals to make a public decision. Temperance speakers constructed their arguments from Scripture, history, medical science, and recently collected data about the social and economic nature, causes, and effects of intemperance. Some famous speakers were former drunkards, and they became quite adept at giving their testimonies in dramatic, passionate, and persuasive ways, while in other cases "the revivalist and the temperance lecturer were often the same person." Some speakers played on emotions with melodramatic stories of the effects of intemperance on helpless and innocent family members. Temperance workers rewrote the lyrics of popular hymns for use during their meetings. All temperance societies closed their meetings with a challenge to sign a total abstinence pledge, reminiscent of the revivalist's call for sinners to repent.

Abstinence-minded revivalist preachers yielded their share of temperance workers. Five such influential antebellum revivalists were Timothy Dwight, Asahel Nettleton, Lyman Beecher, Charles Finney, and E. N. (Edward Norris) Kirk. Timothy Dwight, president of Yale from 1795 to 1817, presided over five student revivals but was most influential in mentoring revivalists such as Asahel Nettleton and Lyman Beecher, and in bequeathing to them certain key theological emphases. Dwight deemphasized complex and controversial doctrines in favor of a life of active Christian service. He preached one of the early published sermons attacking habitual drunkenness. Asahel Nettleton was Connecticut's first and only full-time evangelist during the 1810s. Nettleton was himself converted during the revivals that swept America in 1800 and remained staunchly conservative in his style, theology, and disposition throughout his career. Preaching mostly in smaller Connecticut towns, he opposed emotionalism yet consistently produced converts through a combination of sermons on traditional Calvinist doctrines and intense personal follow-up. Lyman Beecher was an energetic Dwight protégé who pastored both Presbyterian and Congregational churches in New York, New England, and Ohio and served as the first president of Lane Theological Seminary in Cincinnati. Charles Finney, a Presbyterian, was the most prominent antebellum revivalist. He initially made a name for himself in the 1820s in upstate New York through his successful "new measures" revivals, but he also preached throughout the Northeast and served as professor of theology and president of Oberlin College in Oberlin, Ohio. E. N. Kirk, an 1826 graduate of Princeton Theological Seminary, initially itinerated for the American Board of Commissioners for Foreign Missions in the South before pastoring in Albany and Boston. An active participant in many reforms of the period, Kirk was a great fit as president of the American Missionary Association during Reconstruction. The most renowned late-nineteenth-century evangelist Dwight L. Moody was converted under his ministry.

The preaching of Nettleton, Finney, and Kirk produced converts who played leading roles in bringing temperance to Black Atlanta. William E. Dodge, wealthy businessman and founding president of the National Temperance Society and Publication House, was converted under Nettleton's preaching, and under his leadership the society flooded post-emancipation Black Atlanta with temperance literature. Charles Finney was the primary spiritual influence in the life of

Fig. 1—Evangelist Charles Finney, who claimed to have made temperance an "appendage" of revivals. Portrait by Samuel Waldo and William Jewett. Courtesy of Allen Memorial Art Museum, Oberlin College, Ohio, Gift of Lewis Tappan, 1858

Frederick Ayer, the man who organized Black Atlanta's first temperance society. Ayer was inspired to become a missionary under Finney and was ordained by him. John Dougall became a radical reformer after exposure to E. N. Kirk's preaching and distributed free of charge his reform paper, *New York Weekly Witness,* to Black Atlanta clergymen.

"Bringing Men to Reflection": Temperance as Prelude to Revivals

The methodological and personal connections between revivalism and temperance were enmeshed in an intricate web of theology, ideology, and discourse largely designed to defend the practices of revival preachers from theological conservatives, enlightenment-inspired rationalists, and surging Methodism.[11] Revivalists climaxed their services by challenging listeners to repent of their sins and turn to Christ, but America's historically dominant theology—Calvinism—had long held that individuals could not make that choice for themselves.[12] To address this conundrum, several prominent preachers crafted a revised, pro-revival Calvinism by mixing into the revered theology certain elements of enlightenment thought. At the same time, Methodism, which completely rejected the most disputed tenets of Calvinism, fully embraced revivalist practices and was experiencing almost exponential growth, presenting its own challenge to traditionally Calvinist groups like the Congregationalists. Eventually, pro-revival Calvinist theology evolved to the point that it became indiscernible in practice from Methodist theology because they both placed so much emphasis on human ability in the conversion process. The logic of this newly ascendant theology justified—even demanded—temperance. A brief theological overview will set the background.

By the 1830s the vast majority of revivalists came to accept the idea that individuals were able and obligated to respond to God's moral laws, and that failure to do so justified God in punishing mankind, whether temporally through the instrumentality of human government or eternally in hell. This "moral government of God" theology taught that God sought mankind's obedience to moral laws by appealing to his reason through persuasion, not coercion. People were "free moral agents" who, because of their natural, commonsense reasoning capacity, could choose to obey God if they would. Moral government doctrine denied that people were born with a sinful nature, instead arguing that all sin was willful disobedience to God's laws. God had the greatest good of humanity in mind when promulgating his moral law because obedience to his law would remove sin, and by extension, human misery. Likewise, all human efforts designed to persuade people to cease sinning would reduce human misery and, by definition, be virtuous or benevolent acts. Methodist preachers embraced much of this teaching also, so clerical references to God's moral government and man's free moral agency became ubiquitous among pro-revival evangelicals.

Acceptance of the moral government of God doctrine suggested two practical implications for lived Christianity. First, since individuals had the ability to repent, and the Bible nowhere supports a gradual turning away from sin, it soon came to be understood that immediate repentance was a duty after hearing and understanding the Gospel message. This new teaching created in many Christians a sense of obligation to remove all obstacles to understanding the Gospel. Intemperance was clearly one such obstacle. Second, if individuals could repent of their sins, they could certainly choose to stop sinning. One *Oberlin Evangelist* writer explained the relationship between this theology and the temperance movement with exceptional clarity:

> Who does not know that the Temperance Reform finds its very foundation pillars in the doctrine that men have natural ability to cease from sinning? . . . The doctrine that no mere man is able to cease from sinning in the present life has had no agency in working out this glorious reform. . . . It has been held that every drunkard not only *can reform but is solemnly bound to do so.*

A minority of evangelicals carried this thinking to its logical conclusion, arguing that, if people could cease from some sin, they could cease from all sin, and this led to the rise of perfectionism, sometimes called the holiness movement. Perfectionism (of both the evangelical and secular varieties) created some of the most radical leaders of immediate abolitionism and teetotalism, known to some as "ultraist" reforms. The abolitionist poet John Greenleaf Whittier clearly understood this connection between theology and ultraist reforms: "We do not talk of gradual abolition, because, as Christians, we find no authority for advocating a gradual relinquishment of sin. We say to slaveholders—'Repent NOW— today—immediately'; just as we say to the intemperate—'Break off from your vice at once—touch not—taste not—handle not—from henceforth forever.'" Of all the pro-revival theologies, holiness was considered the most extreme, and throughout the century its detractors opposed the theology, but nevertheless, holiness believers were leading reformers into the postbellum years. Pro-revival theology had caused the affinity between temperance reform and revival efforts to blossom into a full-scale symbiotic relationship, a veritable two-member mutual aid society.[13]

By the early 1830s, reformers were touting temperance as a prelude to revivalism. Contemporaries observed that wherever temperance sentiment spread, revivalism followed, and that individuals who had first pledged to abstain were more likely to convert. Albert Barnes experienced a revival in his Morristown, New Jersey, church on the heels of preaching and publishing his *Essays on Intemperance* in 1828. Thomas Hunt, a North Carolina preacher, claimed that revivals occurred in "every neighborhood" that first embraced temperance. In Charles Finney's *Lectures on Revivals of Religion* he called intemperance, or opposition to the temperance movement, one of 24 things that could *stop* a revival. John Marsh, a key leader of the American Temperance Union, urged parents to see to it that their children were converted because, he said, the "wickedness" that "blasts revivals . . . flows from drinking habits" formed in one's youth. Theodore Cuyler attributed the 1866 revival at his Lafayette Avenue Presbyterian Church (Brooklyn, New York) largely to the influence of the temperance society he had organized the previous year. Justin Edwards once counted 300 communities that developed thriving temperance movements and found 275 of them were shortly thereafter "visited with the special influences of the Holy Spirit." But E. N. Kirk presented the most comprehensive articulation of the temperance-then-revival connection in his 1838 sermon *The Temperance Reformation Connected with the Revival of Religion and the Introduction of the Millennium.* After recounting several instances in which revival followed a surging temperance movement, Kirk concluded, "In short, so manifest is the connection between Temperance and revival of religion in this country that we no more expect the latter where the former does not exist." Reformers and preachers alike became convinced that temperance reform was a necessary prelude to revivalism. This is what the General Convention of Congregational Churches of Vermont meant when they declared that "the success of the temperance reformation [is] of vital importance to the interests of religion." Temperance publications such as the annual ATS reports, and pro-Finney publications like the *New York Evangelist*, were filled with references to the temperance-as-prelude phenomenon in the early 1830s, but they tailed off in the latter half of the decade.[14]

Pro-revival theology provided a ready-made explanation for this temperance-as-prelude-to-revival phenomenon. Because intemperance would "darken the understanding, sear the conscience and pollute the affections," it interfered with one's reason, rendered the means of grace "ineffectual," and destroyed one's natural ability to respond to the revivalists' plea, effectively nullifying their "moral sense," their God-given free moral agency. This horrified revivalists and their supporters because the call for immediate repentance presumed the existence of natural ability, free moral agency, and reasoning capacity, and anything that compromised this capacity mitigated the force of the preacher's plea. Conversely, temperance-induced sobriety aided the revivalist by "bringing men to reflection" and causing them to feel their "personal responsibility for personal actions." Justin Edwards put it this way: "Facts . . . show conclusively that the use of ardent spirit tends strongly to hinder the moral and spiritual illumination and purification of men; and thus to prevent their salvation." E. N. Kirk argued that intemperance kept people from church, and even if they went, it made them unfit to respond to the Gospel; it "stupefied" them and "deadened" their "religious sensibilities." The effect of abstinence was reportedly so powerful that even men who became dry through the explicitly non-religious working-class Washingtonian temperance movement were reportedly at an increased susceptibility to the revivalist's pleas.[15]

Becoming "Useful": Temperance as Postlude to Revivals

The focus on human ability in the conversion process fueled an increased emphasis on Christian "usefulness" following conversion. Lyman Beecher in his sermons *The Practicality of Suppressing Vice by Means of Societies Instituted for that Purpose* (1803) and *A Reformation of Morals Practicable and Indispensable* (preached in 1812, first published in 1813), as well as in his 1812 committee report on temperance, established the theological foundations for Christian involvement in moral reform societies. These sermons were classic jeremiads in that Beecher warned of divine judgment if the nation did not turn from its sins, but he also creatively appropriated the doctrine of God's moral government to hold out hope for change. One way he defended the practicality of moral reform efforts by saying that God's Word commanded people to turn from their sins, and if God commands something of people they must be able to do it. "The commands of God, are the measure and the evidence of human ability. . . . We conclude, therefore, that reformation is practicable, because it is the unceasing demand of heaven that nations, as well as individuals, do turn from their evil ways." Beecher was arguing that even the unregenerate could change their behavior based on the three restraints on human behavior: fear of God, public opinion, and the force of law. Moral reform societies could help align public sentiment with God's laws and, thereby, assist into right living those who did not fear God but at least loathed public shame. Beecher preached *A Reformation of Morals Practicable and Indispensable* on the evening he cofounded with his mentor Timothy Dwight, the Connecticut Society for the Suppression of Vice and the Promotion of Good Morals. But Beecher was just one of the earliest preachers to extrapolate from pro-revival theology the Christian's obligation to pursue an active faith. Charles Finney taught that new converts should "aim at being useful in the highest degree possible . . . if they see an opportunity where they can do more good, they must embrace it, whatever may be the sacrifice to themselves. . . . How else can they be like God?" Following his renowned Rochester, New York, revival Finney became convinced that the "very profession of Christianity implies . . . an oath to do all that can be done for the universal reformation of the world." Even in private letters reformers attributed the slow increase in temperance sentiment to a lack of that "self-denyng, self-sacrificing benevolence inculcated in the Holy Scriptures."[16]

From this theology and concerns about settlements in the western river valleys emerged what scholars have termed the "Benevolent Empire," an interconnected group of national, ecumenical evangelical organizations seeking to "do good"— or make themselves "useful"—by producing Christian converts and reducing immorality, thereby shoring up public virtue and increasing the public's happiness. Congregationalists and Presbyterians numerically dominated these groups, although they also included a few Baptists and Methodists. These organizations of clergy and laymen spoke of themselves as "advancing the Kingdom of God" and did so within the context of revivalism. This "empire" included over a dozen societies, but the most well known were the American Bible Society, American Board of Commissioners for Foreign Missions (ABCFM), American Tract Society(ATrS), American Sunday School Union, and American Home Missionary Society. These groups drew on a similar donor base and shared common aims, and several individuals held key leadership positions in two or more societies, creating an interlocking directorate. Comparable denomination-specific groups created by Baptists and Methodists—like the American Baptist Home Mission Society—are traditionally not included in the Benevolent Empire because they were not ecumenical, but they emerged from the same nexus of revivalism, theology, and ideology and together with the ecumenical groups can corporately be understood as "nexus organizations."

These benevolent organizations began forming as early as the late 1790s, and through the 1820s their efforts were the primary institutional expressions of the evolving temperance message. Tract societies published the early temperance sermons and tracts, and home missionaries distributed the literature and organized local temperance societies throughout the West. Sunday school literature often included temperance stories. It was in this context that Ebenezer Porter's weekly meetings germinated the idea of creating a national organization exclusively dedicated to the cause of temperance.

The men who founded the American Temperance Society had previously organized, or were currently serving, in at least five other nexus organizations, and they all understood their work as an outgrowth of their Christian desire to do good, to be benevolent. In fact, 15 of the original 16 ATS members were also members of the ABCFM, and 14 were also members of the ATrS. In the ATrS constitution they had announced they were "busied in discovering every way of access for divine truth into the human heart," and that tract distribution was an easy way of "doing good." In like spirit, the ATS constitution connected intemperance with conversions by lamenting that it had such a "fatal efficacy in hindering the success of all the common means which God has appointed for the moral and religious improvement of men" and declared they wanted to "do all in their power to promote the welfare of their fellow men." ATS founder and agent Justin Edwards advised temperance workers to "Let your object be, the glory of God in the Salvation of men." The same desire to do good works that animated the founders of other Benevolent Empire organizations was at work in the hearts of ATS founders; after all, they were literally the same people.[17]

Edwards's advice points to the fact that temperance served as much as a postlude to revival as it did a prelude. Because pro-revival theology taught an active

Christianity, temperance work was one of many avenues of "useful" activity open to new converts. In July 1827, Eatonton Baptist Church in Eatonton, Georgia, witnessed the beginning of Georgia's "Great Revival." Pastor Adiel Sherwood, a Northerner fresh from Andover Seminary, preached the first set of meetings of this two-year, 40-county harvest of more than sixteen thousand souls. During these meetings Sherwood used his new converts to establish Georgia's first temperance society. The next year, during the Georgia Baptist Convention, Sherwood organized Georgia's statewide temperance society. Likewise, in the middle of Charles Finney's 1830–1831 Rochester revival, Finney convert Theodore Weld preached an impassioned four-hour temperance sermon that stirred businessmen to dump their whiskey in the streets and the Erie Canal.[18] Beginning with this revival it became increasingly common for Finney and other revivalists to expect new converts to sign a total abstinence pledge. Finney actually claimed he and Weld had made temperance an "appendage" of the revival, and bragged about how many of his converts became "temperance men." Revivalist Asahel Nettleton observed that most church excommunications resulted from intemperance, so to prevent this disgrace he recommended that every new convert sign an abstinence pledge. Nettleton argued that if a convert "does not give evidence that he intends to abstain wholly and forever, I feel decided that he ought not to profess religion. If he cannot be willing to do this, he can have no sufficient evidence of his own repentance or conversion." E. N. Kirk agreed, warning that "there is immense temptation to backsliding in the instance of those who are all their days walking on the borders of intoxication," and another preacher announced, "The Church needs the temperance reform for the *purity* as well as the promotion of revivals. Spurious convictions may be expected of those who, in the light of the present day, do not abandon all intoxicating drinks upon conviction of sin." In the minds of some, the temperance pledge had become the immediate postlude to conversion; or perhaps the final stage of conversion itself. Leaders of the evangelical reform nexus had fully merged the discourses of revivalism and temperance, logically arguing that temperance both preceded revivals and "naturally" followed them.[19]

The Notion of Virtue: Temperance as an Element of Christian Republicanism

The societies of the Benevolent Empire also spoke of their work in language that is best identified as Christian republicanism. Americans of all classes, races, and locales claimed to be "republicans" in the years between the revolution and the Civil War. Christian republicanism is best understood as the hybrid social-political-religious worldview through which evangelicals justified the American Revolution, subsequently imagined the moral framework for a republican society, and dissected the social, political, and economic issues of their day.[20] This language enabled Christians to communicate with others in the public sphere about national issues. Although interpreted variously, its basic tenets were nearly universally held by early nineteenth-century American Christians. The Christian republican worldview took for granted the reality of sin, and that God punished it, so fear of judgment by a very real and very personal God inspired evangelicals to fight sin. Evangelicals believed that if they did not at least exert a serious effort to fight sin, God would judge the nation, effectively ending its "republican experiment," not unlike his destruction of Sodom and Gomorrah in the book of Genesis. Reformers viewed the individual immorality of intemperance as the source of social evils like poverty, domestic violence, and unemployment, rather than systems and structures beyond the individual's control. Ending personal intemperance was thus the beginning of efforts to eliminate unhealthy community-wide pathologies. Because evangelicals believed feverish opposition to sin could indefinitely postpone God's judgment, millennialism naturally inhered within Christian republicanism. This latter point contrasted with secular republicanism, which maintained that the stages of virtue, corruption, and decline naturally inhered in every republic. Typical was the writer who maintained, "Without virtue no nation ever prospered—with it, none would ever fail."[21]

Virtue was the sine qua non of all forms of republicanism, and reformers depicted temperance as a virtue essential for the perpetuation of the republic. In the revolutionary and early national periods, public figures frequently expressed concerns about the virtue of the citizenry. Historian Mark Noll argues that one of the reasons a Christian republicanism could evolve was that America was willing to "include several not altogether compatible ideals under the notion of virtue." Christians used it to mean personal, biblical morality, while their more secular contemporaries used it in its classical sense, as disinterested service to the common good. This tacit embrace of ambiguity within the public sphere enabled both secular and religious individuals to patriotically claim the "republican" mantle and unite as "brethren" in the common enterprise of nation-building. Whatever version of virtue one embraced, for the founders and the first generation of Americans, it was a given that it inhered in the nature of a free citizen, that a minimum level had to be maintained to perpetuate a republic, and that religion was at least helpful, if not necessary, to maintain it. Christians loved to cite George Washington's farewell address, in which he asserted that "Of all the dispositions and habits which lead to political prosperity, Religion and morality are indispensable supports," and that "virtue or morality is a necessary spring of popular government."[22]

Antebellum temperance reformers frequently framed their arguments against intemperance in the language of Christian republicanism by calling it a vice that undermined public virtue, republican institutions, and the republic itself. The preamble of the American Temperance Society's constitution warned that "wide-spreading intemperance . . . threatens destruction to the best interests of this growing and mighty Republic." Elsewhere it reported that its members had "often dwelt with deep interest" on several questions, among them: "Shall our republic happily succeed in the interesting and crucial experiment of self-government, and, delivered from the dangers and ruin into which other republics have fallen, remain safe and firm, and be a blessing to the great community of nations?" An endless list of published temperance sermons and lectures continually reaffirmed the Christian republican nature of temperance discourse. In Benjamin Rush's *Enquiry into the Effects of Spirituous Liquors* he argued that "a people corrupted with strong drink cannot long be a *free* people," and Ebenezer Porter's temperance sermon maintained not just that intemperance was sinful but that it was "threatening to the welfare of my native country." The Reverend Heman Humphrey, longtime president of Amherst College, warned in one sermon that "our free institutions are more endangered by the love of ardent spirits, than they ever were by the slave trade," and in another sermon, *The Way to Bless and Save our Country*, that the only "sure basis" of the government was "the virtue and piety of the people. In the absence of these, should Heaven in its wrath ever visit us with so dark a day, it must inevitably fall." Whole sermons were committed to arguing for the interconnectedness of temperance with both the advance of Christianity and the health of the body politic. Perhaps the most detailed exploration of this relationship was Albert Barnes's sermon *The Connexion of Temperance with Republican Freedom*. In Barnes's sermon he lamented the drunkenness that accompanied Independence Day celebrations and then described at length eight "settled" items necessary for the perpetuation of republican institutions (such as right to own private property, right to enjoy the profit of your labor, right to vote, rule of law, and so on) and point by point showed how intemperance undermined each of them. Such reasoning completely blurred the lines between temperance work as a fulfillment of a new convert's obligation to be useful in the Kingdom of God and temperance work as one's patriotic duty to the nation. Being a good Christian and a good citizen had become one and the same for white evangelicals.[23]

Political scientist John Hammond argues that revivalism served as both the motive and the method of antebellum reform, and what he argues about reform in general applies to temperance in particular.[24] Insofar as temperance advanced revivalism it advanced the Kingdom of God on earth, and insofar as it maintained public virtue it preserved the republic. Temperance was far more than an individual act of morality; it had profound ecclesiastical and political implications. The reform represented an optimism long since lost to American Protestantism. Both before and after the Civil War, various secular influences came to bear on the temperance movement, but we do the reformers a disservice and cloud our ability to explain the movement's acceptance among the freed people if we downplay or dismiss the evangelical reform nexus—the intersection of religious practice, theology, and ideology—that birthed the movement, its discourse, and the organizations that brought it to the South. It is to these organizations that we now turn our attention.

Temperance and the Nexus/Missionary Organizations of Post-Emancipation Black Atlanta

In the wake of Union army advances into the Confederacy, "freedmen's aid societies" sprang up across the North. Along with the older nexus organizations, these societies offered relief services to slaves fleeing to Union lines during the war and to freed people following the war, including the teaching of basic literacy skills. Many of the newer societies were "nonsectarian," meaning non-religious, but within a decade the vast majority of them ended their efforts, leaving the older, more established nexus organizations to work long-term among the newly emancipated. The four most prominent organizations in Atlanta coordinated their efforts in the interest of spreading the temperance message among the freed people: the American Tract Society, African Methodist Episcopal (AME) Church, American Baptist Home Mission Society (ABHMS), and American Missionary Association (AMA). Immediately following the Civil War temperance reformers organized the National Temperance Society and Publication House (NTS), but its sentiments, philosophy, tactics, and leadership were fundamentally antebellum in spirit so, although it is chronologically a postbellum organization, I group it with the antebellum nexus organizations. Each organization was fully vested in the temperance movement long before its arrival in Black Atlanta, as the following brief organizational histories demonstrate.

Prior to their arrival in war-torn Atlanta, nexus organizations had years of experience taking their message to western settlers in the Mohawk, Ohio, and Mississippi River valleys (1810s–1830s) and to the non-Protestant, working-class immigrants in eastern cities (1840s–1850s). The fact that western settlers moved to areas without established institutions like schools, churches, and in some cases government bodies greatly unsettled the sensibilities of traditional easterners. The possibility of westerners "going native" and the lifestyles of non-Protestant immigrants both contradicted their understanding of the public virtue required for a successful republic. Christian republican ideology combined with pro-revival theology to create a common discourse with which these groups articulated their institutional mission and defined individual and communal issues such as intemperance. Their goals consisted of persuading the objects of their benevolence to accept evangelical cultural values and living patterns, including temperance, with the hope of shoring up America's experiment in republican government—which, since the American Revolution, leading thinkers presumed was predicated on a virtuous citizenry. As one well-known New England minister extrapolated from an obscure passage in the Old Testament book of Judges, "emigration, or a new settlement of the social state, involves a tendency to social decline . . . nothing but extraordinary efforts in behalf of education and religion, will suffice to prevent a fatal lapse of social order." This lecture, published by the American Home Missionary Society, was ominously titled *Barbarism, The First Danger*, and captures the mentality behind the efforts of nexus organizations wherever they worked. Unsurprisingly, such sentiments produced more long-term "successes" among western Anglo-Americans with a Protestant background than among non-Protestant immigrants or the freed people.[25]

The American Tract Society

The same Monday evening meeting in Ebenezer Porter's study that birthed the American Temperance Society had earlier birthed the forerunner of the American Tract Society. In the fall of 1813 Porter and his Andover Circle organized a local tract society. Tract societies had existed in the United States since at least 1803, so the idea was not new. Their goal was to get "benevolent individuals" to cover the publishing costs of mass quantities of inexpensive gospel literature "best adapted to promote the conversion of sinners, revivals of religion, and experiential as well as practical piety." Within a few months the society relocated to Boston and became the New England Tract Society, and in 1823 it changed its name to the American Tract Society. The society functioned by printing tracts and shipping them to regional depositories where agents sold them to local tract societies, which then distributed them gratis. By 1825 the society had 112 local depositories and 191 auxiliary societies throughout America and had distributed four and a half million copies of 196 different tracts. At the invitation of some New York philanthropists, in May 1825 the American Tract Society (ATrS) reorganized in New York City. Justin Edwards and William Hallock, who had held positions in the Boston-based society, received prominent positions in the new ATrS. Interestingly, however, the American Tract Society-Boston neither disbanded nor fully merged with the New York group. It simply became a "branch" of the American Tract Society in New York and promised to solicit donations only in Massachusetts and upper New England. In 1858 when the American Tract Society voted not to publish tracts addressing any aspect of slavery, the already semi-independent Boston branch reasserted its independence, broke away, and began publishing tracts on slavery. The two societies merged briefly in 1868, only to split again and then reunite in 1878.[26]

The tracts of the ATrS and the pronouncements of its officers consistently testified to the society's commitment to the values of the evangelical reform nexus and to temperance. In the few months between Ebenezer Porter's organizing of a tract society and the formal organization of the New England Tract Society, the Andover Circle raised almost $3,000 and published three temperance tracts, in addition to tracts on other subjects. *On Temperance,* their third tract, was the first of many temperance tracts to come off their press. ATrS tracts employed many narrative and rhetorical approaches to persuade readers and curiously, as often as not, omitted Bible verses, indicating their pragmatic tendency to appropriate any potentially efficacious argument. The American Tract Society-New York did all the printing for the American Temperance Society in its early years. The New England Tract Society's original address to the public asserted in typical pro-revival theology, "A spirit of active benevolence is one of the distinguishing features of Christianity. . . . Where the Gospel has its full influence, it . . . produces the most tender concern for the happiness of mankind." By claiming tract distribution was "an easy way of doing good" they were clearly targeting the mass of new revival converts seeking to be useful. The society viewed the settlers on the western frontier, like other nexus groups, through a Christian republican lens. "What is likely to be the moral and religious character of these new Societies and States? Will it be such to ensure the Divine favour, without peculiar and vigorous exertions to render it so?" At the first anniversary of the ATrS Justin Edwards reminded the society that they were under obligation to the nation to "make a development of character, such as creation never witnessed." The extent to which tracts encouraged public virtue was the extent to which their distribution was deemed a public service, even patriotic.

In 1841 the ATrS adopted the colporteur system. Colporteurs were traveling agents who sold tracts and engaged people one-on-one in religious conversations ("witnessing") and prayer. By the outbreak of the Civil War, the society had employed more than four thousand colporteurs who traveled in all regions of America, both rural and urban. When reviewing the effects of its colportage system on its tenth anniversary, the ATrS boasted that it had helped "check" intemperance, even though no empirical investigation could verify such an assertion. But the point is that the Society wanted to be seen as supporting temperance reform.[27]

The African Methodist Episcopal Church

The African Methodist Episcopal Church was the largest and oldest national black organization in the United States. Its origins date back to Philadelphia,

Pennsylvania, in 1794 when a group of black worshippers left St. George's Methodist Episcopal Church as a body after ushers told them to move to the back of the church while they were in the middle of praying. They began meeting separately in 1794 under the leadership of Richard Allen. Following a successful lawsuit to gain control of their church property from whites, in 1816 Richard Allen was ordained the first bishop of the AME Church. Born into slavery, Allen taught himself to read and write, converted to Methodism as a teenager, purchased his own freedom, and by the time of his death in 1831 had an estate valued in excess of $40,000, a significant sum for an African American in that day.

The creation of the AME Church was the first major Christian schism based on the racial prejudices of fellow parishioners and not on doctrinal differences. This meant that AME theology was essentially the same as that of white Methodists but also that it was strongly influenced by the popular pro-revival doctrines of the day. In fact, many of the revisions of Calvinist theology designed to support revivalism—like the belief that God's benevolence was meant to facilitate man's happiness, that Christians should likewise work for mankind's happiness, the moral government of God teaching, and the idea that sin was in an individual's behavior, and not imputed—aligned exceptionally well with major tenets of the African worldview popular among African Americans at the time. At its First General Conference, the church adopted the *Doctrines and Discipline of the Methodist Episcopal Church* without its pro-slavery provisions. The *Doctrines and Discipline* included a section originally written by John Wesley called the "General Rules," which outlined the requirements for membership in a Methodist "class," the basic unit of Methodism. Each class had about 12 people, plus a leader, who saw to the spiritual needs of each member and held them accountable in the practice of their faith. Several classes comprised a "society" or congregation. To be a class member one needed only "a desire to flee from the wrath to come, and to be saved." Wesley added, however, that the lives of such individuals would show spiritual "fruit." This fruit, or evidence of salvation, included "avoiding evil of every kind, especially that which is most generally practiced," such as using God's name in vain, breaking the Sabbath, and "drunkenness: or drinking spirituous liquors, unless in cases of necessity." All of this meant that the same theology that white Christian' used to support temperance could and was used by AME clergy. Although W' ley only opposed the use of distilled liquors, by the 1830s AME clergy gene' taught and practiced total abstinence from all forms of alcohol, and by the ' the church backed legal suasion—that is, prohibition.[28]

AME Church leaders repeatedly reaffirmed their commitment to ab
The whole church met every four years in its "quadrennial" conference
gional groups, called "conferences," held annual conferences. By the '
lum period there were four conferences. The annual conferences rep

temperance reports. In 1833 the Ohio Annual Conference declared temperance societies were of the "highest importance" to all people but "more especially" to blacks, and the New York Annual Conference also issued a resolution condemning drinking that same year. In 1840 the Quadrennial Conference passed a resolution reaffirming its commitment to total abstinence, and the Ohio Annual Conference called for holding quarterly abstinence sermons and for making ministers give account of themselves if they failed to preach them. Many AME congregations organized temperance societies, and by the 1840s they had enrolled hundreds of their church members. The AME Church was actually ahead of white denominations in its advocacy for temperance and prohibition. In at least 14 different issues between 1854 and 1865,[29] the church's semi-monthly newspaper, the *Christian Recorder*—the only black-edited, -owned, and -financed newspaper that was nationally circulated—published editorials and other articles supporting total abstinence, urging lay participation in the temperance movement, and even defending government prohibition of the liquor traffic, a very divisive idea during that time. Soon after the commencement of hostilities during the Civil War, the *Recorder*'s editor, the Reverend Benjamin T. Tanner, became so disturbed by reports of drinking among Union soldiers that he considered publishing a temperance tract. Then he received from the American Tract Society one of its tracts for the same purpose, which so pleased him that he reprinted excerpts on the *Recorder*'s front page, reminding his readers that the arguments applied to civilians too. Shortly after his ordination, and before the war, Tanner confided in his personal diary that, "Whiskey is as a mighty river of death deluging millions in its fearful course," suggesting that church leaders embraced such sentiments privately as well as publicly. When the AME Church purchased Wilberforce University in 1863, it prohibited its students from using alcohol. During the early years, many AME clergy were illiterate, and this produced noticeable discrepancies on teachings such as temperance, but denominational leaders were firmly committed to teetotalism by the end of the antebellum period and believed if sobriety was widely practiced by blacks it could only improve their treatment at the hands of white Americans.[30]

The American Baptist Home Mission Society

The third important nexus organization in post-emancipation Black Atlanta was the American Baptist Home Mission Society (ABHMS). Concerns (or perhaps fears) about the morality of settlers in the Mississippi Valley led western minister John M. Peck and Massachusetts pastor Jonathan Going to birth the idea of a Baptist home mission society in the summer of 1831. Skirting opposition from antinission Baptists in the General Convention, Baptist believers in revivals and reform came together to form the ABHMS in 1832. This group enthusiastically embraced antebellum pro-revival theology and the full range of benevolent reforms it gave rise to, as well as the Christian republican worldview. Adiel Sherwood, founder of Georgia's first temperance society in 1827, participated in the organizational meeting. ABHMS founders involved themselves in a variety of benevolent works: Peck established schools, Sunday schools, and Bible societies throughout the Midwest, and Going, while pastoring in Worcester, Massachusetts, served as a founding trustee of Amherst College, founded Sunday schools, and became one of the early temperance preachers in his area. The ABHMS's first president, the Honorable Heman Lincoln, supported such benevolent empire groups as the American Bible Society, American Tract Society, and American Temperance Society, and William Colgate, its first treasurer, was active in more than one Bible society. With such leaders at the helm, it is not surprising that their annual reports defined piety as "a disposition to do good to others" and observed that the churches "most active in promoting the benevolent enterprises of the age, are most highly favored with revivals." Regardless of the rivalry between the upstart and less erudite Baptists and Methodists on one hand and the more established and educated Presbyterians and Congregationalists on the other, the pursuit of revivals and reform united many evangelicals behind the same causes. While disparate views on church-state relations may have prevented national level denominational bodies from officially endorsing prohibition, such sentiments in no way prevented multitudes of individual ministers from preaching total abstinence, because moral suasion rested on the same principles as did preaching for conversion.[31]

Unsurprisingly, the ABHMS also incorporated strong Christian republican language in its reports, especially when commenting on the Mississippi valley. Plagiarizing in spirit from the ATrS, the ABHMS asserted that "The character of its population for intelligence, morality, and religion, will determine the national character and the fate of the American Republic." In their ninth report they sanguinely observed that "if" God's blessing on America had been predicated up to this point "upon the intelligence and virtue of the people, and if the perpetuity of those blessings is still dependent upon the holy influence of the religion of Jesus Christ," then there was reason to have hope because of the successful advances of the Gospel. Baptists were as persuaded as other evangelicals that their effort wɜ of the "highest importance" to the "perpetuity of our republican institutions."[3]

The ABHMS also pushed a strong temperance policy. By 1838 nearly ⸳ its missionaries reported giving temperance lectures. The ABHMS suppˡ missionaries with total abstinence pledges before they left for the missi but by 1847 several of them were reporting that the pledges were almosᵗ sary because when they arrived in an area they found many churches v using them. Beginning in 1841 the annual report listed the numbᵣ ance pledges each missionary reported having signed, and by 1857 at least 17,257 people had signed. Annual reports also speak of many Baptist churches either requiring their members to sign the pledge or establishing temperance societies in connection with their church. Late in the antebellum period annual missionary reports speak of thousands of lectures on "moral subjects," some of which presumably included temperance. The ABHMS claim to have provided a "strong impulse" to the temperance reform is well supported by its own annual reports.[33]

The American Missionary Association

The fourth organization that stoked temperance sentiment in Black Atlanta was the American Missionary Association, an interdenominational and interracial missionary society created in New York City in September 1846 by the merger of four organizations: the Amistad Committee, the Union Missionary Society, the Western Evangelical Missionary Society, and the Committee for West India Missions. The target populations of the precursor organizations and the merged AMA included Africans, communities of former slaves, and American Indians. Black Congregational churches had organized the Union Missionary Society. Open to any person of "Evangelical sentiments" (which they defined in a constitution footnote), the AMA's stated purpose was "to send the Gospel to those portions of our own and other countries which are destitute of it." Unlike other missionary societies and boards, the AMA refused to associate with Christians tolerating slavery or any form of "caste discrimination."[34] As the most prominent organization embracing the full range of the logical implications of revival theology, it was known for its abolitionism, its evangelization of people of color, and its insistence on the "brotherhood of man." It opposed not only slavery but the racism that supported it, giving the AMA arguably the most racially progressive ethos of any national antebellum organization. Four of the first twelve men on its executive committee were African Americans, and a total of eight different African Americans served through the 1860s, four of them being ex-slaves. The AMA also supported many African American missionaries to the freed people. The abolitionist Lewis Tappan, a driving force behind its founding, argued that the association offered a "purer and whole gospel to the heathen world." Initially the AMA received funds only from individuals, churches, and schools but not denominations; however, by 1865 the Free-Will Baptists, the Wesleyan Methodist Connection, and most important, the National Council of Congregational Churches had adopted the AMA as their official organization for missions among the freed people. Although its missionaries and leadership included individuals from many denominations (Methodist, Baptist, Presbyterian, Orthodox Friends, Dutch Reformed, Episcopalian, and Congregational), as Reconstruction progressed, Congregationalists came to dominate the organization.[35]

The fact that many AMA missionaries and officials were educated at Oberlin College heavily flavored the organization in its early years. John J. Shipherd, a New England Presbyterian preacher and friend of Charles Finney, founded Oberlin in 1833 about 30 miles from Cleveland, Ohio, with the aim of bringing the Mississippi valley under the influence of the "blessed gospel of peace." Oberlin colony was a Christian community founded on all the principles of the evangelical reform nexus. Its original residents signed a covenant pledging them to "maintain deep-toned and elevated personal piety," which included renouncing all "strong and unnecessary drinks." All "extra" income earned by residents was to be poured into evangelistic, missionary, and reform enterprises. Oberlin was a stop on the Underground Railroad for many fugitives. The college, which initially focused on training teachers and preachers, distinguished itself by being the first American college to accept women and blacks, almost from its founding. One hundred blacks studied at Oberlin between 1835 and 1865, although a much smaller number actually graduated. Asa Mahan and Charles G. Finney, Oberlin's presidents during these years, placed much emphasis on human agency in the conversion process and developed their own influential brand of holiness that came to be known as "Oberlin perfectionism." Residents of Oberlin founded the Western Evangelical Missionary Society to support ministry among the Ojibwe Indians, and when the society merged into the AMA, the new society quickly became the most popular missionary board for Oberlin-trained missionaries to affiliate with. And just as most Oberlin graduates joined the AMA, most AMA missionaries were also from Oberlin. Oberlin graduates comprised 90 percent of all AMA missionaries before the Civil War and held key leadership posts into the 1890s. Heirs of the doctrines and praxis of the Second Great Awakening, AMA missionaries and their benefactors always rejoiced at the news of a revival. AMA missionaries enthusiastically extended this revival tradition to Black Atlanta, reporting in the pages of the *American Missionary* no less than nine separate revivals between 1868 and 1881. The Reverend Michael Strieby, Oberlin alumnus, revivalist, and reformer in his own right, was corresponding secretary for the AMA from 1864 to 1896. The affinity between the two organizations was such that Strieby considered Oberlin and the AMA to be "brothers," and Atlanta's AMA missionarie⸀ called the school they founded—Atlanta University—a "second Oberlin."[36]

The influence of perfectionism on the AMA is suggested by its annual rep⸀ One of the highest priorities of its missionaries was to establish "pure" chu⸀ that is, churches tolerating no known sinful behavior. Although a princip⸀ tus behind the formation of the AMA was to oppose slave-holding amc⸀ tians, the AMA sought much more. Beginning in 1850 its annual repo⸀

a chart summarizing missionary work with a column labeled "pledged to abstinence." Before 1855, missionaries reported a number in that column, but after
1855 every line stated "all." No year passed without the annual report including
missionary tales of either successful temperance work or the sad state of intemperance in their particular field, no doubt designed to inspire increased financial
support. Since intemperance and slave-holding were both sins, they both had to
be eliminated. The AMA drive for pure churches was a direct outgrowth of their
perfectionist theology, as this 1859 resolution demonstrates:

> That the only just mode of conducting missions requires the adoption of the perfect
> standard of holiness given by God in the Bible, and that for missionaries or mission-
> ary societies to allow any sin to go unrebuked among the people where they carry
> the Gospel, or to suffer any members of their churches to practice any sin without
> using all legitimate means in their power to effect church discipline with such trans-
> gressors, is a palpable violation of the spirit and principles of the Gospel, and the
> sure precursor of multiplied mischiefs to missions and the Church of God.[37]

These nineteenth-century Puritans had transformed the seventeenth-century
drive for congregations composed of only the elect into a crusade for churches
full of "perfect" Christians. Missionary John G. Fee, instrumental in establishing antebellum Kentucky's interracial Berea College, best summarized the no-
nonsense approach of AMA missionaries when he declared, "I am engaged in
the effort to build up churches having no fellowship with slaveholding, caste, secret societies, dram-drinking or any known sins." The AMA wanted its churches
not to countenance *any* sin, and when lists of sins were compiled, intemperance
made the short list.[38]

The AMA repeatedly expressed its hostility toward intemperance, even though
the word did not appear in its constitution. At its annual meetings between 1849
and 1859, no less than six resolutions explicitly condemned intemperance, and
members strongly criticized the liquor traffic from America to Africa. At the third
annual meeting a resolution invited "all friends of a pure Gospel" to join the association's efforts to spread the Gospel "without conniving at, palliating, or tolerating the sins of slave-holding, caste, war, polygamy, or intemperance." In 1852
the association explained that ignoring intemperance would undermine the very
Christian character they sought to inculcate: "*Resolved*, That to oppose sin in one
set of relations while we do not in another—for example, to oppose intemperance
while we do not oppose slavery, or to pray against oppression while we vote for
it—is to strike down Christian principle, to deaden conscience, and, in the end, to
undermine and destroy Christian character."[39]

In another resolution they called both slave-holding and intemperance among

Christians "formidable obstacles" to the spreading of Christianity overseas. All sin had to be opposed: institutional (caste discrimination), personal (intemperance), or institutional and personal (slave-holding). Logically, all AMA missionaries were required to sign a teetotal pledge. In 1883 the association distributed a children's choral recitation on the AMA's temperance position for use in its Sunday schools. After quoting several Scripture verses, the leader asks what the AMA position has been on temperance "since its organization," and the response is "It has always taken a decided stand against the use and the sale of intoxicating drink." Temperance did not appear in the AMA's constitution, most likely because its abolitionist position was its raison d'être, and temperance was already a "given" among missionary agencies (in 1830 the American Home Missionary Society ordered its missionaries to preach temperance), but the AMA was obviously a temperance organization.[40]

While the American Tract Society, the AME Church, the American Baptist Home Mission Society, and the American Missionary Association were preaching temperance as just one part of their larger agendas, the temperance-specific American Temperance Union (organized in 1833) was fighting for its life. It was kept afloat by the heroic efforts of its secretary, the Reverend John Marsh, who dutifully prepared its annual reports and oversaw its tract-printing operations. The ATU was the poor stepchild of the Benevolent Empire and was reduced to little more than publishing annual reports on the temperance "advances" and setbacks of the previous year. Although the union successfully supported a range of state-level prohibition initiatives between 1838 and 1855, the political process undermined or overturned most of them, and its reports from the forties and fifties portray an organization (and movement) that was adrift, lethargic, and almost desperate at times. Marsh complained about state legislatures resisting grassroots prohibition efforts, the intemperance of immigrants, the inactivity of churches, apathy within the movement, and a perceived general increase in intemperance. The length of ATU annual reports shrank significantly at the same time as they were increasing their coverage of European temperance news. Indicative of its shrinking stature was one observation that John Marsh himself *was* the Union for its last 25 years. Internal disputes, funding difficulties, and the rise of the national debate over slavery combined to undermine enthusiasm for the movement and its flagship organization. The American Temperance Union was moribund, temperance supporters knew it, and something needed to be done.

The National Temperance Society & Publication House

The National Temperance Society was the last of the organizations to form the evangelical reform nexus. Although it did not exist in the antebellum p organization, leadership, approach to temperance, and religious proclivit perfectly with the spirit of organizations formed decades earlier. Within weeks of Robert E. Lee's surrender at Appomattox Court House, New York Good Templar J. N. Stearns and the American Temperance Union leaders issued a call for a national temperance convention (the fifth one), to be held August 1–3 at Saratoga Springs, New York. This convention brought together a "who's who" list of 378 movement veterans. Their first official resolution enthusiastically offered thanks for the Union victory and the liberation of the slaves, and "for the opportunity now given us to seek . . . a deliverance from intemperance, that other great blot upon our national escutcheon; so that we may under the smile of Divine Providence, move on, through coming generations, in an unparalleled course of liberty, righteousness, and peace." The optimism of this first resolution reveals that the doldrums of war and the excitement attending emancipation in no way caused these men to reject their theological roots in the evangelical reform nexus; they still viewed their world through the prism of Christian republicanism. The emancipation of the slaves meant that abolitionism would never again divide temperance, so in the Union victory they saw the potential for a truly unified and reborn movement. Emancipation and the political and military realities of four years of war not only exposed the common theological roots of temperance and abolitionism but made it convenient for all reformers to embrace their logical implications.

The convention proceedings reveal the extent to which the delegates were still firmly rooted in the mind-set of antebellum temperance. This was such a tradition-bound group that they chose the man who presided over the first national temperance convention more than 30 years earlier, businessman Reuben Walworth, to give the opening address. Walworth, who reminded the audience that "virtue alone exalted the nation," was the first of several speakers to appropriate Christian republican language and encourage increased moral suasion efforts. The delegates spoke of virtue and vice, Divine Providence, and the need for repentance; calls for increased efforts to educate the public about temperance almost became a mantra. While they agreed on these antebellum values, the delegates also revisited old antebellum disputes such as the proper roles for the churches and the government to play in the movement. While all agreed that churches and the religious basis of the movement were essential to its ultimate success, they disagreed about the extent to which churches had supported the reform in recent years. Some argued for the need to reinforce moral suasion with legal suasion, but others countered that until the masses could be properly educated to support it, prohibition would never work. They also discussed such divisive issues as voting for prohibition candidates and the use of grape juice instead of wine for Holy Communion. One delegate called for a new temperance tract publication house since so much of the earlier literature had gone out of print, and a Canadian delegate, John Dougall, called for a special effort to reach the freed people with the temperance message.

John Marsh reminded the convention that the "great mistake" of the American Temperance Union was that it had "no pecuniary basis," except Edward C. Delevan's periodic contributions and subscribers to its publications. The convention ended by approving a long list of resolutions, including one establishing a committee to look into creating a new temperance organization, a call for a new temperance publication house, and one recognizing that the four million freed people were now "thrown open to Temperance efforts" and recommending "their case to the special attention of any national organization that may be formed."[41]

To carry out these resolutions, on September 26, seven men, including three clergy, met in the Manhattan offices of Phelps, Dodge, & Company, of which William Earl Dodge was the senior partner. Dodge, who chaired the meeting, and some of the others present had been involved with the ATU and were particularly concerned with creating a more effective organization. During this and subsequent meetings that fall, the committee organized the National Temperance Society and Publication House, whose mission was to "promote the cause of total abstinence from the use, manufacture, and sale of all intoxicating drinks as a beverage" by publishing and circulating literature, encouraging the use of the teetotal pledge, and "all other methods calculated to remove the evil of intemperance from the community." The NTS purposely revived the temperance movement on the basis of such antebellum values as moral suasion, education, and clergy and church involvement. The respected philanthropist William Dodge was elected the first president, and J. (John) N. Stearns was named its publishing agent. Executive decision-making power was vested in a board of managers, but the publications committee was also powerful because it vetted all publications. Influential and ceremonial (vice presidential) NTS leaders included everyone from the most conservative to the most progressive temperance reformers and eventually grew to include Southerners, blacks, and Canadians. The NTS could embrace such a wide range of reformers because it did not demand ideological conformity but, rather, focused on the lowest common denominators of the movement, namely, educating the public by printing and distributing large amounts of inexpensive literature and defending every local community's right to conduct local option votes. At the same time, it shrewdly refused to endorse specific state and national prohibition campaigns or take a position on the existence or platforms (after 1869) of the national Prohibition Party.[42]

The NTS did all this within a Christian republican framework and with a commitment to revivalism. Although the NTS strategically removed itself from rancorous political debates over prohibition, it simultaneously remained firmly committ to the educational aspect of grassroots political organizing, embracing prohi only where an educated public sentiment demanded it and opposing it els For many years its leaders asserted this was the only meaningful path to pr

Despite this approach, some of the men who wrote its constitution were involved in organizing the Prohibition Party in 1869 and still remained involved with the NTS. Although it struggled with finances like the old ATU, throughout the period of this study it maintained a relatively stronger "pecuniary basis." Its monthly publication, the *National Temperance Advocate*, published without interruption into the 1900s, served as a clearinghouse for all movement news.[43]

As Union armies marched through the South and the enslaved sought freedom behind Union lines, Northern philanthropic energies quickly focused on the contrabands' plight. Long before Robert E. Lee surrendered, Northern emergency aid and relief workers began flowing to the freed people in coastal regions. Although the short-lived organizations did much for the freed people, it was the well-established evangelical nexus organizations that settled in for long-term social development among the former slaves. They brought with them a deeply rooted religio-cultural heritage with all its inherent biases, believing their efforts were the cultural phase of the conquest initiated by the Union army. The agents of these organizations generally did not make temperance their primary message upon arrival in the war-torn South, but they also would not, and could not, excise it from their value system and worldview. These nexus organizations were too closely related to temperance, and while they might be rivals in other areas, like true siblings, at the end of the day they closed ranks in defense of their brother, the temperance movement. If nothing else, they agreed on the teetotal pledge. As a result, despite whatever other educational, political, doctrinal, and institutional designs motivated these organizations' activities among the freed people, they were predisposed to work cooperatively with each other, and with the NTS, to support a temperance reform agenda that was bigger than any one organization. We now turn our attention to exactly what that cooperation looked like.

> The ship called Moderation
> May cruise a little while,
> But soon its wrecks are strewing,
> The rocks of Drunkard's Isle.
>
> The good ship "Total Abstinence"
> Well manned by Christian men
> With Christ our Lord for pilot
> No fear or danger then.
> —"The Light House"

CHAPTER 2

The Message Trickles South

Introducing the Freed People to Temperance, 1865–1876

We have met one slav'ry boys, in blood we put it down;
Now the liquor slav'ry next, our bloodless arms shall crown;
We shall meet it face to face, despite its demon frown;
Down with the rum-curse forever!
—C. L. Shacklock, "Prohibition Battle Cry," fourth stanza

The middle of the city is a great open space of irregular shape, a wilderness of mud, with a confused jumble of railway sheds, and traversed by numberless rails, rusted and splashed, where strings of dirty cars are standing, and engines constantly puff and whistle. In one place I saw beside the track a heap of bones and skulls of animals, collected from battle-fields and the line of march for some factory, moulding and blackening in the wet weather. Bricks and blocks of stone and other rubbish were everywhere. Around this central square the city was formerly built, and is now building again.[1]

If this was what Atlanta looked like to the tourist John Dennett on Christmas Day 1865, it must have not looked even this good when the AMA missionaries Frederick Ayer and his wife arrived in early November. Indeed, conditions improved slowly, as most city streets remained unpaved into the 1880s, and it took years before it could be truly said Atlanta had risen phoenix-like from the ashes. Ayer was born in Ma´ sachusetts in 1803 to a Presbyterian minister but grew up from two years of ag New York's frontier region, where he experienced first-hand the fervor of the f "burned over" revival region. Ayer was a young man in Utica when Charle₅

Fig. 2—Brown & Dwyer's Saloon and Hagan & Co., two late 1860s Atlanta liquor purveyors. Kenan Research Center at the Atlanta History Center

led his great revival there between October 1825 and May 1826, producing over two thousand converts and many revived Christians. Like many other young people in the area, he underwent a conversion experience during this time, and by 1829 his religious commitment moved him to make himself more "useful" by becoming a teacher in an Ojibwe Indian school established by the American Board of Commissioners for Foreign Missions on Mackinac Island, Michigan Territory. Ayer founded Ojibwe mission schools in various parts of Wisconsin and Minnesota over the years but always felt a special connection with Finney, so he visited Oberlin College in 1842, during Finney's presidency. While there, Finney ordained Ayer, and the Oberlin community subsequently became so committed to Ayer's work among the Ojibwe that it organized the Western Evangelical Missionary Society to help finance it. When that society merged with others to form the American Missionary Association, he left the American Board to affiliate with the AMA. Fortuitous for the cause of temperance in Black Atlanta was the fact that Ayer and his wife had witnessed and fought against the negative effects of alcohol abuse among the Ojibwe in the various stations where they worked, developing a particularly strong hatred for alcohol. The Ayers brought a wealth of cross-cultural educational experience with which to establish the AMA's presence in Atlanta and soon became known for their extensive personal relief work among the freed people. Although he arrived as a gray-headed 62-year-old with a life-long respiratory ailment and died within two years, in that short period of time Frederick Ayer successfully organized a school, a six-hundred-member temperance society, and the city's first Congregational church, and became one of the signers of Atlanta University's charter application. Ayer was only the first of several Northerners under the auspices of evangelical nexus organizations to arrive in Black Atlanta with the temperance message.[2]

Recently emancipated slaves led Atlanta's postbellum demographic revolution. Between 1860 and 1870 the population of Atlanta more than doubled, and in line with the South's ten largest cities so too did the percentage of blacks in that population. Between 1860 and 1870, blacks went from being 20 percent of Atlanta's population to more than 45 percent. As in other Southern cities, black immigration eventually slowed, and white population growth soon surpassed black growth. After 1870 the relative size of Atlanta's black population began a long, slow, steady decline lasting into the twentieth century, but Atlanta's overall size relative to other Southern cities was increasing at the same time. In 1890 only New Orleans, Richmond, and Nashville were larger, and by 1900 only New Orleans and Memphis. Atlanta's population growth was not unrelated to its boosters' proud assertion that it was an exemplary "New South" city. Within Atlanta there were spaces—and a space—carved out for and by African Americans.[3]

Black Atlanta and Alcohol

Although difficult, life for blacks in post-emancipation Atlanta and the urban South, generally, was filled with exciting potential. Because whites believed blacks "naturally" belonged on plantations and wanted to keep them there, the presence of urban black migrants suggested they embraced a different vision for their lives. Many newly freed blacks considered city living a way to improve their standard of living for, as ex-slave and Atlanta immigrant Julie Tillory announced, her goal was "to 'joy my freedom."[4] Life in Atlanta possessed all the potential inherent in a fresh start in a new place, but also many challenges, because most black immigrants were illiterate and unskilled, or semiskilled workers at best. Throughout the South, young and old freed people avidly sought at least the rudiments of literacy, and cities were particularly appealing because Northerners often established schools in urban areas. Blacks viewed educational opportunity as a fundamental part of their freedom and essential to improving their standard of livin~ In addition, because Atlanta housed Union troops and a growing black pop~ tion, it appeared to promise a degree of security, community, and respite fro~

Table 1—Black Population in Atlanta, 1860–1900

	Total Population	African American Population	Percent African American Population
1860	9,554	1,939	20.3
1870	21,789	9,929	45.5
1880	37,409	16,330	43.6
1890	65,533	28,117	42.9
1900	89,872	35,727	39.7

Source: Ronald H. Bayor, *Race and the Shaping of Twentieth-Century Atlanta* (Chapel Hill: University of North Carolina Press, 1996), 5.

white-on-black violence of rural areas. Urban population density also facilitated the creation of a network of black churches and fraternal organizations. After the war, these organizations had to be built from the "ground up," unlike other Southern cities that boasted antebellum-era networks of black churches, schools, and societies. Because Atlanta's pre–Civil War free black population was so small, it could only sustain one Methodist and one Baptist congregation, both of which were closely overseen by whites. Black Atlanta was the "wild west" of community development for any black with the gumption to move there. There was no elite class with which to network, or compete, so achievement was based on one's skills, hard work, and luck—and what whites would permit.[5]

Where blacks lived in Atlanta immediately following the war was not as much a function of law or custom as it was of the housing shortage, its market-driven corollary of high rent, and their abject poverty. In 1866 one missionary observed that "a little shed" without a pane of glass went for $15 to $20 per month, while another lamented that "We find them in tents and shanties and cabins of all description made of old cloth, tin and tine, the remains of roofing of buildings destroyed by the army." It is evident that the housing of most freed people improved slowly, for in 1879 the houses in the black neighborhood of Shermantown were still described as "huts." Financial exigencies clearly trumped racial prejudice as the primary determiner of residential patterns in the early years after the war. Choosing the least expensive areas, the freed people clustered on the outskirts of the city near landfills and railroad facilities or on "bottom" lands prone to flooding, all of which the white residents avoided. This resulted in an "urban cluster" residential pattern. By 1880 Atlanta had about ten clusters ranging from 77 to 91 percent black, but freed people lived in all parts of the city, and most did *not* live in the clusters. The clusters, however, had an influence "far beyond" what the numbers of blacks living there might suggest, because their population density provided the demographic basis for the development of black institutions.[6]

The three largest and most well-known black-majority clusters were Summerhill, Jenningstown, and Shermantown. Following the war, William Jennings, a Republican lawyer, owned land in the Summerhill area south of the central business district that had many small houses previously occupied by slaves. Summerhill, which was adjacent to a city dump, had suffered extensive damage during the war. Since whites would not buy his houses, Jennings sold them to blacks for one hundred to $200 each and allowed them to make appealing $2.00 monthly payments. This was the perfect housing opportunity for the freed people, as the daily wages for unskilled labor at that time were less than $2.00.[7] But as former slave dwellings, these houses constituted some of the worst housing in the nation. It was in the Summerhill neighborhood that the Methodist Freedmen's Aid Society founded Clark College and where the infamous 1906 race riot primarily occurred.

Fig. 3—Shermantown, an 1879 sketch. *Harper's New Monthly Magazine.* Kenan Research Center at the Atlanta History Center

Jennings was also the agent for a landowner whose property on the west side of the city contained the remains of Confederate fortifications. He began selling this land to blacks, too, and by July 1867 he had sold 130 of 300 lots in what came to be known as Jenningstown. A hilly area immune from flooding, Jenningstown represented some of the best land blacks could afford to own. Jenningstown also attracted blacks because of the anticipation created by the AMA's 1867 announcement that it intended to build a university nearby. The third area, Shermantown, was originally an eight-block area between North Collins, Wheat, Harris, and Fort Streets. It developed east of the central business district on flood-prone lowlands. This area took its name from the fact that General William T. Sherman's troops camped here during the war. Shermantown grew eastward down Wheat Street (now Auburn Avenue), as well as north and south, comprising much of the city's Fourth Ward in the years after the war, which made it Atlanta's only black majority ward.[8]

Some smaller black neighborhoods had also developed by the 1880s. They were Tanyard Bottom, near a city dump and tannery on the north side of town; Pittsburgh, near the roundhouses of the Southern Railroad to the southwest; and Reynoldstown, near another roundhouse east of Summerhill. By the 1890s a black neighborhood had also grown up around Spelman Seminary, which the Woman's American Baptist Home Missionary Society founded in 1881 for African American girls. Whether large or small, all black majority neighborhoods were characterized by extreme poverty and municipal neglect. Atlanta's white press portrayed the hardships of life in these neighborhoods in sarcastic, demeaning, and sensational language, sometimes referring to blacks as "cullud gentlemen" and "society ladies." One headline read, "A Mulatto boy cuts the entrails out of a playmate with a razor," while another article described Jenningstown as populated by "niggers, bobtailed dogs and babies," whose "migratory" residents usually disappeared about rent day and turned up "again a few days afterwards."[9]

According to the 1880 census no enumeration district was more than two-thirds black or more than four-fifths white. In white neighborhoods it was not unusual for black domestics to live in a house behind their employer or in adjacent narrow alleyways. But despite the relatively integrated housing and the apparently close proximity of the races, unpaved streets made the small distances that separated the races seem even larger than they were. Even within an urban cluster model there was a clear sense of where one neighborhood began and another ended.

It was to this space for blacks that Frederick Ayer and other Northern evangelicals came in the years following emancipation. And when they arrived, it did not take long for them to broach the issue of alcohol use. But was there an alcohol "problem" in Black Atlanta? Did the stresses related to emancipation soon inspire

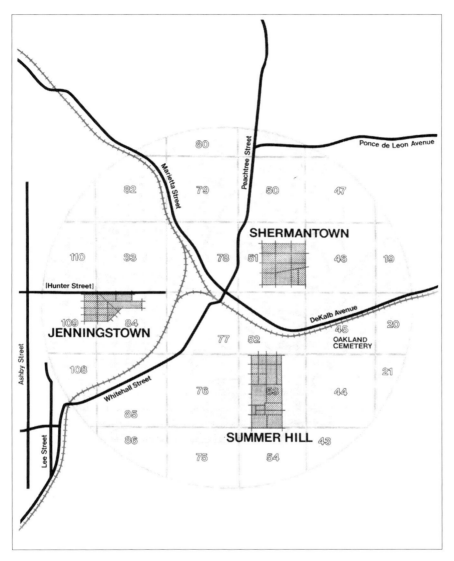

Fig. 4—Black Settlements, 1870. From Dana F. White, "The Black Sides of Atlanta: A Geography of Expansion and Containment, 1970-1870" *Atlanta History Journal* (Summer/Fall 1982): 210. Kenan Research Center at the Atlanta History Center

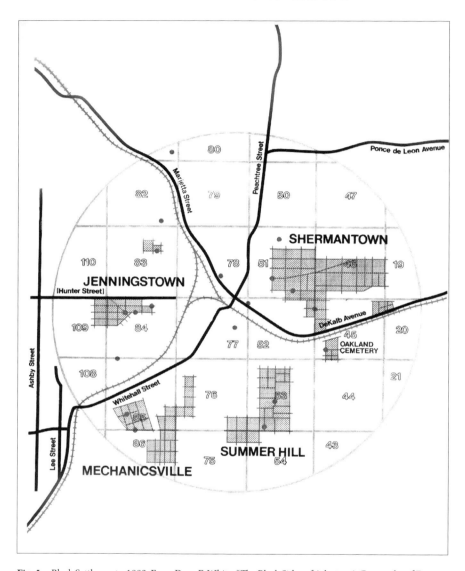

Fig. 5—Black Settlements, 1880. From Dana F. White, "The Black Sides of Atlanta: A Geography of Expansion and Containment, 1970-1870" *Atlanta History Journal* (Summer/Fall 1982): 211. Kenan Research Center at the Atlanta History Center

pathologies of alcohol abuse to which Northern missionaries were responding? How did alcohol use affect freed people's lives? Alcohol abuse was of some consequence in Black Atlanta, but not in the ways one might initially anticipate. The remainder of this chapter explores the impact of alcohol abuse on Black Atlanta, assesses the freed people's attitude toward alcohol use, and explores the first decade of efforts by the American Missionary Society, the American Tract Society, the National Temperance Society, and the AME Church to persuade African Americans to accept teetotalism.

"The Warden and his Deputy Both Stays Drunk Nearly Half the Time":
Law Enforcement, Criminal Justice, and Alcohol

Georgia's notorious convict lease system is a helpful starting point for unpacking the above questions.[10] Although Georgia's Reconstruction-era government invented neither the convict lease system nor forced prison labor, in the postbellum years Georgia initiated what was to become a decades-long regional commitment to convict leasing. This system arose soon after the hostilities ended in 1865 from a convergence of governmental and corporate fiscal exigencies, labor supply shortages, and racist assumptions. In addition to cash-strapped Reconstruction governments and white paranoia that the freed people would refuse to work, the Southern infrastructure desperately needed rebuilding. The war's physical and economic devastation made it difficult for state and local governments to raise enough cash to fund basic government services in the early postbellum years. In addition to providing basic services, governments also had to repair or rebuild much of the war-ravaged public infrastructure. This need was especially acute in Atlanta because General Sherman had burned so much of the city. From the 1870s through the 1890s railroad companies rebuilt their tracks to align them with Northern ones, and extractive industries feeding Northern industrialism like coal mining and lumbering experienced exceptional growth, creating a need for abundant cheap labor. Since this was low-paying and heavy manual labor, whites expected the freed people to provide the bulk of the workforce. Industrialists preferred to hire whites in factories, but then claimed that black laborers hired in the extractive industries so frequently changed their jobs or just did not report to work that they often had to keep as many as 50 to 75 percent more workers on the books than were needed to work on a given day. The combination of a strong demand for cheap labor (in both the public and private sectors) and governmental budget constraints resulted in the convict lease system. So states would not have to foot the costs involved with incarcerating prisoners, they cleverly converted their prison systems from an expense item to a revenue item and did it on the backs of disproportionately black convict laborers.[11]

A December 1866 law established Georgia's convict lease system. Georgia's first convicts were not leased, however, until 1868 when the Georgia and Alabama Railroad and the Selma, Rome, and Dalton Railroad each contracted for one hundred prisoners. These private companies assumed full responsibility for the prisoners, housing and feeding them in camps at the worksite, and hiring guards to secure them on the property. Although considered inmates of the state's penitentiary, leased prisoners did not reside in the actual penitentiary unless they were deemed too ill to work, reducing it to little more than a hospital. As did former slave masters and overseers, private guards whipped prisoners for "slacking," even though Georgia's 1868 constitution prohibited it. In the first year of the program, the principal keeper of the penitentiary, who was responsible for inspecting prison camps, reported that the convicts' "humane treatment" was "entirely ignored." Similar observations were repeatedly reported to the state legislature throughout the duration of the convict least system. Eventually the state appointed a physician to visit the camps, but visitations did little to stem the abuse, for Georgia soon became dependent on convict leasing revenue. By 1870 Georgia's penal system became a revenue-producing arm of government, earning $10,756.48 in 1875 and over $300,000 annually by the end of the century. Business owners, several of whom were political officials or their business associates, were pleased with the dependability of their workforce, labor costs far below that of free workers, and above all, their untold millions in profits. Profiting from criminal convictions thus became normative for Southern governments and businesses in the "New South." As W. E. B. DuBois observed, convict leasing was the logical outcome of the mentality that "the black workman existed for the comfort and profit of white people."[12]

But the convict lease system was not just about finding profitable ways to dispense with otherwise costly governmental obligations. It also served as the state's primary means of controlling black labor, encouraging industrial development, and maintaining white supremacy in a post-emancipation society. Since slave owners had previously been personally responsible for punishing their slaves, it was a new thing for the state to assume responsibility for blacks who behaved criminally. Prior to the war it was rare for Georgia's penitentiary to house black convicts, but by the end of 1865 it held large numbers of blacks, and after 1871 the prison population was always at least 85 percent black. Courts sentenced increasing numbers of black men, at progressively younger ages, and for longer periods of time. In the space of 40 years the total prison population increased ten times, and by the 1890s almost half of the prisoners were under 21. The racism of the system became so blatant that it was not unheard of for officials to use the words "prisoner" and "nigger" interchangeably. Typically, convicts were put to work in industries like railroad building and coal mining, building the "New South" about which Atlanta's business and political leaders crowed so loudly. Convict leasing embodied the contradictions of the New South by reconciling economic development and racial subjugation.[13]

Police and judges fed men and boys into this convict lease system, and Atlanta's law enforcers were among the most zealous. Unlike in some other Southern cities, Atlanta's police force never employed black officers, so the suspicion of discrimination was implicit in virtually every act of law enforcement in Black Atlanta. Black Atlantans were not just sentenced disproportionately compared to whites, but Atlanta's police also arrested blacks at a higher rate than police in other major Southern cities. The most frequent causes for arrest were vagrancy and petty misdemeanors, which likely reflected the large numbers of transient black migrants to Atlanta seeking work or housing. Drinking, to the extent it occurred, would have only exacerbated the situation. A little drinking, the loss of a game of craps, a heated conversation, or a perceived insult to someone's honor could all preface an arrest. The limited extant police records show that 55–60 percent of all arrested individuals before 1890 were black, even though blacks never comprised more than 46 percent of Atlanta's population during these years.[14]

Given the combination of housing shortages, unemployment, underemployment, racial prejudices, and the institutionalized racism of the criminal justice system, the last thing Black Atlanta needed was inebriated on-duty officers, but it had them too! Drunken policemen were a recurring problem, and they exacerbated Atlanta's already tense race relations. Although patrolmen frequently faced charges of drunkenness, the worst year was probably 1873, when 20 percent of the police force (5 out of 26) was charged with being drunk on duty at least once. All were initially suspended pending a hearing, but the final outcomes were not always what would now be considered appropriate. Two received reprimands and a fine, two were dismissed, and one had the charges dropped and reclaimed his back pay. Law enforcement inequities agitated Black Atlanta so much that Howard Rabinowitz maintains, by the 1880s, probably more than in any other Southern city Atlanta's blacks had entered into literal "warfare" with the police. Black crowds frequently harassed policemen escorting suspects to the station, hoping to free them. Police arrests of blacks were inlaid with a broad filigree of racism because policemen, all of whom were white, generally interacted only with the poorest and most desperate freed people, and their superiors tended to believe them rather than any charges of brutality and harassment coming from black citizens. Drunken police working under these conditions only made bad situations worse.[15]

The danger of alcohol use in such a racially hostile environment is suggested by an incident that occurred on July 30, 1883.[16] White and black newspaper reports of this incident were so disparate that one almost thinks they are describing two different events, but this only indicates the vast gulf that existed between the white and black worlds of Atlanta. The *Atlanta Constitution* reported that Officer Holcomb Scarborough's superiors asked him to speak to Eliza Richardson as part of an investigation into an arrest of another person. At some point he decided to arrest Richardson, but blacks mobbed Scarborough in an effort to prevent her arrest. In the ensuing ruckus Scarborough shot and killed Eliza. He was suspended, but an investigation the next day exonerated him. In the investigation Scarborough denied he had been drunk at the time of the shooting. Apparently little more than his race and status were needed to convince authorities of his integrity. The *Constitution* decried the "well-known" practice of black mobs interfering with arrests. In striking contrast, the black weekly, *The Vindicator*, reported simply that a drunken Scarborough shot indiscriminately into a black neighborhood and killed a pregnant Eliza Richardson and wounded a young boy named Willie Scott, whom doctors doubted would live. It then reviewed other examples of anti-black violence in Georgia in recent weeks. Shooting and killing an informer, witness, or a suspect, whatever the case may be, while conducting an investigation apparently did not damage Scarborough's career, for by 1884 he had been promoted to detective, where his primary duty was to investigate crimes.[17]

Police brutality toward blacks was commonplace in Atlanta. It was not uncommon for police to beat blacks while arresting them. Black complaints to the city's mayor in 1876 brought nothing more than a request that "patience and forbearance" should be exercised toward blacks. Between 1865 and 1885 city policemen shot and killed at least twelve blacks while conducting arrests. In only three of these cases were the officers prosecuted, and each time they were acquitted. In the early eighties the black newspaper *The Weekly Defiance* regularly criticized how the police and courts treated blacks. It condemned police who ignored reported assaults on blacks and shot at unarmed fleeing suspects. Police harassed blacks by purposely standing in the way of female pedestrians, forcing them to walk around them, and by making first-class ticket purchasers at the DeGives Opera House sit in inferior seats (before Jim Crow laws required it). In addition, the *Defiance* complained that blacks brought before the Recorder's Court received higher fines than whites for the same crime. The low probability of black complaints about police brutality being taken seriously, the likelihood that charges of drunkenness would *not* result in meaningful discipline or job loss (only 40% in 1873), and the threat of black mobs undoubtedly all conspired to increase the likelihood of on-duty officers showing up inebriated in black neighborhoods.[18] Policing of black neighborhoods might have been perceived as so undesirable that officers would drink to stiffen their resolve, perhaps not unlike lynchers who took a little alcohol to brace themselves in their efforts to "defend" white civilization. While rural Georgia blacks feared violence from the KKK and other vigilantes, Atlanta's blacks feared the drunken police officer.[19]

Blacks caught up in Atlanta's alcohol-plagued law enforcement system were then sentenced to a convict lease camp and had more reasons to fear drunken white authorities. In the spring of 1883, state physician Dr. Thomas Raines visited the camps of the Dade Coal Company for a week. He stayed drunk the whole time, but that did not stop him from certifying as healthy 12 sick prisoners brought in on stretchers. Also, guards were sometimes drunk when they beat prisoners for violating camp rules. One prisoner, Charlie Bailey, complained that at his camp "The warden and his deputy both stays drunk nearly half the time" and claimed to have seen the warden "hit a man 200 licks and he was drunk at the same time." The Durham Coal Company also had an alcoholic "whipping boss," who was ironically named Captain Goode. (Drunken administrators of convict camps, however, could also be "nice" drunks, like the alcoholic superintendent who was so well liked by the convicts that they went on strike after his firing.) Inebriation normally exacerbated the inherent tensions between white law enforcement and black suspects and convicts. Eugene Genovese argues (and antebellum African American fiction writers depicted) that the biggest problem slaves had with alcohol was the drinking done by their masters, and these stories suggest that the freed people's biggest problem with alcohol was its abuse by law enforcement officers, a striking parallel indeed.[20]

"An Astonishing Streak of Sobriety": Black Atlantans' Use of Alcohol

But most black Atlantans were neither convicts nor arrested by the police. What role did alcohol play in the lives of the majority of Atlanta's blacks?[21] What was the day-to-day reality of alcohol use and abuse encountered by missionaries like Frederick Ayer? Did black Atlantans drink as heavily as whites, adopting such common practices as taking a hot toddy before bedtime, or perhaps dram drinking?[22] Were they so frequently inebriated that it interfered with their family life, employment, or citizenship responsibilities? Assuming that the prejudices of Southern whites and the temperance sentiments of Northern whites would give both groups a heightened sensitivity to black drinking patterns and abuse, I closely examined comments made in travel journals, the records of those who went south to work in Black Atlanta, and the city's white press for any reference to freed people and alcohol, expecting abuse to be highlighted and minor incidents exaggerated or condescendingly editorialized. The findings were mixed, and occasionally surprising.

The uses of intoxicating beverages and the definition of inebriation are culturally determined, and we know that it was common in the African cultures from which American slaves came for power, status, and gender roles to determine who drank, when they drank, and how much they drank. Prior to leaving Africa, most Africans would have been familiar with alcohol in palm wine and beer. The way Africans consumed these drinks "taught the lessons of hierarchy" because higher status individuals usually profited from any sale of the beverage, and on special occasions they drank first and then determined the drinking order of other community members.[23]

The ways whites regulated enslaved and free blacks' use of alcohol reinforced the "lessons of hierarchy" learned in Africa societies. During slavery, whites proscribed slaves' and free blacks' drinking by law and custom in cities and on plantations. Beginning in 1853 city ordinances not only prohibited Atlanta's free and enslaved blacks from selling and buying alcoholic beverages but also forbade them from even entering a retail liquor establishment. Such laws were common in the antebellum urban South. Although it was illegal to sell liquor to enslaved or free blacks, many plantation owners gave their slaves several days off at Christmas time and provided liberal amounts of whiskey or beer. Masters permitted slaves to drink on other special occasions also. In Frederick Douglass's experience, masters encouraged slave drunkenness between Christmas and New Years. Douglass thought masters did this to give slaves a perverted sense of liberty by making them think the alternative to slavery to man was slavery to drink. He hated this "grossest of frauds" because he claimed it tended to prevent slaves from thinking about ways to escape, thus perpetuating their bondage. But some masters would provide whiskey, brandy, eggnog, cider, or beer and then monitor their slaves' drinking. According to fugitive slave, temperance speaker, and novelist William Wells Brown, drunken masters treated slaves worse than sober ones. His writings associated intemperance with slaveholders and portrayed sobriety as an instrument slaves used against whites. Charles Stearns, an abolitionist who purchased a plantation after the war, described at length the traits of the freed people, specifically noting that they were neither given to drink nor total abstainers. He found that the freed people did not like to spend money for liquor when they needed other things. The existence of laws prohibiting the sale of liquor to slaves, combined with masters' self-interest in their workers' sobriety, suggests that although slaves drank with and without permission, and sometimes to excess, whites' proscriptions of slave drinking were generally effective. Most historians of the subject agree that the African cultural patterns that slavery reinforced changed only gradually following emancipation.[24]

Travelers in the postbellum South sometimes commented on drinking customs, but they tended to contrast whites' heavy drinking with blacks' lower levels of consumption. Although drinking declined throughout the nation by mid-century, the decline was less pronounced in the South, which had a particularly strong reputation for heavy drinking. Planters' conception of gentility and the South's rural culture meant that fewer Southerners shared the North's evolving bourgeois work ethic, which combined with the evangelical reform nexus to make the practice of abstinence flourish. In late 1865, the *Chicago Tribune* correspondent Sidney Andrews toured Georgia and the Carolinas and declared whiskey drinking the "prevailing vice of the whole people." Andrews noted that on Georgia's trains people were more likely to bring along their favorite alcoholic beverage than lunch. A few years later, the Englishman Robert Somers concluded that Southerners held liquor-drinking "in greater social esteem" than any other people in the world, but he noticed that they mostly drank in saloons and taverns and seldom at home, a change from antebellum times. American Missionary Association field secretary E. P. Smith toured the South each winter specifically to observe the habits of the freed people, and in 1870 he reported that although they drank more than was good for them, they did not drink as much as whites. He said he never saw an intoxicated "Negro," but that he had seen several intoxicated whites. Smith further asserted that stories of black mothers giving whiskey to their babies were greatly exaggerated. In 1867 the AMA missionary Edmund A. Ware equated the freed people's attitude toward liquor with that of antebellum Northern whites. He said there seemed to be "much the same feeling, or rather—want of feeling on the subject that there used to be in New England before the agitation of the temperance question." Just as Northern society had needed a reform movement to inform its conscience, so too did the freed people. But this was a fundamentally optimistic appraisal for it assumed blacks had the same ability to learn and change their habits as whites. Into the 1880s, outsiders who visited America agreed that Southerners drank more than others, and that whiskey was particularly popular, but negative reports of the freed people's drinking practices were rare and usually referenced those in small towns and rural communities.[25]

The Englishman Charles Nordhoff is the main exception to these observations by outsiders. In the mid-1870s Nordhoff toured the South, and his writings reveal a generally unfavorable view of the freed people's "progress." In his book he quoted the following cynical words of an Atlanta newspaper: "In the matter of temperance has there been progress? Nay, in this respect the freedmen are a thousand percent worse off than they were in slavery. Rarely do we find a strictly temperate man. Very nearly all drink." Nordhoff thought the paper was a little harsh, but accurate. Various things could account for his perspective. Perhaps Nordhoff expected to find much less drinking among freed people than he found, or perhaps he discussed black drinking practices with whites who ostensibly "knew their Negroes" and believed them to be heavy drinkers. It is also possible that his travels simply brought him into an exceptionally large number of incidences of inebriated freed people. Whatever the case, Nordhoff's comments and newspaper excerpt confirm others' observations that teetotalism was not a prominent African American value in the early post-emancipation years.[26]

Although explanations for silence in the historical record are seldom obvious, one silence on this matter seems noteworthy, and it comes from John W. Alvord, superintendent of schools for the Freedmen's Bureau and colporteur for the American Tract Society-Boston during the war. As a Congregational minister, Oberlin alumnus, and onetime American Anti-Slavery Society agent, Alvord held impeccable antebellum reform nexus credentials. In 1869 the Freedman's Bureau director General Oliver O. Howard sent Alvord on a tour of the South to report on the condition of the freed people. He sent back a series of letters, and in one of them he mentioned hearing reports of increased intemperance on the Sea Islands. But after five days in Atlanta in January 1870, Alvord made virtually no mention of intemperance there. Earlier, in 1867, in response to reports of intemperance among freed people in Virginia, General Howard had asked him to oversee the creation of temperance societies for the freed people. Given Alvord's personal background, his notice of drinking in other places, and his responsibility to organize temperance societies for the freed people, it is not likely that he would have ignored patterns of intemperance anywhere in his travel report. In fact, in 1867 Alvord had written of intemperance among the freed people that "We do not find them notoriously given to this vice." Given his background, Alvord would have had a relatively low threshold for defining "notorious" alcohol abuse. In the context of Alvord's life and professional responsibilities, his omission of any reference to intemperance in 1870 Black Atlanta strongly suggests that it was not a glaring problem there.[27]

Atlanta's newspapers also shed light on black drinking. The Mayor's Court and Recorder's Court columns in Atlanta's newspapers did *not* indicate a court system swamped with drunken black criminals in the decade after the Civil War.[28] Although they wrote in sarcastic and derogatory ways about the freed people, they did not report or complain about disproportionate numbers of inebriated blacks being dragged to court. Although no week passed without multiple arraignments for public drunkenness or the catch-all category of "drunk and disorderly," the papers often did not indicate race, and when they did, as many whites as blacks were so charged.[29] As might be expected, Atlanta had its coterie of habitual drunkards. When the *Weekly Sun* complained about an increase in crime in 1871 it did not mention alcohol as a factor, but by the 1870s white drinking on Independence Day seems to have been on the rise. On the first court day after July 4, 1870, there were 24 cases in the Mayor's Court. The paper commented that "of course" the majority of the cases were "drunk and disorderly" charges from the "glorious fourth." But the stories did not mention race. On July 4, 1873, the police only charged one of the three blacks they arrested with intoxication, while five of the twelve whites were so charged. In general, the newspapers' court reporting did not create an image of drunken blacks filling Atlanta's streets.[30]

Rather than report daily examples of black drunkenness, Atlanta's newspapers were more likely to spotlight black decorum during holiday celebrations, and Independence Day and Christmas were traditionally heavy occasions for heavy drinking.[31] Although the press's condescending comments mocked the showiness of black-dominated Independence Day celebrations, the press never reported violence, public drunkenness, or criminal behavior at these events. Instead, in the early years following the war, the press considered them to be little more than Republican rallies with politicians addressing integrated crowds sometimes as much as one-fourth white. In 1868 the *Atlanta Constitution* was so impressed with blacks' decorum that it ended its description by saying "the negroes deserve great credit for their orderly demeanor during the exercises as well as during the night of 'The glorious Fourth.'" In 1871 when black benevolent societies participated, the *Daily New Era* reported nothing negative about the celebration. On Emancipation Day 1872, an event irregularly celebrated in Atlanta,[32] the Grand United Order of Odd Fellows held a parade, and the paper described them as "very orderly" and "composed of the very best class of the colored people." Later that year when 19 railroad cars of blacks came to Atlanta to celebrate Independence Day, a tradition that would continue for many years, the press found nothing negative to report. As late as July 1885, the papers said of Independence Day celebrants that the "darkies took little liquor" and that most of the 62 drunks arrested were whites. If anything, the white press showed that it was whites, not blacks, who had a problem with public intoxication on holidays.[33]

Some signs indicated, however, that as early as 1875 the trend was beginning to reverse itself. Following Christmas the newspapers reported many liquor-related crimes and highlighted those committed by blacks. The rise in crime was partly attributable to the new mayoral tradition begun that year to free all prisoners held in the city jail on municipal charges. Most prisoners were black, and as the papers tell it, clemency made Christmas a busy day for the police. After each Christmas the *Atlanta Constitution* ran a "Christmas Crimes" column. "Christmas time and cheap whisky developed an amount of rascality among our darkies which we must confess we were unprepared for," the *Constitution* reported in 1875. "The clemency of Mayor Hammock in releasing from the guard house the roughs and disorderly persons the police had arrested, proved to be a mistake." The police charged blacks in various stages of inebriation with three assaults with attempt to murder, plus multiple lesser crimes, several occurring in saloons. But this report is the exception that proves the rule. The reason the city was "unprepared" suggests that up to this time blacks were rarely known for these public displays of drunkenness. The practice of freeing Atlanta's mostly black jail population at Christmas, which continued for years, is perhaps analogous to the liberty some slave owners used to give slaves during the week between Christmas and New Year's. For Christmas 1876, police restricted the use of firecrackers, creating a quieter city, but reporters claimed they saw more intoxicated men and boys on the streets than they had seen in six months. Seventy-five cases, several times more than usual, appeared on the Recorder's Court docket on December 26. The papers could not report on all of these arrests, but they highlighted black crimes. In 1877 there was so little alcohol-related crime that it prompted the *Constitution*'s editors to exclaim, "You would hardly have known it was Christmas." While blacks did not seem to drink nearly as much as whites in the early years after emancipation, their drinking likely increased with time. For Southern whites, emancipation had raised all sorts of racial control "fears," and thus the parallels between the policies of slave masters and the new postbellum governments toward African Americans could be eerily similar at times.[34]

An event that occurred in Atlanta on Independence Day in 1866 illustrates the nature of the freed people's problem with alcohol in the early years after emancipation. In Atlanta, as in other Southern cities in 1866, blacks dominated public Independence Day celebrations. This year they began with a procession led by a band and a grand marshal, followed by uniformed, banner-carrying members of two groups who have since been lost to history: the Order of the Golden Rod and Rising Generation and the Order of the Hickory Rod and Fallen Generation. The Golden Rod banner depicted Charles Sumner giving a speech from Plymouth Rock, and the Hickory Rod banner had the motto "My God, My Duty, and My Self." Although men and women belonged to both groups, and both participated in the procession, they marched separately. A captain adorned in red, white, and blue on a white stallion preceded the parade, and it ended with a female "Genius of America" dressed in tattered clothes and a gaudy hat, with an old can filled with dirty cotton attached to her neck. Atlanta's blacks had turned the national holiday into a celebration of the end of slavery and the mentality that supported it, for the hickory rod and the "fallen generation" likely referred to the near-death caning of the Republican Massachusetts senator Charles Sumner by South Carolina representative Preston Brooks and the military defeat of his enthusiastic supporters in the Civil War. Sumner was obviously being honored for his presumed faithfulness to the highest ideals of America's Puritan founders. Such celebrations revealed the freed people's readiness to imagine their own narrative of national events.

The procession ended in an oak grove near the city's Oakland Cemetery with speeches and picnicking. After the clubs positioned their banners and took their seats, the audience heard speeches from three black speakers before feasting on corn bread, custard, sweetmeats, and a variety of other foods. Joseph Wood, pastor of the Bethel AME Church, was master of ceremonies. Although the white press reported the whole affair in a conspicuously mocking tone, nowhere did it mention alcohol was part of the celebration or that any celebrants became inebriated, even though the saloons were open.[35]

Before the war whites had commonly celebrated the Fourth publicly, with "big dinners" and "big drinks"—and getting at least a little tipsy—but in 1866 any celebrations by whites were done quietly at home. The *Daily Intelligencer* explained the absence of the heavy drinking by whites with a quote from a well-known temporarily sober local drunkard named "Jones." Jones said that because the Fourth was a "day we of the South have agreed to surrender up to the niggers, Yankee school-marms, and such like, if a Southern gentleman gets drunk, friends might think he is celebrating the day, and I wish to be *above suspicion*" (emphasis in original). The humor of a drunkard self-identifying himself as a "gentleman" who wanted to be "above suspicion" made light of the truth that just as excessive drinking before the war held important social meaning for whites, so too did abstinence in the wake of losing the Civil War. Alcohol use itself was quickly becoming racialized, as most Southern whites segregated themselves from public celebrations of national holidays.[36]

While Southern whites could appreciate Jones's logic, unfortunately for blacks, it was lost on Northern white soldiers stationed in Atlanta. As the mostly black celebrants returned from the cemetery, two drunken soldiers exchanged some heated words with a few members of the crowd, and a row followed, with the soldiers firing shots that injured some blacks. Enlisted men under the direction of a sergeant arrived to restore order, but a little later an inebriated, mounted lieutenant showed up to assume command. As the lieutenant marched the men away from the scene they began balking at his orders, and the sergeant, siding with the infantry, knocked the lieutenant off his horse. Although the newspaper in 1866 downplayed these and other "disturbances of a trifling character" among the soldiers, the following year the commandant of the post ordered the mayor to close all saloons on July Fourth. In 1867 the paper expressed the hope that it would prevent a repetition of the previous year's "disgraceful events."[37]

This overview suggests the subtle truth that alcohol abuse was not so much a problem *in* Black Atlanta as it was *for* Black Atlanta. Although Atlanta's white press and outside observers had plenty of opportunities to expose heavy alcohol use or abuse in the black community, they seldom reported either. While Atlanta's blacks were clearly drinkers, little evidence suggests anything near epidemic levels of abuse in the early years of freedom. As late as the eve of the 1885 local option campaign, the *Atlanta Constitution* observed that the freed people were "not specially given to intemperance" but, rather, had developed "an astonishing streak of sobriety." Atlanta's blacks apparently entered freedom without a widespread custom of heavy drinking, or a significant number of alcohol abusers, but also without a natural tendency toward teetotalism. Even with that being the case, there is no reason to doubt that a significant number of black convicts were drunk at the time they committed their deed, just as was the case with whites. In fact, it was not unheard of for individuals who leased convicts to oppose prohibition, evidently fearing a decreased pool of labor. But in the early years of freedom, the average freed person was likely more pragmatic than ideological in his or her approach to beverage alcohol. For the vast majority of blacks, the excitement and challenges of creating a new life in freedom overrode tendencies toward dissipation, but this was not enough to prevent Northern missionaries from finding an alcohol "problem," for they could easily construe the mere lack of teetotalism as a "liquor problem." The missionaries arrived in Black Atlanta with a religious and cultural predisposition to preach abstinence even if they did not witness public drunkenness on every street corner and were not bombarded with tales of alcohol-induced violence.[38]

"Intemperance Will Soon Lay Hold upon Their Excitable Natures": Northern Missionaries and Roots of Temperance Sentiment in Black Atlanta

The attitude of the missionaries and the nexus organizations toward the freed people was analogous to their attitude toward western settlers and eastern urban immigrants in the antebellum period. In each case their Christian republican worldview discerned a threat to republican government in the masses of uneducated, unchurched, and presumably unvirtuous citizens; this time, those citizens just happened to be of a different race and in the part of the nation that had recently failed to secede from the union. As in antebellum days, this threat was not seen as a cause for hand-wringing but, rather, as a new opportunity to make oneself "useful" in God's kingdom. Using almost the same republican language with which they had previously targeted unchurched whites, evangelical Northern missionary agencies now turned their attention to the freed people. "In their intelligence, Christian culture, and sobriety is the future welfare of the Republic in no small degree involved," opined the *National Temperance Advocate* editor in 1873. Speakers at annual meetings of the AMA and ABHMS, and their annual committee reports, regularly spouted Christian republican tropes when describing their Southern mission work. One AMA speaker reminded his audience that "liberty can not live in this country without Christian morality," while another argued that a "more Christian citizenship" was needed to prevent "our experiment in self-government" from shipwreck.[39]

The North's victory in the war emboldened those committed to the values of the antebellum evangelical reform nexus. Arrogance set in, and James McPherson has aptly labeled this postbellum attitude of Northern missionaries "cultural-ism," a belief in the intrinsic superiority of Northern evangelical culture over all others. This prejudice equally targeted Southern blacks and whites. Missionaries criticized the freed people who claimed to be Christian but found it easy to justify lying and petty theft, although some did recognize this for what it was, namely, a learned response to the exigencies of life under slavery and the hypocrisies of their white Christian owners. But Northern missionaries also took issue with the Christianity of the former slave masters. "We can not trust the cause of Christ to the Judas who has betrayed it," one Northerner charged. Southern Christians were too corrupted by the "spirit of slavery" and "tainted with sympathy for the rebellion" to be entrusted with morally rebuilding the South. Such attitudes ob-viously only added to the existing tensions between the missionaries and local whites during Reconstruction.[40]

Evangelical missionaries' racial attitudes are best described by the term "ro-mantic racialism." Romantic racialism emerged from the nineteenth century's emphasis on passion and feeling and the growing tendency to believe in intrin-sic racial traits. Evangelicals accepted the idea of intrinsic racial differences but argued that the supposedly inherent traits of black people—docility, expressive-ness, impressionability, and religiosity—were childlike, even Christian, because of their supposedly nonaggressive and non-threatening nature. Although these traits were deemed generally positive, blacks' "impressionable" and "emotional" natures presumably made them more "susceptible" to vices such as intemperance. This thinking underlay the AMA's 1867 warning about the freed people: "All evil influences are springing swiftly into activity within and around them. Natural de-pravity, with instinctive force, will germinate its bitter fruits rapidly; intemperance will soon lay hold upon their excitable natures."[41]

Significantly, the missionaries did not consider intellectual capacity a racially inherent trait but, rather, believed that given equal religious, educational, and po-litical opportunities blacks would become as virtuous, as economically produc-tive, and as politically responsible as whites. Henry L. Morehouse, secretary of the American Baptist Home Mission Society, argued that blacks had "essentially the same nature and endowments as the white man" and the same ability to become "self-reliant, aspiring, [and] cultured." An editorial in the Baptist *Home Mission Monthly* expressing this view was appropriately titled "Culture is Colorless." Be-cause Northern missionaries assumed blacks had the same ability to assimilate Northern evangelical culture as other peoples, they were the most racially pro-gressive thinkers of their day. Although it is tempting to dismiss such paternalistic thinking as "racist," to do so obscures the fact that the evangelical missionaries' belief in the pernicious effects of the *system* of slavery made them theological and ideological forerunners of the Social Gospel movement and twentieth-century "public" Protestantism, which traditionally attributes social injustice and racism to inequitable systems and structures of power rather than to individual acts of discrimination or personal moral failures. AMA missionaries derived from the abolitionist theological camp, which developed the concept of "social sin," a key element in the hermeneutical foundation of today's liberal Protestantism.[42]

Many Americans at the time viewed the Civil War as a clash of opposing civilizations or cultures, and evangelical missionaries widely believed that the North's victory would not be complete until their culture dominated the South. The freed people's supposedly tractable nature made them the logical starting point for remaking all Southern society, thereby completing the Union victory. One can see the centrality of culture as a driving force in Northern missionary thought in these comments by the AMA's corresponding secretary Michael E. Strieby about starting Congregational churches among Southern whites:

> There is undoubtedly a large mass of white people in the South as unlettered, impoverished, and shiftless as the blacks. To them we must come with sympathy, education, and the gospel. There is no power like an intelligent Christianity to arouse men from indolence, poverty, and vice. With this gospel thus brought to the lowliest class, it may be uplifted, and its uplifting will move the masses above it.

Northern missionary organizations committed themselves to a long-range plan to conquer the South with New England culture and religion, and they chose to begin with the freed people.[43]

Frederick Ayer was the vanguard of the AMA's cultural uplift effort. On November 27, 1865, he assumed control of a school of 75 students being run by two former slaves, James Tate and Granithan Daniels.[44] The next day he had one hundred students. During the first year, Ayer taught in a reconstructed army chapel he had shipped from Chattanooga, and in the war-damaged building of the Bethel AME Church, the city's oldest black congregation. At the time, a smallpox epidemic was raging, especially among the refugees streaming into the city. Employed freed people, who quickly turned to self-help efforts, did the best they could to fund an infirmary for black smallpox victims, but white Atlantans considered the hospital a nuisance and made the city relocate it beyond the city limits. Events like this inspired one missionary to report on racial attitudes: "The whites, generally do not seem disposed to favor them, any farther than it benefits themselves. Still they do not seem to be discouraged."[45]

The AMA's commitment to temperance as part of its culturalism was evident from the moment it established its presence in Black Atlanta. To begin with, all AMA missionaries had to sign a teetotal pledge. Three of the first five AMA missionaries in Atlanta were former Oberlin students: the sisters Lucy and Rose Kinney, who arrived in November 1865, and Jennie Barnum, who arrived a few weeks later. Lucy returned to Oberlin in 1866, but in 1867 Eliza Mitchell arrived, and more "Oberliners" followed. Whether or not AMA teachers were Oberlin alumni, they all had a personal commitment to abstinence that showed in their teaching and missionary work. One example of how a teacher's personal commitment to abstinence could affect her teaching is the AMA missionary in South Carolina who wrote a mnemonic verse about the presidents for her students. When she wrote the line for Franklin Pierce, she conveniently forgot his effective lobbying for the controversial Kansas-Nebraska Act and instead turned his personal life into a moral lesson by calling him "A drunkard whom we blush to name." As always, the teacher was the most important element in a child's education; but the influence of the educational literature itself should not be overlooked.[46]

Textbooks were even more central to education in the nineteenth century than they are today, and Northern evangelicals sought to capitalize on this fact. Because rote memorization was the pedagogical norm, students regularly suffered through their "recitations," making the textbook the sine qua non of education. Well aware of the textbook's importance, during the war the newly independent American Tract Society-Boston published a series of readers for the freed people called the "Educational Series," as well as other literature, most of which seems to have circulated in Atlanta after the war. The ATrS-Boston modeled its readers after the popular New England readers of the day but added special religious and civil emphases that betrayed their culturalism and romantic racialism. Just as much as they taught literacy, they conveyed cultural values that Northerners believed the schoolhouse of slavery had ignored, twisted, or contradicted.[47]

Early Temperance Literature for the Freed People

ATrS literature initially arrived in Atlanta despite the best intentions of Gilbert S. Eberhart, Georgia's first superintendent of schools for the Freedmen's Bureau (October 1865–September 1867). In order to gain the confidence and cooperation of Georgia's Southern whites, Eberhart had announced that blacks would not be taught social equality and suffrage in Bureau schools. Accordingly, he adopted the A. S. Barnes & Co. readers, which, compared to ATrS-Boston texts, included relatively few exhortations on civic duties or warnings about vice, and no references to the war, Southerners, or the new civil rights of the freed people. Despite Eberhart's decision, the ATrS-Boston sent him more than five thousand books and other educational materials during his first year on the job, and he consented to distributing the literature throughout "half" of the state. It is not clear which areas received the literature or whether Atlanta was included. But regardless of what Bureau schools did, Frederick Ayer founded an AMA school, and he chose to use ATrS publications. Less than two months after Frederick Ayer arrived, he received 50 copies of *The Freedman* and 20 copies of *Freedman's Journal*, two small monthly newspaper-readers produced by the ATrS-Boston not only for students but also for families to use at home for literacy training and moral instruction. *The Freedman,* first published in 1864 and the simpler of the two publications, included writing lessons and stories geared for young children, while the *Freedman's Journal* contained facts about the government, nature, history, and current events (relevant to the freed people) written for slightly more literate and mature audiences. Both journals printed stories and sometimes direct messages from "friends" of the freed people like Methodist layman and temperance advocate General Clinton Fisk, urging such virtues as sobriety, honesty, thrift, and self-reliance. *The Freedman* and *Freedman's Journal* immediately attracted some interest, and within a month 15 blacks wanted to purchase their own subscriptions at 25 cents per year. Ayer thought there was enough interest—and literacy—for him to distribute more than a hundred copies each month, so the AMA began placing monthly orders with the ATrS on his behalf.[48]

"The Cure of the Drunkard," in the January 1866 issue of *The Freedman*, was probably the first printed temperance message to arrive in Black Atlanta. In this little vignette the character John Abbot signed a pledge to abstain from intoxicating beverages for one year. At the end of the year he renewed his pledge, this time for 999 years. A few days later John visited the tavern where he used to drink, and he told the keeper, as though he were in pain, that he had a lump on his side. The proprietor said the lump was the result of his abstinence. John asked if drinking would take away the lump, and the tavern keeper said yes, and then poured him two glasses of whiskey. John replied, "'I guess I won't drink, especially if keeping the pledge will bring another lump; for it isn't very hard to bear after all'; and with this he drew the *lump*, a roll of greenbacks, from his side-pocket, and walked off, leaving the landlord to his reflections." The story was shrewdly designed to cause its readers, most of whom were living from hand to mouth, to engage in some practical "reflections" of their own. Stories of this nature graced the pages of both publications on multiple occasions.[49]

Both newspapers presented a consistent temperance message with a wide variety of arguments, consistent with antebellum ATrS tracts. *The Freedman* actually never cited Scripture in defense of teetotalism, instead emphasizing the unhealthy effects of drinking and arguing that it was a waste of money. It also warned children that tobacco was a gateway to worse substances, like liquor. The *Freedman's Journal*, however, on occasion did use Bible verses. In "What You Cannot Afford,"

Clinton Fisk listed first that "you cannot afford to drink any kind of spirituous or malt liquors." He then quoted several Bible verses and warned that drinking would squander people's money and destroy their self-respect. The *Journal* also printed a short dialogue called "Drinking by the Acre." When Tim McMoran asks John Nokes to have a drink, the following conversation ensues :

> "I've made up my mind that I can do better with land, than to drink it."
> "Who's asked you to drink land, I'd like to know."
> "Well, I find, that every time I drink sixpence worth of liquor, I drink more than a good square yard of land worth three hundred dollars an acre."

Whether rural or urban, blacks placed a high priority on land ownership, and it is easy to imagine this pragmatic approach resonating with many. By the end of the century, the assets of several of Atlanta's more well-off blacks were based on land ownership because it was a way to improve one's status that whites' discriminatory practices could do little to prevent.[50]

More important than these monthly papers, however, were the ATrS-produced classroom readers (textbooks) that AMA missionary-teachers began using almost immediately, for they also incorporated a strong temperance message. In the first three "classes" of the *Freedman's Spelling-Book* students were taught one-letter words, two-letter words, and then three-letter words and syllables.[51] Even at such a rudimentary linguistic level, the authors could include a clear condemnation of drinking:

> It is a sin to sip rum.
> A sot is a bad man.
> Do not get in a pet.
> A la-zy man can not get a job.
> God is ho-ly; he can see if men sin.
> If a man sin, he is bad.
> A sot has rum or gin in his jug.

In this simple lesson, students were introduced to the concept of sin, given examples of good and evil, taught about God's nature, and repeatedly warned about the evil of intemperance—and all that within the limits of a three-letter-word vocabulary! As the lexical and syntactic complexity increased, the author conveyed more complex messages, such as this one with strong undertones of pro-revival theology and a hint of Christian republicanism: "Strong drink not on-ly stim-u-lates: it stu-pe-fies the sens-es and the mind, and leads one to vi-o-late du-ty, and per-pe-trate hor-rid crimes." The passages also incorporated a millennial optimism: "When we dine we drink no wine, in nine-teen hundred and nine-ty nine."[52]

The *Second* and *Third Readers* used short readings to teach new vocabulary words, proper pronunciation, and lessons about abstinence. One story from the *Second Reader*, "Mary and the Drunkard's Children," contained a list of five new words with their definitions. The story told about a drunkard's family who had recently moved to town. His two children came to Mary's house looking for food. Mary and her mother fed them breakfast, and Mary's mother promised to look after them in the future and hoped to be able to convince their father to become sober. "Sober" was one of the words defined at the end of the story. The second and third readers mixed poetry with prose. For example, "Bertie Rand's Temperance Pledge" was a three-stanza poem:

> Though I am only ten years old,
> Said little Bertie Rand,
> Upon the side of Temperance
> I proudly take my stand;
> And naught that can intoxicate
> My lips shall ever pass:
> For there's a serpent slyly coiled
> Within the drunkard's glass.
>
> Poor Allen Benton's little Will,
> In tattered garments clad,
> Whose blue eyes oft are full of tears,
> Whose heart is seldom glad,
> Has learned, through fear of angry blows,
> His father's face to shun.
> It must be very, very hard
> To be a drunkard's son!
>
> When others round their wine shall sit,
> I'll never bear a part,
> And thus disgrace my father's name,
> Or break my mother's heart
> But I am weak; not of myself
> Can I resist this sin:
> The Savior aids the weakest child
> That putteth trust in him

This little poem caused students to pledge every time they recited the poem, reminded them of how drunken fathers made their families miserable, and taught them that only through faith in Jesus Christ can one hope to overcome the temptation to drink. This last point was as old as the temperance movement itself. Through practice sentences, stories, and poems, American Tract Society readers and newspapers served purposes beyond just teaching reading—and temperance was one of them.[53]

But ATrS publications reached not only African Americans enrolled in missionary schools. Although Eberhart did receive and distribute thousands of "school books and papers" from the American Tract Society, and in 1868 Georgia received more ATrS-New York literature than any state except Virginia, as far as Atlanta is concerned, it is also important to note that AMA missionaries Frederick Ayer, Malvina Higgins, Lizzie Stevenson, and Cyrus W. Francis each received free shipments of ATrS literature, and that from 1871 to 1874 the ATrS sponsored colporteurs in Fulton County. After school and on the weekends, missionary-teachers conducted home visits in Black Atlanta, during which time they distributed primers, copies of the *Freedman's Journal*, and tracts, and of course, colporteurs were doing the same thing. Children used these materials before enrolling in school, for Malvina Higgins reported that the primers she distributed during her visits were so effective that some students enrolled in school having already taught themselves up to the third reader in the A. S. Barnes & Co. series. Many who could not attend school also achieved a basic level of literacy using these materials in their own homes.[54]

Among the items missionaries and colporteurs distributed were temperance tracts designed specifically for the freed people. A handful of such tracts were published between 1863 and 1873. The American Temperance Union published the *Temperance Tract for the Freedmen* during the war, which was probably distributed by AMA and ABHMS missionaries working behind Union army lines along the Atlantic coast. No evidence exists that the National Temperance Society reprinted it after the war, so it probably never reached Atlanta. In 1863 Isaac Brinckerhoff, a former colporteur and the first ABHMS missionary to work with the freed people, published with the ATrS-New York a tract titled *Advice to Freedmen*, in which he directly addressed temperance, among other issues, using traditional Christian republican language and pro-revival theology. He warned that although they were under army control at the time (he was working on St. Helena Island, South Carolina) and did not have much access to liquor, there would come a time when they would have access, and that they should abstain from drinking because it would deprive them of the use of their reason and "blight" their "prospects for usefulness." He called ignorance an "evil" imposed by slavery and urged them to get an education that would make them "useful, virtuous, and Christian." Although it was written in the context of the war, Frederick Ayer received copies of this tract for distribution in 1866. At the end of the war, the ATrS-New York published another Brinckerhoff tract, *A Warning to Freedmen against Intoxicating Drinks*, which discussed how the temptation comes, how to overcome it, and the consequences of yielding to the temptation and ended with an abstinence pledge for readers to sign. Among other arguments, again Brinckerhoff warned that drinking "unfits" one for the "required heart power and mental power necessary to escape from the wrath to come," traditional revivalist language about one's need to have uncompromised reasoning abilities to respond to the Gospel in order to escape God's judgment at the end of the world. Colporteurs undoubtedly distributed this tract in Black Atlanta. In addition to receiving Brinckerhoff's tracts from the ATrS, by 1867 the National Temperance Society was also sending tracts to Frederick Ayer, although it is not clear what they sent since their first tract for the freed people, *Freemen, or Slaves*, was not published till 1868.[55]

Following emancipation, the freed people pursued literacy at an almost frantic pace, and Northerners' distribution of these various readers and tracts played well into this passion for education, the existence of which has been thoroughly demonstrated by Herbert Gutman and Heather Andrea Williams, among others. Before the war, slaves "stole" an education anyway they could, and as freedom spread during the conflict they rushed to establish schools, with or without the help and sanction of whites. Freed people's drive for literacy underlay their push for enfranchisement, financial sacrifices for their children's education, multiple conflicts over control of black schools, and the beginning of public education in the South. According to Gutman, Georgia's blacks led the way in education. He maintains that "between 1865 and 1867, black people in Georgia did more to educate their children than those in any other Southern state." One Atlanta manifestation of this drive was the school operated by former slaves James Tate and Granithan Daniels that Ayer found upon his arrival. They learned anywhere they could, from whomever they could, and free literature in their homes on any subject, even temperance, only facilitated this passion. At the same time, this literature introduced the freed people to the timeworn discourse of temperance that had previously targeted northern and western white audiences.[56]

Temperance Societies in the Freed People's Schools

In 1866 the nexus organizations began appropriating Abraham Lincoln for the temperance cause among the freed people. Both *The Freedman* and the *Freedman's Journal* printed a story of the night Lincoln first received the Republican nomination; it was a story subsequently made popular by temperance reformers. Lincoln was not at the convention when nominated, so a party of men brought him the news. Lincoln declared that such an occasion called for treating his guests, which he purportedly did with cold water because "it is the only beverage which our God has given to man; it is the only beverage I have ever used or allowed in my family, and I can not conscientiously depart from it on the present occasion." In the wake of emancipation, there could be no more influential temperance spokesman in the eyes of the freed people than the "Great Emancipator" himself.[57] Also in 1866 the AMA asked the NTS to compose a "Lincoln" Temperance Pledge card. The AMA openly admitted that they named it the "Lincoln" Temperance Pledge "to make it attractive as well as more impressive" to the freed people. The card was handsomely designed, with the pledge printed over a shadow image of an interracial group of adults and children gathered around a table watching a black man sign the pledge. The Emancipation Proclamation and a likeness of Abraham Lincoln hung over the scene. Five of the most popular pro-abstinence Bible verses framed it. NTS president William E. Dodge donated $100 toward the printing and distribution of the pledges.[58]

The power of Lincoln's image was not lost on Frederick Ayer either. In December 1866 the AMA opened a new school building, the Storrs School, named for the Reverend Henry M. Storrs, the Cincinnati pastor whose church had made the initial donation. The former building was rented to the Methodist Freedman's Aid Society, which operated the Summer Hill School out of it. For many years black Atlantans regarded the Storrs School as the best school in Atlanta for their children. The school included a four-hundred-seat chapel in which Frederick Ayer taught Sunday school. Images of Jesus blessing the children and of President Lincoln flanked each side of its platform. This iconographic juxtaposition undoubtedly seemed entirely appropriate to both missionary and student. In January and February 1867, under the watchful gaze of both "saviors," Ayer taught a series of temperance lessons that resulted in more than three hundred students signing the pledge and the creation of a temperance society whose membership exceeded six hundred by the time Ayer died in September. Within two years of emancipation black Atlantans had their first temperance society.[59]

In the early years of Reconstruction the lines between the evangelical missionary organizations and the federal government's Freedmen's Bureau were blurred, and in terms of temperance work they were effectively an interlocking directorate. For example, John Alvord worked as a colporteur for the ATrS-Boston with the Union army during the war and afterward was made general superintendent of education for the Bureau; Edmund A. Ware was an AMA missionary before being appointed the Bureau's superintendent of schools for Georgia; and General O. O. Howard, the commissioner of the Freedmen's Bureau, simultaneously served on the AMA's executive committee and was a vice president, and later president, of the National Temperance Society.

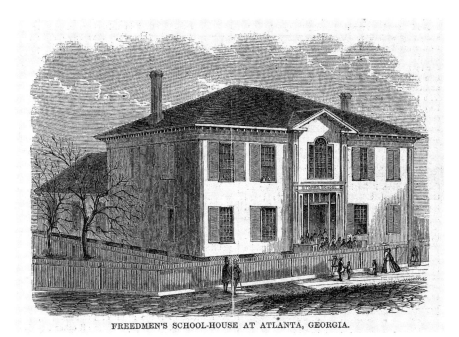

FREEDMEN'S SCHOOL-HOUSE AT ATLANTA, GEORGIA.

Fig. 6—The Storrs School, opened in December 1866. In the chapel in the rear, missionary Frederick Ayer organized Black Atlanta's first temperance society in February 1867. From *Harper's Weekly*, March 30, 1867. Courtesy of HarpWeek

This interlocking leadership meant that signs of intemperance among the freed people were as much of a concern to the federal Freedmen's Bureau as they were to the nexus organizations. About the same time that the AMA began using its Lincoln Temperance Pledge cards, General O. O. Howard received reports from Virginia and South Carolina of increasing intemperance among the freed people as well as reports that the Sons of Temperance insisted on segregating its black members into separate chapters. In June 1867 Howard ordered Bureau agents to organize local "Lincoln Temperance Societies" and "Vanguards of Freedom" for children enrolled in Bureau schools. Together the societies comprised the Lincoln National Temperance Association, an interracial organization designed to "suppress intemperance among the colored people" and "such white persons as may choose to unite with them." Howard found "great appropriateness" in calling them "Lincoln" societies because of Lincoln's character and the "love the freedmen bear him." Howard then ordered John Alvord to request of the AMA a donation of five thousand copies of their Lincoln Temperance Pledge for the Bureau's teachers and agents. The AMA gladly obliged. Howard appointed John

Alvord to the executive committee of the national association and made A. E. Newton, involved in a non-religious relief organization, general secretary of the Vanguard. Newton promptly tweaked the *Band of Hope Manual* to turn it into the *Manual of the Vanguard of Freedom*, which the NTS published in December. The manual explained how to organize a society and included a sample constitution, a pledge, and suggestions for conducting "interesting" meetings. While Bureau agents never reported functioning Vanguard chapters in Atlanta, in 1869 the NTS reported "several" black temperance societies in Atlanta, which may have been local Vanguard chapters. It is possible that teachers at the AMA's Storrs School and the Methodist Freedmen's Aid Society's Summer Hill School were pushing the message so effectively on their own that no need for Vanguards existed in Atlanta. Whether or not they were Vanguard chapters, many young black Atlantans were surely receiving the temperance message. When they were not hearing it in their classrooms from their teachers, they heard it with their families in church.[60]

The First Congregational Church and Temperance

Frederick Ayer's last major initiative was to organize the First Congregational Church in the Storrs School chapel on May 26, 1867. The congregation began with three missionary families and several students and was intended to be an interracial church. After Ayer's death in September, his colleague Cyrus W. Francis assumed the pastorate until 1873. He was followed by a succession of Northern white pastors into the 1890s. The AMA viewed the church and their schools as complementary institutions in their effort to "raise" the freed people to their level of culture. As an appendage to the Storrs School and Atlanta University, First Congregational's existence created some friction with Atlanta's black-pastored Methodist and Baptist congregations. Northern missionaries were accused of steering their students toward attendance at First Congregational and of criticizing traditional Southern black worship styles, but despite chafing at these expressions of interdenominational rivalry and paternalism most black pastors shared the same commitment to temperance that First Church's white pastors did.

First Church, as it was called, maintained high expectations for its members and excommunicated members for persisting in less than "pure" behavior after receiving correction and exhortation. In the early months the church was mostly young single males, and Reverend Francis found it challenging to keep them focused. Because drinking was undoubtedly an issue he had to deal with, he was quite pleased when in the summer of 1868, following a period of revival, the members of the church's literary society decided to turn their group into a temperance society also. Francis praised them for "awakening" a much needed interest in abstinence. By the 1880s it was becoming routine for all new members to sign abstinence pledges in First Church, as well as in other Congregational churches. As temperance became increasingly associated with middle-class values, First Congregational's strictness in this area strengthened its reputation as a church for the better class of blacks.[61]

First Congregational is the only Black Atlanta church from this period whose discipline records are extant, and a review of its alcohol-related cases is illustrative of the ways the AMA missionaries worked through churches to reinforce their temperance message. In traditional AMA fashion, its missionary-pastors worked to create a church as free from sin as possible. Church discipline was a serious matter, and nearly every one *charged* with violating church standards suffered the ultimate penalty of excommunication. Between its founding in 1867 and 1876, 205 people became members of First Congregational. Of those members, 22 came under church discipline charges, and 21 (10 men and 11 women) experienced excommunication, with one being successfully restored. Only 5 of the 21 excommunicated members faced alcohol-related charges. Members' behavior was judged against the church's covenant. Although the first members did not sign abstinence pledges, membership entailed subscribing to the church's covenant, which included some of the basic evangelical doctrines and the following sentence: "I promise to live a holy life to strive against sin in my heart and in my conduct to be temperate, pure, and prayerful."[62]

All of the liquor-related charges were against men, reflecting the contemporary reality that men drank more than women and did so in public places. The first person excommunicated for drinking was Styles Dougherty, who had been a member for less than 18 months. The public statement of his excommunication quoted from the portion of the church covenant he had violated and said he had "repeatedly" violated his temperance pledge and often been angry, used abusive language, skipped services for no good reason, and generally failed to perform "even the outward duties of a Christian." Worse still, when confronted, he exhibited no remorse or desire to change his ways.[63] Appearing on virtually all excommunication statements, lack of remorse was the ultimate reason for this most extreme form of discipline. On September 29, 1869, the same day that Dougherty was excommunicated, William Duncan and George Payne, who joined the church in April 1868 during a revival, were both suspended because of intemperance, profanity, and association with people of "bad character." Suspension was considered temporary, an opportunity for individuals to reform their ways. The church was particularly "long-suffering" with Duncan and Payne. In February 1871 Duncan confessed his sins and was received back into full fellowship, but in April 1871 Payne was excommunicated after a committee reported that it had failed to get Payne to "abandon his evil ways." William Duncan, however,

Fig. 7—First Congregational Church, founded by AMA missionary Frederick Ayer. From Henry Proctor Papers, Amistad Research Center at Tulane University, New Orleans, Louisiana

apparently lapsed again, and being unrepentant, was finally excommunicated in November 1875. James King was excommunicated in December 1871 because he "publicly" violated his "publicly" signed temperance pledge and then refused to show up to a meeting to respond to the charges.[64]

But First Church did more than insist on teetotal members. Bradford Garner, whom the church "esteemed so highly as a Christian," apparently disagreed with the church's stand that bartending was "not consistent" with the church covenant. A bartender, Garner repeatedly resisted attempts to persuade him to change his livelihood, and he was subsequently excommunicated. A few years later he left bartending to become a railroad porter, but he never rejoined the church. Finally, the church also charged Perry Kieth with selling liquor. The church held an incredible seven meetings about his case in the summer of 1871. Kieth initially defended himself and was suspended for four weeks. Later he confessed his sin and was restored to full communion. Kieth subsequently relocated to Alabama, and the church gave him a letter to transfer his membership.[65]

Of the almost two hundred blacks who voluntarily submitted themselves to the spiritual oversight of First Congregational's white AMA missionary-pastors before 1876, only 2 percent were ever charged with inebriation, suggesting that alcohol abuse was not a major problem for the church. First Congregational's disciplinary procedures seemed to have followed a relatively conservative pattern in that charges were not brought until the evidence was overwhelming and excommunication was sure. Most members were not charged and removed until they had already voluntarily absented themselves from services for an extended period of time, developed a widely known sinful lifestyle, and could be charged with multiple violations of the church covenant. Then they usually refused to change their ways and were excommunicated. The high rate of conviction under these circumstances suggests that First Congregational's pastors were genuinely concerned with removing those who had become members in name only and were tarnishing the church's image and not with divisive witch hunts based on members' peccadilloes. Although the reason is not clear, the annual rate of excommunications declined beginning in 1877. From 1873 to 1888 the church regularly excommunicated a lower percentage of its membership than the average for other churches in its regional conference. AMA missionaries probably would have attributed this lower rate to the effect of the Storrs School and Atlanta University because many, if not most, of First Church's black members were also students in one of these schools, and this would have validated the AMA's policy of founding schools and churches in tandem. At the 1880 Georgia Congregational Conference, former pastor C. W. Francis presented a paper on "The Object and Method of Church Discipline." In his paper Francis maintained that church discipline is a statement to a "member who walks unworthily . . . that such is the fact, and is a recognition in formal action of that state of things which in fact exists before such action." Such a decision must be made by all of one's brethren, not the minister or some committee drawn from the membership, he argued. Congregational church discipline undoubtedly differed in important ways from that of other churches because studies show that other denominations convicted a much lower percentage of those charged or a lower percentage of their membership.[66] Although no discipline records from individual black-pastored churches are extant, we know that many black pastors proclaimed the message of abstinence in the early years following emancipation.

AME Churches and Temperance

Northern blacks could share the same culturalism embraced by Northern whites. AME Bishop Daniel A. Payne was well-known for his insistence on an educated clergy and his opposition to emotional African American worship practices such as the ring shout. Payne was born free in Charleston, South Carolina, but had moved north in 1835 to pursue his education, eventually earning a degree at a Lutheran seminary. He joined the AME church in 1840 and was ordained a bishop in 1854, but his stance on congregational worship and an educated clergy created its share of friction between him and others within the church. Following emancipation, Payne wrote that the brightest freed people should be trained up North in "northern sentiments" so they could return to the South as "propagandists of these sentiments" and admitted to dreaming about a time when "New England ideas, sentiments, and principles" would rule the "entire South."[67]

In May 1865, while he was president of Wilberforce University, the AME church sent Payne to organize the denomination in South Carolina and Georgia, but he also traveled with financial backing from the AMA. Payne was one of several agents sent by his church to enroll preexisting Southern black Methodist congregations. On May 15 he organized the South Carolina Conference and immediately commissioned nine missionaries to traverse South Carolina and Georgia to enroll congregations and establish AMA schools. One of the missionaries Payne sent out was William Gaines, a native of Georgia and brother to the better-known future AME bishop Wesley J. Gaines. The Gaines brothers had grown up on plantations in various Georgia "black belt" counties.

William Gaines arrived in Atlanta in the summer of 1865, several months before Frederick Ayer, and he enrolled the Methodist congregation named Bethel, that had been worshiping separately from whites since the 1840s. Joseph A. Wood, the group's leader since 1855, was ordained as an elder in 1866. In 1866 a group of blacks from the Summerhill neighborhood requested an AME church, so Wood began holding meetings there, organizing what was initially called Wood's Chapel (its name was changed to Allen Temple in the mid-1880s), and pastored there from 1867 to 1869, and again from 1879 to 1883. Wesley J. Gaines was first ordained in 1866 by Daniel Payne when he organized the state of Georgia into its own annual conference. From 1867 to 1869 Gaines pastored Bethel and built a 2,000-seat building in Shermantown, which at the time was the largest black church in the South. The church soon became known as "Big Bethel." Gaines went on to pastor churches in Athens, Macon, and Columbus before returning to Atlanta in 1881. Black Atlanta's continued population growth had led to the founding of Shiloh AME in 1872, and in 1874 the Georgia Annual Conference was divided into the North and South Georgia annual conferences because of the rapidly increasing number of congregations.[68]

Atlanta's AME leaders frequently spoke out against intemperance. The first bishop of the Georgia Annual Conference was John M. Brown, a free-born black from Delaware who was educated in several Northern schools, including Oberlin College. During one annual conference sermon he warned his ministers not to stand around street corners smoking but, rather, to become teetotalers and early risers. Elders Wesley J. Gaines and Joseph Wood were committed teetotalers, as was Henry McNeal Tuner, who, free-born in South Carolina, lived in Maryland and Washington, D.C., until after the war and was appointed superintendent of Upper Georgia in 1866, ordained bishop in 1880, and made his home in Atlanta. Undoubtedly these men endorsed abstinence on multiple occasions, even if it might have been just one of many points in a sermon. At the Fifth Georgia Annual Conference, held at Big Bethel in 1871, the clergy engaged in a lengthy discussion of temperance. More than ten clergy denounced alcohol, each seeking to outdo the previous speaker. This is the first year for which evidence exists that the Georgia Conference had a temperance committee. The committee's resolution stated, "That the Holy Scriptures are a testimony against the use of intoxicating liquors" and that their church discipline also testified against it. The strength of their Methodist tradition, dating back to the eighteenth century, was not lost on these men. Reverend J. W. Randolph pushed the cause a step further by asking all conference members to cease using "tobacco, snuff, and cigars" as well as intoxicating liquors. Wesley J. Gaines, Henry M. Turner, and F. J. Peck, a future Bethel pastor, were among those who spoke in favor of abstinence. The following year Gaines suggested that the tobacco ban again be included with the Temperance Committee report, and it was. This report also ordered pastors to preach quarterly temperance sermons and called on them to "reclaim" inebriates through both precept and example. It is not possible to know to what extent ministers complied with this directive, but Atlanta's AME adherents were potentially hearing four temperance sermons a year in the early 1870s, as well as being disciplined by abstinent church leaders.[69]

At the first meeting of the North Georgia Annual Conference (1874) a standing temperance committee was organized. For some unexplained reason, the first thing the committee did was to lower the standard for pastors by requiring only "one or more" sermons on alcohol each year. Perhaps pastors had been ignoring the earlier directive or opposing it for some reason, and the clergy thought that lowering the standard would elicit greater compliance. Perhaps members were complaining about what they perceived as an overemphasis on temperance. Or, more optimistically, perhaps the ministers perceived a reduced need for such sermons. At the same time, the conference created a temperance society, with Joseph Wood as president. The conference minutes do not make clear what the society's function was or how long it existed. In 1876 the temperance committee reinstituted the call for quarterly temperance sermons, which suggests the ministers perceived an increased need for them.[70]

Literate AME adherents in Atlanta would have also encountered temperance in their church library. As a service to their members, many of whom lived in poverty or on the edge of it, and to encourage literacy, AME churches maintained lending libraries. By 1871 Wood's Chapel owned 250 volumes, and Big Bethel 500. Big Bethel's library doubled in size in the next year, and undoubtedly some of these books promoted temperance. In these libraries members could also find the most recent copy of the AME Church's stridently pro-temperance *Christian Recorder*.[71]

The only AME Church discipline statistics for Atlanta-area churches are found in the 1890 Minutes of the North Georgia Annual Conference. According to these minutes, Bethel AME excommunicated 6 out of 2,100 members (0.03%) and Allen Temple excommunicated 16 out of 735 members (2.18%). No reasons for excommunication are provided. Although we do not know the number of members charged, the percentage excommunicated is only a fraction of the 10 percent evicted at First Congregational. It seems that in these early years of establishing black churches, any tendencies toward strict disciplinary standards would have been checked by the overwhelming economic, educational, and political needs of their people, as well as the low literacy rates, which would have complicated efforts to maintain formal written records.[72]

How many black Atlantans actually heard this temperance message in the early post-emancipation period? A close review of the evidence presented in this chapter suggests that the American Missionary Association, American Tract Society, National Temperance Society, and African Methodist Episcopal Church reached relatively large numbers of black Atlantans early in their efforts. Between 1866 and 1876 Black Atlanta's population grew from roughly 8,000 to roughly 13,000. In 1867 the AMA had 1,900 students enrolled in its day school classes, 225 enrolled in night school, and 1,200 enrolled in its Sunday school, but many of the Sunday school children also attended the day school. In 1870 there were 2,000 children attending AMA schools. One can reasonably suppose that each child represented a household of several individuals, because underemployment and high immigration rates encouraged the creation of extended families and multi-generational households.

In addition to teaching, AMA missionaries also conducted family visitations where they distributed literature. Elizabeth Ayer reported that, in addition to Bibles, every Sunday during her home visitations she distributed about 50 "papers," and these would have included literature from the American Tract Society and National Temperance Society. It is not clear whether these visitations included only the families of their students, but in all likelihood at least some other families were visited. It seems reasonable, then, to imagine AMA missionaries personally reaching perhaps as much as half of Black Atlanta's population with the temperance message. While the Summer Hill School records during these years are very limited, it is reasonable to assume that its Methodist teachers were also instructing their charges in abstinence at this time.

As for the AME Church, in 1872 the combined membership of both Atlanta congregations was 1,460 parishioners, and two more congregations organized that year. Bishop Payne estimated that the number of people influenced by the denomination's work was three times its actual membership. If this optimistic estimate was near correct, it suggests that AME teachings alone could have reached more than 40 percent of the black population. Many AME families were likely exposed to temperance from multiple sources because their children attended AMA schools and heard the message there, as well as at church. One must also consider the receptivity of children to the temperance materials, combined with their influence on their own parents who themselves were scrambling to learn to read and function successfully in their new and trying circumstances. One Alabama AMA missionary told of a boy in her school who excitedly reported that he was able to single-handedly convince his mother to forgo eggnog one Christmas and his father to stay "dry" the whole holiday season. There is no telling how often children persuaded their parents to stop drinking because they had been taught its evils at school. Scenes like this were probably repeated in more homes than we can ever know.[73]

But hearing a message is not the same as accepting it. From the freed people's perspective it is unlikely that many of them perceived a need for teetotalism. In the first few years following emancipation, given their immediate food and shelter needs, grinding poverty, limited literacy, and harassment by law enforcement, temperance qua temperance could not have been a primary concern. Increasing rates of incarceration and the drunken policemen and security officers likely troubled blacks more than any inchoate liquor-related pathologies. Despite the rise of missionary-run primary schools for blacks (and public schools in the 1870s), there were never enough seats for all of Black Atlanta's school-age children. Illiteracy remained high throughout this period, and even with all the literature being distributed, missionaries repeatedly complained they did not have enough to go around.

It is true that reports of temperance societies existed in Black Atlanta in the late 1860s, but we will never know how many joined them and maintained their pledges over the long run. What is certain is that those attending the Storrs School, First Congregational, Big Bethel, and Wood's Chapel during these years received a consistent, and perhaps constant, temperance message. But this was a relatively small percentage of Black Atlanta. These factors suggest that although relatively large numbers of freed people may have been exposed to the temperance message, for most of them its strength was mitigated by the harsh exigencies of daily living and limited contact with Northern institutions, and thus it probably gained little traction during the early post-emancipation years.[74]

While by most standards Black Atlanta likely did not have a "drinking problem," that reality did little to influence the strength of the temperance message brought by Northern evangelicals. It is clear that Northern evangelical missionaries arrived in Atlanta with their own worldview and its inherent biases. Given their pro-revival and Christian republican language, perfectionist theological proclivities, culturalism, and romantic racialism, they did not need to see widespread alcohol abuse to teach temperance. All they needed to see was the lack of teetotalism, and that *is* what they saw. Everything about their collective and individual pasts predisposed missionaries to teach temperance, whether or not the freed people themselves perceived a need for it or wanted it. Because the missionaries embraced their own evangelical culture of revivalism and reform so enthusiastically, temperance inevitably arose as part of their mission to educate and Christianize, regardless of actual on-the-ground conditions.

From time to time evangelicals succumbed to their urge to be alarmist about the less than teetotal ways of the freed people. Perhaps it was because they could not shake their culturalism, or maybe it was because of their need to attract donations. In February 1867, the same month the AMA warned about intemperance and the freed people's "excitable natures," the editor of the AME Church's *Christian Recorder* reminded all AME ministers to form temperance societies "everywhere, that intoxicating drink may not find victims among our people." It was also in 1867 that General Howard ordered the creation of the Lincoln National Temperance Association. These early concerns remained relatively latent during the first decade or so following emancipation but increased as the freed people became more socioeconomically stratified and the national political climate changed. As Northern whites wearied of the politics of Reconstruction, the Freedmen's Bureau closed up shop, and the non-religious freedmen's aid societies withdrew, Northerners from evangelical nexus organizations found themselves the only ones left working among the freed people. Beginning in the mid- to late 1870s, temperance rose again in the national consciousness with the presence of a national Prohibition Party, the successes of the Ohio Women's Crusade, and the notable rise of the Woman's Christian Temperance Union. By the early 1880s the temperance movement was advancing in every region of the nation and at every level of government, with more and more to show for its efforts. Temperance once again became the primary concern of many Northern evangelicals, and this quantitatively transformed their delivery of the message to the freed people. We now turn our attention to that transformation.[75]

> Right in the track where Sherman
> Ploughed his red furrow,
> Out of the narrow cabin,
> Up from the cellar's burrow,
> Gathered the little black people,
> With freedom newly dowered,
> Where, beside their Northern teacher,
> Stood the soldier, Howard. . . .
>
> And he said: "Who hears can never
> Fear for or doubt you;
> What shall I tell the children
> Up North about you?"
> Then ran round a whisper, a murmur,
> Some answer devising;
> And a little boy stood up: "General,
> Tell 'em we're rising!"
> —John G. Whittier, "Howard at Atlanta," first and fifth stanzas

CHAPTER 3

The Trickle Becomes a Flood

Northern Temperance Targets Southern Blacks, 1877–1890

An essential condition of permanent prosperity and success for Republican Government in America, on the part of both its colored and white constituents, is sobriety as well as freedom.

—*National Temperance Advocate* (January 1873)

In the summer of 1877 Reverend J. L. Smith, pastor of Atlanta's Shiloh AME church, began receiving free year-long subscriptions to the *New York Weekly Witness* and the *National Temperance Advocate*. Smith was one of hundreds of Southern black clergy who received free and unsolicited subscriptions to Northern temperance publications beginning in the late 1870s. Times were changing. As the Reconstruction era ended and political opportunities for blacks decreased, Southern black leaders turned increasingly to self-help and moral uplift measures, once common among antebellum Northern blacks, to build their community. These efforts included building institutions like churches, schools, and fraternal societies and embracing many of the social and moral norms of middle-class America. As Northern evangelicals learned of these uplift efforts from their missionaries, they began to underwrite newspaper subscriptions to reinforce the temperance component of that effort. These free subscriptions signaled a new period of intensified efforts by Northerners to disseminate the temperance message. Atlanta's missionary-sponsored schools became the vibrant center of temperance education in Black Atlanta and throughout much of Georgia. These schools adopted cutting-edge Scientific Temperance Instruction (STI) with the assistance of the National Temperance Society and the even more recently organized Woman's Christian Temperance Union. But temperance instruction involved far more than coursework; it became the topic of chapel speakers, the goal of extracurricular activities, and the focus of summer proselytizing. The decade-long trickle had become a flood by 1880.

This new emphasis was part of a national surge in temperance activism occurring at this time. The reenergized national movement included more activity, new forms of activity, and new leadership. Although finding ways to end the liquor traffic (prohibition) became the dominant new focus of the movement, preexisting groups like the NTS, the AMA, and the ABHMS retained the old emphasis on moral suasion, believing it to be complementary to legal suasion tactics. They believed that molding public opinion was a necessary precondition for successful prohibition at every level. Social change needed to precede political change. This education-then-politics approach blended old and new temperance tactics into an increasingly vocal and influential movement in many localities, including Atlanta.

The first indicator of the revitalized national movement was the increased frequency of national gatherings by the critical community of reformers. While only four national temperance conventions were held in the 30 years before the Civil War, five were held in the first 16 years following it. Conventions were opportunities for reformers to network, hear motivational speeches, assess various strategies, and pass resolutions refining and articulating their definition of the "problem" of alcohol in America. Delegates from local and state temperance organizations learned about temperance activities in other places and were inspired to adapt them for their area.

In 1867 some temperance newspapers began calling for a political party committed to national prohibition. The new national tax on alcoholic beverages imposed during the war, and subsequent related developments, had effectively turned liquor regulation into a national issue. Because reformers increasingly viewed the end of slavery as a result of the Republican Party's efforts, some became convinced that reforms on that magnitude were best handled politically. It soon became evident, however, that the Republican Party was unwilling to back the temperance/prohibition movement fully, so a new reform party had to be created. The International Order of Good Templars and the Sons of Temperance took the lead in calling a convention in Chicago in 1869. At least two of the leading organizers of the Chicago convention and the Prohibition Party were also founders of the NTS and active Templars, publishing agent J. N. Stearns and James Black, a Methodist lawyer and delegate to the first Republican national convention. But the Prohibition Party did not begin as the one-issue group its name suggests, for its initial platform also contained such progressive planks as a call for the direct election of senators and woman's suffrage, among other issues. Although the party openly proclaimed its Christian character, its focus on ending the liquor traffic largely precluded the necessity of appropriating pre-revival theological language, which was more conducive to individual moral suasion efforts designed to produce teetotalers. In 1872 the party nominated James Black as its first presidential nominee, but it was not until the eighties that the party won enough votes to gain the attention (and occasional concern) of Republicans and Democrats.[1]

Despite the existence of a national Prohibition Party, the most politically effective activities of the seventies and eighties were grassroots efforts to create state-level prohibition by constitutional amendment. The previous movements for statewide restrictions on the sale of alcohol, attempted in the 1850s, had been only statutory, so they were easily subverted by legislatures and state courts. This time, reformers sought more permanent prohibition by amending state constitutions. Although procedures varied by state, all amendments required significant support from the will of the people and were more difficult to overturn than statutory laws. At this point the movement still required the persuasion of a majority of voters as opposed to a majority of elected officials, which became the case in the twentieth century. In the years leading up to the passage of Georgia's 1885 General Local Option Law, a national groundswell produced prohibition campaigns in more than 20 states, many of them successful. Temperance once again became a leading news story in the American press.

While the political arm of the movement was revising its tactics, the social arm, as represented by the evangelical reform nexus missionary groups, experienced its own renewal. In the wake of the war, Baptist women began forming missionary societies, and in November 1877 New Englanders organized the second such society, called the Woman's American Baptist Home Mission Society (WABHMS). One of the WABHMS founders was educator Sophia Packard, who became the organization's first treasurer and then its corresponding secretary. A trip through the South in 1880 inspired her to found a school for black girls. After returning to Massachusetts, she and longtime friend and colleague Harriet E. Giles made arrangements to open a school in Atlanta.[2] In April 1881 Packard and Giles established the Atlanta Female Baptist Seminary in the basement of Friendship Baptist Church, Black Atlanta's oldest Baptist church. Although it was almost 20 years after emancipation, they approached their work as Frederick and Elizabeth Ayer had done in the sixties. In addition to regular teaching, they each conducted weekly prayer meetings and Bible studies, did home visitation, and distributed Bibles and other literature, just as AMA missionaries had been doing. Partly inspired by the bourgeois cult of domesticity, Packard and Giles viewed the woman's role in the home as particularly crucial for uplifting the black race, but their worldview continued to be expressed in the discourse of Christian republicanism; Giles confided to her diary, "Surely something must be done for them and to prevent whiskey drinking if we would save our country." In 1883 the school's three hundred students relocated to a tract of land containing the former Union army barracks on the west side of town, adjacent to the Atlanta Baptist Seminary. John D. Rockefeller Sr. helped pay off the mortgage on the property in 1884, and the school changed its name to Spelman Seminary in honor of his abolitionist in-laws, Mr. and Mrs. Harvey Buel Spelman. The Spelmans, Rockefellers, Packard, and Giles were all teetotalers, and abstinence became a "cardinal virtue" of the school.[3]

The WABHMS schools worked closely with those of the American Baptist Home Mission Society, which came under new leadership around this time. In 1879 Henry L. Morehouse became the new corresponding secretary of the ABHMS, and for the next 38 years under his leadership (as corresponding secretary, 1879–1892 and 1902–1917, and field secretary, 1892–1902) the ABHMS greatly expanded its work with former slaves and their children. In 1896 Morehouse articulated what had all along been the guiding principle of schools run by Northern missionaries when he declared his intention to create a "talented tenth" of freed people who could educate the masses of their own people. This phrase, later popularized by W. E. B. DuBois, came to be used synonymously with the phrase the "better classes" of blacks.[4] The same year that Morehouse became corresponding secretary, the ABHMS's Augusta Institute relocated to Atlanta, becoming Atlanta Baptist Seminary, and in 1912 it was renamed Morehouse College. By the early 1880s, four missionary-sponsored schools were clustered in Atlanta—Atlanta University (1869), Clark University (1877), Atlanta Baptist Seminary (1879), and Spelman Seminary (1881)—and two more organized later in the decade.[5]

In 1873 a group of Ohio women began praying in front of and inside saloons and used other face-to-face tactics to pressure saloon owners to close up shop. Their successful "Women's Crusade" quickly spread to other Northern states, with Lucy Spelman, John Rockefeller's mother-in-law, participating in one in Brooklyn, New York. In 1874 veterans of these crusades organized the Woman's Christian Temperance Union (WCTU). The NTS initially printed its literature. In 1879 the charismatic Frances Willard rose to the presidency, launching the organization's most influential years. Although she embraced various spiritual traditions during her life, Willard was a product of the same evangelical reform nexus as other reformers, being born in upstate New York, growing up in Oberlin, Ohio, and experiencing conversion under holiness preachers. In the 1870s she participated in the temperance meetings Dwight L. Moody sponsored during his revivals. In 1880 the WCTU created the Department of Scientific Temperance Instruction, headed by Mary H. Hunt until her death in 1906. Hunt directed successful campaigns in virtually every state for legislatively mandated STI in public schools. In addition, she persuaded physiology textbook publishers to increase their coverage of alcohol and other drugs to 25 percent of each book. The first temperance textbook adopted by Spelman Seminary with support from the National Temperance So-

Fig. 8—Friendship Baptist Church, E. R. Carter, pastor. The first home of Spelman Seminary. Kenan Research Center at the Atlanta History Center

ciety was written upon the urging of Mary Hunt. The WCTU did as much as any postbellum organization to bring temperance and prohibition to the forefront of the nation's collective consciousness.

In 1881 President Willard made a much touted tour of more than 50 Southern cities, including Atlanta, where she addressed students at Atlanta and Clark

Universities. Her trip reenergized the temperance movement throughout the South and was viewed by many as a major step in reunifying the nation in the wake of the Civil War and Reconstruction. Willard proclaimed a "Do Everything" motto that encouraged local union chapters to engage in whatever reforms they desired, and this decentralized approach effectively activated the WCTU for several years. This localism meant that, although black women were welcome to attend and participate in national conventions, the organization did not force local chapters to admit them. Although some Northern chapters were integrated, in Georgia and most of the South black women formed their own separate local and state unions called the "Colored WCTU," or "WCTU No. 2." Under Willard's leadership more than half of all U.S. counties created a local chapter, making the WCTU the first truly national voluntary organization since the end of the Civil War.[6]

While each of the above postbellum temperance developments has attracted its share of recent scholarly attention, none has been given to the Northern temperance work done with freed people during this period. This chapter examines these aspects of the temperance reform insofar as they relate to Black Atlanta. Free newspaper subscriptions were only one of the rivulets that fed the flood of temperance propaganda reaching the freed people beginning in the late 1870s. As one might expect, this flood most deeply affected those closely associated with the Northern missionary institutions. Although the temperance message was not promoted in Black Atlanta solely by Northern whites, to a large extent it was, and their efforts are the focus of this chapter.

"The Best Paper That Has Ever Passed through the South": John Dougall and the *New York Weekly Witness*

One of the pioneers in providing Southern black preachers with a "continual supply of Gospel and Temperance matter, and thus to elevate them" was John Dougall, founding publisher and editor of the *New York Weekly Witness*.[7] From Scotland via Montreal, Canada, Dougall was part of an influential Montreal community of Scots-Canadians who were successful merchants, devout Presbyterians, and committed temperance reformers. In his 30s he came under the influence of the abolitionist revivalist E. N. Kirk, and that experience launched him into a life of rigorous piety and enthusiastic reform without regard to his personal well-being or that of his family. He switched to the more evangelical Congregational Church and eventually embraced holiness teachings. Among Dougall's favorite reforms was abolitionism. Before the Civil War he assisted fugitive slaves and helped lead a mass public meeting memorializing John Brown. Although one scholar has likened Dougall to William Lloyd Garrison, Dougall invested most of his reform energies in temperance. Dubbed the "prophet" of the movement, Dougall was a founding member of the Montreal Temperance Society, editor of its newspaper, and delegate at a few national temperance conventions, including the one in 1865 where his call that special attention be paid to the newly freed slaves went largely unheeded in the short run. Dougall's commitment to teetotalism was an outgrowth of his perfectionism and post-millennialism, and he sincerely believed that widespread societal transformation would result from prohibition. In 1845 he founded the *Montreal Witness*, and he successively aligned his reform agenda with the following U.S. political parties: Whigs, Know-Nothings, and Republicans. Dougall was also one of the first vice presidents of the National Temperance Society.[8]

Seeking a new challenge, in 1871 Dougall moved to New York City, where he established the *New York Weekly Witness*, which by the mid-eighties had a circulation ten times that of the *Montreal Witness*. He attended Lafayette Avenue Presbyterian Church, pastored by fellow NTS founder and future president Theodore L. Cuyler. Dougall proudly described the *Witness* as aligning with the National Temperance Society on temperance and the American Missionary Association in regard to the "oppressed races." The paper quickly garnered praise from the editor of the AME Church's *Christian Recorder*.[9]

Dougall proved particularly committed to African Americans and the issues that concerned them. He regularly reported the injustices endured by Southern blacks, editorialized in their favor, and railed against Southern racism. Dougall reported extensively on the "Exoduster" migration to Kansas in 1879, not needing to await the findings of the congressional investigation to reach his conclusions. He forthrightly asserted that blacks had created "all the wealth" of the South and thus deserved all the aid they could get in their effort to "flee from oppression." Dougall preached a version of self-help by admonishing blacks to "trust in God and in themselves, and not in the President or Congress." On another occasion he sympathetically reported a declaration of complaints issued by Orangeburg, South Carolina, sharecroppers. Dougall chastised Southern whites for "persecuting" blacks and blamed deceitful landlords for the fact that blacks had been able to save so little since emancipation. He castigated one South Carolina newspaper editorial by saying that it did not even sound like a citizen of a republic had written it. Dougall's sympathies clearly lay with the radical wing of the Republican Party.[10]

In addition to being sympathetic toward the plight of the freed people, the *New York Weekly Witness* also offered a strong temperance message. Dougall was a moral suasionist who primarily concerned himself with molding a public sentiment

that would eventually demand prohibition from political leaders and then support its enforcement. The front page and editorials regularly included news and
letters to the editor pertaining to liquor legislation, law enforcement, and temperance activities. In one front-page article Dougall argued that it would be cheaper
for society to educate children about the dangers of alcohol than to try to cure
drunkards and punish criminals later. One issue featured as many as four front-
page temperance stories. Dougall spoke glowingly of state prohibition in Kansas
and Iowa and on more than one occasion directed readers to the resources of the
National Temperance Society. Occasionally there appeared a column titled "Temperance Sermons," which included one or more stories about individuals whose
death was the direct or indirect result of inebriation. Dougall's regular "Temperance Column" included short temperance stories, anecdotes, and facts relating
to alcohol use and abuse from such well-known temperance activists as John B.
Gough, Julia Coleman, and Neal Dow.[11]

John Dougall believed the message and sympathies of the *Witness* were especially suited to educate and uplift African Americans. Within weeks of issuing the
paper he asked Southern missionary subscribers to share their copies with the
freed people. Apparently too few did—or he had no way of knowing—so he finally took matters into his own hands with an editorial titled "How are the Freedmen
to be Educated?" Here Dougall argued that education was the key to black uplift.
While he believed schools and seminaries were necessary, Dougall also argued
that reading the *Weekly Witness* would benefit black preachers in their "ministra-
tions and intercourse with their people." In a list of seven reasons why he thought
the *Witness* was so appropriate for the freed people Dougall included the fact that
the paper was "thoroughly in sympathy with the negro race" and "very strong on
the temperance question and inserts the most convincing extracts, articles and
stories bearing upon it." He then asked his readers to donate toward a fund to
send the *Witness* gratis to every black minister. Total annual subscription and
postage costs per subscriber were $1.50, so for every dollar donated, the *Witness*
contributed 50 cents. To obtain clergy names Dougall requested lists from the
black denominations and asked readers to send in names and addresses of black
clergy they knew. The *Witness* regularly listed donors, their gifts, and the names
and addresses of the receiving clergy.[12]

By November 1877 Dougall had received about $2,200 and sent out the
same number of free subscriptions. Of Atlanta's 17 black clergy recipients, 4
were Baptist, 8 were AME, and 5 could not be identified. Included were the
pastors of Macedonia, Mt. Pleasant (Wheat Street after 1884), and Pleasant
Grove Baptist churches, and Big Bethel, Wood's Chapel, Shiloh, and Union
AME churches. Apparently concerned about ongoing costs and to assess the
degree of interest, in April 1878 Dougall announced to black clergy readers that

unless they specifically requested their subscriptions to continue, they would end. He also reissued an appeal for donations to the "colored preacher's fund." While some readers complained that the clergy should have been able to purchase their own subscriptions by now, Dougall argued that they were still too poor to be able to afford even the $1.50 annual price. While many fewer donors responded in the second year, so also did many fewer clergy. In 1878–1879 only 800 free subscriptions went out, 5 of which went to Atlanta clergy. Only the Reverends Charles O. Jones (pastor, Pleasant Grove Baptist) and W. H. Tillman (pastor, Third Baptist and Mt. Pleasant Baptist), and B. Scott received the *Witness* for a second year. This outreach continued into the 1880s, when the number dropped to about four hundred. At the same time Dougall also supplied black schools such as Spelman Seminary and the AMA's Fisk University in Nashville, Tennessee, with free subscriptions. The AME clergy were so grateful for the free subscriptions that at their 1880 General Conference they passed a resolution offering Dougall and his donors "sincere thanks for the past, and prayers for their future continuance."[13]

Letters published in the *Weekly Witness* indicate that some black clergy genuinely appreciated the editorial slant of the paper and valued its temperance message. Several clergy reported reading excerpts from the paper in their sermons and expressed great appreciation for its support of the "colored race." More specifically, one minister from Kentucky praised it for having "just such matter as is needed in the southern States, especially temperance." Another minister reported one of the paper's "success stories" when he reported on a fellow clergy recipient who had ceased being a braggadocio drinker and instead "joined a temperance council, and is [now] doing all in his power to elevate his people." A New Orleans pastor appreciated its usefulness for combating both intemperance and Catholicism. Some clergy were so excited about the paper that they took it upon themselves to sell subscriptions. Although it was praised by many as the best paper they read, the minister who perhaps most eloquently captured the clergy's positive sentiment called it a "grand way to diffuse Christian intelligence among a down-trodden race." No records exist of the responses of Atlanta's pastors, but it is likely that at least some of them shared these positive sentiments.[14]

Such accolades lead one to question the declining subscription list. Dougall suggested some plausible reasons. He thought that perhaps some pastors who initially received it were illiterate, while others might not have understood that it was free. Also, some who did understand that it was free might have been too proud to receive a free paper, which Dougall recognized as a good thing, except that it was harmful if it prevented clergy from receiving a valuable resource. He also knew that some Southern postmasters intercepted the *Witness*. Combined, these factors account for the declining distribution of the *Weekly Witness*.[15]

The "Balance-Wheel" of the Temperance Movement: The National Temperance Society and Publication House

Although *Witness* distribution was declining, receptivity to its temperance message and evangelical efforts to spread it were not necessarily in decline. In the spring of 1881, the National Temperance Society and Publication House (NTS)[16] decided to focus its resources on the freed people, and it coordinated its efforts with the ABHMS and AMA. While this refocusing should be understood within the context of the national surge of the temperance movement, it also reflected changes internal to the NTS and the evolving sentiments of missionaries and Southern black leaders. As a result, the NTS transformed itself into an organization that, for the next 20 years, would claim that its "great work" was among the "colored population of the South."[17] At the same time, its leaders and agents perpetuated the discourses of the evangelical reform nexus, romantic racialism, and culturalism, closely aligning it with the spirit of the older AMA and ABHMS.

Through the 1880s, William E. Dodge and J. N. Stearns were the two most influential leaders of the NTS. Both men were involved from the beginning and shared a similar outlook as transplanted New England Congregationalists. Stearns was also active in the Sons of Temperance and the Good Templars and a founder of the Prohibition Party. At the NTS he edited both NTS monthlies, the 16-page *National Temperance Advocate,* and the 4-page *Youth's Temperance Banner.* As the movement's standard bearer, the *Advocate* not only included national and international stories about temperance activities and related legislative and judicial actions but also articles drawing on a potpourri of moral, religious, social, medical, and economic arguments promoting teetotalism and opposing the liquor traffic. By 1871 Stearns had also assumed the positions of recording and corresponding secretaries, making him the "face" of the organization until his death in 1895. He kept such a grueling schedule that on a few occasions the NTS board gave him several weeks' leave with pay to regain his health. Stearns began touring the South during the winter of 1875, slowly developing an interest in intemperance among the freed people by visiting schools like Atlanta University and the Storrs School and speaking with citizens in communities that held local option votes. After hearing stories of black opposition to prohibition, he brought his concerns to the board of managers but remained optimistic, arguing that with just "half the [temperance] instruction" given to whites, blacks would be "far ahead of them in practice and example."[18]

William E. Dodge, president from 1865 till his death in early 1883, was a well-respected New York City businessman and philanthropist. He was probably the single largest NTS benefactor during his lifetime, donating even more through his will and indirectly through his sons and widow. Although never an abolitionist, during the Civil War Dodge developed an interest in black education, and in 1862 he became a trustee of the Ashmun Institute near Philadelphia, Pennsylvania, the first school opened in the United States for the higher education of blacks (renamed Lincoln University in the spring of 1866). Among his many reform and philanthropic interests, Dodge endowed Lincoln's chair of Sacred Rhetoric and partially endowed another chair, and he also made substantial contributions to Zion Wesley Institute (established 1882), an AME Zion school in Salisbury, North Carolina (the name was changed to Livingstone College in 1887). Dodge became such a respected philanthropist of black higher education that John Slater sought his advice before establishing his famed Slater Fund, one of the main late nineteenth-century philanthropies focused on Southern black education.

Dodge personified the experiences and values of the evangelical reform nexus. He was converted under the preaching of the New England revivalist Asahel Nettleton, and he financially backed the New York City revivals of Charles G. Finney and Dwight L. Moody. He even made a hobby of reading about revivals. Involved with organized temperance and other groups in the Benevolent Empire since the 1830s, Dodge staunchly embraced the old temperance teaching that the surest way for a drunkard to reform was through "repentance towards God, and faith in Jesus Christ."

Following the war, Dodge purchased timber rights in Southern Georgia and arranged for the creation of a county bearing his name in the area. While on trips to inspect his business interests, Dodge visited and often addressed audiences at Atlanta University and various black and white Atlanta congregations. Dodge also made a point of identifying and sponsoring needy AU students. These visits continued into the eighties, and he did not miss an opportunity to admonish students about abstinence. During these visits Dodge also befriended the Georgia businessman and politician Alfred Colquitt. Colquitt was a member of the famed Bourbon Triumvirate—a group of politicians who, from the 1870s through the 1890s, rotated between Georgia's governor's mansion and the U.S. Senate seats as though they were in a game of musical chairs. Although they all actively promoted Georgia's industrialization in the postbellum era, unlike other members of the group Colquitt was a Methodist who was also a committed prohibitionist and was actively involved in Atlanta's 1885 and 1887 votes. Partly as a result of Dodge's increased consciousness of Southern issues, in 1872 the NTS published six small tracts for the freed people using only monosyllabic words. In the same year the board of managers voted to raise a special fund of $5,000 just for Southern literature distribution, but the fund-raising apparently never occurred. The NTS's commitment to provide vast amounts of inexpensive temperance literature, combined with its anemic fund-raising efforts, kept the organization's balance sheets in the red most months, and in the seventies its publications budget averaged an annual

$5,000 deficit. Dodge repeatedly launched matching donation drives but failed to establish any meaningful "permanent working capital" throughout the 1870s.[19]

While Dodge and Stearns were developing their interest in the cause of temperance among the freed people, some other NTS members had similar and even stronger African American connections. We have already discussed the abolitionist John Dougall, but Peter Carter, who chaired the important publications committee for 30 years, was also an immigrant from Scotland, and he taught in a New York City African American Sunday school for more than 30 years. Then two new people joined the NTS in the mid-1870s. In 1876 Reverend Theodore L. Cuyler nominated Joshua L. Baily, a Quaker, for the board of managers. A successful merchant from Philadelphia, Baily had a long history of involvement with temperance causes and African American philanthropy. Baily harbored sympathies for the plight of African Americans almost on a par with Dougall's radical views. In 1880 he told a friend that the "future of the negro" was as much a concern to him then as it was before the war, since the federal government refused to "afford them adequate protection." This was a truly radical view for a Northern white man to hold in 1880, when most Northerners were tired of hearing about Southern blacks. Then, in 1877, longtime abolitionist and John D. Rockefeller Sr.'s father-in-law, Harvey B. Spelman, joined the board of managers, and from 1879 to 1881 he was the treasurer. Before the war, Spelman had been an Underground Railroad "conductor," and his home a "station." Spelman's daughter Laura, John D. Rockefeller Sr.'s wife, said her household was so pious when she was growing up that she was only allowed to violate the Sabbath if it was to prepare food for fugitive slaves. Spelman used his family ties to enlist financial support from Rockefeller, and after Dodge died Rockefeller became the organization's largest single donor for the next 20 years. Spelman, Baily, Carter, Dodge, Stearns, and Dougall together steered the organization to focus its efforts on the freed people, but they were not the only influence.[20]

By the end of Reconstruction the growing cohort of missionary-educated freed people was just beginning to emerge from the masses of African Americans in terms of their lifestyle and values. Attitudes toward alcohol use were becoming one of the social markers of the better class of blacks. Just as much as missionary-educated individuals increasingly shunned alcohol, it is likely that those more distant from the influence of Northern evangelical culture who were experiencing dwindling opportunities for upward mobility were increasingly embracing its use. It did not take long for missionaries and blacks associated with them to spot this growing divide. In 1875 AMA secretary Michael Strieby warned that although the freed people initially demonstrated a "marvelous enthusiasm" for learning, inadequate educational efforts were causing them to degenerate and "sink into idleness and intemperance." It is telling that the nascent class formation he observed included a distinction in regard to temperance:

Fig. 9—William E. Dodge statue in Bryant Park, New York City. Founding president of the National Temperance Society. Financier of revivalists Charles Finney and D. L. Moody. Photo by Sasithon Pooviriyakul

> I have thus far called your attention only to the foreground of the picture—a foreground made bright by the little homes of the people, their cultivated land, their growing intelligence and virtue. But there is that dark and deep background which it is my duty to point out, and yours to examine. The one is a narrow strip, the other the broad area; the one contains a few thousands of the people, the other millions; the one is occupied by the industrious and intelligent . . . the other by the comparatively idle, who are not drawn to the schools, and who . . . are more or less a prey to their vices—indolence, intemperance, licentiousness and theft.[21]

Strieby likely overstated the contrast to motivate the AMA's donor base, but in any case, his description reveals that practicing or not practicing abstinence was emerging as one among several ways to demarcate class boundaries within the black community.

But Strieby's concern was not just an expression of Northern culturalism; Southern black clergy began making similar observations at about the same time. In 1875 the North Georgia conference of the AME Church called intemperance a "growing evil," and in 1882 the *People's Advisor*, a black newspaper from Jackson, Mississippi, declared whiskey to be the "greatest curse to our people . . . worse than poverty, worse than ignorance." In 1875 and 1876 the Missionary Baptist Convention of Georgia complained that the "evil of intemperance" had reached "alarming proportions" and called for pastors to organize temperance societies in their churches. In 1877 the Ebenezer Baptist Association, containing several Atlanta congregations, lamented that intemperance was not only found among unbelievers but had "also found its way into Christian families, and many of our useful members have been brought to disgrace and poverty." Although Ebenezer's previous temperance reports had called on ministers to preach and practice temperance, the 1877 report had a mournful and urgent tone, which distinguished it from previous reports. Ebenezer's report was part of a broader trend among Southern black clergy. That same year the Louisiana Baptist Convention refused to consider a resolution requiring ministers to be teetotalers, but when proposed again in 1879, the same resolution was not only entertained but passed. What makes these black Baptist observations so significant is that of all local black leaders, they likely had the least amount of contact with, and obligation to, Northern institutions rooted in the antebellum evangelical reform nexus. Unlike AME pastors, Southern black Baptists had no national church hierarchy or polity to which they were accountable but, rather, were subject to the whims of their church members' votes, and even *they* began to notice alarming changes in the use of alcohol among blacks. While the practice of, or failure to practice, abstinence served various socioeconomic functions, just as in antebellum times, it was evangelicals who formed the critical community that shaped the discourse defining the problem.[22]

The "Great Work" of the NTS among the Freed People

Beginning in late 1880, the National Temperance Society reported receiving "constant and pressing" requests from both whites and blacks to distribute literature among the freed people. Barely breaking even each month, for years the NTS had not been in a position to launch a special campaign. By March 1881, however, fund-raising efforts had begun to yield the desired results, and the organization's financial health had never been better. Wasting no time, the NTS called for a special meeting on April 13, 1881, to discuss intemperance among the freed people. About 20 people attended, including several NTS members and officials of the WCTU, ABHMS (Henry Morehouse), and AMA (Michael Strieby). Peter Carter presided, J. N. Stearns reported on his recent trip to the South, and Henry L. Morehouse announced that the ABHMS had concluded that its mission work among the freed people would be useless if they did not become teetotalers. Stearns reported that although there was a tremendous revival of temperance in the South, blacks generally voted against prohibition in the increasingly common local option elections. But Stearns's observations had convinced him of the influence of the clergy on the freed people, so he called for a mass distribution of literature to Southern black clergy. Attendees discussed various ideas before passing a resolution calling on the NTS to raise $5,000 for literature distribution among the freed people.[23]

The NTS board of managers resolved immediately to flood the South "knee deep" in temperance literature by appealing for donations to "reach the freedmen" and by creating a Missionary Committee to coordinate its efforts. The committee held its first official meeting in September, and during its first year it made more than 500 literature donations and mailed 3,250 copies of *Gospel Temperance* to theological seminaries. Stearns, having added secretary of the Missionary Committee to his portfolio, continued his Southern winter travels, and after four weeks in 1882 that included visits to Atlanta and Clark Universities accompanied by President Dodge, recommended to the board of managers a 3-part plan of action: (1) create and disseminate to every black minister in the Southern states a "pamphlet containing temperance fact, argument, and appeal"; (2) send textbooks and literature to every black school for study and free distribution; and (3) hire agents to travel throughout the South to address black audiences, distribute literature, and organize temperance activities and organizations. Fund-raising challenges made the board initially reluctant to approve formally any more than the first item, but two years later it finally agreed on the following 6-point program:

1. Sending missionaries or lecturers to visit churches, conferences, educational institutions, schools, etc., delivering addresses, introducing temperance text-books into schools, and endeavoring to enlist ministers and teachers to help carry on the work among this people.
2. To organize societies for colored people wherever practicable in all parts of the country.
3. To circulate a literature with the view of reaching every cabin-home in the South.
4. To introduce temperance text-books into schools and educational institutions wherever possible.
5. To continue the work of supplying the ministers of colored churches with documents covering every phase of the temperance question.
6. To issue an appeal or address on temperance to the colored people of the South, to be circulated as widely as possible.[24]

The delay of the managers in formally adopting an outreach agenda did not hinder Stearns or the Missionary Committee, however. From the beginning the Missionary Committee worked toward its fund-raising goals and spent the money as they received it, and then some. It sent its first missionary, a YMCA worker, to the South in the summer of 1882. He went to South Carolina, where he gave speeches and sold 50 subscriptions to the *National Temperance Advocate*, which so pleased the committee that it extended his stay by a month and hired him back the following summer, fall, and winter. Beginning in January 1883 the committee sponsored the travels of NTS vice president Edward Carswell in Virginia and North Carolina and of the Reverend Charles H. Mead in Georgia and Alabama. Mead, a Prohibition Party member since 1872, was a former Methodist pastor and former president of New York City's Bowery Mission.

Of the two, Mead was a particularly frequent speaker in Black Atlanta. Between January and March 1883 Mead delivered more than 70 speeches, and he claimed that he spoke before 25,000 black church members. While in Atlanta, he addressed the students of Atlanta and Clark Universities. During Stearns's annual trip he joined Mead to speak at schools in Atlanta and elsewhere. In 1884 Mead and Stearns visited Atlanta and Clark Universities again and also spoke at the Storrs School and Spelman Seminary. In addition, they spoke at Big Bethel AME and Friendship Baptist churches to standing-room-only crowds. School visits entailed getting students to renew their abstinence pledges (Atlanta's schools already required them for attendance), encouraging them to get others to take the pledge, and meeting with administrators and faculty to discuss incorporating Scientific Temperance Instruction into the curriculum and supplying their needs for textbooks and literature. The committee was so pleased with Mead's work that in June 1884 it issued him an open-ended invitation to travel for the society as long as funds were available and as long as he had an open door into the freed people's schools, churches, and ministerial conferences. During his winter 1884–1885 trip Mead spoke at Clark and Atlanta Universities again, and by his own account, he held about 12 nonchurch, nonschool meetings a week, addressing a total of about 150,000 Southern blacks. In 1885 Mead estimated that he spoke before 1,700 black clergy in various church conventions. In 1886 Mead and Stearns spoke at Spelman again. Unfortunately there is no record of individual student responses to these addresses. Most students would have been enrolled in either the primary or secondary grades and therefore would not have been in a position to voice any meaningful opposition, but we do know students at these schools actively campaigned in Atlanta's 1885 and 1887 local option votes. Although Mead continued his travels until 1888 and Stearns continued his annual trips until he died in the mid-1890s, in 1886 the missionary committee altered its approach.[25]

"The whole matter of the work among the colored people of the South came up for discussion and it was finally resolved to recommend" the employment of "colored men" to work as temperance missionaries among their own people. So read the minutes of the September 1886 Missionary Committee meeting. This decision had been long in coming and the minutes do not record discussions, so we are left to speculate about why it took so long to "finally resolve" this matter. Undoubtedly the committee held long conversations about the pros and cons of such a policy, taking into consideration such matters as the organization's image among Northern donors and Southern whites and blacks. Perhaps committee members questioned the logistics of travel for black men or even their relative effectiveness compared with that of whites. A strong dose of culturalism surely pervaded their discussions, for in one annual report they patronizingly announced that it was the North that "gave the negro his freedom and the ballot" and that it was now its responsibility to make him a "sober citizen." In any case, the change was wholesale, for after 1886 the society rarely employed white missionaries.[26]

As one would expect, the society sought out educated black men with good reputations. The first two approved African American missionaries were L. A. Rutherford, M.D., of North Carolina, and Baptist minister and editor Reverend James J. Spelman, a New Englander who had relocated to Mississippi during Reconstruction and become politically active. Among those hired in the next two years were E. E. Smith, principal of North Carolina's State Colored Normal School, Reverend A. Barry of Kentucky, and George Wassom of North Carolina. Recent Atlanta University alumnus Antoine Graves represented the NTS from early 1888 to the spring of 1889 in parts of Georgia. One of the ways men came to the attention of the committee was by personal application, but it is not clear how blacks learned of the opportunity. Its tight budget forced the committee to reject several missionary applicants.[27]

By far the most celebrated black NTS temperance missionary, however, was the Reverend Joseph C. Price. President Dodge had a special relationship with Price because he had paid Price's way through Lincoln University. Beginning with his valedictory speech in 1881, Price's oratorical skills quickly distinguished him as one of the outstanding speakers of his day. Following Price's graduation, Dodge paid for him to go on a speaking tour through North Carolina in support of its upcoming prohibition amendment vote. An AME Zion minister, Price was such a committed educator that he turned down three federal patronage offers and three opportunities to join his church's bishopric. In 1882 he reopened the Zion Wesley College in Salisbury, North Carolina. Professor Price visited Atlanta in January 1887 and spoke at Friendship Baptist Church and the Zion Presbyterian Church (colored), all of the missionary schools, and a conference of over 150 ministers of the Colored Methodist Episcopal Church. *The Conflict*, a short-lived Atlanta temperance newspaper, was quoted in the *National Temperance Advocate* calling the NTS's employment of black missionaries to work with the freed people "a fine stroke of diplomacy." NTS leaders were so enamored with Price that they scheduled a ten-day Northern tour with several speaking engagements between Philadelphia and Boston in January 1887. The highlight of the tour was a special reception held in his honor at the Broadway Tabernacle with major donors such as John D. Rockefeller Sr. present. Price's Northern appearances certainly allayed any apprehensions that NTS leaders would have had about the elocutionary abilities of black missionaries.[28]

Whether using white or black temperance missionaries, however, the NTS's primary mission remained "scattering" temperance literature, and its missionaries were simply one means of accomplishing this larger goal. In addition to lecturing at churches and schools, missionaries distributed large numbers of free tracts and sold periodical subscriptions. To encourage subscription sales, missionaries' salaries were partly commission-based. S. C. Kennedy's original remuneration agreement was $100 per month plus expenses, but when the committee learned he sold fifty dollars' worth of *Advocate* subscriptions, they decided to let him keep the money and reduced his pay to $50. From then on he was paid $100 "provided that he take one half in literature." Other missionaries were also funded on the same commission system. When C. H. Mead traveled in December 1883 the missionary committee promised him literature "according to his discretion," and in the next meeting Stearns reported that most donated literature in the last month had gone to Mead. For his winter 1884–1885 trip, Mead took five hundred dollars' worth of NTS publications. In December 1885 Mead received another five hundred dollars' worth of literature to distribute at a special exposition in New Orleans. Reverend J. J. Spelman requested supplies of specific books and tracts because of their perceived effectiveness. Another missionary specifically requested thirty thousand

Fig. 10—Antoine Graves (second from right) while a student of Atlanta University in the early 1880s. In 1888–89 he served as a missionary for the National Temperance Society. Kenan Research Center of the Atlanta History Center

TEMPERANCE AMONG THE FREEDMEN.

A PUBLIC TEMPERANCE MEETING

WILL BE HELD IN THE

Fourth Congregational Church,

HARTFORD,

UNDER THE AUSPICES OF THE

NATIONAL TEMPERANCE SOCIETY,

Tuesday Evening, January 18th, 1887,

COMMENCING AT EIGHT O'CLOCK.

To be addressed by Rev. J. C. PRICE, *President of Zion Wesley Institute,*
North Carolina, and J. N. STEARNS, *Cor. Secretary of the Society.*

Prof. PRICE, who is one of the ablest Colored Orators in the land, is the special
Missionary of the National Temperance Society among the Freedmen, and has recently
been laboring in several of the Southern States with great acceptance. He thoroughly
understands Negro life and Negro characteristics, and has taken great interest in the
education and elevation of his race. His visit to England a few years ago was the
occasion of great interest and enthusiasm. He will give some account of his work
and the progress of his race up toward a better life and a higher manhood. No one
should fail to hear this gifted "Brother in Black."

THE PUBLIC CORDIALLY INVITED. ADMISSION FREE.

Fig. 11—Announcement of J. C. Price speech being given in the North to showcase his speaking talents on behalf of temperance. Price was president of Livingston College and a missionary for the National Temperance Society. The Library Company of Philadelphia

copies of one-page tracts so he could print his own comments on the back. Within two years black NTS missionaries sold seven hundred subscriptions of the *National Temperance Advocate* to black families and introduced the NTS publication *Water Lily* into many Sunday schools. Just as black pastors shared their denominational publications with their parishioners, black lay subscribers to the *Advocate* undoubtedly shared it with their friends, multiplying its impact.[29]

Another way the missionary committee disbursed literature was through unsolicited direct mailings to individuals and schools. During the 1880s, the NTS annually donated millions of pages of literature worth thousands of dollars. In September 1883 a Dr. Ellis donated $1,300 toward the cost of mailing copies of that month's *National Temperance Advocate* to every preacher (65,000) in America. Beginning in 1886, funded by donations made by *Advocate* readers, about four hundred black clergy began receiving free subscriptions to the *Advocate*, and this continued until at least 1897. A special booklet for black pastors that was proposed in 1881 was financed by Dodge's widow in 1883. At least two different versions were produced: a 336-page book in 1883 and a 226-page book in 1884. They were mailed shortly before the year-end holidays to about 5,000 Southern black clergy. Ministers from throughout the South expressed their appreciation, and some requested a package of tracts to distribute in their community. In 1886 the committee agreed to raise money to print and mail another 5,000 copies. In May 1885 the Reverend J. M. Van Buren donated enough money to mail 10,000 copies of his NTS-published *Gospel Temperance* to clergy of both races. In 1887 he financed another 5,500 copies for seminaries and churches. The NTS also gave thousands of pages of literature to missionary groups such as the AMA and the WABHMS for their missionaries to distribute.[30]

Although the NTS mailed unsolicited literature, much literature was also solicited. In 1885 the Atlanta Baptist Seminary (Morehouse College) requested abstinence pledge cards, a "roll of honor" (a poster designed for recording the names of pledge signers), and tracts for its students to distribute. In 1889 the Gammon Theological Seminary, newly independent from Clark University, requested and received one hundred books that its library housed in a special "National Temperance Society Alcove." Two NTS donors underwrote Gammon's request. On several occasions Atlanta University's students raised money for the NTS, receiving in one instance more than 77,000 pages of literature in return. As with missionary applications, however, limited finances prevented the committee from filling many requests.[31]

In the early 1880s Spelman Seminary's administration sought to form a Band of Hope for its youngest students but had no temperance literature. After Stearns's and Mead's 1884 visit, and partly because the school's namesake was the late NTS treasurer Harvey B. Spelman, the NTS donated five hundred *Primary*

Temperance Catechisms and forty *Alcohol and Hygiene* textbooks. In addition, Spelman received a subscription to the *National Temperance Advocate*, several *Band of Hope Manuals*, and other books for its library. The total value of the donation was more than $150. As new schoolbooks came off the NTS press, the missionary committee provided Spelman's library with free copies.[32]

The outreach to Southern black clergy reflected the culture of the antebellum evangelical reform nexus. Some tracts mailed south, like the "Physiological Action of Alcohol," were long, detailed, scientific works while others were the chintzy short stories that had made up much of temperance literature for years, such as "A Bank for Losings," written by Theodore L. Cuyler, the NTS's third president. Another piece mailed to clergy was President Dodge's "The Church and Temperance," a paper he read at the 1880 Pan-Presbyterian Council in Philadelphia. *Freemen, or Slaves*, the first tract written by the NTS specifically for freed people (1868), was also included. This literature contained the same timeworn temperance discourse used since antebellum times because NTS officials believed the black man's reason could be appealed to in the same manner, and with the same effect, as the white man's. Dodge's speech warns about intemperance preventing salvation and draws on the old emphasis of being useful in his self-assertion that he was "actuated" by Christ's principle of "self-sacrifice for the good of others." In *Freemen, or Slaves,* the author draws heavily on the parallels between slavery and intemperance, urging the freed people not to become enslaved to liquor now that they are free from their old masters. He warns that alcohol will prevent them from being influenced by the "spirit of piety" and that "temperance is the handmaid of virtue."

In J. N. Stearns's editorials and in communications from NTS temperance missionaries one finds Christian republican language ("every hindrance to virtue must be suppressed"), romantic racialist language ("The negroes are naturally amiable and affectionate"), condescending attitudes ("It is a tremendous work to lift a whole race, but it has got to be done"), and yet optimism ("The colored people take more strongly to temperance as they understand it than do the white people"). Much of the NTS outreach was financed from solicitations made at revival meetings. Between 1881 and 1887 the NTS annually sponsored or participated in four to fourteen revivals or camp meetings in popular New York and New Jersey venues. Fund-raising for the freed people remained strong through the 1880s, for by the middle of the decade the NTS was seeking to raise $10,000 annually, although they most likely never reached that goal.[33]

The National Temperance Society was clearly passionate about its mission. A conservative group, it operated within the framework of the evangelical reform nexus, kept religion central to its work, and sought to disseminate the values of the critical community of temperance reformers, believing that Americans, one locality at a time, would eventually demand prohibition on their own if properly educated. Like other Northern missionary groups, they accepted the incremental and long-term nature of the reform and were content to work on shaping public sentiment rather than organizing political activity. Its relative singleness of purpose prevented the NTS from experiencing the types of divisive internal struggles that plagued the WCTU and Prohibition Party during the 1880s and 1890s. The biggest problem the NTS faced was its lackluster fund-raising and liberal literature distribution policy, but even with its financial struggles the organization remained the nation's single greatest distributor of temperance literature in the second half of the nineteenth century, and perhaps the single greatest source of temperance indoctrination among Southern blacks.

"The Colleges They Founded Were Social Settlements": Northern Missionary Schools and Temperance

The full impact of the NTS can only be appreciated when one considers the integration of its efforts with those of Atlanta's missionary schools.[34] The first organization to offer elementary-level instruction to Black Atlanta was the AMA, and when it opened its Storrs School in late 1866 it sold its first building to the Methodist Freedmen's Aid Society, which then operated its Summer Hill School in that location. Clark University evolved from that school. The opening of Atlanta's public school system in the early 1870s allowed the AMA and Methodist Freedmen's Aid Society to shift their efforts to secondary and teacher and preacher training programs, since Atlanta refused to open a high school for blacks. Along with other missionary schools throughout the South, Atlanta and Clark Universities—and in the 1880s the newer Spelman and Atlanta Baptist Seminaries—became institutions focused on the training of "competent, consecrated Christian leaders for the uplift of the race," the so-called talented tenth. As culturalists who believed in the assimilative ability of black people, the schools stressed "character" creation rather than "making better servants for the white race." The schools sought to inculcate the sentiments and behaviors of middle-class Northerners in black ministers, teachers, mothers, and wives.[35]

As mentioned earlier, Spelman Seminary's founders embraced the cult of domesticity, which asserted that since the woman's "proper sphere" was the home, she was responsible for maintaining its moral purity, training the children, and providing a refuge for her husband from the "contaminating" influences of the outside world. (Teaching was equally appropriate, but only for the unmarried woman.) Such thinking meant that training for the roles of mother and wife was no less important for racial uplift than training teachers and preachers. In 1884 the annual ABHMS report declared that the atmosphere of the home was more important than that of the school in character development, and it asserted, "it is not to be lost sight of that knowledge . . . of family and household duties, is an important factor in all schemes that are designed to improve the condition and to elevate . . . those who are to be influential in giving direction . . . especially who are to be the *mothers* of the coming generation" (emphasis in original). This nineteenth-century philosophy crossed racial lines, for Northern black divine Alexander Crummell commended the WABHMS educational efforts by declaring "the greatness of all peoples come from the home and . . . there can be no home . . . if a people have no true, plain, practical, pious and enlightened women." Such a value system provided a powerful impetus to educating black women about temperance.[36]

During the 1880s the AMA, ABHMS, WABHMS, and Methodist Freedmen's Aid Society each enforced strong temperance positions for their schools. A few months after the NTS-sponsored meeting in April 1881, the AMA bragged that its schools were "citadels of drill and equipment" in the temperance battle. To further fortify these "citadels" the AMA executive committee ordered all of its schools to incorporate temperance textbooks into their curriculum. Also that same year, Atlanta University's abstinence pledge, which had existed since at least 1872, for the first time was placed at the top of the list of items in the catalog required for school "membership." In 1883 the Congregationalists claimed their churches were "practically temperance societies" because total abstinence was an "article of their faith." In 1883 the ABHMS declared its schools an important "ally" of the temperance movement, and one of the movement's biggest weapons was the large number of totally abstinent future preachers being trained in institutions like Atlanta Baptist Seminary. The schools happily used NTS resources for Scientific Temperance Instruction and for their students' summer missionary work. Wilbur Thirkield, founding dean of Clark University's Gammon School of Theology, arrived in Atlanta in 1883 and immediately became an active campaigner for prohibition in Atlanta and elsewhere in Georgia. In 1886 the local conference of the Methodist Episcopal Church, North, issued a strong temperance resolution calling for total abstinence and government prohibition and advocating that ministers strictly enforce the church's discipline and teach their parishioners to uphold prohibitory laws. Black students at all of Atlanta's missionary schools, regardless of their faith traditions, were bombarded with the temperance message that was increasingly uniting all American evangelicals.[37]

Missionary School Students and Temperance Societies

Advanced students in Atlanta's missionary schools spent their summer vacations teaching in rural schools to raise tuition money.[38] In addition to teaching from Monday through Saturday morning, the students also taught in Sunday schools, organized temperance societies or Bands of Hope, and made home visitations. Over the years these students taught thousands of children not only literacy but also Bible stories and Christian virtues such as abstinence. NTS literature was a key part of these efforts. By the late 1870s more than one hundred or more Atlanta University students annually used their summers to teach in rural Georgia. Missionary educators shamelessly touted the cultural and political benefits of this tuition-raising process, believing in the effectiveness of their students' temperance work. "We must have no such defeat as was seen in North Carolina," claimed one teacher while soliciting more NTS literature. She was referencing the recent defeat of a prohibition law in North Carolina that was widely attributed to black voters. Annual shipments of NTS literature to AU for summer distribution began in 1878. In 1883 the NTS shipped 35,000 tracts in 200 packages for AU students to distribute. NTS shipments probably continued into the 1890s. The AMA candidly dubbed its students "temperance propagandists." Among the literature they distributed was "Appeal to the Colored Race," a one-page NTS leaflet written by an AME minister from Texas. In his short appeal he begged his fellow freed people to avoid whiskey because it put so many in state prisons and made so many orphans. He argued that whiskey will make us "slaves to death and destruction," but that "as a race" we can "advance our Redeemer's Kingdom" by abstaining. He argued that another source of inspiration should be the "better class of white citizens," who are teetotalers and who vote against whiskey. Although this black minister had imbibed the language of the antebellum evangelical reform nexus, he obviously remained grounded in contemporary racial reality.[39]

Predictably, students' experiences in promoting abstinence varied. Many happily reported their successes. One AU student who had taught in the same community for two consecutive years proudly reported that of the sixty who pledged the previous year, only three had broken their vow. A Spelman student teaching in Tennessee organized a society and asked one of her teachers for literature: "I have formed a temperance society of one hundred men, women, and children; and now I ask you to assist me a little by sending me some pledges and regulations to go by. This is a very bad place; it seems that the people's study is alcohol and beer. I am trying to do all I can to destroy king alcohol and his followers." Others were discouraged by the difficulty of the work. While one young woman was saddened to learn that her students' own parents gave them whiskey, another student said he did not bother with pledges because he knew they would be broken at Christmas. Then some students were more cautiously optimistic, such as Spelman's Sarah Lay, who happily reported organizing a Band of Hope but prayed, "May the seed sown bring forth good fruit."[40]

But Spelman students did not just form Bands of Hope during their summer breaks; their entire student body became a temperance society. Spelman's Band of Hope, established during the 1883–1884 school year, was one of the first clubs organized on campus and included nearly every student. The NTS and Atlanta's white WCTU donated literature. Meetings included local WCTU speakers, programs by the students or teachers, or sometimes simply a discussion about how to conduct summer temperance work. In addition, in 1885 a Young Women's Christian Association (YWCA) chapter was established on campus, and it had a temperance "department" that held monthly meetings. All of these groups were active during the 1885 and 1887 local option campaigns. The Atlanta Baptist Seminary formed a Young Men's Christian Association (YMCA) during the 1884–1885 school year, and while nothing is known of its activities, the national organization supported total abstinence. Atlanta Baptist's Ciceronian Lyceum, an extemporaneous speech club whose members practiced the rules of parliamentary procedure, made the idea of national prohibition the topic of one of its meetings.[41]

The Storrs School and Atlanta University also sponsored extracurricular temperance organizations. Founded in the spring of 1880, the Storrs School's Young Woman's Christian Temperance Union was the first Colored WCTU in the South. The Storrs School's Band of Hope met every Wednesday and in 1888 had 125 members, with an average of 75 attending weekly meetings. Atlanta University's YWCTU members were young women in the Higher Normal department, that is, teachers-in-training. They had a very active union, made up of a committee to visit the poor, a press superintendent, a social purity superintendent, and a literature superintendent. At meetings, the social purity superintendent gave a reading, and the literature superintendent reported how much the various members read during the week from their circulating library. The two YWCTUs met quarterly with the West and East Side Colored WCTUs in citywide mass meetings. The Young Woman's Christian Temperance Unions circulated the NTS's *Youth's Temperance Banner* among their members.[42]

Classroom Temperance Instruction

But students in Atlanta's missionary colleges received even more exposure to temperance than club membership offered because they enrolled in cutting-edge Scientific Temperance Instruction (STI) courses decades before Georgia mandated them for all students.[43] Although the AMA did not mandate temperance instruction for its schools until 1881, Atlanta University adopted the NTS's *Temperance Lesson Book* as soon as it came off the press in 1878. This text was the first major scientific temperance textbook published in the United States, and AU was the first school in the nation—white or black—to adopt it. Since the early 1870s, AU and Storrs School students had studied Alex M. Gow's *Good Morals and Gentle Manners for Schools and Families,* which included a strong biblical abstinence message. Spelman's administration instituted STI for its students by requiring younger students to use Julia Colman's *Primary Temperance Catechism* and older students to use her *Alcohol and Hygiene* text, which was also used by some AU students. By the late eighties, AU students had switched to Jerome Walker's *Anatomy, Physiology and Hygiene.* A brief look at these texts and their authors reveals the nature of STI at Atlanta University, Spelman Seminary, and the Storrs School during the 1880s.

The first textbook used in the AMA's Atlanta schools that directly addressed abstinence was Alexander M. Gow's *Good Morals and Gentle Manners.* This text taught that all good manners are based on good morals, which in turn were based on the Bible. *Good Morals* perpetuated the republican notion that governmental stability is rooted in the virtue of the citizenry, and it defined the "good society" as one made up of moral people. Its chapters addressed such topics as courage, chastity, dress, the poor, amusements, hatred, property rights, and temperance. The "Temperance" chapter is essentially a Bible study divided into sections on "Wild oats," "Temptation," "Put it out of sight," "Touch not, taste not, handle not," and "Moral courage." AU students studied this text in the first year of either the college preparatory or normal course, roughly equivalent to today's ninth grade. It was probably taught to students in their seventh or eighth year at the Storrs School. AU used the text from 1872 to 1899. Spelman teachers also used the book in the 1890–1891 school year.[44]

With only one chapter on temperance, Gow's book had its obvious limitations, so in 1878 AU teacher Mary Chase persuaded the school to adopt Benjamin Richardson's newly published *Temperance Lesson Book.* Chase believed a more thorough understanding of alcohol's dangers would deepen the abstinence commitment of AU students. A Fellow of the Royal Society, Richardson was a British doctor whose research into the effects of alcohol persuaded him to become a teetotaler. Schools in the United States, England, Scotland, Canada, New Zealand, and Holland adopted his highly regarded text. AU students studied Richardson in either the last year (third) of the college preparatory or in the third year (of four) of the normal course. The *Temperance Lesson Book*'s many three-page chapters covered the latest science on alcohol in various types of beverages and its effects on the body.[45]

Beginning in 1882 and continuing through 1897, students in Atlanta University's eighth and final year of grammar school studied Julia Colman's *Alcohol and Hygiene: An Elementary Lesson Book for Schools,* another NTS publication. Her own study of health and diet led her into the temperance movement, and Colman built a career as a temperance teacher, lecturer, and writer. In addition to being an NTS-endorsed lecturer who once spoke at Spelman, she published more than five hundred juvenile temperance tracts, books, pamphlets, and lessons and was superintendent of the WCTU's Department of Temperance Literature from 1880 to 1891. Colman published extensively in the *National Temperance Advocate*, *Youth's Temperance Banner*, the WCTU's *Our Union*, and the Methodist *Sunday School Advocate*. At the suggestion of the WCTU's Mary Hunt, in 1880 Colman wrote *Alcohol and Hygiene: An Elementary Lesson Book for Schools*. While it explained the nature of alcohol, as did Richardson's book, it did so in less technical terms and with many suggested experiments. Colman takes her readers through the steps necessary to create alcohol, starting as simply as suggesting that students watch a sealed jar of apple juice and stewed apples decay in 70° heat. She notes the contradiction of saying that the decay of apples makes them sour and unfit to eat while the decay of the juice makes it fit to drink. Colman explains the various sources of alcohol and the processes of fermentation and distillation in simplified terms. She then discusses alcohol's effects on the various parts of the body. Several chapters are overtly preachy, with titles such as "Crimes Caused by Alcohol," "Would you like a Clear Head?" and "Achievements of Abstainers."[46]

A few years later Colman wrote a text for even younger children called *The Primary Temperance Catechism*, also published by the NTS. Its lessons followed a simple format: a statement, a question-and-answer sequence, a picture, an explanation of a few lines, and a short mnemonic poem. Spelman's grammar school students used the *Catechism*.[47]

The 1880s, then, witnessed the most intense period of STI in Atlanta's missionary schools. By the end of the decade more than three hundred Spelman students had signed the school's temperance pledge book, which was stored with official student records. All of Atlanta's black schools required students to sign abstinence pledges, including the AME Church's Morris Brown College, which opened its doors in 1885 and modeled its program after Wilberforce University. Expulsion for violating the pledge at these schools was not unheard of. James Weldon Johnson had four friends who were expelled for drinking and smoking at Atlanta University. AU students who attended from elementary through one of the secondary or collegiate programs would first encounter Gow, then Colman, and finally Richardson. At Spelman they began with Colman's *Catechism* and later studied *Alcohol and Hygiene*. In addition to several pro-temperance Baptist periodicals, students also had library access to the *New York Weekly Witness*, *National Temperance Advocate*, and *Youth's Temperance Banner*. An important part of graduation at Spelman was four days of public examinations, and one of those days was devoted to recitations on temperance. During mandatory chapel services college students heard the leading temperance and prohibition speakers of the day, such as J. N. Stearns,

Julia Colman, John B. Finch, Frances Willard, William E. Dodge, and Frances E. W. Harper, and for their extracurricular activities most belonged to the Band of Hope or YWCTU. Members of the YMCA and YWCA also received constant abstinence messages. When the school year ended they were expected to travel to some rural community and, when not teaching, to set up temperance societies. The NTS stocked school libraries with literature and partially or wholly funded the purchase of textbooks as well as literature for summer distribution. The intensity of Atlanta's missionary schools' teetotal message could not be greater.[48]

The temperance message was apparently quite compelling. For one young student the temperance message was even more compelling than efforts to convert her. She announced that even though she was not a Christian she had promised "the Lord" that she would never drink any rum. When Gammon's first class of ministers graduated in 1886, at least two class speakers called for respect from whites to be based on the personal moral purity of blacks. The line calling for every preacher to "blaze with eloquent and earnest appeals to his race for the casting of their ballots for the speedy and complete destruction of the liquor traffic" met with hearty applause. Even after the defeat of prohibition in Fulton County in 1887, Spelman students optimistically continued to establish Bands of Hope in city churches in anticipation of electing dry candidates in upcoming municipal elections.[49]

Although the free distribution of the *New York Weekly Witness* was short-lived, the flood of NTS literature and the temperance programs of the missionary schools reflected a "relatively coherent, unified discourse" on temperance, and Thomas Rochon argues such is required of any reform movement trying to influence culture. The evangelical reform nexus organizations created that discourse, transported it to Black Atlanta, and funneled it through their schools toward the freed people.[50]

It is well established that the missionary schools created controlled environments to instill evangelical culture into their students. Teachers gladly reported the number of Christian converts each year and the percentage of the graduating class who were professing Christians. Spelman's motto was "Our whole school for Christ," and Sophia Packard was so intent on conversions that she called a week with none the "saddest failure."[51] But Northern missionaries understood evangelical Christianity to be as much about one's behavior following conversion as it was about conversion itself, so all students were made subject to the right rules, the best teachers, and extensive interaction with their (white) teachers. Having as many students as possible live on campus was designed to maximize contact with, and the influence of, the primarily Northern faculty. AU had dorms from the early 1870s, and Spelman opened its first ones within

Fig. 12—Atlanta University Chapel (in Stone Hall) where William E. Dodge, J. N. Stearns, Frances Willard, and others addressed the student body on the subject of temperance. From undated, Atlanta University Photos, Buildings/Grounds, Atlanta University Center Robert W. Woodruff Library

two years of its founding, but Atlanta Baptist Seminary did not have any until 1890, which greatly disturbed Baptist leaders. They complained that off-campus boarding exposed students to the "distractions and temptations of the city" and was therefore a "great hindrance to our work." Obviously they meant the "work" of character building, and those "temptations" most certainly included the city's various watering holes. Without dorms, the enforcement of abstinence pledges must have been more difficult at Atlanta Baptist than at Spelman or Atlanta University. When AU students lived off campus they were required to live in a "home-like environment." To maximize the influence of the teachers, AU's first president decided to have teachers and students sit together at mealtime, and it apparently had the desired effect, at least for some, because one alumnus recalled "that intimate association three times a day exercised an influence over manners, speech, personal appearance and attitude that could not be exerted so effectively in any other way." Observers reported that faculty influence outside of class created a more rapid rate of spiritual and academic growth among boarders than nonboarding students. AU's president believed the matron in the men's dorm re-created the "refining, elevating, and restraining influence" of family life. Parent-like, teachers worried each spring when the students left the campus cocoon for summer vacation. Giles and Packard took some comfort from the fact that the students had signed total abstinence and social purity pledges, but they still solicited prayers from their donors.[52] In sum, these Christian schools were "combinations of Christian forces . . . to mold character."[53]

Discipline, discipline, discipline summed up life for Atlanta University's students. First Congregational pastor and AU professor Cyrus W. Francis described his school as a closed system: "The course pursued in this school consists essentially in separating the pupils by means of a family school from all old associations and habits, and subjecting them for months and years to a strong and watchful discipline, in surrounding them with the most earnest and aggressive religious influences." W. E. B. Du Bois, a product of the AMA-founded Fisk University and professor at Atlanta University for many years, described the missionary schools as "social settlements":

> The teachers in these institutions came not to keep the Negroes in their place, but to raise them out of the defilement of the places where slavery had wallowed them. The colleges they founded were social settlements; homes where the best of the sons of the freedmen came in close and sympathetic touch with the best traditions of New England. They lived and ate together, studied and worked, hoped and harkened in the dawning light.[54]

In the eyes of the missionaries, the depths of the moral and spiritual destitution slavery created justified such extreme measures. Students choosing to attend these schools arrived knowing and accepting the fact that they were to going to be literally "trained" in a mode of behavior that was quite foreign to them.[55]

An education at Atlanta University, Spelman Seminary, Clark University, and Atlanta Baptist differed from an education at other Christian secondary and post-secondary schools. Atlanta's missionary schools were much more than just schools. DuBois said AU embraced a fourfold cultural mission: higher education, racial equality, academic freedom, and increased democratic and social power. Students at these schools knew they were a select minority within a minority, Morehouse's "talented tenth." They were being made into "race leaders" to uplift and transform their race. Because Northern teachers could never educate all the freed people, the preachers, teachers, and mothers they trained were expected to impart the ostensibly superior cultural values of Northern evangelicals to the masses of their people. The ABHMS unashamedly called its schools "assimilating apparatuses" designed to make black students "thoroughly homogenous" with middle-class culture. Atlanta University clearly conveyed the talented tenth cultural transmission model to its students. James Weldon Johnson said he had not been in school long before he realized his education was designed to prepare him for his "peculiar responsibilities due to my own racial group." According to historical sociologist Joseph O. Jewell, the AMA's Atlanta schools were central to the creation of Black Atlanta's middle class. Evidence suggests that the early graduates from these schools largely accepted the mission to uplift their race.[56]

Temperance indoctrination in Atlanta's missionary schools affected blacks differently than similar practices in white schools. Because of WCTU pressures, increasing numbers of white children were receiving mandated Scientific Temperance Instruction in America's public schools throughout the 1880s, but many of the teachers were ill-prepared to teach it, opposed teaching it, or both. Public school teachers and administrators bristled at lay people telling them as professionals how to do their job. By contrast, in the missionary schools, teachers and administrators thoroughly embraced and personally modeled abstinence. The schools aligned both their curricular and extracurricular programs to push the temperance message. During the first two decades of the twentieth century there was a per capita increase in alcohol consumption in America, suggesting the general failure of years of STI efforts, but the closed system approach of the missionary school guaranteed a more complete reception of the temperance message by the emerging black middle class. Scholar Ivan Light argues that in order for voluntary associations and institutions to impose ethical discipline they need to achieve as nearly as possible "total rather than segmental control over members' motives, beliefs, associations, and conduct," and this accounts for the degree of success the schools achieved.[57]

Missionary school alumni largely accepted the values of the antebellum reform nexus, which were fast becoming the core of bourgeois middle-class values, but this was a relatively small number of blacks. These values, including abstinence, increasingly separated missionary school alumni from other blacks. By the mid-1880s the inchoate "better class" of blacks who pastored, taught in the public schools, and led fraternities was just beginning to coalesce around these values. As the years passed, their numbers and solidarity grew—they intermarried, created their own residential neighborhoods, and eventually their own social clubs. But in the 1880s, these processes were just beginning, and only the most prescient contemporary observers perceived them.[58]

Temperance in 1880s Black Atlanta had long, tangled roots in culture, religion, and education and manifested increasingly important ramifications for race and class relations. Northern missionaries did their best to drive home the temperance message, but after graduation it was up to the alumni to spread the message through the black-controlled institutions of Black Atlanta—churches, mutual aid, and fraternal societies. It is to their temperance efforts in these institutions that we now turn our attention.

> Let us help the colored people,
> Help the colored people,
> Let us help the colored people,
> Along the temp'rance way.
> —"Let Us Help the Colored People," chorus

Part II

Reformers in the South

Haste, Lord, the time when all mankind,
Black, white or copper hue,
All shall have signed the Temperance Pledge,
And to that Pledge are true!
—Phoebe A. Hanaford, *Hymn of the Temperance Man*

The hope of our race is as much dependent upon this virtue, as any
other, and possibly more.
—*Star of Zion* (January 1886)

CHAPTER 4

Taking Ownership

*Black Atlanta's Efforts to Institutionalize a Temperance-
Based Moral Community*

We need more education and less whiskey, more morals and less
politics, (we do not say no politics but less politics), more pure
Christianity and less bigotry in religion, more of mental culture
and less pampering our bodies and appetites.
—William M. Dart, alumnus, Atlanta University,
The Helping Hand (April 1881)

One fateful day a teenager "full of liquor" meandered down the street near the
Storrs School just as a temperance meeting was about to begin. Rose Kinney, a
teacher, invited him inside, and by the end of the meeting the young man had
signed the teetotal pledge. His name was George V. Clark, and he was one of the
many former slaves who poured into Atlanta following the war. At the time he met
up with the missionary work of the AMA he was a porter at a saloon. Miss Kinney
and the Reverend Cyrus Francis saw potential in the young man, enrolled him at
Storrs, and began to deal with him about his soul. Before long George Clark underwent a conversion experience and joined First Congregational. He eventually
graduated from Atlanta University, and in 1881 from Howard University's School
of Divinity. Following his graduation, Clark responded to an invitation to plant a
new Congregational church in Athens, Georgia. His church was duly organized,
and he was ordained, in April 1882. His new church plant, with only 17 members
at first, was initially supported with AMA funds, and when Clarke County held a

local option vote in early 1885, he was proud to report that his whole congregation voted "dry," helping to make the county dry. In the nineties, Clark moved on to pastor self-supporting black Congregational churches in Memphis, Tennessee, and Charleston, South Carolina. Clark was clearly an AMA "success story."

George V. Clark was not the only "success story" from Atlanta's missionary schools, and they did not all leave Atlanta. Many remained, becoming local pastors, teachers, and journalists, forming the nucleus of Black Atlanta's "better classes." With few exceptions, through the eighties, all of Black Atlanta's "leaders" had some connection with Northern evangelicals and were overwhelmingly supportive of temperance.

Up to this point this study has focused on the theology, motivations, and activities of Northern evangelicals who insisted on introducing black Atlantans to temperance, regardless of their need. From this point forward it concentrates on the freed people themselves, first examining how the clergy functioned as a critical community by defining Black Atlanta's intemperance problem and then taking leadership in collective action to address it, first through moral suasion efforts and then through Fulton County's local option elections. These chapters also argue that black temperance leaders were strongly connected with the religio-cultural traditions of both black and white antebellum evangelical reformers.

Northern free blacks were immersed in the antebellum evangelical reform nexus, which partly accounts for the AME Church's embrace of temperance. But at the same time, the severe socioeconomic, political, and religious ostracism endured by Northern African Americans encouraged them to perpetuate elements of a distinctly African worldview or cosmology, and this worldview also encouraged temperance values. In the South the continued experience of slavery, combined with the ongoing illegal importation of slaves after 1808 and the general absence of Northern revival theology, created even more intense spaces for blacks to perpetuate elements of traditional African spirituality, although not to the extent of slaves in the Caribbean and Brazil. The Christianity taught by Northern missionaries to the freed people sounded different from what they learned under slavery for more than one reason, but what concerns us here is that Northerners taught a benevolent God, downplayed or rejected the doctrine of original sin, and understood God to be the moral Governor of the universe. None of these ideas would have been the common fare of white clergy employed to preach to slaves, but such ideas connected in meaningful ways with latent and explicit African elements of African Americans' worldview.

This chapter will briefly review the common elements of traditional African spirituality widely believed by nineteenth-century African Americans and will identify where they intersect with evangelical reform nexus theology. I will then identify ways that the temperance discourse and activism of both Northern antebellum blacks and postbellum black Atlantans reflected these traditions. Subsequent chapters will suggest the ways that these traditions informed black Atlantans' response to the city's experiment with prohibition.

"When the Occasion Comes, the Proverb Comes": The Pragmatic Syncretism of African and African American Spirituality

Just as the Puritans brought their version of Christianity to Massachusetts and the Quakers brought theirs to Pennsylvania, the African immigrants who had come to America involuntarily brought their own religious thought. Over time, the creolization process turned African cultural practices and belief systems into African American ones, as slaves blended elements of their various African cultures with elements of the dominant white culture.[1] While scholars debate much about this historical process, it is generally agreed that developing an African American cosmology required slaves to draw on their commonly held beliefs about the nature of, and relationship between, the spirit world and the material world. Some ideas were jettisoned because they were so ethnically unique, while others died out because they did not seem to work in America as they had in Africa. Despite the fact that slaves hailed from many disparate societies, as religion scholar Dianne Stewart notes, there was still a "great deal of cross-cultural consistency . . . especially with regard to metaphysical orientation and religious logic, expression, and function." These principles coalesced and perpetuated themselves in the black-only spaces created by slavery and the racial segregation following emancipation, and provided the lens through which African Americans interpreted their experiences in America.[2]

Although U.S. laws generally permitted owners to make almost limitless demands on the time of their slaves, discipline them at will, and sell family members as needed or desired, the one thing a master could not do was control the perceptions and thoughts of his slaves or their conversations when they were out of sight and earshot. While scholarship is divided on the relative cultural importance of these independent spaces, they did exist, and within them, as much as they could, slaves developed their own worldview by telling stories, teaching, preaching, praying, and talking of—and sometimes planning for—individual and corporate freedom. The African American cosmology that coalesced in these spaces was blended, or syncretic. Further syncretism occurred as African Americans adopted and adapted elements of European Christianity to their experience of oppression. The creolization process was multi-generational, and traditional beliefs died hard. Discussed below are the beliefs likely to have had the most influence on how nineteenth-century African Americans interpreted the temperance message and responded to its politicization in local option elections.[3]

The first, most basic assumption of African cosmology is that the universe is hierarchical and functions on an "ethic of reciprocity." While names varied, African peoples widely believed (and believe) in a Supreme Being whose duty is to always seek the order and preservation of the human community. Beneath the Supreme Being are various types of lesser spirit beings, mankind, the various plants and animals, and phenomena and objects. The "ethic of reciprocity" meant that "those of higher rank are obligated to protect their subordinates and the duty of the latter is to acknowledge their dependency by always seeking the good will and blessing of the former." This applies within and between the natural and spiritual worlds. In many African people groups, powerful men were such because they protected and provided for so many people in their clan or lineage, and because large numbers reciprocated by publicly recognizing these individuals' status and power. Likewise, lesser spirit beings were expected to protect and favor their human devotees in return for lavish worship rituals. Prominent Africanist Karin Barber has argued that in Yoruba culture, spirits (òrìṣà) who fail to answer their devotees' supplications are ignored and can fade into insignificance because people are free to switch their allegiance to a spirit who will answer their prayers. The relationship between humans and spirit beings is so intimate in African thought that distinctions between the sacred and secular are often blurred in practice, if not in theory.

The second major African concept relevant to this study concerns beliefs about the relationship between the community and the individual, and the nature of evil. In African thinking, an individual's behavior is judged according to its impact on the community. Behaviors that benefit the community are deemed virtuous, while evil behavior is the opposite. Anything that violates the social order or insults or offends the spirits is evil. An individual's behavior is never only about himself. Charges of witchcraft are sometimes accompanied by evidence that the individual's wealth compared to that of others in the community has improved too rapidly. Such exceptional success is enough to raise suspicions of foul play. Evil, then, inheres in the deed, not the person, as Christianity has historically taught. The results of an evil act are presumed to affect the whole community, so often the whole community is expected to respond. Illustrative of this principle is the African tale about a tortoise, an iguana, and a snail hiding under a tree. Birds and monkeys arrived to eat the fruit on the branches, and in the process became very noisy. The tortoise became concerned that the noise would attract a hunter, so he whispered to the iguana to relay a message to the birds and monkeys to quiet down, but a hunter came along before the iguana could hear clearly what the tortoise wanted him to do. The tortoise had warned the iguana that "death begins by one person," by which he meant that all the animals might die even if only a few of them were acting inappropriately. Such folktales encouraged Africans to be their brother's keeper "or else suffer for sins that he has not committed."[4]

It is from this individual-community relationship that African thought, per se, arises. African thought—ethics, philosophy, and theology—largely arises from efforts to address disorder within the human community. As a result, traditional African ethics is situational and theology is contextual, as reflected by the Ashanti proverb, "When the occasion comes, the proverb comes." People judge actions according to their effectiveness. One's position or status could be contingent on their efficaciousness. For example, if a shaman's prophecies or cures repeatedly fail, it is not unheard of for them to be rejected, dismissed, or even punished by the village. Facilitating this utilitarian or pragmatic orientation was the absence of the concept of orthodoxy from African religions. Africanist John Thornton argues that the belief in continuous revelation and a historically weak priesthood prevented the rise of orthodoxy. While there have always been Christian traditions that accept limited forms of continuous revelation, the faith asserts a closed canon of writings, which has no parallel in African religion. Furthermore, historical Christianity developed a relatively strong priesthood that reserved to itself the privilege of interpreting the closed canon in order to form doctrine. In stark contrast, African cultures do not entertain the concept of an "official" version of a folktale or proverb, for they all exist in several forms, undoubtedly designed out of the exigencies of varying contexts. The absence of a closed canon and a strong priesthood combines with a belief in spirit beings' ongoing revelations through dreams, visions, spirit mediums, and divination to create a constantly evolving and inclusive religious and ethical orientation. Pragmatic syncretism, then, heavily colored African Americans' worldview, and they could not help but interpret personal calls for abstinence and the politics of prohibition within its parameters.

African American Spirituality and Reform Nexus Theology

Some African elements of African American thought intersected with key doctrines of the evangelical reform nexus. Increasing numbers of antebellum Americans came to believe that traditional "Five Point" Calvinism—with its emphasis on God's predestination of only some to heaven, leaving the rest for eternal damnation regardless of their efforts—characterized God as capricious and unreasonable. Partly in response to people's revulsion to such a characterization of God, the new pro-revival theologians downplayed, and sometimes outright denied, the doctrine of original sin, instead stressing each individual's ability to work out their own salvation. In a complementary manner, moral government teaching portrayed God as a rational, consistent, and just "Governor" who designed laws to maximize mankind's happiness. This emphasis on the human ability to do good and God's benevolence toward mankind is functionally identical to key elements of traditional African spirituality. Finally, the doctrine of disinterested benevolence, the teaching that new converts are obligated to demonstrate their salvation through their benevolent deeds to relieve others' suffering, bears much resemblance to the African belief defining virtuous behavior as that which benefits the whole community.

The pro-revival theological innovations of the reform nexus, however, did not go unchallenged. Theologians like Archibald Alexander, Charles Hodge, and James Henley Thornwell, among others, mounted vigorous attacks on these "New England" revivalist doctrines, and their attacks found their greatest acceptance in the antebellum South. In fact, the leading historian of antebellum theology, E. Brooks Holifield, argues that the pro-revival doctrines discussed here had "only a token presence" in Southern life. To this reality must be added the fact that slaveholders who arranged for preachers to address their slaves intended such instruction to serve primarily as a motivation "for slave obedience and deference." The goal of slave submission yielded routine sermons from a relatively small number of Bible passages. Slaves largely dismissed such preaching, seeing it for what it was, and preachers fretted over what seemed to be a low number of conversions. Although many slaves accepted Christianity and practiced much of it out of sight of their masters, they had no sense of the intersections between their worldview and Northerners' innovations in Christian theology. Since Southern white preachers could only teach abstinence as a form of obedience to the master, if at all, it could be nothing more than an expression of the master's concern for labor efficiency, which obviously was of little to no concern to the slaves.[5]

All of this changed when AMA and ABHMS missionaries arrived in Black Atlanta after the Civil War. Whether or not Northern evangelicals delved into the finer points of their doctrines, they taught, preached, and prayed in the presence of the freed people in their schools and churches on the assumption that their nexus doctrines were true, and this could have only made their version of Christianity sound qualitatively different—and more appealing—than that of their former masters. Southern freed people, like Northern blacks before them, probably discerned the overlay between elements of their African American worldview and those of the evangelical missionaries. These similarities likely facilitated the diffusion of temperance values and discourse within Black Atlanta. Similar to Northerners before them, black Atlantans drew on both evangelical and African themes in their temperance efforts. A brief overview of the key elements of Northern antebellum black temperance will provide the basis for discerning these continuities.

"A Subject of Peculiar Importance to Colored People Generally": Northern Antebellum Black Temperance

Antebellum black temperance discourse and activism evolved within the confines of a painfully racist society.[6] Nineteenth-century American white supremacy placed so many economic, political, social, cultural, and religious restrictions on free blacks that they lived as second-class citizens, enjoying a "quasi-freedom." Their inability to find employment, to advance in employment, to be paid the same as whites for the same work, to vote, to receive an education, to be treated courteously by whites in personal encounters, and sometimes even to assemble peaceably, among other things, made a mockery of blacks' freedom or, worse, threatened their continued existence as independent individuals and a community of free persons. Their limited economic and political opportunities created a contingent, dependent state of being for Northern African Americans. They lived a precarious, unstable existence with little or no opportunity to improve themselves, as white institutions and structures were mostly closed to them. Complete dependence is the essence of enslavement, so free blacks' inability to live independently—their continuing state of "dependence," even though they were ostensibly free—created an existential crisis for Northern blacks. Despair led some to emigrate to places like Haiti, Liberia, or Upper Canada, and even more to talk about doing so. The vast majority, however, remained and fought for the human and civil rights that were rightfully theirs. Successes were so minimal that multiple approaches were tried, and those leading the fight could not easily agree on the best way to make their case for full equality before white society.[7]

One helpful idea black leaders facing this crisis rallied around was the concept of virtue. The concept of virtue was located at the intersection of African spirituality and reform nexus ideology. As discussed in chapter one, beginning with the era of the American Revolution virtue had repeatedly appeared in American public discourse as the central element of the malleable and ubiquitous ideology of republicanism. Classical republicanism equated economic independence with public virtue, while the Christian version of republicanism equated virtue with personal morality. Using either or both definitions, revolutionary-era patriots had often claimed that because of their virtue they would not, indeed *could not*, accept being "enslaved" to Britain, and to remain rhetorically consistent they turned and argued that the actual (African) slaves in their midst lacked virtue, thereby justifying their enslavement. Whites even denied that free African Americans were virtuous, which helped them rationalize the less than full citizenship rights extended to free blacks well into the nineteenth century. While the revolutionary generation argued that virtuous people by definition could not be enslaved and were thus compelled to fight for their freedom and independence, in the era of the early republic whites carried their argument to its logical conclusion by arguing that one could not retain one's freedom and independence without remaining virtuous. Thus, virtuous people would naturally become an independent people, and conversely, all independent people must logically be virtuous and remain virtuous people. This circular reasoning remained a truism of American civic thought for decades.[8]

Whites' denial of African Americans' virtue meant they felt no obligation to respect their freedom and independence, personally or collectively. The racism of the young nation gave free blacks anything but a sense of human dignity or the confidence that they, like whites, could improve themselves by dint of their own hard work, skill, and intellect. Black leaders argued this was unacceptable in a nation whose founding philosophy asserted that "all men are created equal," and they sought to nurture and demonstrate the existence of virtue (independence) among their own people. In each Northern city, African Americans organized mutual aid societies, fraternal lodges, literary societies, and most importantly, churches. In these spaces they learned to look to each other for strength independently of whites. The independence might be economic, in that mutual aid societies assisted the sick and needy, or it might be political, as each organization elected its own officers, giving those with leadership abilities a place to exercise them, since they often could not vote and definitely could not win public office. These demonstrations of independence were ultimately about creating a virtuous community.

In addition to the independence demonstrated by these community groups, their constitutions stipulated that members lead personally virtuous lives or risk being expelled. Several years before Richard Allen led the walkout from St. George's Church, he and Absalom Jones had organized the Free African Society of Philadelphia, one of the nation's first black mutual aid societies. The society's constitution prohibited any "drunkard or disorderly person" from being admitted to membership. The 1796 constitution of Boston's African Society stipulated that "any member, bringing on himself any sickness, or disorder, by intemperance, shall not be considered, as entitled to any benefits, or assistance from the society." And so it went, as society after society required members to lead virtuous, moral lives, and intemperance was banned. This language reflected much more than a unilateral effort to coerce individuals to lead moral lives. Drawing on broad African principles about the relationship between an individual and community, these societies presumed that it was *natural* that "personal morality should motivate one to participate actively in the welfare of the group." Insofar as these societies facilitated individual virtue, they facilitated corporate virtue, resulting in genuine independence and existential wholeness. Ethicist Samuel K. Roberts argues that by using virtue in this manner antebellum blacks were able to resist the contingency and precariousness imposed by their racist society and instead establish a viability that "may be understood as the quality of existence without which a person or group is devoid of an interior generative force capable of achieving and sustaining life." For Northern free blacks, the concept of virtue "impelled" them to "struggle against injustice and oppression and to forge communities and structures that could ensure the development of the furthest moral and material possibilities." Just as white Americans asserted their virtue and defied British tyranny in the 1760s and 1770s, likewise, in the first half of the 1800s free African Americans asserted their virtue and defied the oppression of white Americans. All African American community groups did not define temperance as teetotalism, but the character trait of temperance, broadly conceived, was a virtue expected of members of Northern black societies.[9]

Other ideas besides virtue had currency with both reform nexus doctrines and African spirituality, and the overlap makes it difficult to determine the true source of antebellum black temperance discourse. For example, in an 1834 temperance speech the Pennsylvania businessman William Whipper argued: "To assert that we are morally bound to support the cause, is only to say that our obligations to our Maker and society impose upon us the duty of promoting the welfare of our species." Was Whipper assuming a well-churched audience familiar with Charles Finney's theology of benevolence, or was he appealing to an African ethic of reciprocity—or both? Similarly, the Sixth National Convention of Colored People (1847) issued a temperance resolution praising the movement for its positive effect on the "social happiness" of humanity. Since both nexus theology and the African American worldview defined virtuous behavior as an obligation to God and as that which benefited the community, it is not easy to discern whether the speaker had simply assimilated white evangelical theology or had found language that was familiar to whites yet actually was understood slightly differently by a black audience. It is likely that, even though white and black temperance audiences heard the same language, it resonated differently with blacks because they arrived at it from a slightly different direction. Since both groups arrived at the same language by different routes it is not unreasonable to assume that, even if that language persuaded different peoples to embrace abstinence, it did so for slightly different reasons.[10]

At other times it was clear that the discourse was borrowed directly from white reformers. An example of this was when four men who issued a call for the creation of a New England Temperance Society for people of color said, "We long to stand among the men of our country, as fellow-citizens, worthy of our country and the human race. Our first step is to put far away vice and every immorality." In 1839 the Reverend Amos G. Beman, a Connecticut minister active in temperance societies, published a series of five temperance articles in *The Colored American*. Beman devoted the entire fifth article to the premise that "intoxicating liquors are the enemies of the religious interest of man." He asked, "how can it be expected that men should understand and regard the best interest of their souls, when they habitually allow themselves to be under the pernicious influence of intoxicating liquors?" Beman's concern here is best understood as nothing more than an expression of the moral government of God theology, which highly valued the unfettered reasoning capacity of sinners.[11]

Then there was temperance discourse that drew most definitely from African traditions. "As a people, our interests, our prosperity, and our happiness call upon us to forsake this course," announced one colored temperance convention, clearly judging intemperance on the basis of its effect on the whole community. One argument that was popular for a time was that if blacks became temperate it might convince whites they actually were virtuous, giving the lie to whites' charges and removing a pillar of racism. One call for a state temperance convention expressed how this behavior harmed the whole community: "Prejudice is, alas! too strong without any cause. None of us, therefore, by intemperance or any vicious indulgence, should contribute in the least to foster it." This is widely known as the "moral reform and racial uplift" response to racism, of which many scholars have been critical, seeing in it little more than a failed assimilation effort. It is more culturally authentic, however, to interpret this language in the context of an African-inspired ethical system that evaluates an individual's behavior based on its effect on the whole community. This approach to ethical behavior has roots deep in the collective African heritage.[12]

Perhaps the favorite approach of black temperance speakers was to equate intemperance with slavery, arguing that both harmed the African American community, and that an attack on one was an attack on both. This connection could easily be drawn from a consistent reading of moral government of God theology, which many white temperance reformers were loath to do. A key theme here was that slaves to human masters and to the bottle both, by definition, lived dependent, that is, non-virtuous, lives. "The same principles that sustain the system of slavery will apply, equally well, to the justification of rumselling," declared one writer. Another speaker insisted that "Our freedom must show itself in the fact that we are not slaves to intemperance," while the Fifth National Colored Convention resolved that, "as intemperance and slavery are closely allied, this convention recommends to our people the formation of temperance societies which we believe will facilitate the cause of immediate and universal emancipation." Their precarious freedom made rhetorical connections between virtue, freedom, and independence especially poignant for African Americans. Besides African Americans, the other group for whom such connections were particularly salient was slave owners. Temperance literature designed for plantation owners argued that "Drinking could lead to loss of control, where the distinction between freeman and dependent was blurred or destroyed." After all, no one understood better the inherently demeaning nature of the dependency of slavery than the slave master who enforced it with violence.[13]

Even African American fiction writers depicted the interdependence of virtue, temperance, and freedom in their narratives. Perhaps the best example of this is Martin R. Delany's novel *Blake: Or, The Huts of America,* serialized in the *Anglo-African Magazine* from 1859 to 1862. This novel repeatedly associates intemperance with slave ownership. The protagonist, Henry Blake, is a fugitive slave who travels through the South to stir up rebellion. On one occasion, a white man who figures out that Henry is a fugitive unsuccessfully offers him whiskey in a false attempt to befriend him. In another scene a slave posse drinks and eats in Henry's presence, totally deceived into thinking he is a local slave. On yet another occasion a slaveholder uses brandy as a sedative for a visitor who is horrified at his treatment of a slave. Finally, a slave insurrection is exposed through some inopportune comments from a drunken slave. Delany viewed intemperance as supportive of black oppression, while temperance was a tool of resistance, even revolution.[14]

The Northern antebellum African American temperance movement was integral to blacks' quest for meaningful independence, full citizenship rights, and full recognition of their humanity—or "manhood," as many termed it. It was logically an outgrowth of both their evangelical Christianity and their African heritage. The temperance work of blacks in postbellum Atlanta shows that they inherited this dual Northern antebellum tradition.

"It is Ruining our People": Temperance and the Church in Black Atlanta

Through the 1880s Black Atlanta's clergy led the way in temperance reform in their community and also left the most extensive record of their rationale for supporting the reform. Their most dedicated allies were non-clerical alumni of the various missionary schools. Through their leadership of churches and various societies, these men sought to institutionalize a temperance-based moral community in Black Atlanta and eventually turned to politics and cooperated with white secular and religious leaders to make the whole city dry.

The Dual Heritage of the Critical Community of Black Clergy

The local and state associations, conventions, and conferences to which Atlanta's AME and black Baptist churches belonged had standing temperance committees as early as the late 1860s, and they remained in place well into the twentieth century. The reports of these committees collectively expressed the temperance views of Atlanta's clergy. This is how the committees functioned: After members were appointed, the committee drafted the report and presented it to the whole body for their comment and all-but-guaranteed approval. Usually one Atlanta area clergy served on each committee. These reports included some combination of a rationale for abstinence; an assessment of the extent of intemperance in their churches, community, or nation; recommendations for clergy action; and commentary on the local or national temperance movement. In spite of their often cursory nature, these reports collectively provide the best window into the thinking of Atlanta's black clergy.

Since clergy penned these reports, it is not surprising that one of their most prominent aspects is the bemoaning—not unlike that of their Northern antebellum white counterparts—of alcohol abuse in their churches. These admissions became more frequent and assumed a more urgent tone in the mid-1870s. In 1875 the North Georgia Conference of the AME Church recognized intemperance as a "growing evil," and the Ebenezer Baptist Association declared, "Great reproach is brought upon the cause of Christ by the practice of some professed Christians in visiting drinking saloons, and drinking whiskey and other liquors as a beverage." The following year the Baptist state convention announced that intemperance had to be defeated in the Church first, before it could be defeated in the world, a sentiment shared essentially verbatim with many antebellum temperance clergy. The problem did not go away, for in the 1880s committees were still bemoaning that intemperance had "entered the Sanctuary of the Lord" and brought "many of our useful members" to "disgrace and poverty." Some reports even went further, exposing a drinking problem within the ranks of the clergy. The New Hope Baptist Association lamented "that by alcohol the judgment of ministers is prevented, the purity of deacons is blasphemed and the church is sacrilege." To help address the problem of drinking in the church, the editor of the *Christian Recorder*, the AME's national newspaper, suggested that churches make the annual temperance report the topic of a class meeting and offer the pledge to class members. Such a practice would ostensibly "add immensely to the value of the often hastily drafted and more hastily adopted" report. Although lacking details, clergy reports with this tone were noticeably absent in the late sixties and early seventies but began appearing in 1875 and continued throughout the eighties, suggesting that by the mid-seventies abuse of alcohol had increased in black churches.[15]

But just as much as black clergy complained of intemperance within their churches, there were also echoes of the Christian republicanism that had animated Northern white antebellum reformers. Yet this language was much more common from AME committees than from Baptist ones. One AME committee warned that because the nation was spending an inordinate amount on liquor the "vigor" of the nation was being destroyed and the "alms-houses and prisons are being filled." In 1889 the same committee said of intemperance, "Let it alone and it will destroy the place and prospect of our church, and corrupt our government, and will ultimately destroy our nation." This was wording with which almost any antebellum Northern white clergyman could agree. Undoubtedly the national, centralized structure of the AME Church gave its local conference reports a slightly more Northern (or national?) flavor than Baptist reports, thus reflecting the Northern theology.[16]

Equally understandable was the clergy's concern about the effects of intemperance and the liquor traffic on the "cause of Christ." Reports mentioned that when Christians drank they brought "reproach" to the cause of Christ or "retarded" the church's progress. Lamenting a nationwide increase in intemperance, the New Hope Baptist Association declared, "Even in proud America 'King Alcohol' sways the largest kingdom ever established on earth; even outnumbering the church of Christ and rivaling the kingdom of heaven." One committee claimed intemperance stopped the "progress of the kingdom of God," while another said it "dethroned reason." Such language clearly had its roots in antebellum revival theology.[17]

Over half of the temperance reports cited Scriptural authority by direct quote, summary, or reference, to assert the personal sinfulness of intemperance.[18] The most widely used verse was Solomon's warning in Proverbs 20:1 that "Wine is a mocker and strong drink is raging, and whosoever is deceived thereby is not wise," but committees found other verses appropriate when stressing things like temperance education ("In all thy getting get wisdom") and the importance of lifelong temperance habits to one's spiritual well-being ("Let us lay aside every weight and the sin which doth so easily beset us"). Some reports included a simple reminder that the Bible condemns drunkenness and warned that drinking "enslaved" and damned the soul. By the 1870s evangelicals had well-mined Scripture for antidrinking verses, and black clergy frequently cited examples from the standard list.[19]

Temperance reports also reflected the traditional African emphasis on the relationship between an individual's actions and communal well-being. The second most frequently used defense of abstinence highlighted the social disorder occasioned by intemperate drinking: financial, medical, and criminal problems, family conflict, and destitution. One committee warned that intemperance "promises to destroy friends and rob us of our senses. It promises to make friends and neighbors become enemies of each other." Liquor-related crime destroyed peaceful relations within the race as well as between races.[20] The committee of the Eleventh North Georgia Conference of the AME Church lamented that intemperance was destroying the youth of the community. Their depiction has so much pathos that one wonders if the committee members did not have one or more specific individuals in mind when drafting the report:

> It is the means of interfering with, and often stopping the progress of a promising young man; one who has received the best training in the best institutions of our country; one who has been the idol of a loving mother and a doting father, just when his prospects were the brightest and the expectations of this friend the greatest. But all of their hopes are blighted by the "worm of the still."[21]

Obviously some young men's lives went the opposite direction of George Clark's. Nearly as impassioned, but with more sweeping language was the attitude of the Ebenezer Baptist Association:

> It dethrones reason, dwarfs understanding, reddens the eyes, impairs health, impoverishes the rich, widows our fair daughters, ravishes the heart of woman, the main spring as well as the ornament of society, orphans our children, supplies our jails, chain-gangs, penitentiaries and gallows. . . . This flagitious, diabolical, and inexorable demon fathers most of all of the crimes that are committed, and points to hell as the best proof of its appalling work.[22]

Clergy loathed intemperance not just because they considered it an individual sin but because people lived in families and communities, and it violated and ruptured the vital social bonds of a healthy community. As the Missionary Baptist Convention said in 1875: "Families beggared, business destroyed, children hungry, naked; character lost, souls lost, are only a few of the dreadful consequences of intemperance." Intemperance undermined the social order and, as such, was evil. While such arguments had historically been made by whites, they sometimes incorporated concern for the financial costs to the community, but in the context of African American life, with so few economic assets, these concerns are best understood against the backdrop of an African worldview that required a community response to individual violations of the social order.[23]

The third most frequently mentioned rationale suggested that intemperance had reached such alarming proportions it posed an existential threat to Black Atlanta—it called into question the continued existence of the community as it was then known. Using traditional African worldview language, these reports lamented the impact of intemperance on "our people." Often it is unclear whether "our people" meant only church members or blacks generally, but in either case, it meant African Americans, and the reports expressed real concerns about the effects of drinking on the corporate well-being of blacks. Ever hopeful that their children's lives would be better than their own, the clergy fretted that alcohol abuse was destroying any possibility of that. In 1876 the New Hope association lamented intemperance's destruction of potential future community leaders: "This evil is destroying many of our young men and women that might be filling important stations in life." Over the years the Ebenezer association, which had more Atlanta congregations than any other Baptist association during these years, made several particularly strong pleas for abstinence in the interest of the race. The Reverend W. H. Tillman, the self-educated pastor of Third Baptist, moderated the annual meetings throughout most of the eighties. In 1882 the association lamented intemperance's effects on the current generation: "we find the evil of intemperance among our people to be deplored; year by year it is slaying its hundreds, it has entered the homes of many, it has robbed many a wife of a good husband or a comfortable home." In 1885 the Ebenezer temperance committee, which included W. L. Jones, pastor of Atlanta's Mount Zion Baptist Church, drafted a most desperate plea on behalf of the race:

> We do say that whiskey is the leading sin, and we do say that it is the life destroyer . . . for we see and know that it is ruining our people; lay it down; Oh! may God help us to lay it down. It is driving away the Holy Spirit. It is driving our children down to degradation. This great demon fills our country with disgrace, and also our chain gang, and fills the place of a murder. It fosters quarrels; it degrades the person; it causes sickness, and we urge the Baptists of the State of Georgia to go to work to condemn it in the pulpit and then we can convince our congregation.[24]

In 1889 the committee requested the clergy to "use every effort to drive it from our midst and save our people." The temperance committees of the Sunday School Convention of the New Hope association echoed the concerns of the Ebenezer committee. The concern for the long-term health of the African American community could hardly be clearer.[25]

When the committee reports turned to suggestions to combat the "growing evil" of intemperance, the recommendations of Baptists and the AME Church were quite similar. Both repeatedly reminded their clergy that the example of their own abstinence was one of their most powerful weapons. Several committees endorsed non-ecclesiastical temperance organizations like the Woman's Christian Temperance Union and the United Order of True Reformers and encouraged their clergy to work cooperatively with other individuals and groups to combat intemperance. The AME Church and the Missionary Baptist Convention of Georgia encouraged the creation of temperance societies in churches and Sunday schools. One of the most common suggestions, however, was also the most vague, to simply "use all your efforts" or "influence" to fight the "great enemy."[26]

These temperance committee reports make it clear that a variety of factors informed the temperance thought and discourse of Atlanta's black clergy. The language of the committee reports strongly suggests that many preachers were influenced by the antebellum nexus ideas promulgated by Northern missionaries, the *Weekly Witness,* and National Temperance Society literature. But the clergy's temperance discourse also reflected African elements of the African American worldview. The pragmatic syncretism of the African American worldview made it relatively easy for the clergy to merge the temperance values and language of Northern evangelicals with their own concerns and defend abstinence from several angles. Historian David Wills has argued that nineteenth-century AME Church leaders sought to create a "working synthesis"—a "black Christian culture"—between the realities affecting historic Christianity and those affecting the contemporary situation of black Americans. The preaching of abstinence was clearly one element of this synthesis, and a similar claim could probably be made for Southern black Baptists.[27]

"Fearful Hypocrisies": Temperance and Church Polity

The Baptist and AME communities also made use of their different polities to fight intemperance in the pulpit. The extreme congregationalism—or localism—of the Baptists meant that each congregation was autonomous. Baptist beliefs, like local church autonomy, the authority of the Bible, and the priesthood of all believers comprise what is called the "Baptist democracy." All Baptist church associations were voluntary, whether at the local (associations), state (convention), or national (convention) level. Associations and conventions could also include individuals or organizations, like Sunday schools, as members. Associations and conventions legally existed only while they were meeting, so no permanent hierarchy or bureaucracy existed. Decisions made by delegates were little more than recommendations for their members. Drafters of association and convention pronouncements relied on their moral authority and hoped they would be received in the spirit with which they were written. Being so beholden to the laity, the Baptist polity effectively prevented their pronouncements from being too far removed from the laity's actual experiences or sentiments. Considering the nature of the Baptist polity, since their association committee reports admitted that a drinking problem existed, it is reasonable to presume not only that it existed but also that the laity supported both admitting it and condemning it.[28]

The AME Church, on the other hand, had centralized governance under a board of bishops, an Episcopal polity. Every year the bishop in charge of each annual conference appointed the minister for each church in the conference. Many pastors changed congregations annually or biannually. In addition, as discussed in chapter two, from its beginning the AME church adopted John Wesley's "General Rules of the United Societies of 1739," which prohibited Methodist class members from drinking ardent spirits, "unless in cases of necessity," but in the 1830s AME ministers began teaching total abstinence from all intoxicating beverages. In the postbellum years, the quadrennial conferences of the AME Church maintained temperance committees, which repeatedly reiterated the church's position. The AME's organizational structure, *Discipline*, and church traditions conspired to create a unity of theology and praxis that Baptists never experienced—or desired to experience.[29]

The process of licensing and ordaining ministers differed significantly between the two denominations. The seminary-educated Bishop Daniel Payne, among others, had struggled since the 1840s to create a high standard for the education of AME clergy. Consistent application of this standard proved challenging and was uneven, but ordination generally required passage through three stages, creating an apparently rigorous process. After being recommended by the quarterly meeting of their conference, clergy had to be approved by a majority vote of the annual conference for a probationary period and then approved again two years later by the annual conference to become a traveling elder or preacher.[30] Among other requirements, candidates had to answer "yes" to these two questions: "Are you temperate in all things?" and "Do you choose and use water for your common drink, and only take wine medicinally or sacramentally?" In the 1872 quadrennial conference the church revised its statutory laws so that clergy or laity who "give, distil, drink, buy or sell spirituous liquors" would be considered to be in "gross immorality" and subject to censure or suspension.[31]

Baptists, on the other hand, ordained men through ad hoc ministerial councils convened for that purpose. According to historian Paul Harvey, the Baptist process encouraged "freelance exhorters to shop around for credentialing." Such a decentralized process was relatively friendly to intellectually and morally underprepared individuals seeking ordination. The high value that African Americans place on clergy oratorical skills and political savvy enabled some men who might be otherwise undesirable to become ordained, only exacerbating the shortcomings of the Baptist ordination process. If an intemperate person slipped through the system, the best a Baptist congregation could do was refuse to vote him in as pastor (as Augusta's Springfield Baptist Church once did to a candidate) and warn other churches through their association to avoid the "jackleg" preacher. Although lacking coercive authority, the American National Baptist Convention "recommended" that member congregations "not call or retain a pastor who is not strictly temperate." Baptist congregations could call a pastor, dismiss him for immorality, but not defrock him, as the AME hierarchy could. Occasionally Baptist associations would publish the names of specific preachers for congregations to avoid.[32]

On the face of it, the AME ordination process appeared to be designed to produce "higher quality" preachers. The AME church discipline included detailed procedures for defrocking ministers accused of drunkenness or other moral turpitudes, and they were used from time to time. During the late 1800s several candidates for ordination in various conferences, including Georgia, were denied advancement for failing to show adequate educational progress. NTS missionary C. H. Mead thought that the AME's ordination process ensured "much stronger" temperance sentiment among its clergy than the Baptist process, but ironically, ten months later the AME's *Christian Recorder* called for "absolute abstinence" among ministerial applicants because of "fearful hypocrisies regarding this temperance subject." Obviously no process could be "foolproof."[33]

The AME Church's *Discipline* gave its leaders leverage in the temperance cause that Baptists did not have. The *Discipline* served two different functions. In 1871 the temperance committee of the Georgia Annual Conference could support its call for AME members to "discard the use" of "all intoxicating liquors" on the basis of the testimony of the Bible *and* "our Book of Discipline." Second, there must have been some cases of AME members using intoxicating beverages, because the committee reminded clergy in 1874 to "enforce the law of the General Conference" relating to intemperance and in 1885 to "strictly enforce" the laws in the discipline. In one sense the AME *Discipline* seemed to make temperance committee reports redundant, but at another level it invested them with an extra layer of moral authority that comparable Baptist reports could never claim. While Baptists occasionally criticized Methodists for having "another book" besides the Bible to abide by,[34] Baptists had to come to terms with the irregularities resulting from the fact that "Baptists neither in conventions nor associations nor churches can enact laws of morality or utter directions to their brethren."[35]

Both Baptist and AME temperance committees repeatedly urged clergy to preach and teach on the subject, but the different polities of the denominations affected this simple request. On two occasions the AME annual conference ordered quarterly sermons, and Baptist committees asked pastors to show clearly from Scripture why drinking was wrong. Baptist ministers like W. H. Tillman and Charles O. Jones and AME minister F. J. Peck, who received the *National Temperance Advocate* or the *New York Weekly Witness*, were particularly well equipped to expound on the biblical argument for total abstinence. Because of the different polities of the two groups, their committees used different language. One Baptist committee exhorted pastors to preach on temperance "whenever convenient," and on more than one occasion committees asked pastors to "tenderly urge" the topic on their people. In 1869 the national Consolidated American Baptist Convention "recommended" that all people over whom they had "influence" completely abstain from intoxicating drinks, and in their 1879 convention they "requested" that all members of the convention abstain. In contrast, the Fifteenth Quadrennial Conference of the AME Church approved a committee report that read, "each pastor shall preach or lecture upon the subject of temperance" four times a year. If certain members, or enough members, of a Baptist congregation did not like constantly being exhorted about their habits they might try to stir up the congregation to vote the pastor out during the church's next annual business meeting or use lesser ways make his tenure difficult. This was a threat AME pastors did not have to worry about since they served at the pleasure of their bishop, not their congregation. Both Baptist and Methodist traditions had elements of their polity that helped or hurt them in their fight against intemperance, but dry ministers in each tradition did their best to use their church structures to fight "demon rum" anyway.[36]

The problem of drinking in the black church continued throughout the seventies and eighties, and clergy efforts had less effect than they desired, partly because the clergy were not all abstainers themselves. During the 1885 prohibition campaign a speaker accused 80 percent of the members in Bishop Henry M. Turner's conference of being drinkers. This might have been little more than electioneering hyperbole, but if it was too far from the general public perception of AME members it would have been politically overreaching or perhaps even scandalous, and there is no indication it was either. It is also striking to note that temperance committees did not *begin* complaining about intemperate black clergy until the 1880s. While the meaning of this is uncertain, one possible interpretation is that drinking clergy were not a major problem until the 1880s, suggesting that perhaps drinking in the church became worse with time, not better, just as it likely did in the black community in general. If this is true, it provides a stark contrast to trends among Southern white evangelicals, Baptists particularly. The white Baptist Convention of Georgia complained twice in the 1870s about intemperance in its churches, but in 1879 it declared them "comparatively free from the evil." The only other complaint about drinking in white churches came in 1880 when the Convention complained about the "baneful practice" of church members using liquor moderately. During the eighties, state-level white temperance committees took comfort in the fact that the few cases of intemperance that did crop up were swiftly and strictly handled.[37]

Although clergy temperance committee reports reveal the durability of antebellum evangelical and African worldview–inspired temperance arguments, the exigencies of church polity could undermine that message. When ecclesiastical realities hindered the temperance message, one thing a preacher could do was take his temperance message outside the church's four walls and become a leader of a temperance lodge or fraternity and hopefully reach those not in the pews on Sundays. Black Atlanta's most outspoken temperance clergy were AME ministers Joseph Wood, Henry McNeal Turner, Wesley J. Gaines, and E. R. Carter, who was raised as a slave, trained as a shoemaker after his emancipation, and graduated from Atlanta Baptist Seminary in 1884. Carter was the second pastor of Friendship Baptist, Atlanta's oldest black Baptist church. These men eagerly involved themselves in lodges and the rough-and-tumble world of city politics.

Fig. 13—AME Bishop Henry McNeal Turner. One of Atlanta's leading black prohibitionist clergymen. From *Shadow and Light: An autobiography with reminiscences of the last and present century,* Manuscript, Archives, and Rare Book Library, Emory University

Respectability: The Social Reform Efforts of Black Atlanta's Lodges

Blacks from all social levels expressed their temperance sentiments through membership in a lodge. Church members who joined lodges might have seen their pastor again as an officer of the lodge. Like freed people elsewhere in the wake of emancipation, Atlanta's blacks formed dozens of fraternal and benevolent societies. Among both whites and blacks, the postwar years were the "Golden Age of Fraternity" in America, with 40 percent or more of all adult males belonging to either a fraternal lodge or a benevolent society.[38] Seen from the perspective of the temperance movement, there were three categories of black societies in Atlanta: national temperance fraternal orders, local benevolent and mutual aid societies, and "parallel" fraternal orders.

Fig. 14—AME Bishop Wesley J. Gaines. One of Atlanta's leading black prohibitionist clergymen. Pastor of Big Bethel. From *African Methodism in the South*, Manuscript, Archives, and Rare Book Library, Emory University

Fig. 15— Reverend E. R. Carter, pastor Friendship Baptist. One of Atlanta's leading black prohibition- ist clergymen. Archives Division, Auburn Avenue Research Library on Afri- can American Culture and History, Atlanta-Fulton Public Library System

National Temperance Fraternal Orders

Two national temperance fraternal orders arrived in Black Atlanta in the 1870s: the United Order of True Reformers and the Independent Order of Good Samaritans and Daughters of Samaria. The Independent Order of Good Templars (IOGT), a national temperance fraternity begun in upstate New York's "burned-over district" in 1852, organized True Reformer "fountains" across the South for blacks. The Templars, an openly Christian organization that admitted no atheists and accepted the Bible as "the standard of faith and practice,"[39] distinguished themselves from other fraternities by admitting women on a basis of "nominal equality" and by purposely refusing to include insurance benefits. This latter practice kept dues low enough to attract the young and the lower classes. The IOGT also distinguished itself by vigorously supporting national prohibition. Templars comprised a majority of the Prohibition Party's organizing convention, and for many years the two organizations worked together closely. Templar lodges spread quickly through the North, and in the wake of the Civil War entered the South and crossed the Atlantic. U.S. membership exploded, peaking at over half a million in 1868. But racial troubles arose when the IOGT moved south.[40]

William Washington Browne, a freedman, spread Good Templary among Southern blacks. The Georgia-born Browne, an army veteran, attended Clark University briefly and then settled in Alabama as a schoolteacher. Personal experiences led him to become a passionate opponent of alcohol. Inspired by an integrated temperance meeting in Montgomery, Alabama, Browne became a temperance speaker, often addressing standing-room-only crowds. His speeches presented intemperance as a major threat to the African American community. Browne argued that intemperance disfranchised blacks because not only was public drunkenness a crime but drunken people were more likely to commit other crimes, and convicted criminals were not permitted to vote. The fact that many blacks were convicted without a trial further increased the numbers of the disfranchised. In the early seventies, under Browne's leadership, several black men from Alabama sought a charter from the Grand Lodge of the Independent Order of Good Templars.[41] Afraid of the social implications of creating a black lodge on an equal basis with white lodges but also not wanting to hinder temperance work among blacks, the Grand Lodge offered a "compromise." It created a separate organization just for blacks called the United Order of True Reformers, whose lodges would be called "fountains" and be authorized to use Templar-like rituals. Disappointed at being forced into a segregated organization, Browne reluctantly accepted the offer as a step in the right direction and began organizing "fountains" in Alabama. By March 1874 he was a full-time organizer.[42]

Shortly after Browne began his work, the Grand Lodge appointed a white man, James G. Thrower of Atlanta, as the general superintendent to oversee the organization of all True Reformer fountains. Thrower was an English immigrant who had lived in New York and Minnesota before the war and moved to Atlanta following the war to work in construction. In the North, Thrower had been active in the IOGT, and within a year of arriving in Atlanta he had organized 18 men into Atlanta's Lodge, No. 1. Thrower became the first of four Northerners instrumental in energizing and organizing Atlanta's postbellum white temperance movement.[43] During the seventies Atlanta's IOGT hosted J. N. Stearns of the National Temperance Society on several occasions, and in the eighties Thrower helped plan NTS missionary C. H. Mead's Georgia itinerary. The Grand Lodge possibly chose Thrower to organize blacks because they believed his foreign/Northern roots would increase his appeal to the freed people. Or perhaps he was chosen simply because they could not find a Southern white man willing to work with the freed people in potentially "compromising" social situations. In any case, Thrower expended considerable energy organizing True Reformer Fountains, in which role he proved to be divisive, yet he remained a leader in Atlanta temperance circles through the 1880s.[44]

In addition to his regional oversight responsibilities, Thrower also organized Georgia's fountains. He organized the first True Reformer Fountain on November 28, 1873. Among the other white IOGT members present to bless the new venture were the pastors of Atlanta's First and Second Baptist Churches. Thirty-five blacks turned out to organize Pioneer Fountain No. 1, and after listening to Thrower's presentation they elected AME minister Joseph Wood as worthy master and Oliver Cromwell, a drayman, as worthy secretary. Eighteen fountains and 11 months later, 47 delegates met in Atlanta's Wheat Street Baptist Church (black) to organize Georgia's Grand Fountain, the first state grand lodge of the United Order of True Reformers. A succession of black and white speakers addressed the delegates, among them were William Pledger, alumnus of the Storrs School and current Atlanta University student; E. W. Warren, pastor of First Baptist (white); C. A. Evans, pastor of Trinity Methodist Episcopal Church (white); Thomas N. Chase, teacher and administrator at Atlanta University (white); and Andrew Jackson, pastor of Wheat Street Baptist (black). Following instructions from Thrower, the delegates, representing some two thousand fountain members across the state, selected a committee to draft a constitution and elected William A. Pledger as their grand worthy master.[45]

A peripatetic figure, William Anderson Pledger was a leader in Republican Atlanta politics and temperance from the time he arrived in 1870 to attend school. After leaving school in 1876 he moved back and forth between Atlanta, Athens, and other Southern cities but always considered Athens his home. He edited several newspapers, held government patronage jobs, practiced law, and was an influ-

Fig. 16—William A. Pledger, Grand Worthy Master of Georgia's Grand Fountain of the United Order of True Reformers. From *Shadow and Light: An autobiography with reminiscences of the last and present century,* Manuscript, Archives, and Rare Book Library, Emory University

ential member of Georgia's Republican Central Committee and delegate to the national convention for more than 20 years. Pledger also represented Georgia's blacks in several national black conventions. When he became grand worthy master in 1874 Pledger was only 22, but like many other men he did not stay involved in the organized temperance movement past his twenties. Like many Northern antebellum black temperance reformers, his argument drew on the power of the concept of virtue to transform African Americans' quality of life in a racist society. In an 1876 memo to members he explained:

> As a general thing, we are credited as being a vicious, lazy people, which is not as a whole people true, but as a part really true, and it is our mission to make our people a sober people indeed. The chain-gang has now over eight hundred colored, to only ninety white convicts. It is said the augmentation of this number of colored, is because of intemperance; of course we know this is not wholly true, . . . yet many of them are sent there for that reason, and should be a warning to us in the cause. . . . Never can we own land, shares in Railroads, College, Academies, and other sources of wealth and knowledge, till we practice temperance.[46]

Not only did Pledger believe that abstinence would improve economic prospects for blacks by reducing their crime rate and freeing up money for wealth-producing activity, but a secondary effect would be to produce "that harmony which is so much needed in the South between races." Pledger believed that the influence of preachers and teachers was so important that he refused to give money to or serve under ones who drank. He challenged all True Reformers to follow his example. It is not insignificant that Pledger, like Browne, sat under Northern missionary teachers. Their temperance work could have only made their teachers proud, and there is little reason to think they would have opposed the race-specific ends each man pursued through the lodges.[47]

The True Reformers maintained high ethical standards for their members, which generally earned them a good reputation. True Reformers were required not only to abstain from alcohol but also to be above reproach in financial matters and not to associate with "persons of suspicious character." Because failure in any of these areas was grounds for expulsion, members could proudly claim to be "some of the best people of our race." As Willard B. Gatewood and other scholars have argued, values and behavior were often more important indicators of status than income for the better class of blacks. Clergy, skilled and unskilled workers, and university students were counted among True Reformers. In 1876 the Missionary Baptist Convention of Georgia specifically commended the work of the United Order of True Reformers.[48]

The True Reformers' high moral standards, however, failed to undermine the prejudices and fears of local whites. The Reformers met every Friday evening in a hall on Broad Street. In 1875 someone leaked information about one of their meetings where they had discussed how difficult it was for blacks to earn a living and had suggested some causes and possible solutions. They had apparently even dared discuss some recent incidents of racial violence in central Georgia, the upcoming elections, and the enfranchisement of Confederate loyalists, all politically sensitive issues. Some members reportedly blamed white people for blacks' slow economic progress since emancipation, while others said it was unjust that individuals who supported the Confederacy should be enfranchised. Even worse, rumor had it that some members supported a violent response to a recent white-on-black episode of violence. An *Atlanta Constitution* reporter interviewed an anonymous member who produced all the "right" answers to calm white Atlantans' fears, but some members still felt compelled to issue a formal statement asserting the respectability of their membership and organization, and to assure whites that nothing had been said "to which the best citizens of Atlanta could object." While the comfort of this black-only space encouraged "free" conversation on current events, this incident revealed the limits of such "independence" in the era of Reconstruction.[49]

Between 1876 and 1887 the IOGT suffered a schism that destroyed True Reformer fountains. Insisting on the right of blacks to join the order on equal terms with whites, the English and Scottish Grand Lodges seceded and organized the Right Worthy Grand Lodge of the World. They immediately began organizing black lodges in the South. The original Good Templars' Grand Lodge, representing the United States and Canada, decided to compete with the secessionist branch for black members by reorganizing True Reformers into a Good Templars' "dual grand lodge" system in each state. In this competing system blacks would now be considered Good Templars—not True Reformers any more—and would have their own segregated local lodges and (state) grand lodges. Almost simultaneously with the split of the IOGT, Pledger resigned as head of Georgia's Grand Fountain, despite the fact that under his leadership he had more than quadrupled statewide membership. Just when Georgia's True Reformers were most in need of leadership, they had none.

With the True Reformers in disarray, James Thrower was able to pressure Atlanta's—and many of the state's—fountains to become colored Good Templars' lodges under the auspices of the original IOGT, and in the fall of 1876 he organized the first colored "Dual" Grand Lodge in the South.[50] But confusion reigned, as Thrower enrolled local lodges by falsely claiming that the two IOGT factions had reunited, and at least one Dual Lodge member secretly worked to persuade local lodges to join the British-based Right Worthy Grand Lodge. Thrower asked Pledger to return to lead the Grand Lodge, which he did briefly. In the confusion of the period, Pledger claimed to be recognized by both Templar bodies, but in 1879 he left Atlanta and the organization again, moving to Athens to teach school and edit the *Athens Blade*. In 1880 Atlanta still boasted about two hundred black Good Templars in three lodges, but despite the installation of a new black grand worthy master from Savannah, a statewide decline followed Pledger's departure, and the grand lodge had ceased operating by the end of 1881. In the spring of 1882 Thrower tried to revitalize the Grand Lodge with a meeting at Big Bethel AME, where Wesley J. Gaines had been pastor. The speakers included NTS president William E. Dodge and his friend Governor Alfred Colquitt, but even this star power could not overcome the unappealing confusion of the IOGT schism, and in 1883 the Dual Grand Lodge collapsed.[51]

In 1886 Thrower tried yet again to reorganize Georgia's 23 remaining lodges and 2,300 members into a state Dual Grand Lodge. Atlantans filled eight out of the fourteen elected positions, and three of them were clergy: Friendship Baptist's pastor E. R. Carter, a graduate of Atlanta Baptist Seminary, became grand worthy chief templar; former Big Bethel pastor and AME presiding elder Wesley J. Gaines was made representative to the national Grand Lodge; and Allen Temple's pastor, J. G. Yeiser, became grand chaplain. Another prominent black Atlantan, Alice

D. Carey, principal of Morris Brown College, was made grand worthy secretary. Even with this who's who of Atlantans, Georgia's Dual Grand Lodge fizzled. Black lodges struggled not only because of the IOGT's internal conflicts but also because of the limited resources and literacy of their members. By 1900 black Good Templary in the United States was all but dead.[52]

Black Atlanta's more enduring temperance order was the Independent Order of Good Samaritans and Daughters of Samaria. The Samaritans were also a Northern antebellum lodge founded on the principle of total abstinence, but from the beginning the order differed from the IOGT in important ways. Samaritans not only signed an abstinence pledge but also committed themselves to caring for the "distressed families of those who pledge themselves to abstain from all intoxicating drinks." Openly benevolent, the order aimed to "spread the principles of true charity in the hearts of members." Jesus's parable of the Good Samaritan illustrated the values it promoted and was the "centerpiece" of its rituals. The order originated in New York City in 1847, and although it welcomed any abstinent person, it particularly sought to "reform and restore" drunkards. From its first year the order organized women and blacks into separate lodges but allowed them representation at the Grand Lodge and National Grand Lodge levels. The Good Samaritans' history is unique in that during the 1870s the order became a majority black group because freed people organized so many of the new lodges. By 1877 black representation in the National Lodge had increased so much that they elected a black national grand sire. Under black leadership white membership dwindled. From the end of the 1870s the Samaritans became essentially a black temperance fraternity.[53]

As with the True Reformers, black Atlantans organized Georgia's first Good Samaritan lodge, named Crystal Fount Lodge, No. 1. Crystal Fount was organized in July 1875, but in 1876, to stimulate growth, the Grand Lodge No. 1 of New York appointed Smith W. Easley Jr. the district deputy in charge of organizing lodges throughout Georgia. A correspondent for black newspapers in the seventies, by the eighties Easley had become a railway postal clerk. Easley had founded ten lodges by 1885, so that year he organized the state Grand Lodge, and the delegates elected him right worthy grand chief. In 1886 and 1887 he was elected right worthy grand secretary. Easley worked for several publications as writer, manager, editor, and correspondent, but perhaps most importantly, like Browne and Pledger, he had also sat under Northern missionary teachers in Atlanta. Easley attended the Storrs School briefly in the late 1860s. Although Easley did not remain in school long, the Lincoln Temperance Pledge he signed there started him out on a life of war against "King Alcohol." The similarity of the Storrs School and Good Samaritan pledges made Samaritan membership seem natural to him.[54]

Like the national Grand Lodge, Atlanta's Good Samaritans were a modestly successful order. The Crystal Fount Lodge, No. 1, began with 28 members. In 1876 Easley organized Atlanta's second lodge, Morning Star Lodge, No. 4, with 164 members, under AME minister Joseph Wood. It was the third temperance society of which Wood had become leader since 1873. The Samaritans grew steadily and prospered. Although Crystal Fount Lodge's membership shot up to 123 within three years, Morning Star's membership dropped to 57. By 1891 there were 2,000 members in six Atlanta lodges, and 100,000 members nationwide. Like the True Reformers, the Good Samaritans' members represented a range of socioeconomic levels, from AME bishop Wesley J. Gaines and financially comfortable grocer Charles H. Morgan to the lumber mill worker Joseph Hankerson. Several women, many of whom appear to have been wives or daughters of male members, also held elected office.[55]

Until the mid-nineties Atlanta's Samaritans were a well-run order. Attentive to the needs of others, during the seventies and eighties they donated to yellow fever victims in Savannah and to cholera victims in Memphis. They were Atlanta's first black fraternal group to purchase real estate. They purchased lots in Atlanta's black-owned South-View Cemetery for their members and built their own four-story brick building on Ivy Street in 1890, hiring Alexander Hamilton, a local black contractor. The building dedication was a five-day celebration that included addresses from Governor John B. Gordon, the Reverend E. R. Carter, and Bishop Henry M. Turner. In September 1891 Atlanta's lodges hosted the national Good Samaritan convention, with more than three hundred delegates. In 1895 Fulton County taxed the Samaritans on $7,500 worth of property, making them the wealthiest black order in Atlanta at the time, but by 1898 they had lost their building because of financial mismanagement.[56]

Mutual Aid Societies and Temperance

Far more common than temperance fraternities in Black Atlanta were mutual aid and benevolent societies. The desire for independence—or the fear of dependence on whites—made these societies extremely popular among African Americans throughout the United States, even among the poorest. Continuing a free black practice dating to at least 1780, Atlanta's mutual aid societies served as reciprocal aid societies (or proto-insurance companies) by providing financial assistance to their members in case of sickness, unemployment, or death. Some of these societies evolved into commercial life insurance companies. Historically, benevolent societies often originated with the members of a particular church, as ministers sought to provide an economic safety net for their largely working-class parishioners, but

Fig. 17—Good Samaritan Hall. From *The Black Side,* Kenan Research Center at the Atlanta History Center

in some cases churches grew from benevolent societies. The AME Church is an example of the latter, as it grew from Richard Allen's Free African Society of Philadelphia.[57]

Atlanta's mutual aid societies retained the antebellum practice of requiring their members to lead virtuous lives. The Reverend E. R. Carter observed of the Colored Men's Protective Association that "Those who are received must take most solemnly the pledge which strictly requires good morals, decency and up-rightness of character, and so soon as one violates this pledge he is excommuni-cated." Intemperance would certainly have disqualified anyone for membership in the Colored Men's Protective Association. Some societies were so insistent on abstinence that they included temperance in their name. By 1886 the Temperance Mutual Benefit Association of Philadelphia, probably an interracial group, was so-liciting blacks in Georgia. Its state office was in Atlanta, and James Thrower was on its local board of managers. Founded in 1870, the Temperance Mutual Ben-efit Association offered benefits to sick members and provided accident and life insurance. Women's groups maintained the same standards. In 1883 an *Atlanta Constitution* reporter identified 15 African American female benevolence soci-eties composed primarily of working-class women and noted that among them "temperance obligations" were "very strong and binding." Big Bethel's pastor F. Jesse Peck founded one of them, the Daughters of Bethel, in 1870, but it ran into difficulties. Former members reorganized it into the Independent Daughters of Bethel in 1880.[58]

It is difficult to estimate the number of black Atlantans belonging to benevo-lent societies. Some societies existed for only a few years, new ones were con-stantly organizing, their sizes varied significantly, and few if any records have been preserved. In 1880 the Gospel Aid Society had about 250 members, while the Brothers of Love and Charity had only 75. By 1890 Atlanta had over 30 of these societies, with probably over 1,000 members, out of a total black population of almost 30,000. But the numbers may have even been much higher, because in antebellum times Northern free blacks were known to maintain as many as 70 or 80 benevolent societies in one city, with as many as one-half of all adults holding membership in at least one society. Long after the eighties mutual aid societies remained popular among blacks.[59]

Parallel Fraternal Societies and Temperance

The final category of society is what some scholars have called "parallel" so-cieties, because they modeled their name and rituals after white societies. The two parallel societies with Atlanta lodges in this period were the Odd Fellows and Prince Hall Masons. Both orders began in the antebellum North, but because American lodges refused to charter them they received their original charters from England. Neither of these orders (nor the Knights of Pythias, which organized in Atlanta in the early nineties) made abstinence a cornerstone of membership, but they were concerned with the "respectability" of their members. Members could likely drink moderately at home and retain their "good standing."

Both orders organized lodges about the same time in Atlanta. In the fall of 1870 the Grand United Order of Odd Fellows organized the St. James Lodge and the Star of the South Lodge. Within two years they claimed 275 members, and by 1880, 600 members. By the end of the eighties the Odd Fellows had probably 1,000 members in seven lodges, making it Black Atlanta's largest fraternity. The Odd Fellows had simultaneously become one of the largest fraternities in America, with more than 52,000 members in 29 states by 1886. In 1870 Big Bethel's pastor, F. Jesse Peck, who had become a Prince Hall Mason while living in Boston, received a charter to organize a Masonic lodge. In March 1871 the St. James Lodge No. 4 became Atlanta's first Prince Hall lodge. Because of their selectivity, Masons grew at a relatively slow rate; they had only 50 members in 1880. Both groups had ladies' auxiliaries. The Households of Ruth complemented the Odd Fellows, while the Order of the Eastern Star complemented the Masons.[60]

These traditional secret fraternal orders insisted upon their members being models of middle-class bourgeois respectability. While the Odd Fellows functioned as both a benevolent and a fraternal society, the Masons set initiation and other fees so high the very fact that members could afford them probably meant they were unlikely to need assistance. The Masons designed their admission process to admit only those who were already demonstrating a commitment to middle-class values. Having steady work, a good reputation in the community, and a character that modeled "producer" traits such as thrift, sobriety, and regularity were essential for membership in the Masons. Although the Odd Fellows were not known to be as selective, Atlanta's white press found them "respectable" and "intelligent" and always spoke positively of their decorum during their anniversary parades and other social activities. Their connection to accepted standards of morality was strengthened by their relationship to the black church. Anniversary celebrations were often held in churches—usually Bethel AME or Wheat Street Baptist—and participants were usually addressed by local pastors, even when the events were not held in a church.[61]

All three types of African American societies projected an image of middle-class morality that embraced temperance. The AMA praised all three for encouraging "habits of sobriety and economy," and the local press praised the Odd Fellows for availing themselves of the opportunity to improve their "morals and mental culture." Mutual aid societies and parallel fraternities, however, tended to be more opposed to drunkenness than to drinking per se.[62] Despite the fact that not all fraternal lodges demanded teetotalism of their members, stories like that of Atlantan Lena Edwards, who was picked up for public drunkenness, demonstrate that nonlodge members were well aware of the *image* of the sober black lodge member. While before the judge, Edwards mocked her situation by arguing that her disorderly conduct assisted lodges in spreading the abstinence message. (She brought up lodges on her own initiative; they had nothing to do with her trial.) Since many people did not attend lodge meetings, she argued, they would not receive the temperance message, but her public display of drunkenness educated them about the dangers of whiskey. Despite Edwards's quick-wittedness—or humor—she still had to pay the customary fine.[63]

Social Reform in Black Public Schools

Sources on Black Atlanta's fraternal and benevolent societies during the 1870s and 1880s are extremely limited, but even more limited is information about black teachers in Atlanta's public schools, who were also agents of temperance. Once the Atlanta Board of Education agreed to hire black teachers for black schools in the late 1870s, Atlanta University fed its graduates into the schools in disproportionate numbers relative to the other missionary schools. In 1888, 23 of the 28 black teachers in Atlanta's public schools were AU graduates. In 1890 all of the teachers in the Houston Street School were AU graduates. By the late nineties, grads from the other schools were making inroads, as AU alumni comprised only 70 percent of the city's black teachers. While it is clear that AU alumni had been well instructed in temperance, it is not clear how much time they dwelt on the subject in the public school classroom. Atlanta first mandated scientific temperance instruction in 1887. Also, black teachers taught significantly larger classes than white teachers and had far fewer resources, compromising the effectiveness of instruction. But black students in Atlanta's public schools at least had the personal example of teetotaling teachers educated in the "social settlements" known as Atlanta University and Spelman. Their employment in the Atlanta Public Schools showed the "talented tenth" principle at work. So even those African Americans of lesser means were implicitly "reached" with the temperance message that had traveled across many decades, through multiple institutions, being reinterpreted all along the way.[64]

From emancipation through the eighties one searches in vain for African American opposition to the Northerners' temperance message. Black Atlantans had their share of complaints about how the schools were run, their failure to employ black teachers, and the racial attitudes of some Northerners, but never does one find a complaint about their constant harping on temperance. It is important to remember this was not a white message, but a *Northern* message, because Northern blacks like Bishop J. M. Brown and Southern-born but Northern-educated blacks like Henry M. Turner and Bishop Daniel Payne also preached the temperance message. One element accounting for the ease of acceptance could well be the relatively high esteem the freed people placed on Northern life and culture in the wake of emancipation. But this chapter has more importantly argued that there was an intersection between key elements of Northern revival theology and traditional African spirituality. This intersection made it seem almost "natural" to some Northern antebellum blacks to embrace temperance, and when this brand of Christianity presented itself in the persons of the newly arrived Northerners, Southern blacks likewise readily accepted the message insofar as they accepted the broader Northern religio-cultural message at all. Temperance seems to have been an issue on which for some, the unique "twoness" of black identity—as African and American—might have ironically mutually reinforced acceptance of a cultural value. Blacks who embraced temperance saw it as an exemplary individual virtue not unrelated to the health of the whole community. To provide an even stronger image, the analogy may be stretched. For those who participated in the social wing of temperance reform by joining an abstinence-based society, the act was psychologically and socially analogous to singing call-and-response spirituals, for as Lawrence Levine has observed, such performances offered a potential outlet for one's "individual feelings even while it continually drew him back into the communal presence and permitted him the comfort of basking in the warmth of the shared assumption of those around him." To be a black teetotaler in 1880s Black Atlanta was to make a social statement.[65]

But not all black Atlantans embraced the temperance implications of this fortuitous theological/worldview convergence. The second half of this chapter has demonstrated how the talented tenth principle functioned to spread Northern temperance values in black Atlanta. In an effort to create a temperance-based moral community, pastors preached temperance sermons, ministers organized lodges, blacks joined benevolent societies, and the emerging better class of blacks through their lodge membership exemplified moderate use of intoxicating beverages, if not outright teetotalism. Temperance permeated all major institutions in Black Atlanta, whether controlled by whites or blacks. Despite these efforts, throughout the 1880s black clergy continued to complain about intemperance in the church, and black temperance fraternities struggled and failed, calling into question the effectiveness of their efforts.

Although the talented tenth seem to have been effectively trained by Northern missionaries, once they attempted to convey the temperance message to the masses of their own people they faced daunting obstacles. The grinding poverty of blacks limited participation in fraternal groups, and black churches and lodges were, by definition, voluntary, competitive associations, which diluted the rigor of their discipline relative to that of the missionary schools. Black-run institutions had limited resources and relatively little leverage over their members. The hostile racial environment only seemed to worsen with time, and opportunities for upward economic mobility shrank as the nadir of black life approached at the end of the century. Undoubtedly many blacks seriously questioned the economic and social "benefits" the virtue of temperance promised. Perhaps, as W. J. Rorabaugh argued for antebellum America, all the talk about intemperance in Black Atlanta simply proved that it was becoming a bigger problem as the years passed. If this was the case, and moral suasion efforts proved ineffective, then the logic of the next phase of the movement became readily apparent. If voluntary social efforts at reforming people did not work, then why not move to the political arena? Temperance reformers turned to legal suasion—prohibition—to reinforce their message, replicating the trajectory of antebellum Northern temperance.

> The Temperance wave o'er the South is spreading;
> It is what saloons are dreading.
> Look away! Look away!
> Look away! Dixie Land.
> In Dixie land where I was born in,
> People are 'gainst rum a-stormin'
> Look away! Look away!
> Look away! Dixie land.
>
> Down South they fight it by local option;
> "No rum sold by our adoption."
> Look away! Look away!
> Look away! Dixie Land.
> That motto should all men inspire
> To rise and fight this rum-fiend's fire,
> Look away! Look away!
> Look away! Dixie Land.
> —"Dixie Land for Temperance," first and third verses

CHAPTER 5

"The Most Enthusiastic Election Ever Held in This Country"

Atlanta's 1885 Local Option Election

> Look away, Look away,
> Look away, sunny land;
> To duty they are waking, oh yes, oh yes!
> In Dixie's land they'll take the stand,
> To live and die for Temperance.
> The South, brave South, the South will
> Stand for Temp'rance.
> The South, brave South, the South will
> Stand for Temp'rance.
> —"Look Away, Look Away," third stanza

Prohibition is the political expression of the temperance movement.[1] Ever since the 1830s, there had always been some temperance reformers pushing for a ban on the sale of all alcoholic beverages. Some arguments were as specific as trying to help inebriates who could not help themselves, while others were more abstract, claiming that public attitudes toward liquor would, over time, be transformed by the law's hostility toward it. But the public also dreamed of more lofty goals, such as removing liquor industry money from the political process and "advancing" the Kingdom of God. Whatever argument was employed, prohibition was part of a grand scheme to reform, purify, and Christianize not only individuals but the nation.[2] Those who genuinely anticipated these results viewed contrary votes as having grave moral implications for society. The almost infinite number of variables impacting individual voting decisions meant that it was not unusual for drinkers to vote for prohibition and for teetotalers to vote against it. These variables split both black and white voters during the South's many local option elections.

In the wake of Reconstruction, prohibition emerged as one of the most talked-about public policy issues of the 1880s. The times created a space where the ideas of temperance could rise to an unprecedented level of political prominence. During this decade, 19 states held statewide prohibition referenda.[3] In the South, Texas, North Carolina, and Tennessee held statewide referenda, and hundreds of counties and municipalities across the old Confederacy either sponsored local option elections or petitioned their legislators for special prohibitory legislation. Some efforts failed, some succeeded, and some "dry" areas reverted to "wet" after a year or two. Prohibition was a "wave . . . going over the Southern country," observed one journalist. It was almost impossible to pick up a secular or a religious newspaper without finding a reference to prohibition somewhere, and most African American publications—whether religious, like the *Southern Recorder* or *Georgia Baptist*, or secular, like the *Savannah Tribune* or *African Expositor*—openly endorsed temperance and prohibition. Virtually every white and black denomination had a "standing" temperance committee. In this brief period of African American enfranchisement before the nineties, black votes were hotly contested.[4]

Many black and white teetotalers supported legal prohibition in principle, but voting for it was politically tricky, at best. The Georgia Press Association probably summed up the thoughts of the majority of teetotaling American voters when it announced that it endorsed prohibition "without any intention to disturb the party lines." A lot of prohibitionists were Republicans, and because of their party's abolitionist heritage they argued it was "naturally" the party of temperance, but not all Republicans agreed. Prior to 1888 national party leaders refused to take a stand either way on prohibition because when state and local Republican parties took a position it usually backfired on them in subsequent elections. Teetotalers in the Democratic Party had to contend with their national party's "personal liberty" plank, which simply maintained that drinking was a strictly personal matter and prohibition would be an unnecessary sumptuary law. Turning to a third party was also problematic. Supporting the Prohibition Party, founded in 1869, had strong negative political ramifications for both whites and blacks. Although some blacks joined the party because of its strong reform agenda and connection to the Republicans (in the 1880s two-thirds of its leaders were former Republicans), these factors were not sufficient to move most blacks from the party of Lincoln. Both the fiercely competitive two-party system in the North and West and Southern whites' commitment to a "solid" Democratic South prevented most white temperance people from voting for the Prohibition ticket. Also, many Southern evangelicals who were otherwise attracted to the Prohibition Party could not support its endorsement of women's suffrage. These various political alignments consigned the Prohibition Party to a decade of slowly increasing, but always insignificant, popular vote totals. Political allegiances rooted in deep-seated regional, racial, and economic attitudes and institutions forced prohibitionists to develop extra-party tactics.[5]

By the eighties, many reformers had come to believe that the local option election was the best way around the political obstacles to prohibition. During these referenda the only issue decided was the retail sale of liquor, thus removing party politics from the discussion. Local option elections could be held at the county or municipality level. Many prohibitionists supported local option laws because they understood, as modern political scientists do, that "political movements always require manifestations of societal support." As Reverend Theodore Cuyler, the NTS president from 1885 to 1893, argued, "Law can rise no higher, nor can it go beyond popular sentiment." Only a community that voted for prohibition could be expected to demand its enforcement subsequently and thus ensure its success. If prohibition won an election, that would be proof positive that the masses were "ready" for it. The social arm of the movement first had to educate the masses through moral suasion (evangelical reform nexus organizations). When a critical mass of voters supported abstinence, a local option vote could be called for. If their side won, the social arm of the movement would then continuously need to educate citizens about the need for vigilant law enforcement. This is how the components of the temperance movement were theoretically interrelated. Since the war, Georgia's legislature had permitted counties to hold a local option vote if they requested one, but the WCTU and other activists desired a "general" local option bill that would standardize and simplify the process, and they agitated annually until they got one in September 1885. Atlanta's presence in Fulton County made the county's local option vote the center of national attention. Blacks, prohibitionists, and the Northern and Southern press closely followed the campaign and editorialized extensively on its course and outcome. Prohibitionists praised Atlantans for drying out the city without using party machinery, and for a brief moment many thought prohibition would spread rapidly throughout the South.[6]

Against this backdrop of national temperance resurgence and political jockeying, two decades of rising temperance sentiment among black Atlantans converged with rising local white temperance sentiment to produce the city's first local option vote. Although these were two separate movements, they were both largely instigated by Northerners. Four Northerners organized Atlanta's white temperance movement: James G. Thrower, John W. Drew, "Mother" Eliza Stewart, and Frances Willard. While Thrower came to stay, brief visits by the last three individuals between 1879 and 1881 politicized white reformers, resulting in Atlanta's hosting the organizing convention for the state WCTU (1883) and the Georgia Prohibition Association (1884), as well as hosting state temperance conventions in 1881 and 1885. Atlantans were also briefly able to support the publication of a temperance newspaper called *Temperance Watchman*. Prominent Methodist and Baptist clergymen increasingly spoke out for the cause, yet a significant number of white laypeople remained uncomfortable with prohibition into the nineties. Finally, the 1880s witnessed the rise of the "New South" ideology, whose leading proponents included a unique mixture of businessmen, politicians, and clergymen. This regional "civic nationalism" embraced a variety of initiatives deemed essential to a strong, diversified Southern economy, and prohibition was one of them. Georgia's spokesmen for this new vision of Southern life included *Atlanta Constitution* editor Henry Grady, famed for his "New South" speech; Methodist minister Atticus G. Haygood, president of Emory College; Methodist evangelist Sam Jones; and Alfred Colquitt, governor (1877–1882) and U.S. senator (1883–1894). Combined with two decades of black temperance growth, this white movement made Atlanta a veritable hotbed of temperance activism. By the mid-eighties Atlanta was primed for a prohibition vote.

During the campaign, the prohibition rhetoric targeting black voters reflected both the virtuous and the pragmatic themes of classic black temperance discourse. Black clergy accepted the standard evangelical prohibitionist arguments and frequently reminded voters in no uncertain terms that this was a "moral" crusade. This line of argument was particularly effective in facilitating cooperation with white clergy. But probably more effective with the average black voter were race-based arguments, which directly or indirectly promised improved race relations with the "best class" of white men. This promise was no small matter to Atlanta's blacks. Strong interracial cooperation characterized the prohibitionists' campaign, and this was portrayed as a harbinger of things to come. Both the cooperation and the promises were duly noted by friends and foes of prohibition.

Anti-prohibitionist rhetoric targeting the black voter highlighted the difference between (personal) temperance and (legal) prohibition, stressed the economic costs of prohibition, and offered an alternative critique of race relations. It was a strictly pragmatic approach. The most popular anti-prohibition argument maintained that ending the liquor trade would cripple Atlanta's economy, especially the service sector jobs on which blacks depended. In addition, white anti-prohibitionists argued that they had been better friends to the black man than the drys, and that prohibition would never work, except against the poor. The complex political, economic, and social implications of outlawing the liquor traffic that voters had to consider meant that one's personal alcohol use was not a reliable indicator of one's voting predisposition.

The greatest legislative achievement of Georgia's temperance movement prior to the creation of state prohibition in 1907 was the governor's signing of the General Local Option Bill in September 1885, for which white Atlantans justly took much credit. The excitement over the law energized Atlanta's prohibitionists, but they still had an uphill journey to convince voters to use the power of the state to end the retail liquor traffic, a proposition fundamentally different from personal abstinence and one that an American city the size of Atlanta had never tried. Nearly all black and white clergy backed prohibition, giving it a strong moral tone, but New South businessmen also defended it with purely secular arguments. The prohibitionists' enthusiasm put the anti-prohibitionists on the defensive, giving them the more difficult task of campaigning *against* something. Although Northern personalities, ideas, and literature influenced the electioneering, this was an opportunity for Atlantans to debate among themselves the merits of prohibition—a family affair if you will. This was a distinctly Southern prohibition debate that could have occurred only in the 1880s.

This chapter begins with a review of Atlanta's white temperance movement in the years leading up to the passage of the General Local Option Bill, provides a narrative of the unprecedented rhetoric and events of the election campaign, and concludes with contemporary observers' predictions about its implications for race relations and politics. Although the 1885 and 1887 votes occurred in the postbellum years, they belonged culturally to the antebellum reform nexus because they were the logical conclusion to decades of temperance activism heavily informed by antebellum sentiments, but conditioned by their Southern context.

Atlanta's White Temperance Movement and the Local Option Law of 1885

Georgia's antebellum temperance movement began during the 1827–1828 "Great Georgia Revival" under the preaching of Adiel Sherwood, a Baptist preacher from upstate New York trained in pro-revival theology at Andover Seminary in Massachusetts. Sherwood personally oversaw the organization of scores of temperance societies throughout the state and organized Georgia's first statewide temperance society in 1828, during the meeting of the Georgia Baptist Convention. While most believed conversion was the best way to ensure one's abstinence from ardent spirits, some pushed for prohibition. In 1839 and 1853 two unsuccessful attempts were made to petition the legislature for state prohibition, but then the movement fizzled. Prohibition legislation returned in the 1870s, as the state legislature responded favorably to many requests for local dry zones from localities across the state. In some places a "three-mile" law requiring the assent of all landowners or voters within a three-mile radius of a proposed saloon was enough to create a dry county. In other places legislators mandated dry zones around churches, schools, and factories, or authorized counties to conduct local option votes. Some counties set exorbitant retail liquor license fees to create de facto prohibition. This patchwork quilt of laws had effectively "dried up" 108 of Georgia's 136 counties by the time the 1885 General Local Option Law took effect.[7]

Although James G. Thrower had established Georgia's first Good Templars' lodge in 1866, widespread excitement for the cause did not begin until the fall of 1879. In early November a reformed drunkard and temperance speaker named John W. Drew arrived in Georgia, after having been invited by Sam Small, an Atlanta journalist.[8] Originally from Concord, New Hampshire, Drew traveled in the North and Midwest giving speeches challenging moderate drinkers and drunkards to reform their ways and sign the abstinence pledge. He bragged of being able to get more than 500 people to sign the pledge in one day. Before moving on, Drew would organize pledgers into "reform clubs" for mutual support and the perpetuation of the movement. When he turned his attention to the South, he chose to visit Atlanta first because of its central location and belief that it was "representative" of the region. Drew reasoned that his treatment in Atlanta would suggest how the rest of the South would receive him.[9] After soliciting and receiving the endorsement of Atlanta's pastors, Drew held nightly temperance meetings between November 15 and December 18, successfully persuading 4,122 people to sign the pledge, many of whom were known drinkers. His meetings incorporated testimonials from local reformed drunkards and temperance workers. As was his custom, Drew organized a "reform club" before leaving town. He also brought WCTU literature and held meetings with a group of women, including Governor Colquitt's wife, planting the seeds for the state's first WCTU chapter. Although Drew reached all classes of whites, press reports give no hint that blacks participated in his meetings.[10]

Building on this enthusiasm, James G. Thrower and the Good Templars invited "Mother" Eliza Stewart to Atlanta. Stewart was a well-known veteran of the 1873–1874 Woman's Crusade in Ohio that birthed the WCTU. In April 1880 Stewart visited Atlanta while touring the South in her capacity as chair of the national WCTU's Department of Southern Work. In the basement of Trinity Methodist Church, Georgia's largest and most renowned Methodist Episcopal Church (South), Stewart organized the state's first WCTU with two hundred members and a "who's who" list of society ladies as officers. James G. Thrower's wife was an officer, and while Governor Colquitt's wife declined the presidency, she hosted union meetings in the governor's mansion. James Thrower also took Stewart to the Storrs School, where she spoke several times and organized the South's first Colored WCTU. The white teacher Lizzie Stevens was made president, but all other officers were either students or alumni.[11]

One of the Atlanta WCTU's first major projects was its 1881 petition campaign for a general local option law. The Good Templars joined the WCTU in sending out thousands of petitions across the state. To bolster their efforts, they invited the WCTU president Frances Willard to visit Atlanta during her 1881 Southern tour. Willard gave several stirring speeches before white and black audiences, including one to more than 1,200 people at DeGive's Opera House, but the WCTU efforts were for naught, for more than 30,000 signatures failed to sway the state legislators. Subsequent unsuccessful petition drives yielded incremental tactical advances, until eventually the General Local Option Bill passed the legislature in the summer of 1885 and was signed into law in September.[12]

Georgia's General Local Option Law stated that "upon application by petition, signed by one-tenth of the voters who are qualified to vote for members of the General Assembly, in any county of this State the ordinary shall order an election to be held . . . to take place within forty days after the reception of such petition, to determine whether or not . . . spirituous liquors . . . shall be sold within the limits of such designated places." No matter what the outcome, there was a two-year waiting period before a county could hold a second referendum. Some important loopholes existed. For example, the law did not ban the sale of domestic wines or the ordering of liquor by mail, and "domestic" was undefined.

"The Most Remarkable Campaign Ever Waged in the South": The 1885 Local Option Campaign

Despite the loopholes, Atlanta's prohibitionists immediately capitalized on the momentum from their legislative victory.[13] Four days *before* the governor signed the bill into law, a group of white Atlanta prohibitionists met in the Good Templars' Hall to make preliminary plans for a petition drive. By September 19, the day after Governor Henry McDaniel signed the bill, two more meetings had been held, a petition drawn up, racially integrated ward committees established, and a campaign strategy devised. The prohibitionists' enthusiasm spread like wildfire. The excitement was so extreme that the *Atlanta Constitution* wildly predicted that almost one hundred local option elections would be held in Georgia by the end of the year. Now a U.S. senator, Alfred Colquitt credited National Temperance Society literature with stirring up the popular support needed for the law to pass, and the Society itself predicted that its Georgia literature distribution would ensure a strong prohibition vote from Atlanta's blacks. Early in the campaign Bethel's pastor Wesley J. Gaines announced his confidence in a large dry vote from blacks. The press and black and white leaders from across the nation viewed Atlanta as the bellwether of Southern sentiment and predicted that if Atlanta went dry other

Southern cities would follow. The campaign began in earnest on October 23, after the county ordinary had validated the petition signatures and set the election for November 25.[14]

The growth of Atlanta's saloon industry gave prohibitionists something to complain about. Between 1880 and 1885 the number of saloons in Atlanta had grown more rapidly than the population. While in 1880 the city had 82 saloons, in June 1884 alone the city council approved over 100 licenses. By January 1, 1885, the *Atlanta Constitution* reported that one could "get their toddy" in nearly 150 places in Atlanta. By the beginning of 1885 there were approximately 333 people for every saloon in Atlanta, the lowest ratio the city had experienced to date. The city council increased the retail liquor license from $300 to $500 in early 1885, which caused about one-third of the saloons to close, but that was obviously not good enough for prohibitionists (see appendix 2).[15]

Hastily assembled "prohi" (or "dry") and "anti" (or "wet") organizations coordinated the campaign, which revolved around a series of rallies, extensive newspaper coverage, and exciting public displays. The prohis organized ward committees to canvass the city and county for petition signatures and to distribute literature. Each ward organized a white and colored "Young Men's Prohibition Club." WCTU members also secured petition signatures, and after the election date was announced they collected thousands more signatures from people pledging to vote dry. Between October 14 and November 9, prohibitionists held at least nine citywide rallies, drawing between one and six thousand people each time. Some blacks attended most, and perhaps all, of these rallies. In addition, the ward committees hosted local meetings, and many churches held their own rallies. Clergy attended planning meetings, held prominent positions in public rallies, and were frequent speakers, adding a heavy religious flavor to an already moral crusade. The prohibitionists' campaign climaxed in mid-November with the raising of evangelist Sam Jones's tent in downtown Atlanta for daily meetings. The most frequent tent speaker, ironically, was not Jones but journalist Sam Small, who had just given up drink a few weeks earlier at a Sam Jones revival and begun traveling with the revivalist. Small spoke eleven times to Jones's three times. The twice-daily integrated tent meetings, which lasted almost two weeks and included local and visiting speakers, created all the excitement of a revival meeting for the prohibitionists' cause.

The smaller "anti" campaign did not hold its first rally until October 28. They held nine mostly integrated citywide rallies, with attendance ranging from 150 to 2,000. The "Committee of Twenty-Five," which coordinated the anti efforts, also published a pamphlet explaining its position.

Atlanta had not seen such clearly drawn battle lines since Sherman passed through town. The drys gave out blue ribbons, and the wets distributed red ribbons emblazoned with an eagle and the word "liberty." The three papers most closely reporting the events held strong editorial positions. The *Atlanta Journal* openly favored prohibition, the *Macon Telegraph* opposed it, and because the *Atlanta Constitution*'s two editors (Clark Howell and Henry Grady) disagreed, it did not run editorials. Instead, the paper allowed partisans from both sides to submit news articles about their campaigns if they paid for publishing them. Such articles were labeled "communicated" and brought in thousands of dollars for the *Constitution*. Campaign events have been well documented elsewhere, so my goal is to examine the campaign and its implications from the perspectives of black Atlantans generally, and from that of black Atlanta's temperance reformers specifically.[16]

The Prohibitionists, or "Prohis," Organize Their Campaign

The dry campaign was integrated from the beginning. Years of exposure to missionary education and Northern temperance literature, combined with the efforts of their AME and Baptist preachers, had primed many African Americans for this moment. At the beginning, white prohibitionists invited Big Bethel's Wesley J. Gaines to join them in their efforts to hold a local option campaign in Fulton County. Although white Atlantans understood much less than they thought they did about the black community in their midst, they were not far from the mark in discerning Gaines and his Big Bethel congregation as an influential pro-temperance voice among African Americans. Following his first meeting, Gaines conferred with several black ministers, who decided unanimously to cooperate with the white prohibitionists. The *Constitution* reported that, at the third organizational meeting, a "good number of the best colored men of the city" participated. The attendees at this meeting finalized the wording of the petition and organized three-person ward committees to coordinate its distribution and plan the rallies. They formally invited the Good Samaritans and Good Templars to help distribute petitions. The committee appointed blacks to four of the six ward committees: a shoemaker and member of Reverend E. R. Carter's Friendship Baptist church, Nick Holmes; porter R. J. Henry; and ministers Jerry M. Jones and J. G. Yeiser. Gaines joined the finance committee, and he and Reverend Carter worked on the petition drive. William Pledger, former True Reformer and Good Templars' leader, sent greetings by letter. By this time Pledger was back in Atlanta as the coeditor of the *Weekly Defiance*.[17]

Blacks had been involved in Atlanta's politics since emancipation, but whites always made sure they remained insignificant players. The greatest achievement of Atlanta's Republican Party had been the December 1870 election of blacks

William Finch and George Graham to the city council, a position they held for one year. Although black citizens retained the right to vote throughout the seventies and eighties, whites did away with ward-based elections to prevent neighborhoods with large black populations from electing one of their own to the city council. In lieu of ward elections, there were citywide "general ticket" elections so that whites, because they were always the majority, could be assured of winning. To further complicate matters for blacks, the city's Republican Party collapsed in the mid-seventies, and its Democratic Party ceased functioning soon after that. Whites claimed to have made peace with the existence of enfranchised freedmen, and they regularly sought black support by including them in political meetings and campaigning in their neighborhoods, but that was the extent of their "acceptance" of black voters. Jackson McHenry and other blacks ran for office, and whites successfully prevented their being elected. On one occasion, a candidate dropped out of the race and urged white voters to cast their votes for other white candidates, thereby consolidating the white vote. Although black voting was normative in postbellum Atlanta, it was consistently rendered ineffectual. This election held out the prospect that, this time, things would be different.[18]

Men proudly touting the New South provided much of the white leadership for the dry campaign. Urban-focused individuals, New South men sought to diversify the economy beyond its agricultural base, and they did so partly by networking with like-minded Northern investors and industrialists. Hence, William E. Dodge and Alfred Colquitt became good friends. Colquitt and his fellow Bourbon Triumvirate members John B. Gordon and Joseph E. Brown were New South men, although Gordon and Brown did not support prohibition. New South men tried to deemphasize the South's slave past, praising instead the many benefits of emancipation. New South men generally had either a mercantile or an industrial focus, and they wanted to bring the South into line with the North's industrial economy and value system as quickly as possible. Since Atlanta's economy was trade-based, its New South prohibitionists were mostly commercial, professional, and governmental figures, and not industrialists as in other cities. Some of these leaders had spoken in John Drew's crusade six years earlier. Of the 27 men initially involved in organizing the campaign, only two were industrialists: George Winship, who owned a heavy machinery company, and James W. English, an owner of the Chattahoochie Brick Company and member of the Board of Police Commissioners, among other high profile civic positions. Prominent wholesale and retail merchants, including A. D. Adair, E. P. Chamberlin, and Samuel Inman, participated, as well as journalists (C. W. Hubner of the *Journal* and W. A. Hemphill of the *Constitution*), Republican "carpetbagger" politicians (A. E. Buck and John E. Bryant), and various lawyers and realtors. The most prominent governmental officials were the mayor George Hillyer, Judge James A. Anderson of the Recorder's (police) Court, and Judge W. A. Hammond of Fulton's Superior Court. The most prominent white clergyman of the campaign was Dr. J. B. Hawthorne, pastor of the First Baptist church. James G. Thrower, a building contractor, had such a long history with temperance in Atlanta that following the election some observers considered his work the chief cause of the prohibition victory.[19]

The press reported no less than 16 prohibition meetings with black majorities. In fact, the very first public prohibition meeting of the campaign—a Fifth Ward meeting—was mostly black. Jerry M. Jones, the pastor of Macedonia Baptist Church and vice chairman of the Fifth Ward committee, hosted the meeting on October 13. Its sparse attendance of 20 was an inauspicious beginning, but several people spoke, including Judge Anderson, and most attendees signed the petition. The following day witnessed the first citywide rally, with about 1,500 in attendance in the courthouse basement, a site used repeatedly by both sides during the campaign. The highlight of this rally, which undoubtedly had some blacks in attendance, was a speech by Sam Small. The next day Bethel AME was the site of the first citywide rally for blacks. Even though it was specifically organized for blacks, about one-third of the audience was white. (Whites constituted a significant minority at most African American rallies.) Once evangelist Sam Jones set up his tent, organizers reserved four nights for blacks. The first black tent meeting (November 12) drew four thousand blacks and two thousand whites, and the platform was filled with an impressive biracial display of leaders. Over a dozen black pastors and 30 other black leaders sat opposite the mayor and several white prohibition leaders. With only one or two exceptions, Atlanta's black pastors supported prohibition, and each church formed prohibition clubs to persuade others to vote dry and build enthusiasm for the cause. In addition to tent meetings for blacks, Bethel AME, Friendship Baptist, Mount Pleasant Baptist, Mt. Zion Baptist, New Hope Presbyterian, Macedonia Baptist, and St. Philips AME were among the black churches hosting special meetings. The students from the missionary schools joined in with much enthusiasm. Atlanta and Clark Universities and Spelman Seminary also held meetings, and their students provided music for the tent rallies. Spelman's girls held daily prayer meetings for the prohibition cause.[20]

Atlanta's women were also deeply involved in the prohibition campaign. This was the one time that white WCTU members acknowledged and cooperated with their African American sisters, as colored chapters were never welcomed in Georgia's white state WCTU conventions. Local white WCTU leaders invited Charlestonian Sallie Chapin to return to Atlanta to help organize black women, and her efforts yielded Atlanta's East Side Colored WCTU. Chapin, the most influential Southern WCTU worker of the 1880s, was Mother Stewart's successor as chair of the WCTU's Department of Southern Work and president of the South Carolina WCTU. Chapin gave speeches at Allen Temple, First Congregational,

Fig. 18—Spelman High School Class of 1888. Most of these students were likely involved in Atlanta's 1885 or 1887 local option campaigns. Spelman Archives

Bethel AME, and Clark University. Unfortunately her Atlanta speeches were not recorded, but if her reports to the national WCTU regarding her other work with blacks are any clue, she came across in the paternalistic manner one would expect from a member of a former slave-holding family, such as she was. Chapin claimed black audiences received her enthusiastically, and other WCTU leaders praised her for her ability to "influence" the freed people.[21] The East Side Colored WCTU joined with the Young WCTU of Atlanta University and the other schools to conduct door-to-door literature distribution and various get-out-the-vote activities.

Of course black clergy addressed black voters during the campaign, but so too did white Republican leaders John E. Bryant and Colonel A. E. Buck, and New South men like Samuel Inman. Other local speakers included Sam Small; H. I. Kimball, Northern-born builder of Atlanta's premier Kimball Hotel; and

Fig. 19—Clark College Class of 1889. Most of these students were likely involved in Atlanta's 1885 or 1887 local option campaigns. Clark College Photographs, Atlanta University Center Robert W. Woodruff Library

the African American Jackson McHenry, who migrated to Atlanta following the war, held various jobs as a blacksmith, porter, and janitor, and served as a delegate to several district and state Republican Party conventions. As with other prohibition contests of the eighties, both sides invited speakers from other cities and states to aid their cause. Three Atlanta University graduates returned to stir up voters: the editor of Augusta's *Weekly Sentinel* Richard R. Wright, Reverend George V. Clark from Athens, and Edward A. Johnson from North Carolina. From Philadelphia came the AME bishop Jabez P. Campbell and Reverend Benjamin T. Tanner, by this time editor of the *AME Church Review*.

Prohibition Campaign Rhetoric Targeting Black Voters

The standard prohibitionist argument included the following elements: Saloons existed to sell liquor, which was not a food product, and had only harmful

Fig. 20—Jackson McHenry, an aspiring Republican politician who sometimes campaigned for prohibition. From *The Black Side,* Kenan Research Center at the Atlanta History Center

physical and social effects. Since saloon owners wanted to sell all they could, it was in their best interest to violate laws forbidding the sale of liquor on Sundays and to minors and known drunkards. Prohibitionists seized every opportunity to expose violations of these laws. Such behavior indicated a dangerously arrogant attitude, they argued, as did the efforts of saloon owners to influence legislation. Perhaps more persuasively, however, they marshaled statements and statistics from law enforcement officials that demonstrated that liquor was somehow related to a large majority of crimes, although the actual percentage varied according to the source. They would then wax eloquent with extravagant projections about the savings to city government because the police court would need to sit less often and jail expenses would decrease. They could always dig up statistics from some dry community that supported their argument. (This point—that "prohibition prohibits"—was also a direct rebuttal to the anti argument that "prohibition does not prohibit.") In one of their most emotional appeals, prohibitionists lamented the victimized women and children who lacked proper clothing, shelter, or food because the man of the house squandered his income on liquor. This argument was as old as the temperance movement itself. Finally, the fact that these alcohol-related problems still existed after years of moral suasion and high license was the ultimate "proof" that prohibition was the only recourse left. In the name of self-preservation, society had the right to destroy the otherwise legitimate trade in alcoholic beverages. It was a small step for clergy then to equate saloons, liquor, and the liquor traffic with "evil" or "forces of darkness," which immediately implied that no self-respecting Christian could possibly oppose prohibition. Portraying prohibition as part of a cosmic struggle between good and evil was as old as the movement itself. Many people agreed with Reverend E. R. Carter when he called the prohibition campaign "the battle of the Lord and of the people" against evil.[22] But prohibitionists continued to embrace moral suasion, as the Young Men's Prohibition Club banner slogan revealed: "Persuasion for the tempted, but law for the tempter." Finally, as in any heated political contest, this one had its fair share of ad hominem attacks. Opponents of prohibition were regularly accused of being "lovers" of every form of evil, from greed and drunkenness to the Devil himself.

Although all these arguments reached black voters, prohis designed another set of arguments specifically for black consumption. According to press reports, three themes came up repeatedly. One theme was racial uplift through the projected reduction in crime because of reduced numbers of black drunkards. This type of argument had long been used by black temperance workers locally and in the North. Early in the campaign Jackson McHenry pointed out that as a result of blacks drinking in saloons they were doubly taxed for the city's streets. The city taxed the liquor blacks bought in saloons, he argued, and then drunken blacks were convicted of crimes and given fines they could not afford. As a result they served time on the gang, where they physically built the roads their taxes had just paid for. Bishop Henry M. Turner spoke as though he was providing a modern media sound bite. He proclaimed that those who voted with the wets were voting for "degradation, ruin, chain gangs, lunacy and everything low and degrading." Sam Small put it this way: "The pathway to the penitentiary leads through the bar-room. [applause] Back of the bar-room stands the sheriff, back of the sheriff the jail, back of that the coal mines. [applause]." Black audiences understood this sequence all too well. They knew liquor was not the sole explanation for most convicts being black, but they also could not deny a connection. By supporting prohibition, many blacks believed they were doing what was within their power to elevate the race, stem the flow of their young men into the quasi-slavery of the convict lease system, and improve the image of the race before white society.[23]

A second theme aimed at black audiences was that of improved race relations. Like others, Bishop Henry M. Turner believed properly enforced prohibition would greatly reduce drunkenness, and he argued that since whites controlled the levers of power, anything that would keep both races sober and clearheaded would primarily benefit the powerless blacks. But the one who stressed race relations the most was John Emory Bryant. The son of a Methodist minister from Maine, Bryant was a product of the antebellum reform nexus. He had been a teacher before the war and embraced a variety of reforms, including temperance and abolitionism, as was common in New England in the later antebellum years. An early activist in the Republican Party, he was attracted to it for its reform emphasis and volunteered to fight when the war began. He served in the Eighth Maine Infantry Regiment on the South Carolina Sea Islands, where he was known to lecture fellow soldiers on the evils of liquor. Following the war he moved to Atlanta and became a leader in Georgia's Republican Party, working with such Reconstruction-era black politicians as Henry M. Turner. As recently as 1879, hoping to capitalize on temperance's resurgence as a political issue, Bryant had claimed his party was "naturally" the party of temperance. In the 1885 campaign, however, he announced that prohibition was neither a Republican nor a Democratic issue but a moral one that, more important, if supported by blacks would improve their relationship with the "better class" of whites. "You have an opportunity," he announced, "as you have never had before to gain their sympathy, their confidence and co-operation." Bryant presented this argument at least three times, and at least four other white speakers reinforced it in various ways. But this was not just white rhetoric. On the biracial platform of the first tent meeting for blacks, Reverend Carter's declaration that "Your friends are men like Dr. Hawthorne and Mr. Anderson, who, forgetting all self-interest, are battling in this cause for God and the right and for you," received cheers from the crowd. In that heady atmosphere Carter overzealously announced that if prohibition caused an economic downturn as its detractors warned, Atlanta's businessmen would make sure blacks did not suffer. The eagerness and consistency with which white prohis collaborated with blacks during the campaign made this argument seem all the more plausible but only set blacks up for big disappointments later.[24]

Although racial uplift and improved race relations were of great importance to blacks, the issue that speakers before black audiences addressed more than any other was more of a warning than an argument. Because early in the campaign word spread that the antis could buy enough black votes to win the election, prohibitionists repeatedly pleaded with blacks not to sell their votes.[25] Buying votes with free-flowing whiskey was a time-honored white tradition in the antebellum South, and although it continued sporadically in Atlanta into the late nineteenth century, after emancipation whiskey became increasingly associated with black voters. Historically the candidate who "treated" voters most liberally received the most votes. In 1880, when the state Republican Party split along race lines, whites accused blacks of not being loyal enough to the party. They claimed that blacks sold their votes to Democratic candidates for 50 cents or a pint of whiskey. Although trading votes for whiskey declined, the public nature of voting subjected individuals to the influences of peer pressure and intrusive authority figures. Candidates printed their own ballots that voters carried to the polls and cast in full view of poll watchers from the various campaigns. During the local option vote, citizens received their ballots before election day from the side they planned to support. Prohibitionists feared that on election day—or election eve—the antis would corral large numbers of black voters into one place, fill them with whiskey, and lead them to the polls in a group, making the most of peer pressure and the public spectacle. In fact, on election eve, both sides feted black voters, although the drys obviously did not use intoxicating beverages.[26]

But liquor was not the only thing used to buy votes, and the poverty of most blacks increased their vulnerability to outright cash offers. Because vote buying was a known characteristic of American politics, and because the wets bragged about the size of their treasure chest, it is likely they made some cash payments, but they received at least two significant public rebuffs. The well-known black building contractor Alexander Hamilton provided one rejection. A white saloon owner and a building contractor jointly offered Hamilton $500 to stump for the anti side. Taking great offense, Hamilton refused the offer, and the white men immediately severed all business relations with him. The mailman James Parker was stumping for the antis until the first prohi tent meeting for blacks. He entered the meeting late, and his presence elicited such cheers from the crowd that the speaker had to pause for several minutes. Invited to sit on the platform, Parker announced that he was switching to the prohibition side. Speaking of his work for the wets Parker said, "I don't know, but I suppose that the fellows who went with me to those meetings had the money of the liquor men in their pockets. I know I did." The idea of being directly paid for one's vote gained wide circulation and had a certain practical appeal to some blacks, for obvious reasons. The press quoted one blue-ribbon-wearing member of Wesley Gaines's church, who admitted, "I belong to the society of six hundred who wear it, but I haven't made my arrangements for wood and coal for the winter yet and am liable to change and all the others are about in the same boat." He evidently held out hope for casting a financially profitable vote. Whether or not Atlanta had saloons was relatively unimportant to a man who could not afford to heat his house for the winter.[27]

No less than seven speakers of both races pleaded with blacks not to sell their votes. Some, like Wesley Gaines, simply tried to speak positively. During the first rally for blacks, which was held in his church, he announced, "I know of one society of colored people in this city, with a membership of over six hundred who are entitled to vote, and they will march solidly to the polls on election and cast their ballots for prohibition." Samuel M. Inman, while speaking at Atlanta University, used the positive approach and simultaneously praised the school by declaring his confidence that education and Christian training had done so much for blacks that far fewer of them would sell their votes than some were predicting. On the other hand, Dr. J. B. Hawthorne proposed an aggressive stand against the wets by demanding his listeners report anyone who offered to buy their votes. Hawthorne promised to personally give any such solicitor an "immortality of infamy." It was an African American minister, J. G. Yeiser, however, who produced the harshest language and starkest metaphor on the matter. He announced, "The man who would buy a vote ought to be put in the penitentiary and the man who would sell his vote ought to be disfranchised.... Soldiers never sold their rifles and ammunition. The ballot is the people's weapon of defense."[28]

The most culturally powerful attacks on vote selling were couched in appeals to the voters' sense of "manhood." At a black rally on November 5, Bishop Turner told his listeners that if they wanted to vote wet they should at least do it like a man and not be paid for their vote. Two weeks later, in Sam Jones's tent, E. R. Carter and Richard R. Wright both admonished their listeners along the same lines. The news reporter summarized Wright as having said it was time for "all honest colored men to stand up and assert their manhood, to rise above all bribes and low motives and to vote as their consciences told them." Carter followed by challenging blacks to "stand up like men" and prove that charges of black vote selling were a "false aspersion." He mocked black antis by saying every time he saw one wearing the red ribbon he started listening for the auctioneer's bell. At the same meeting, Wilbur P. Thirkield, dean of Clark University's Gammon School of Theology, reminded blacks that it was "useless to aspire to a higher social or political station unless they cultivated the virtues of manly character."[29]

These appeals played to the century-old assertions that virtue was essential to true independence, and that independence was a central component of black manhood. Embedded within the individual's vote for prohibition was a manly commitment to the independence of the community. Dry speakers assumed that the conscience of most black men would tell them to vote for prohibition, but they also knew that the exigencies of their economic deprivation and desperation could pull them the other way. Arguing that accepting a bribe was tantamount to surrendering one's manhood appealed to a powerful and deeply rooted sentiment. A couple of years before the election, the *Weekly Defiance* ran an editorial titled "Manhood," which strongly criticized sycophantic blacks in government patronage jobs who did not speak out in defense of abused members of their race. "If colored men appointed to positions would . . . not be the boot-lick of their superiors or employers, they would prove a surer promoter of the race." True African American manhood, then, was as much about the community's advancement as it was about the individual. On election eve, Bishop Turner reminded voters that if they voted dry they would be proclaiming the dignity of all black people before the entire country, and that could only have positive results for the race. The fact that such appeals were so frequently used suggests the extent to which black men desired to assert their virtue and independence in opposition to white society's continuous painful demeaning of their manhood. In a number of ways, then, despite an emphasis on the moral nature of the vote, prohibitionist arguments targeting African Americans turned on issues empowering the race and improving race relations. Prohibition campaign rhetoric clearly reflected the dual heritage of the black temperance movement.[30]

Organizing the Wet, or "Anti," Campaign

The goal of the anti-prohibitionists was to defend the status quo of Atlanta's liquor regulations, but this presented a public image challenge for them. By 1885 Southern temperance reformers had achieved some success in setting the terms of the public debate on alcohol consumption. Claiming to be a "temperance man" (whether or not one meant total abstinence) was increasingly deemed socially respectable, politically desirable, and all but religiously required. Supporters of both personal abstinence and legal prohibition presented their values as the most forward-looking, the most progressive; they sought to improve, even purify, society. They were progressives before the "Progressive era" began. It appeared, then, as though the antis were working against reform, against progress.

To address this image problem, antis frequently announced that they actually were abstainers themselves and then honestly reasoned with voters about the difference between being for abstinence and being for prohibition. Antis charged prohibitionists with unfairly conflating only a vote for prohibition with opposition to intemperance, and only opposition to prohibition with intemperance. For the sake of their image, antis also publicly distanced themselves from saloon owners. Speakers employed all of these tactics at the first wet rally. The person who opened the meeting announced it was "not a liquor men's meeting," and the first part of the resolution passed that night declared, "It is the sense of this meeting that all excesses and intemperance, as well in passing laws as in drinking should be avoided." When the Committee of Twenty-Five published its pamphlet, they wanted to make it clear they had no personal interest in making or selling liquor. Their pamphlet cover read, "This Pamphlet is issued by the Committee of Twenty-Five appointed at the Mass Meeting of Citizens who are Not Interested in the Manufacture or Sale of Liquors."[31]

The anti-prohibition campaign held only a third as many meetings as the prohibitionists and attracted fewer people, but the closeness of the vote demonstrated the wets' disproportionately strong appeal. Formal anti-prohibition rallies began two weeks to the day after the first prohibition rally. The first anti rally occurred on October 28 and attracted about one thousand people, but it is not clear whether blacks attended. The next night, however, a group of black employees of the Kimball House, the Kimball House Employees Committee,[32] called a general meeting, and about four hundred showed up. The Kimball House was Atlanta's hotel of choice for visiting businessmen and dignitaries. The committee issued a resolution condemning, as "citizens of Fulton County . . . the movement of a set of fanatics that will result in the ruin of the prosperous and growing city of Atlanta." They asked citizens to vote to prevent the "consummation of sumptuary legislation to the end that all men may as prescribed by the Bible be their own free moral agents, eating and drinking what they please and doing as they chose, so long as they do not injure the rest of mankind." Antebellum reform nexus language had become sufficiently culturally normative and malleable to be drafted into both sides of the fight over alcohol. At their second rally these black antis issued a resolution especially inviting the "co-operation of our colored friends who are employed in the various bars and restaurants . . . and who would, in the event of the closing of such places, be at once deprived of their daily earnings." Blacks organized three more rallies, on November 5, 13, and 20.[33]

Black speakers at anti rallies included both well-known and some not-so-well-known individuals. The officers of the Kimball House Employees Committee were W. E. Thompson and N. C. Robinson, of whom little is known. Other black leaders included dentist Roderick Dhu Badger, the wealthiest black man in Atlanta; lunchroom owner and barber Moses Bently; *Weekly Defiance* editor Alonzo W. Burnett; and Baptist pastor Alexander S. Jones. Prior to his conversion

Fig. 21—Honorable Jefferson Franklin Long, an anti-prohibitionist speaker from Macon. Library of Congress, Prints & Photographs Division [LC-DIG-cwpbh-00556]

on November 13, the mailman James Parker was an important black anti speaker. Another important speaker was from Macon, the former slave and former U.S. congressman Jefferson Franklin Long, a merchant-tailor. After 17 years, Long had become disillusioned with party politics and left public life in 1884, but he returned briefly to fight prohibition in Atlanta. Black Atlantans knew Long because of his association with local political leaders such as Henry M. Turner, William Pledger, Alfred Colquitt, and Dr. William H. Felton, a Cartersville-area U.S. and Georgia representative.[34]

Black anti-prohibitionists allied their efforts with "respectable" white leaders as much as black prohibitionists did. Among the white anti spokesmen were cur-

Fig. 22—Dr. Roderick Dhu Badger, an anti-prohibitionist. DeKalb History Center

rent and past government officials (former mayor John B. Goodwin and former Republican governor Rufus Bullock[35]); Julius L. Brown, son of U.S. senator and former governor Joseph Brown; *Atlanta Constitution* editor Clark Howell; and various lawyers and merchants.[36]

Surprisingly, the best-known and most frequent black anti-prohibitionist speaker turned out to be William A. Pledger, who had led the state's True Reformers temperance fraternity in the mid-seventies and had since become a newspaper editor and leader in Georgia's Republican Party. Touted as the "foremost colored man of the state," Pledger had, as recently as February, effectively worked with George V. Clark and others to turn out the black vote for prohibition in Athens, Georgia (Clarke County), but a personally unfortunate turn of events seems to have caused him to side with the wets out of spite. By the spring of 1885 Pledger was a coeditor with A. W. Burnett of Atlanta's *Weekly Defiance*, known for its non-accommodationist stance on race relations. That same spring, H. A. Rucker, a black man who later became Atlanta's Internal Revenue Collector, bought a bakery from a white man. Rucker's white landlord evicted him after a month, forcing him to sell his business at a loss. In June, Pledger wrote an editorial naming the landlord, George W. Adair, and advising blacks not to rent from him, recommending instead two African American landowners by name. Adair brought a libel suit against Pledger, who was convicted on October 27 and given a $200 fine or eight months on the gang. He paid the fine. George Adair happened to be a prohibitionist leader. Rumor had it that Reverend E. R. Carter somehow played a role in Pledger's conviction. Pledger was such a popular personality in Black Atlanta that during his trial the courtroom could not contain all the spectators. Although Pledger had sent a friendly letter to the September 20 prohibition campaign planning meeting, at the end of October he attended the first black wet meeting and spoke publicly against prohibition. The *Macon Telegraph* wondered if Pledger's support might be enough to give wets the edge among blacks. Ironically, the leading black prohibitionist of Clarke County's February 1885 prohibition campaign had become the leading black anti-prohibitionist of Fulton County's November 1885 campaign![37]

Public opinion forced Pledger to justify his change of heart. He initially claimed that, in Athens, inebriated white college boys at the University of Georgia threatened black girls but since this was not a problem in Atlanta prohibition was not necessary. Pledger then produced letters from individuals in Athens who had supported prohibition there but now said it was ineffective. Finally, he asserted that prohibition would never truly prohibit in Atlanta but that it would hurt Atlanta's economy. On at least three occasions Pledger's public comments were laced with personal attacks against Reverend E. R. Carter, portraying him as a morally hypocritical lackey of white prohibitionists and perhaps inadvertently revealing his *real* reason for switching sides. Pledger's closing salvo was an open letter to blacks published in the *Atlanta Constitution* the day before the election.[38]

Anti-Prohibition Campaign Rhetoric Targeting Black Voters

The anti-prohibitionist rhetorical strategy, like that of a defense lawyer, sought to establish reasonable doubt about the prosecution's argument in the minds of the jury (voters). Accusations of dishonesty underlay most of their arguments against the drys. The charge worked equally well before white and black audiences. The foremost argument was that prohibition would be economically devastating for Atlanta. Unemployment, vacant properties, and declining rents, property values, and tax and license revenues were the sure fruits of prohibition, they argued, and prohibitionists refused to say how they would address these problems. This even led some to speculate publicly that the wealthier prohibitionists were conspiring to depress property values so they could buy up land, knowing that one day saloons would return and property values rise again. Antis charged that the drys' moral sensibilities caused them to be reckless with the city's economic health, but worse still, they were dishonest while hypocritically claiming the high moral ground. Such an argument resonated in a commerce-driven city like Atlanta.

Speakers trotted out other arguments too. They frequently claimed that prohibition could never really prohibit in a city the size of Atlanta (about fifty thousand). Speakers marshaled statistics and quotations from citizens and officials of other cities, such as Springfield, Massachusetts, which had tried prohibition and abandoned it, to argue that it only worked in rural communities and small towns. Attacking prohibition leaders was also a major element of anti arguments. Because prohi leaders presented the campaign as a struggle of good versus evil, and God versus Satan, their every act and association suggesting any degree of compromise received immediate scrutiny, exposure, and condemnation, not unlike what occurs among politicians today. Anti-prohibitionists accused drys of being dishonest about the local option law by talking as if it would only end the sale of whiskey. They pointed out that the law banned the sale of malted alcoholic beverages and prohibited physicians from prescribing drinks such as brandy. Calling prohibitionists and their arguments "fanatical," the wets identified their own position as the "truly temperate" one. Whatever arguments were used, however, they always concluded with a line declaring the speaker's goal of only wanting what was best for Atlanta and its people.[39]

The most popular anti argument, however, was also the one most frequently cited before black audiences, namely, that prohibition was bad for the economy, with the corollary that blacks would be hurt the most. The primary occupational niche of blacks was the service sector—the food, beverage, and hospitality industries. Also, a disproportionately large percentage of all draymen and hackmen were black. "The prosperity of the city means plenty of work for the colored people," asserted James Parker, "and prohibition would drive prosperity from its door." Atlanta's largest economic sector—trade and transportation—was absolutely critical to the black economy.[40] Since the masses of blacks were beginning to realize the obstacles to their upward economic mobility, they were increasingly desperate to preserve at least their existing employment status. The more people bought and sold, moved around, and transported goods, the more employment opportunities blacks could anticipate. Suggesting that unemployment would hit blacks the hardest, Jefferson Long predicted that 1,500 men would be "without a dollar to support their families." In William Pledger's open letter he specifically mentioned jobs vitally important to blacks: "Men will lose employment: hackmen, draymen, hotel waiters, clerks, and others employed, because of the travel induced by the sale of liquors here failing to longer stop here." Over the course of the campaign at least six different speakers warned blacks of the impending economic decline if the drys won. Combined with the fact that most blacks were unskilled workers, institutionalized white racism made unemployment and underemployment unrelenting facts of life in Black Atlanta. The economic argument played well to blacks afraid of losing the only jobs they were permitted to work—those at the bottom of the occupational ladder. The argument also appealed to the voters' sense of independence and manhood, for few things undermine men's self-confidence, dignity, and independence like removing their ability to earn their living from their own labor. The freed people's felt need for meaningful independence was broad and deep enough to be used by both sides of the liquor debate.[41]

If the predictions of economic decline proved true, most job loss probably would have occurred outside of the saloon industry, and the 1,500 figure was most likely an exaggeration. According to the 1880 Atlanta City Directory only 177 people were employed in retail liquor sales, 10 percent of whom were black. Only 76 people, including 14 blacks, were directly employed by saloons. But the industry grew rapidly after 1880. Between 1880 and 1884 the number of retail liquor licenses granted annually more than doubled, from over 60 to well over 100, so that by early 1885 the city had 150 licensed retail liquor establishments. In the spring of 1885 the city council increased the license fee from $300 to $500, and this reduced the number of saloons to 95. By the time of the November vote no more than a few hundred people were directly employed by saloons, but the rapid growth during the preceding years probably made the industry seem larger than it was.[42]

Prohibition was not likely to injure black entrepreneurship in the liquor industry. Only occasionally did blacks hold retail liquor licenses. Usually they were unskilled employees, like George V. Clark had been. Not only did blacks find it difficult to acquire the start-up capital, but the city council was reluctant to approve their licenses. E. R. Carter claimed that no black man in Atlanta owned a saloon "without a white man at his back," which was probably true. Blacks undoubtedly needed white business partners for both finances and character references. In the ten years leading up to the local option vote, only six blacks owned a saloon (Robert Stephens, William Cummings, Robert Stevenson, William Gaines, Thomas Stafford, and Jackson M. Ryan), and at the time of the vote probably only Robert Stevenson and Jackson Ryan remained owners. Although blacks did not experience much *upward* occupational mobility, they did experience plenty of occupational mobility, as Thomas Stafford's life illustrates. A longtime Atlanta resident, Stafford worked as a porter in the state capitol and for a railroad delivery company before purchasing a billiards hall. He had saved up enough money to purchase a saloon by 1881 but was out of business the next year and became a

Table 2—Atlanta Saloon Ownership

Year	Number of Non-Black Saloon Owners	Number of Black Saloon Owners	Total Number of Saloon Owners	Black Saloon Owners as a % of all Saloon Owners
1870	36	0	36	0
1880	78	3	81	3.7
1890	100	1	101	1.0
1900	113	3	116	2.6

Data compiled by author from business and residential sections of the city directory.

common laborer. In 1883 Stafford went into partnership with a white grocer and opened the "Marion and Stafford" saloon. After disappearing from the directory for a couple of years, Stafford shows up again, as a saloon employee, in 1888. Stafford and other black saloon owners were not stable, successful entrepreneurs and likely were not significant employers. Prohibition, therefore, was more likely to hurt blacks employed in the transportation and hospitality-related sectors because of the presumption that fewer business and pleasure travelers would visit Atlanta.[43]

The wets' second-most-frequent argument aimed at black voters was to challenge the suspiciously sudden and cozy interracial dynamics of the prohibitionists' campaign. Black-white relations in the prohibitionist camp were so close that they blurred traditional social distinctions and raised eyebrows everywhere. At least five black speakers addressed this issue. Some challenged the assumption that white prohibitionists were better friends of blacks than white antis. Jeff Long and Moses Bently claimed that, because black schools received a "large" part of their money from liquor dealers, it would be not only ungrateful to vote against them but actually harmful to one of the most important institutions of racial uplift.[44] Wets also exposed the hypocrisy of the apparent racial harmony and predicted its quick collapse. The Reverend Alexander Jones spoke of a prominent prohibitionist who until a week ago had addressed him as "Hello boy!" Now when this gentleman met him it was "How are you today, Brother Jones?"

The antis played on the legitimate fears and distrust blacks harbored toward whites. Robert Hayden, one of the *Macon Telegraph*'s Atlanta correspondents, became actively involved in the anti campaign. At one meeting he prophesied of the

Table 3—Atlanta Saloon Employees

Year	Number of Non-Black Saloon Employees	Number of Black Saloon Employees	Total Number of Saloon Employees	Black Saloon Employees as a % of all Saloon Employees
1870	17	1	18	5.6
1880	62	14	76	18.4
1890	111	53	164	32.3
1900	150	120	270	44.4

Compiled by author from business and residential sections of the city directory.

prohibitionists that "when the election is over they will meet in their churches and gather pennies to send to Africa and China, and leave the negro just as ragged as before." Hayden continued with the following story to expose the prohibitionists' chronic racism:

> I met a negro the other day and asked him to have a drink. He said he felt bad, as he had had a bad dream.
> "What did you dream" I inquired.
> "I dreamed I died and went to hell."
> "Did you see any prohibitionists down there?"
> "Yes, sir; lots of them."
> "What were the prohibitionists doing?"
> "Most every one of them had hold of a negro."
> "What were they doing with the negroes?"
> "They were holding them between themselves and the fire."[45]

Playing to the same fears, Moses Bently applied the title of an old song to the dangers he foresaw in the black-white prohibitionist alliance: "There's a snake in the hole and that snake won't bite you till next fall. It will come out then if we are defeated. There used to be an old song: 'Run, nigger, run,' and if prohibition carries you all can prepare to hear that song again. The prohibitionist will catch you; you will be his meat—sweet, juicy meat too."[46]

These speakers were clearly striking a chord in the black community. Twenty years of concerted efforts to deny the freed people the full extent of their freedoms had undoubtedly taken a toll on their ability to trust local whites. Certainly some thought that whites were too consistently opposed to black progress for prohibition not to be just one more scheme designed to hurt them. Bently further expressed this cynicism when he compared voting for the dry ticket to voting for white Republicans who did not keep patronage promises: "The nigger did the voting and the white men got the money and the offices."[47] He could easily imagine that when nomination and election time rolled around in 1886 prohibitionists would conveniently forget any "alliance" they ever had with blacks. Black antis believed the prohis' interracialism was developing a hubris in black prohibitionist leaders and inspiring a false hope in rank-and-file voters, setting up both for a big disappointment, so they cautioned voters not to believe what they were seeing or hearing. This kind of warning about race relations was undoubtedly persuasive to many, and it eventually proved to be completely accurate.

Another popular approach taken by black wets was to argue that under prohibition those who had money would still be able to get all the liquor they wanted, and only blacks and the poor would lose that freedom. Alexander Jones, James Parker, and Pledger all made this argument, which appealed to the listener's sense of obvious class inequities.[48]

Closely related to the class argument was the idea that prohibition limited personal liberty and was therefore a step backward from the independence of emancipation. "Liberty," the motto of the anti campaign, was written across their red ribbons and was emblazoned on the banners and sashes used on election day. The press more frequently reported prohis responding to this argument than it did antis using this argument with blacks. It probably was used more before black audiences than press reports indicate. Dentist Roderick Badger was one of the speakers who embraced the personal liberty argument.[49]

"The Greatest Victory for the Cause of Temperance Ever Won in America": The Campaign Climaxes

"Literally a craze," was how the *Atlanta Constitution* described the disposition of Atlantans on the eve of the election.[50] The weeks of debate were anything but dispassionate. "Men of all classes are almost wild on this question," commented one newspaper, while another editor perceived, "bad blood is brewing." Atlantans were so caught up in the campaign meetings that even theater attendance dropped to a level where DeGives Opera House operated at a loss for four weeks. On Monday, two days before the election, rival groups of blacks debated prohibition so fiercely that the police dispersed them to prevent a fight.[51] The decision about how to vote could emerge from very personal situations and hardly need show deep reflection, as Pledger's case illustrated, but James Parker's switch to the dry side, recounted earlier, was just as personal. While stumping for the wets early in the campaign, Parker had accused black ministers of being "sugared" by white prohibitionists. Reverend W. H. Tillman and other dry acquaintances of Parker's began publicly attacking his character; but the clincher came when Parker's girlfriend told him she would break up with him if he voted wet. When Parker related the story of his girl-friend's ultimatum as he publicly switched sides in Jones's tent, Reverend Yeiser spontaneously called for cheers for the girl, and they were enthusiastically given.[52] The ad hominem attacks used by both sides created predictable backlashes. Some activists argued with each other through open letters published in the press, and the press itself was openly partisan, especially the *Macon Telegraph* and the *Atlanta Journal*. However, the absence of racist attacks was *also* a hallmark of the campaign. I could locate only one example, which was when the *Telegraph* said AME Bishop Jabez P. Campbell "looks like a monkey and talks like an ass." There were efforts to sabotage the opposing campaign. For example, an anti group posing as a prohi group asked, and received, permission to meet at Ebenezer Baptist church.[53] When they printed their flyers they called it an anti meeting. To keep the people out of the church the pastor had to call for police protection.[54]

This craze came to a head on election eve, Tuesday, November 24, as scores of reporters and spectators descended on Atlanta. People began wagering on the election results. At the Kimball House the odds were three to one in favor of the wets. The headquarters of each camp swarmed with people finalizing the night's events and get-out-the-vote efforts. Because of expected disturbances at the polls, the entire police force was put on duty.[55]

The wets and drys produced dramatic spectacles to rally their troops. From seven till ten, antis paraded around town by torchlight, with several bands, and joined spectators in the "wildest enthusiasm." Perhaps as many as three thousand antis marched, carrying banners depicting empty stores, workers leaving the city, and a mother with a dying child and a doctor unable to administer brandy. The *Atlanta Constitution* claimed, "No such procession has ever been seen in Atlanta as this one." After their parade, the antis marched off to the West Point Railroad depot to enjoy a barbecue with plenty of free food and drinks. They danced into the wee hours of the morning.[56]

Meanwhile, more than 5,000 mostly black prohibitionists gathered for one last tent rally to hear speeches from Bishop Henry M. Turner, John E. Bryant, and Wesley Gaines. More than 1,200 members of the various colored prohibitionist clubs, each with its own band and banners, paraded through the streets to the cheers of onlookers on their way to the tent. Their banners proclaimed: "No more coal mines" and "We can't be bought." Before a highly charged crowd Turner reminded blacks one last time that more was at stake for them in this election than for whites. "The negroes are on trial before the country to see whether they will vote as honest, sober men or whether they can be purchased with money and mean liquor [cheers and cries of 'No! No!']." Reflecting the nascent class divisions within Black Atlanta, Turner derided the red badge wearers as lower-class, saying he had not seen even half a dozen of them "decently dressed. If I was a liquor man in Atlanta and could not get up a better crowd than that I would quit [cheers]." Drawing on the clout of the Great Emancipator himself, Turner appealed to blacks to vote so that "if Abraham Lincoln looked down from heaven he would not be ashamed of the people whom he set free [great cheering]."

Following their rally, black prohis went to their various churches to eat, listen to music, and pray till morning. The antis tried one last time to sabotage dry efforts by spreading a rumor that the opossums being provided by a black vendor to Friendship Baptist Church were really cats. The rumor caused such a stir that people not only refused to eat the meat but threatened to vote wet, the ultimate threat. The vendor was eventually able to persuade diners that it really was opossum meat. Some people stayed in their church all night while others went home to sleep. Many visited fellow members' homes to bring them to church for the evening and to make sure they did not go to the depot. The first prohibitionist historian of the election praised the brilliance of this move and revealed his prejudices at the same time by noting that "when a fellow, below the average in intelligence, got into the right crowd in his own church, surrounded by his brethren, and amidst their prayers and songs, and speeches, he was not apt to go out, when he had been provided with a good warm, substantial supper; he generally accepted the invitation to spend the night in the church." Undoubtedly the celebratory atmosphere did much to turn out the vote.[57]

On the morning of the election the various ward clubs rounded up their members and marched to the polls. Some churches marched as a group. Nearly all voters arrived with their blue or red ribbon firmly affixed, and those who arrived in groups appeared with banners, uniformed leaders, and rousing marching bands. Most voters cast their ballots according to the badge they wore, but some switched. The largest voting precinct, South Atlanta, early in the day witnessed the most colorful demonstrations. The antis left the depot 322 strong, marching behind a 20-piece band, with Moses Bently leading the way. They marched in companies, with each "officer" wearing epaulets and red sashes inscribed with "Liberty." Their grand procession arrived at the polls 15 minutes before they opened and before the time the leaders of the respective camps had agreed to go to the polls. The reason the antis came so early was that all night long, church members had been going to the depot and persuading men to come to church and vote with them, causing wet leaders to assume they had already lost about half their crowd. Moments after the wets arrived, the 52 members of the colored Third Ward Prohibition Club marched to the polls behind a band brought in from Macon just for the occasion. They were soon followed by the Reverend E. R. Carter leading the 95 members of his church's prohibition club to the polls under a large blue silk banner reading "Down with Liquor." In the North Atlanta precinct two hundred black "Kimball House Boys" marched to the polls carrying banners and flags and shouting cheers for "liberty." The press reports suggest that only blacks went to the polls in organized groups, but not all blacks went that way, or even with a badge. When the occasional black voter without a badge appeared, there was intense competition for his vote. Longtime teetotaler William Finch, one of the two black Reconstruction-era Atlanta councilmen and an ordained AME minister, urged one such voter to vote the "morality side."[58]

Prohibition women were busy all day. Some black and white women spent the day praying together in black churches while others prepared and served lunches from donated food outside polling stations to prohibition voters. Black and white voters ate in separate facilities.[59]

Given the intensity of the competition, the press was pleased to report no major "incidents." Fourteen arrests were made Tuesday night through Wednesday, including a couple of blacks arrested for selling their votes and one saloon owner for trying to buy them. Also, one person violated state law by trying to sell liquor on an election day, but these were minor events. Given all the talk of violence

Table 4—Atlanta Registration for 1884 Municipal Election and 1885 Local Option Election

	1884 Municipal Election Registration	1885 Local Option Registration by Race		1885 Total Local Option Registration
		Black	White	
South Atlanta	1,378	1,735	2,327	4,062
North Atlanta	1,695	1,399	1,752	3,151
Total Registration	3,037	3,134	4,079	7,213

Data compiled by author from "An Army of Voters," *Atlanta Constitution*, November 15, 1885.

at the polls, challenging ballots, and anticipated logistical obstacles, the election transpired more smoothly than expected. Careful planning by city election officials, last-minute "gentlemen" agreements between leaders of the two camps, and a "general good humor" among voters helped assure an orderly election day.[60]

One indicator of engagement in the election was voter registration—more citizens registered than for any previous election in Atlanta's history. More than 7,200 voters registered, compared to only 3,947 who had registered the previous year for the annual municipal elections. In addition, 1,753 people from the "country districts" of Fulton also registered (see tables 4 and 5). One reason for such a high registration was the fact that both sides eagerly paid the past due poll taxes of any black who promised to vote for their side.[61] Whites from both campaigns literally escorted black voters from the tax office to the registrar's office. Some claimed the antis were more successful with this tactic than drys, but the competition to register voters remained intense and deceitful. To reduce their costs and simultaneously undermine dry efforts, on one occasion the antis put blue badges on two hundred blacks and sent them to the prohis to pay their back taxes under false pretenses. E. R. Carter encouraged black drys to get wets to pay their back taxes but then turn and vote dry. To justify this behavior, Carter drew on the complex moral imagery of Brer Rabbit tales so familiar to his audience.

> Liquor men . . . remind me of a man who told a rabbit he could have all the peas he wanted if he would let the man eat him for breakfast when he got enough. [Laughter] So the rabbit he pitched in. He ate peas, he ate peas, and peas he ate. [Laughter] After a while the man said, "Look here, Brer Rabbit, you done eat up most a patch of peas. Come on; I want you for breakfast." The rabbit threw up his tail and said, "Good bye, Mr. Man!" [Great laughter] You let them pay your taxes, if they want to, and you do right and vote the dry ticket. [Cheers] And if any man come blowing around you about doing it, you tell him you'd have him indicted for the crime of buying votes. [Cheers and cries "We'll do it."]

Adaptations of African trickster tales that obsessed over "reversing the normal structure of power and prestige," Brer Rabbit tales reflected the moral and ethical complexities inherent in being powerless in a world full of powerful people. Always humorous, Brer Rabbit was known for using his weak body and strong mind to play the "boundary lines of what was defined as right and wrong, good and evil over against each other," and as such often pushed the limits of traditionally absolutist Christian morality. But this was a language of ethics that resonated with a people trying to make their way in a world that was so limited in opportunities and so liberal with limitations. The audience obviously loved Carter's story, but there is no way to know how many blacks played the trickster for the drys—or the

Table 5—Comparison of Atlanta and Fulton County Registration and Voting, 1885 Local Option Election

	Registered	*Voted*
Atlanta	7,213	4,927
Fulton County outside of Atlanta	1,753	2,502*
Total	8,966	7,429

Data compiled by author from "Results of Registration," *Atlanta Journal*, November 16, 1885; "The Inside of Atlanta," *Macon Telegraph*, November 27, 1885; "Dry It Is," *Atlanta Constitution*, November 26, 1885.

*This number is so much higher than the registration because of the large number of city voters who went or were taken out of the city to vote. Voting officials in conjunction with the railroads arranged this so that everyone who wanted to would get a chance to vote.

wets, for that matter. Unsurprisingly, Carter was criticized because as a Christian minister he encouraged dishonesty, but he was not Atlanta's only black minister to endorse this deception in the name of prohibition. In total, about two thousand voters paid (or had paid for them) back taxes that averaged $3 per person.[62]

The final count was a majority vote of 229 for prohibition, and blacks, not rural folk, probably gave the drys the victory. The large dry majorities in the county polling stations (550) made it look like the rural voters made the city dry. But because voters could legally vote at any polling station, as many as one thousand were transported from the city to county precincts (to alleviate precinct back-logs), and a few hundred came into the city to vote, creating a situation where more people voted in the rural parts of the county than actually lived or registered there, so county precinct totals do not reveal anything about the sentiments of county voters. The leaders of each camp had predicted from 500- to 2,000-vote margins of victory, revealing either how little they understood public sentiment or how intent they were on encouraging their side. The vote was far closer than anyone predicted and was not carried because of a strong rural prohibition vote. Based on the membership of the colored ward prohibition clubs and reports of poll watchers, prohibition leaders estimated that 1,600–1,800 black Atlantans voted for prohibition, out of a total registration of 3,134. Assuming not all regis-trants voted, this would be a clear, perhaps significant, majority of the black vote, and this would have given blacks a larger vote spread in favor of prohibition than the overall margin of victory for prohibition. If Atlanta's whites were evenly di-

Table 6—Local Option Election Results, 1885

	"Against the Sale"	*"For the Sale"*	*Totals*
Atlanta	2,303	2,624	4,927
Fulton County outside of Atlanta	1,526	976	2,502
Totals	3,829 (51.5%)	3,600 (48.5%)	7,429

Data compiled by the author from "The Inside of Atlanta," *Macon Telegraph*, November 27, 1885; and "Dry It Is," *Atlanta Constitution*, November 26, 1885.

vided, the dry margin of victory would probably have been greater, but since the margin of victory was *only* 229 it is conceivable that a very slim white majority actually voted against prohibition.[63]

As part of the white prohibitionists' get-out-the-vote efforts, the WCTU ladies made a banner for each colored prohibition ward club, and a special two-sided satin banner for the club that got the most men to vote dry. The satin banner, displayed for the first time on the eve of the election during the last tent meeting, was blue on one side and portrayed a white dove with an olive branch in its mouth, with the words "Peace on Earth, and Good Will to Man." The other side was white and had the WCTU motto: "For God, Home and Native Land." On January 15, about six weeks after the election, Reverend Virgil Norcross, pastor of the Fifth Baptist Church, presented the banner on behalf of the WCTU to the First Ward colored club, which had polled 351 voters. The club also received $100. Atlanta University's glee club rendered several selections, and E. R. Carter gave the acceptance speech, but it was the Reverend Norcross's comments that struck most people. Norcross proclaimed that black prohibitionists "erected a monument to your Christian manhood" and proved to those who denied they had a conscience that, "in the soul of the colored man, the spirit of the living God had a temple." His comments climaxed with a rousing call for interracial unity and opened him up to charges of negrophilia:

> Let us make a great pile of all unreasonable race prejudices, all political animosities, all sectional bitterness, and partisan hate, all narrowing and belittling views of public questions; then, with the sacred torch of Christian love, lighted from the pure altars of heaven, set fire to these works of the devil, and, as the

> smoke rolls up to the skies, shout "Glory to God in the highest, and on earth peace, good-will toward men."

This grandiose imagery capped off several weeks of the most conciliatory racial rhetoric and behavior Atlanta's blacks had ever witnessed from local whites—or ever would witness for many decades to come. Some blacks believed it, but others remained incredulous.[64]

"The Importance of This Event . . . Can Hardly be Overestimated": Implications of the Vote

Atlanta had been truly "torn up from the lowest foundation of her emotions," and in the immediate aftermath of the election those pent-up tensions burst forth uncontrollably.[65] Confrontations arose between the drinkers who voted for prohibition and those who voted against it. The latter believed the former had forfeited their right to drink. The day after the vote Mr. Hughes (a wet voter) accused Mr. O'Neil (a dry voter) of drinking, saying he had no right to do that since he supported prohibition. Hughes threatened and cursed him until O'Neil punched him. Hughes pulled a knife, but O'Neil threw a rock, cutting Hughes badly. The police arrested O'Neil for assault. Students at Emory College, in Oxford, three counties removed from Fulton, organized a celebratory march and were pelted so badly with rocks and rotten eggs that they had to flee for their safety. In another case, two men got into a fight because the one did not permit drys on his property. There were also reports of saloon owners not serving prohibitionists who came in for a drink after the vote. One prohibitionist, Samuel Blackburn literally went crazy. The night after the election Blackburn began ranting and raving, using threatening language toward antis, and his family, fearing he was losing his mind, called a doctor. The doctor immediately administered morphine, but when its effects wore off the next day, and he began chopping down the fence around his house, his family had him arrested. The judge pronounced Blackburn insane and sent him to the state asylum, where he died several months later. The voting even ended marital plans, as one newspaper reported that "not a few engagements and marriages were broken off" on account of the vote.[66]

The tensions also ran high between family members. The dentist brothers Robert and Roderick Badger had a falling out related to the campaign. During the campaign Robert had used Roderick's name in an "unwarrantably slanderous way," so Roderick forbade Robert from ever again speaking to him or about him. Eleven months later Roderick learned of a rumor about his character. Convinced

Robert had started it, Roderick confronted Robert on the sidewalk outside of their office. Robert denied any connection with the rumor and punched and stabbed Roderick. Roderick had his brother arrested and charged with stabbing and disorderly conduct. Campaign-related pressures had begun literally to rend the fabric of Atlantans' social life.[67]

"The Breaking Up of Party and Color Lines"

Besides generating tension on the street and in homes, the election results also produced a voluminous commentary on its political and racial implications.[68] Observers were most passionate about the campaign's implications for race relations. Atlanta was the nation's largest city to choose prohibition by plebiscite, and commentators now surmised that theoretically no large city was "safe" from prohibition when done the local option way. The national Republican Party took notice, and local prohibitionists immediately called for wet/dry reconciliation in the best interests of the city. Basically everyone had a reaction and an interpretation. Analyses of the election often attributed its outcome to the vote being kept outside of politics.[69] Some wanted to crow about the triumph of righteousness over evil, and Atlanta's "redemption."[70] However, the most discussed matter was the campaign's unprecedented violation of traditional racial etiquette and the new political lines that seem to have been drawn.

Blacks quickly took credit for the election results and, very tellingly, praised the interracial nature of the campaign as something of equal importance to the prohibition victory. Even though the AME's *Christian Recorder* praised the election results as a "mighty movement in favor of civilization and Christianity," it also called the union of whites and blacks on both sides of the issue a "hopeful sign." Beyond prohibition, blacks just wanted to be treated like men, and both wet and dry white campaigners offered black voters unprecedented levels of respect. When Richard R. Wright saw how closely the black and white women associated, he exclaimed he was "not prepared to see the ladies coming so close together . . . as they hadn't done it in Christianity." He concluded that "It was the ballot that did it; the ballot is a powerful leveler." The ballot did level but, unfortunately, not for long. Other blacks called it a "star of hope" and a "happy omen of peace and good will among all our people."[71]

Whites also noted the unprecedented interracial cooperation but drew very different conclusions. They were concerned about the ideas one could get from a campaign that "compelled deference to the negro," as one Northern paper put it. If passing prohibition meant that the races had to relate on "terms of perfect equality," another paper opined, then whites needed to be much more cautious. The week after the election, the *Atlanta Constitution* responded to Richard R. Wright's "leveling" remark with an editorial titled "Was It a Mistake?" It excused Atlanta's women for acting out of the "purest motives" but announced that, since it was now clear how blacks understood such actions, their "mistake" should "not be repeated by ladies of other Georgia cities where prohibition elections are about to be held." The blurring of the race lines encouraged by white prohibitionists unsettled many whites but also contributed to making Atlanta the nation's largest dry city.[72]

But the campaign's "most remarkable" feature lay in the fact that it *simultaneously* blurred both racial and party lines, surprising virtually all political camps: Northerners, Southerners, Democrats, and Republicans. Atlanta's black voters had been divided before, but it was new for its post-Reconstruction white electorate to be likewise so divided. For years Southern Democrats had been working to consolidate the white vote, and their Georgia successes had been magnified by the internal weakness of the state's Republican Party, which experienced almost continuous internal feuds. The fact that Democrats and Republicans, blacks and whites, joined forces to win Atlanta's local option vote challenged this seemingly unassailable Democratic hegemony, as well as the assertion of Southern whites that black voting had declined because blacks were uninterested in the franchise. Although the "Compromise of 1877" signaled the end of the national Republican Party's commitment to blacks, and what remained of the party's reforming zeal lay submerged beneath newer economic and industrial priorities, some members still dreamed of restoring the party's competitiveness in the South, and this victory encouraged them to fight harder within the party for their values.[73]

While this division of black and white votes was shocking and unsettling to many observers, one group had foreseen at least four years earlier that voting for prohibition held just this kind of potential, and they longed to see it overturn the status quo in American politics. During Frances Willard's 1881 tour of the South she attended a North Carolina temperance convention, where she said the best speaker was black, and there were 75 black delegates. After returning to Illinois she gave a speech where she declared that the "color-line has been broken from within North Carolina, as it should be, and not by foreign intervention." She optimistically asserted that a new prohibition party would arise in the South "out of the breaking up of old lines." In an 1884 speech Willard said she pined for the day when the color line would be broken in the South "by ballots from white hands and black for prohibition." A year before Atlanta's election, NTS official Theodore Cuyler ended his opposition to the Prohibition Party and signed an open letter with NTS secretary J. N. Stearns and others, which included the following assertion: "A National Prohibition party will end the 'solid South' and 'solid North' in our politics. Prohibition made the dominant issue will divide the negro and the white vote in the South, and will force a redivision of the voters in the North. . . . Divide the negro vote, and *it will be counted."*

Other writers made similar predictions about the effect that prohibition voting could have on race relations and the suppression of the black vote. These were certainly radical individuals for their day. They envisioned prohibition producing a threefold positive fallout: (1) strengthening the Republican Party in the South, (2) ending the fraud that effectively disfranchised blacks, even though they legally could vote, and (3) reuniting all "moral" Americans around another reform crusade roughly comparable to abolitionism. At a time of declining national interest in the civil rights of blacks, the last thing party leaders were interested in doing was sacrificing the national party structure to guarantee black voting rights. The plan was never seriously considered by the most influential political leaders, but Atlanta's election was an "I told you so" moment for these prohibition radicals.[74]

In the wake of the vote other activists belatedly "discovered" this power of prohibition that others had anticipated. One New York editor said the outcome of Atlanta's local option vote demonstrated that "The true solution of the Negro problem (and there is such a problem) is to so reorganize parties that the Negro vote and the white vote of the South will be divided between the two parties." The editor went on to claim that prohibition was the *only* issue that could reshape Southern politics, and he might have been right, at least for a brief moment in the mid-1880s. Another Northern editor proclaimed that it was obvious blacks cared about the franchise, but certain "ordinary and needful" measures were necessary to ensure a large black turnout. Perhaps the editor was referencing the paying of back taxes, although he did not say.[75]

But it was not just journalists and activists who took note of Atlanta's blurred color lines. The Republican Party leadership began to get nervous. In the 1884 presidential election the Prohibition Party's vote tally had increased 1,386 percent over 1880. While that only represented an increase from 0.1 percent to 1.5 percent of the popular vote, when added to the Atlanta victory 12 months later, it raised some eyebrows. These events emboldened the already disgruntled and marginalized Northern prohibitionists within the party. They now made the case more forcefully that a prohibition plank could simultaneously revitalize the party in the South and ensure blacks' voting rights. The following August, James G. Blaine, former presidential nominee and the most prominent Republican of the 1880s, announced that he was considering urging the national party to add a prohibition plank to its next platform because of its potential to break the solid Democratic South. As it turned out, Blaine never did support prohibition,[76] but he was not alone in his ruminations. The following month the *Atlanta Constitution* reported that a majority of Republican senators and "many" congressmen supported the idea. Among others, a *Washington Post* editorial and an independent writer in Bishop Turner's *Southern Recorder* both predicted that the Republicans would soon have to decide whether to endorse prohibition. The *Post* further projected that whatever decision the party made, large numbers of Republicans would be upset, and the results from a "vote-getting standpoint" could only be "bad." The urgency of this matter was only exacerbated by some black clergy who were encouraging blacks to vote for the Prohibition Party. One black Texas clergyman and state legislator said he thought prohibition sentiment was so strong among the better classes of blacks that they would be willing to "break down" both political parties to create prohibition in Texas.[77]

All this talk, combined with the inaction of party leaders, resulted in several northern and western Republicans organizing the Anti-Saloon Republican National Committee in the spring of 1887. They sought, albeit unsuccessfully, to pressure the national party to insert a "declaration of hostility to the saloon" plank in its platform. The Committee argued that a clear anti-saloon statement that was purposely vague about the method of implementation would give the Republican Party a "fighting chance" in Southern states lacking a "large black belt, and secure three or four for the republican column this year." The group did not seek a plank endorsing national constitutional prohibition; rather, it wanted the national party to follow the lead of the ten state Republican parties that were already calling for the submission of prohibition to popular votes. In a half-hearted nod to the prohibition lobby and as the last act of platform writing during the 1888 convention, Republicans added a mildly worded clause declaring their support for "all wise and well directed" temperance efforts. The plank remained through the 1896 platform. For a short while following Atlanta's vote, and largely inspired by it, a vocal group of Republicans argued that the right type of prohibition endorsement could give the party the edge in the South and thus return it to dominance over the Democrats. Their arguments fell on deaf ears.[78]

The prohibition victory also reverberated through local Atlanta politics. Observers wondered if voters would vote for municipal candidates based on their prohibition stance, as reformers had sometimes done in other places. Some argued that this was the best way to guarantee prohibition's enforcement, but others condemned this as "dragging prohibition into politics." Opponents feared that this type of voting might alter local Democratic hegemony and, if successful, spread to other places. The *New York Times* rejoiced in the possible effects of prohibition spilling over into Georgia politics, which it said "seemed certain": "It will doubtless help the process of breaking up the old political associations, based upon national issues of a past generation, and of effacing the color line in politics. So far it cannot fail to have a beneficial effect." But newspaper editors in Baltimore and Augusta perceptively assured readers that prohibition would never undermine the strength of "the Democracy," as the Democratic Party was often called.[79]

In a matter of days the facts began to support the hunches of Southern editors. Six days after the local option vote the city held its annual municipal elections, and Atlantans resorted to the common approach of "keeping prohibition out of politics." First of all, there was very little interest in voting for city officials. Only 66 percent of the whites and 38 percent of the blacks who had registered for the local option vote registered for the municipal elections. White prohibitionists called for carrying the "temperance banner high above politics," which meant supporting the slate of candidates that had been nominated six weeks earlier and not opposing the anti-prohibitionists among the nominees. Against the warnings of some leaders but in line with the practices of other places that had instituted prohibition by local option, Atlantans by an overwhelming majority elected a "fusion" ticket, and it included several city officials who were personally opposed to prohibition. The ticket had so many antis (a slim majority) on it that the *Macon Telegraph* announced that the "honor of the victory to-day rests with the anti-prohibitionists" and "conservative" prohibitionists. White prohibitionists accepted anti-prohibitionist municipal leaders because they assumed that once they took the oath of office they would feel bound to execute the law whether or not they agreed with it. White prohibitionist leaders used the election to salve intra-racial divisions created by the local option campaign. How these leaders, and men chosen in subsequent elections during prohibition, implemented the law and treated black residents would greatly impact black Atlantans' perception of prohibition.[80]

Why did prohibition win in Atlanta in 1885? A major reason was that so many African Americans voted for it. Atlanta had experienced a historically unique convergence of ideologies, movements, and resources. By December 1885, a well-informed and impartial observer might reasonably have identified four plausible explanations for the outcome of Atlanta's election and for the extent of black support for prohibition.

Blacks voted for prohibition to the degree they did partly because of the 20 years of temperance work by Northern evangelicals. Also, the relatively high social status of the clergy, combined with their exceptionally cohesive united front, was not unimportant. Early in the campaign the *Weekly Sentinel* (a black paper from Augusta) astutely discerned that two types of people supported prohibition, those acting on "principle" and those on "reputation." By "reputation" the writer meant a concern with being perceived as respectable. In 1885 Black Atlanta, "respectable" was still heavily defined by the culture brought by evangelical Northerners and preached by the clergy. Even Reverend J. G. Yeiser, who was accused of frequenting saloons and running up unpaid tabs, campaigned for prohibition.

Only one black preacher joined the antis' campaign. The truth is, for some—perhaps many?—African American voters, framing this as a moral issue was sufficiently persuasive.[81]

The relative influence of Northern evangelical culture was magnified in 1880s Black Atlanta because of the absence of organized and respected alternate routes to success and respectability. Secular and non-evangelical freedmen's aid societies never established schools in Atlanta. These societies existed only briefly following emancipation, but they resolutely omitted all religious instruction from their schools, thus offering a different model for "uplift" than evangelical schools run by such organizations as the AMA and ABHMS. Also, Black Atlanta had yet to develop a self-conscious entrepreneurial class whose rise to prominence occurred independent of reform nexus culture. Such a "petit bourgeoisie" class did eventually develop in Black Atlanta, but it would take 10 to 15 more years before it coalesced and offered an alternative route to the better classes. When this group did find its voice in the early 1900s, it espoused a much more pragmatic approach to social, political, and racial matters than those under the influence of the reform nexus organizations.

Of course the mass of black voters already embraced a pragmatic approach to politics, and in 1885 it manifested itself by positively responding to promises (and examples) of better race relations from prohibitionists, which were just too compelling to ignore. The success of this appeal reflected the harsh reality of Southern race relations. No matter how they voted, most black Atlantans at least hoped that their vote would yield better race relations.

The fourth major element of the dry victory would have to be the quantity and quality of the resources and leadership white prohibitionist activists brought to the campaign. Traditional white prohibitionist organizations like the WCTU and the Templars effectively merged their efforts with New South spokesmen, people for whom prohibition was just one of many concerns. But white leaders' efforts were not focused on, nor successful with, white voters. Historian Joe Coker has persuasively argued that several deeply rooted religious and cultural traditions had yet to be inverted or co-opted by prohibitionists before the masses of Southern white evangelicals could accept their cause; that would take almost 20 more years. In the 1880s, white prohibitionists seem to have brought more resources and enthusiasm to the campaign than they did white votes, but as far as black voters were concerned, they produced a better "get-out-the-vote" effort than the wets. In the end, an ideal alignment of factors had set up Atlanta for an unprecedented two-year "dry" experiment. Some would be surprised by the results; some would not.

Oh, come, let your manhood be plighted,
To help us again to restore
The Freedom with Virtue united
Our forefathers brought to the shore;
When law never licensed temptation,
And Conscience to Right was so true;
Oh, bring back those days to the nation
That gave us the Red, White and Blue.
—"For Home and the Red, White, and Blue," first stanza

CHAPTER 6

The "Dry" Years, 1885–1887

O the conflict now is past, we have gained the day at last,
And we celebrate a glorious victory;
Let us heartily rejoice, and with thankful heart and voice
Praise the Lord whose arm has made His people free.

All the skirmishing is done, and the victory is won,
And a million homes with happiness are bright;
All the sorrowing is o'er, drink will crush their lives no more,
Praise the Lord for giving triumph to the Right.
—"The Conflict Is Past," first and second stanzas

From December 1885 to November 1887 Atlanta was the nation's largest "dry" city. Hubris-filled prohibitionists announced that their slim electoral victory guaranteed sufficient public support for prohibition's enforcement. In reality, voters and the newly elected city officials were so divided that enforcement was undermined every step of the way. It took almost a full year for the city to close all legal venues for selling liquor, and even then alcohol was still accessible to any Atlantan who wanted it. July 1886 was widely touted as the "real" beginning of Atlanta's experiment because all the city's saloons closed on June 30. Prohibitionists in the government were almost constantly under attack from anti-prohibitionists and from other prohibitionists who thought they were either too strict or too lenient in enforcing the law.[1]

The two-year experiment revealed that all along there had been two types of black prohibitionist voters in 1885: the opportunistic and the principled. Opportunistic prohibitionists had three basic characteristics. First, they viewed a vote for prohibition as a means to some other end. Their goal might be the promise of a government job or increased political leverage for black voters in city politics. Second, they understood temperance and prohibition as fundamentally different things. The former was apolitical, a personal matter, while the latter was a political idea that should be treated like other political issues, something over which to negotiate, bargain, and compromise and ultimately accept or reject based on pragmatic considerations. Third, they had little to no contact with reform nexus organizations.

Principled prohibitionists, on the other hand, conflated temperance and prohibition, accusing everyone opposed to prohibition of being *for* whiskey, *for* drunkenness, or *for* poverty. Even if they did not fully believe their own campaign rhetoric, their words nonetheless reflected their deep commitment to ridding society of liquor. Principled prohibitionists were likely to be teetotaling clergy or members of fraternal temperance organizations with relatively strong connections to reform nexus organizations. They assumed prohibition would lead to decreased drinking by removing the temptation of the saloon, which could only benefit blacks, most of whom were very poor. Even more importantly, principled prohibitionists viewed the reform as primarily a moral issue, and as such, no more subject to compromise than any other moral issue.

Opportunistic prohibitionists supported or opposed prohibition based on their view of what was the best tactical move for black people in terms of politics or race relations. Prohibition turned out to be a great disappointment to these men; they felt betrayed. Typical of the opportunistic prohibitionists was the aspiring Republican politician Jackson McHenry. Although he was a member of an AME church, he had received no formal education. In 1885 McHenry supported prohibition because of the benefits to the race he was sure it would bring. But after he witnessed the first few months of prohibition in 1886 he announced that the prohibition/anti-prohibition debate was a white man's debate that blacks should ignore. Then, further observations led him to reverse himself again, and he served as a prohibitionist ward leader during the 1887 campaign. Bishop Turner praised him as a "staunch advocate" of ending the rum traffic. Among the other black leaders who changed their position on prohibition were mailman James B. Parker, discussed in the last chapter; barber and lunchroom owner Moses Bently; and *Weekly Defiance* editor Alonzo W. Burnett. Bently and Burnett both became drys in time for the 1887 campaign. Not products of Atlanta's missionary schools, these four men's decision making seemed more influenced by the situational ethics of African thought than by unchanging Christian principles.[2]

The smaller group of principled prohibitionists did not vote dry because of some political quid pro quo but because of a deeply held belief that prohibition was the next logical step following their commitment to total abstinence. Through their relationship with reform nexus institutions they became vested in the re-ligio-cultural system that birthed and conflated temperance and prohibition, so they remained unmoved by the contradictions of prohibition or the hypocrisy of white drys. Bishop Turner, who perceived that prohibition was in America's future, believed that if blacks wanted to become fully accepted in white society they had no option but to move in the direction the nation was moving, namely, toward prohibition. Smith W. Easley, Reverend Wesley J. Gaines, Reverend E. R. Carter, and Bishop Henry M. Turner are representative of this group.

"A Put-Up Job": The Contradictions of Prohibition

Prohibition means banning the sale of alcoholic beverages, and so strictly speaking Atlanta never had total prohibition.[3] The General Local Option Law, while banning the sale of any beverage "which if drank to excess will produce in-toxication," exempted domestic wines. At the time of the 1885 election people generally expected the law to close saloons because it prohibited the sale of dis-tilled spirits by the drink, but previously issued liquor licenses had to be honored and this delayed prohibition for many months. The inherent complexity and in-evitable contradictions arising from this state of affairs quickly soured blacks on prohibition.

Legal impediments delayed the introduction of prohibition until July 1, 1886, but even then all the liquor venues the law meant to shut down did not close un-til late October 1886. Immediately following the election, anti-prohibitionists mounted a legal challenge to the results, which was finally settled in favor of the prohibitionists on Christmas Eve. In addition, the city granted 12-month business licenses, and most retail liquor licenses took effect on July 1. There were about 100 saloons in Atlanta, but only about 30 closed down within three months of the vote. Upholding its obligation to these license holders, the city announced that current saloons could remain in business until their licenses expired on June 30, 1886. Although "wine rooms" were legal, only a few saloon owners announced plans to operate them after July 1; most thought they would be unprofitable. Those who purchased a wine room license contested the legal definition of "domestic" wines. Because Georgia's wine producers pressured the legislature to create the wine loophole, some saloon owners thought they could only sell wines produced in Georgia. However, the city government announced that in accordance with recent judicial decisions it would define "domestic" to include wine produced in any state of the union. The wine room operators also announced that they would sell tobacco products and non-alcoholic "temperance drinks," such as lemonade.[4]

Atlanta also had one brewery, the Atlanta City Brewery. The brewery announced that it would continue making and selling beer as usual. The brewery sold beer in large quantities by delivering directly to homes. To close the doors of the $150,000 facility, it explained, would cause a property devaluation of approximately 90 percent. Its legal counsel advised that closing the brewery would amount to the unconstitutional seizure of property without "due process," conveniently exploiting a clause in the otherwise despised Reconstruction-era Fourteenth Amendment. On July 1, when Atlanta's saloons finally closed, it appeared that wine and beer would be sold indefinitely.[5]

In addition to saloons and breweries, Atlantans could also continue to purchase alcohol at pharmacies, which the law did not close. In addition to providing alcohol in prescriptions, pharmacists also sold other alcohol-containing products such as bay rum, which was a popular ingredient for barbecuing. One pharmacist reported a significant increase in demand for bay rum after prohibition began, but he assured the reporter that because of the responsibility resting on a man in his position he did not sell it to known drunkards.[6]

July 1, 1886: "Real" Prohibition Begins

The press gave detailed reports on the last days and hours of wet Atlanta and the first days of dry Atlanta. At the end of June people bought thousands of jugs that saloons filled with their favorite distilled beverage. "Respectable" white businessmen who wanted to stock up but did not want to be discovered sent black employees to purchase their liquor. On the last night, the faithful—as well as the nostalgic—filled the saloons until barkeepers gave the truly "last call" and darkened the lights at midnight. Although local papers claimed it was a rather peaceful night in the city's watering holes, the *Augusta Chronicle*, less concerned with boosting Atlanta, suggested it may have been a more raucous evening. The *Chronicle* reported that it was "safe to say there are more drunken men in Atlanta to-night than any night in a year past." July 1 and 2 contrasted sharply with June 30 because the only sounds emerging from saloons were those of workmen breaking down counters and shelving.[7]

The contradictions and hypocrisy of "dry" Atlanta became apparent even before July 1. On June 30 the *New York Sun* published a report claiming that Mayor Henry Hillyer, an outspoken prohibitionist, was among those who had procured their own personal barrel of whiskey in the days leading up to prohibition. The rumor caused the NTS's J. N. Stearns to write James Thrower, asking for an explanation. Thrower passed the letter on to Hillyer, who called it a "mere canard," and the *Atlanta Constitution* published the story at Thrower's request. Despite Thrower's attempt to squelch the rumor, the moral clarity of the prohibition experiment and

Fig. 23—City Brewery (c. 1890). Kenan Research Center at the Atlanta History Center

its leadership had been clouded. This would not be forgotten by anti leaders over a year later.[8]

But the contradictions of prohibition soon transcended the personal and symbolic. Those with the financial means regularly found legal and quasi-legal methods for buying liquor, while blacks and poor whites were forced into illegal venues. On July 1 the *Atlanta Journal* reported that the wholesale liquor dealers received their licenses from the county instead of the city, and that those licenses did not expire until August or later. By the end of the first week of July one of the proprietors of the famed Kimball House saloon welcomed into partnership Miles J. Mabry, an individual whose county quart license (the minimum wholesale volume) did not expire until October 9. Added to its recently acquired wine room license, the Kimball House's quart license shored up business from its white-only clientele, but customers were not permitted to consume their whiskey on the premises, although they could drink wine there. Before long, nine holders of quart licenses surfaced. Shortly afterward the police began filing charges against some of them for allowing customers to drink on the premises, including one saloon that sold quart measures in open buckets, allowing drinkers to pass them around until they were empty. The difficulties of enforcing prohibition immediately became apparent. The last quart license finally expired on October 26.

Although the police began tracking the Atlanta Brewing Company's sales almost immediately, it took until late October before the right combination of legal and political maneuverings successfully closed its doors. Although the *Atlanta Constitution* claimed that prohibition was well enforced in the early weeks after July 1, the *Macon Telegraph* correctly reported that beer and whiskey by the quart could "be had on all sides" for several more months in "dry" Atlanta.[9]

Although subject to repeated police investigations, prosecutions, and sporadic criticism from prohibitionists, wine rooms remained open after October 1886. Within four months after prohibition began, complaints arose about the 30-plus rooms in the city, because the word on the street was that drinks other than wine could be obtained there. Secret codes, gestures, and lists evolved to allow "regular" customers surreptitiously to purchase liquor and prevented detectives and others from procuring it. Because stories got out that wine rooms mixed wine with various types of liquor but still called it "wine," a call spread for the authorities to submit wine room beverages to chemical analyses. Several fights also broke

Fig. 24—City Brewery's interracial workforce (c. 1890). Kenan Research Center at the Atlanta History Center

out in wine rooms, giving them an increasingly saloon-like aura. By the fall of 1886 one city official openly admitted that, since wine rooms were essentially the same as saloons, prohibition was a failure. "A man can go into one of them and get as drunk as he could when we had saloons and straight liquor."

Critics called for indirectly outlawing wine rooms by creating a prohibitive license fee. This proposal divided prohibitionists, however, because some claimed that the original law had not been sufficiently tested and that the proposal unfairly altered the local option bill approved by the people. In December 1886, state representative Dr. Latimer Felton submitted a bill to the legislature for a $10,000 state wine room license fee. Fulton County's representatives opposed the bill and the legislature rejected it. As the pressure on wine room proprietors increased, they decided as a group to stop permitting customers to drink on the premises, hoping that self-regulation might undermine the movement for the $10,000 license. But Felton resubmitted his bill in 1887, and it passed. The governor signed it into law in September. However, license holders were allowed to remain open until their licenses expired in January 1888. By that time Fulton County voters had overturned prohibition, making the bill's provisions moot.[10]

Those who did not drink in public could purchase whiskey to consume at home through agents for companies based in wet Georgia towns such as Augusta, Griffin, Gainesville, and Macon. Atlantans were technically supposed to travel to these cities to make their purchase, but agents crisscrossed Atlanta taking orders for out-of-town liquor companies. Hundreds of jugs containing one or more gallons of whiskey arrived in Atlanta daily by train. Sometimes Atlantans participated in this "jug trade," as it was called, in a group, buying a ten-gallon barrel and dividing it among themselves. They formed clubs in which they could communally enjoy the liquor they had collectively purchased. Few blacks seem to have purchased liquor jointly, probably because bulk purchases were cost prohibitive.[11]

Most blacks and poorer whites who wanted liquor during prohibition had two options: to buy some form of alcohol from a pharmacist or get it illegally from "blind tigers."[12] "Blind tigers" referred not only to the person doing the selling but also to the business itself; thus some were said to "run a blind tiger." Blind tiger whiskey was frequently a cheap, mixed form of whiskey sometimes supplied by moonshiners. There were plenty of both black and white blind tigers, and they appeared immediately after prohibition began. On July 2 an arrested drunk claimed to have purchased his liquor from a blind tiger, but the first police prosecution of blind tigers came on July 20, when they charged four people with running blind tigers. Tellingly, the *Atlanta Constitution* gave the most attention to Lucy McCall, a 16-year-old black girl charged with being a tiger. The paper's editor indicted her in the public's eye with the article title "A Girl Runs a Blind Tiger," only to have the judge exonerate her the following day, charging her instead with furnishing liquor to minors, which was a violation of a pre-prohibition law. During the nine months between July 1886 and March 1887, 43 separate times white individuals were charged with illegally selling liquor, and 13 times blacks were so charged. Some individuals were charged repeatedly, and several charges were dismissed for insufficient evidence. One controversial tactic the police developed to convict blind tigers was to arrest individuals who possessed whiskey to use them as witnesses against their provider, but it is not clear that this tactic increased conviction rates.[13]

It did not take long for blacks to respond to the obvious contradictions of prohibition, namely, that whites retained legal access to liquor but blacks had to use primarily illegal means. Within two weeks of the "official" start of prohibition, the *Atlanta Constitution* candidly reported that many blacks "all over the city . . . announced loudly their belief" that prohibition had been a trick on them. They said the fact that the Kimball House and Big Bonanza saloons only sold liquor to whites proved prohibition was purposely designed to keep liquor from blacks. The most pithy indictment came from an unidentified man who declared, "Prohibition's a put up job by the democrats and these high-hat negro preachers." The only attempt at an organized black response to prohibition came with the municipal elections in October. Several leaders gathered to nominate black candidates for city council. Atlanta's blacks rarely nominated their own slate of candidates, but the tensions between white antis and prohis and the black sense of betrayal caused some to question the value of interracial cooperation. During their meeting several speakers spoke out angrily against both Democrats and white prohibitionists, expressing a strong sentiment that blacks should support their own candidates in the interests of the race. Former prohibitionist leader Jackson McHenry announced that he had only supported the drys out of a sense of spite, because blacks had been consistently denied retail liquor licenses and he wanted to deny the same to whites. He called on others to ignore the prohibition/anti-prohibition debate because it was only an attempt to use blacks. No preachers spoke at this meeting, suggesting that some secular leaders sought to distance themselves from the clergy and provide an alternative model of black leadership.[14]

Crime and Prohibition

But what about the much ballyhooed reduction in crime and public drunkenness predicted by prohibitionists in all corners of the country? Were the jails emptied and did the judges have to cancel court sessions? While most of the Police Court dockets from the eighties are nonexistent, complete records for the months of July 1886–March 1887 still exist. While these do not allow a pre and post comparison, one can see trends during the "real" prohibition period, some of which are almost stunning. The first thing the data show over time was a decline in the total number of individuals charged by the court, from the high to mid-400s per month to the low 300s per month. The extent to which this might have been a direct result of prohibition cannot be determined, but it is true that the police charged decreasing numbers of persons with crime as the months passed. While that statistic might seem favorable to the drys, the percentage of people charged with drunkenness actually showed no long-term decline. In fact, the percentage of charges for public drunkenness increased and then decreased, ending at about the same place—the low 20 percent range—where it began. Prohibition seemed to do little to keep alcohol from those who wanted it.

But the most striking statistic from the Police Court Docket is the percentage of charges, by race, for public drunkenness. As graph 3 shows, throughout this period, a much higher percentage of whites were arrested for public drunkenness than blacks. Monthly arrests for public drunkenness as a percentage of total white arrests ranged from three to almost seven times higher than that for blacks. While never more than one-fifth of black arrests were for drunkenness, for whites that number was never less than one-third, and more than once approached two-thirds. For all the difficulties blacks had with law enforcement officers and for all the prejudice whites harbored against them, relative to whites blacks either drank more moderately or they more frequently drank at home. Of all things that might be said of Atlanta's streets, one could not say they were full of drunken blacks. This relative lack of black public drunkenness might account for the lack of "black beast" rhetoric, which characterized Atlanta's and the South's prohibition discourse by the early 1900s. There likely was not even a modicum of reality for people to exploit. In light of this data and the argument about blacks and alcohol presented in chapter two, it appears that white leaders such as Henry Grady and NTS president Theodore Cuyler, who claimed blacks needed prohibition because of their "special weakness" for liquor and the saloon, only revealed their prejudices and ignorance and the gulf that existed between the races.[15]

A Return to the Status Quo: Race Relations in Dry Atlanta

Compounding the contradictions of prohibition itself was the frustration and disillusionment experienced when race relations with prohibitionists quickly returned to their pre-campaign standards of inequity and exclusion in the interest of white supremacy. Blacks witnessed this in three areas: politics, religion, and law enforcement. Although blacks' support for prohibition gave them marginally more influence in the 1886 municipal elections than they had ever had before,

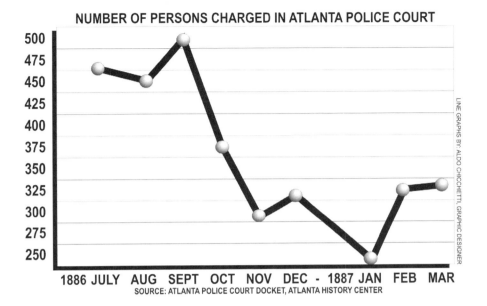

NUMBER OF PERSONS CHARGED IN ATLANTA POLICE COURT

SOURCE: ATLANTA POLICE COURT DOCKET, ATLANTA HISTORY CENTER

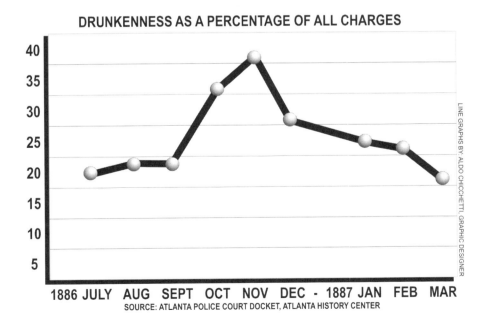

DRUNKENNESS AS A PERCENTAGE OF ALL CHARGES

SOURCE: ATLANTA POLICE COURT DOCKET, ATLANTA HISTORY CENTER

both groups of whites continued to prevent blacks from exercising any real political power. It was soon evident that white prohibitionists had only countenanced
blurring the lines of racial etiquette for the short-term goal of gaining votes. No
real change of heart had occurred, as some blacks had hoped and some whites had
feared. The first evidence that white Atlantans had no intention of making real
changes in the status quo of race relations came with the city's fall 1886 elections.

Atlanta had not had a two-party political system since the early seventies. After the Republican Party collapsed, a variety of forces combined to destroy the
coalition that was the Democratic Party. For several years municipal candidates
had presented themselves directly to the citizens without party affiliation. Elites
began complaining that this free-for-all system catered to the lower classes too
much and encouraged the election of poorly qualified individuals. Beginning in
1884 Atlanta's business and professional elites reformed the election process to
assure that the city's "best people" (themselves) would be elected and that there
would be minimal opposition to their candidacies. The new process began with
a call for a mass citizens' meeting to select a committee that contained ward and
at-large members. This committee then nominated a "Citizen's Ticket" for councilmen, aldermen, and the mayoralty. The committee reported back at a second

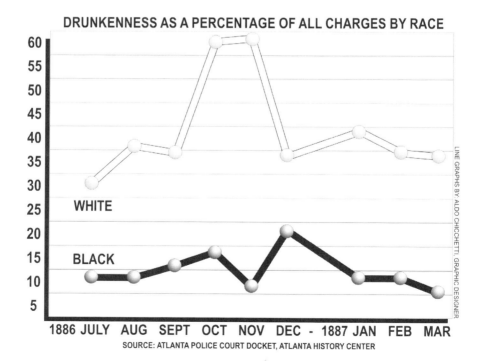

SOURCE: ATLANTA POLICE COURT DOCKET, ATLANTA HISTORY CENTER

mass meeting, which then held a discussion and a ratifying vote. The hope was to gain widespread support for the ticket while carefully managing the selection of candidates, but local representatives of the Knights of Labor frequently protested the lack of workingmen on the ballot and sometimes nominated a competing slate of candidates. Blacks, too, sometimes nominated their own candidates. On several occasions white workers unsuccessfully sought to create an alliance with blacks. With the exception of 1890, Atlantans used the citizens' mass meeting process through the 1891 elections. When combined with the issue of prohibition, this process empowered blacks to a greater degree than anything else in Atlanta city politics to that time. Nevertheless, blacks still could not elect their own to city government.

The first citizens' mass meeting held during prohibition occurred on October 22, 1886. The chair announced the intention to unite all Atlantans behind one municipal ticket, regardless of how candidates stood on the issue of prohibition. This meeting convened several days after blacks had held their own separate nominating convention, but several blacks, including Reverend E. R. Carter and Reverend Wesley Gaines, *Weekly Defiance* publisher Alonzo W. Burnett, and lunchroom owner Moses Bently, attended this meeting. The continuing animosity between the prohi and anti camps caused the meeting leaders to divide the crowd into prohibition and anti-prohibition meetings so each group could select 25 men for the nominating committee.[16]

In the prohi meeting speakers stressed the necessity of cooperating with the antis and the importance of nominating "conservative" men. During the selection process one individual reminded the group how important blacks had been during the local option campaign and suggested that they should have some representation on the committee. Others agreed, so they put Reverend Carter and Reverend Gaines on the committee.[17] This was the first time blacks had served on a nominating committee, and although they continued to serve in subsequent years they were never able to put a black man on the ticket.

Things were different in the anti committee meeting. The antis were militant, even hostile, toward the prohibitionists and dismissive toward blacks. The first speaker predicted that the bipartisan 50-member committee would not be able to agree on a slate of candidates and urged the antis not to make any concessions to the "fanatics." Others argued, however, that since their side had enough public support to win on their own, if the cooperative effort failed they could afford, for the sake of the city's unity, to try to be conciliatory. As blacks saw no interest in including them in the discussion or on the committee, they began leaving the meeting. When messengers from the prohi meeting arrived and read their list of committee members, the antis responded with derisive "shouts of laughter." But the remaining black antis at the meeting noticed that the prohibitionists had included two black members, and Moses Bently asked for a similar addition, warning that otherwise blacks might vote dry. Two members agreed to resign, and Moses Bently and Alonzo Burnett were chosen to replace them.[18]

After two consecutive nights of wrangling, the equally divided committee of 50 finally produced a compromise slate of candidates known as the "fusion" Citizen's Ticket. It was so evenly divided that both prohibitionists and antis claimed victory. A "balance of power" between the two camps was ostensibly created by nominating a wet mayor and a dry majority for the city council. Seeking public ratification, the committee presented the slate at a raucous public meeting on November 4. Several men addressed the crowd, but attempts by three blacks—the tailor William Finch, mail carrier C. C. Wimbish, and editor William Pledger—to speak were ignored. Speakers pleaded with the audience not only to accept the slate as given but to accept the spirit of compromise that it represented. Responding to a call to replace two prohibitionists with antis, Henry Grady argued that that would "cause a renewed fight among the citizens of Atlanta," the very thing the "best" white Atlantans wanted to avoid at all costs. One man shouted out from the crowd, "Did the colored men on the committee of fifty ask for anything?" When the answer "no" came back from a white committee member, people applauded, and several cried out, "The colored men are for Atlanta! They don't want a division among the people!" It may or may not have been true that the blacks asked for nothing, but what is certain is that whites, whether prohibitionists or anti-prohibitionists, refused to nominate blacks for elective office. That snub helps explain why blacks were so unexcited about the election. Only 471 blacks registered (16.5% of the total), and certainly less than that voted. The inclusion of blacks in the nominating committee caused the most prominent blacks to support the Citizen's Ticket, and none of the independently nominated black candidates polled even three hundred votes.[19]

Like other municipal elections in the 1880s, the 1886 vote stirred little excitement, but more importantly for the city's elites, it stirred little opposition.[20] The Citizen's Ticket won a large majority of both white and black votes, but only 20 percent of eligible voters bothered to register. The *Atlanta Journal,* which opposed the committee's choice for mayor, supported the ticket anyway, candidly commenting that "From a personal standpoint the ticket is probably acceptable as a whole to very few citizens, but it must be admitted that with the very pronounced views entertained by each member of the committee the result of their labors is commendable . . . the interests of the city cannot suffer at their hands." The ideas that the rule of "conservative" men was best for Atlanta and that both sides needed to compromise to heal the division over prohibition, served the cause of white supremacy not the best interests of all Atlantans.[21]

Social relations between the races also reverted to old patterns in religious affairs. In the spring of 1887 Bishop Turner claimed that every time he returned to Atlanta from a trip he received complaints that blacks were not being treated respectfully at white religious meetings. One example occurred on March 13 when two white Clark University teachers took ten of their black female students to a tent revival held by traveling evangelist Reverend J. L. Tillman. The teachers and students all sat together undisturbed until an usher asked the students to move to empty seats in the colored section because the white seats were all taken and several white ladies had no seats. The teachers asked what difference color made and refused to let the girls move. The usher brought in a policeman, who explained that Tillman did not want the races sitting together. The whole Clark group left the service in protest, while reminding the usher and the officer that they had been allowed to sit together when they attended Sam Jones's tent meetings. Unfazed, the policeman reminded them that "In this section we have nothing like social equality and never will, in church or out of church." Both Sam Jones and Sam Small put in appearances during Tillman's revival, giving their blessing to the event, and were apparently indifferent to the return of segregated seating.[22]

The third area of race relations resistant to change was law enforcement. On at least two occasions before 1887 black Atlantans had sought to be employed on the police force, only to be ignored. Most blacks would have been happy with black police officers in black neighborhoods, as some other Southern cities permitted, but the fact that all police officers legally had authority over any citizen made even that idea anathema to white Atlantans. In 1887 the Board of Police Commissioners consisted of a slim majority of prohibitionists, and during its biannual restructuring the small majority removed anti-prohibitionist officers deemed to be too lax in their enforcement of prohibition. This action elicited a firestorm of criticism from anti-prohibitionists, who believed the commissioners exhibited a lack of "good faith." Some blacks thought the existence of a prohibitionist majority on the Board of Police Commissioners created an ideal opportunity for them to secure a place on the police force. In March 1887 prohibitionists Jim Palmer and James Parker applied, as well as W. A. Pledger, even though he had opposed prohibition. Blacks felt they were owed positions on the police force, and white prohis knew they would need black support if another prohibition referendum occurred in the fall. But the political and racial implications of prohibitionists empowering Atlanta's blacks with police uniforms and badges were enormous. The antis made it known that if the police commissioners appointed black officers they would charge prohibitionists with being fanatics who had overturned Atlanta's entire system of race relations. Even though James Parker claimed prohibitionists promised him a police position as payoff for his support in the 1885 election, he, along with the other two black candidates, abruptly withdrew their applications. Parker wrote to the *Atlanta Constitution* that he withdrew because of the "racket" that had been made over his application and to prevent the anti-prohibitionists from making an issue out of his candidacy. But the *Macon Telegraph* reported that Parker was telling people around town that he had accepted a $200 payoff to withdraw his application. When Parker switched to the prohibitionist side during the 1885 campaign he claimed that previously the antis had been paying him off, and that he switched because he was losing his "better class" of black friends and his female companion had threatened to break up with him. Whatever really happened in the election and with his police application, both cases clearly reveal his keen-witted pragmatism. He was not interested in leading any "crusade." The mechanics of white supremacy often required blacks to test its boundaries and to employ multiple approaches to find cracks in the system.[23]

One of the reasons blacks were so determined to get on the police force (they tried again in 1889) was the poor treatment they received from white police officers. Southerners designed postbellum urban policing to control the black population. As in other Southern cities, Atlanta's police served as what historian Howard Rabinowitz called the "first line of defense" against the freed people and their supposed proclivity to disturb the peace of the city through petty robbery, vagrancy, and general "disorderly conduct." Atlanta's police arrested more people on the catch-all charge of "disorderly conduct" than any other single charge. As discussed earlier, incidents of excessive force against blacks were not uncommon, and blacks rarely had any recourse. When it came to enforcing prohibition, a particularly egregious example of disregard for black citizens' rights stands out. Three detectives who had been assigned to work on cases of prohibition violation suspected an older freedman named Giles Moore of being a blind tiger. He lived in his own house, which he said was just outside the city limits but the detectives thought was within the city limits. On Saturday, April 2, 1887, the detectives searched his house for liquor and, in the process, admitted they did not have a warrant. The next day they went through his home again while he was in church, even having the temerity to take him from the church service to unlock a particular chest. Their efforts never yielded more than one bottle of wine. Moore was so angry that he had the detectives arrested for trespassing, and he told his story to an *Atlanta Constitution* reporter, who kindly printed it without trying to make the detectives appear innocent.[24]

Other ongoing abuses of police power also occurred. Officers began arresting blacks who possessed whiskey to hold them as witnesses against the seller, even though no law banned the possession of liquor. On one occasion when an officer crossed paths with a black man carrying a bottle of whiskey, he asked him to stop so he could talk to him. The man fled instead, dropping and breaking the bottle. The officer fired two shots at the fleeing witness and missed. The irony of the situation was not lost even on the white press, which questioned where the justice was in risking the murder of a *possible* witness to a *possible* crime. After all, the officer had not even determined whether, or where, the man bought the liquor. Actions like this suggested that at least some whites wanted prohibition to keep liquor away from blacks. Abuse from law enforcement only further soured blacks who had voted for prohibition in 1885.[25]

By the end of Atlanta's prohibition experiment most blacks could point to little or no benefits from prohibition or their votes for it. The animosity between white prohis and antis remained as strong as ever, but they masked it whenever they wanted to exclude blacks. Whites had legal access to liquor that was not available to blacks, and blacks were now not just being arrested on the usual "disorderly conduct" charges, but for the new crime of being a blind tiger or for nothing more than to be held as a witness. Every time blacks looked for improved race relations, they only found disappointment and growing discontent, and they even spread stories of their discontent with prohibition to other areas of the South.[26]

Telling Their Story: Principled Black Prohibitionists

Although prohibition was riddled with inconsistencies and stagnated race relations, principled black prohibitionists were busy touting their campaign successes. Between the 1885 and 1887 votes, black and white prohibitionists started three short-lived newspapers to get their story out: *The Conflict, Southern Recorder,* and *Herald of United Churches.* Both white and black prohibitionists capitalized on the success of Atlanta's local option vote by crisscrossing Georgia and the nation giving speeches to temperance organizations and in other prohibition campaigns. Senator Alfred Colquitt and Dr. J. B. Hawthorne were in great demand in both the North and the South. Although at least one speaker accused Hawthorne of not being a teetotaler himself, no one ever questioned the abstinence of the most outspoken black ministers—Carter, Gaines, and Turner. In early 1886 Reverend Carter spoke in Milledgeville, Georgia, and Gaines accompanied Sam Jones to the same city for a speech, sharing the platform with him. Carter not only traveled in Georgia but also brought the prohibition message to Virginia, Mississippi, South Carolina, Alabama, and Indiana. During Staunton, Virginia's local option campaign, James Parker spoke for prohibition and William A. Pledger spoke against it. In 1887 Good Samaritan leader Smith W. Easley became business manager of a new Atlanta publication *Herald of United Churches,* a short-lived prohibition paper that represented both black and white churches. But the black leader whose words on the subject have been best preserved is Bishop Henry McNeal Turner. In addition to touring Georgia towns, Turner spoke in Tennessee, Louisiana, and Alabama, and gave 37 speeches in Texas as part of its statewide prohibition campaign in the summer of 1887.[27]

But Turner was more than an active speaker. In September 1886, he stopped contributing to Alonzo Burnett's *Weekly Defiance* and began publishing and editing his own paper, the *Southern Recorder*, initially with assistance from Smith W. Easley and James B. Parker. The masthead read, "Devoted to Temperance, Religion, Justice, Industry, Economy, Education and African Civilization." Suggestive of its first position in the motto, temperance was one of the most frequent topics in the early issues. In the first issue Turner delineated seven reasons why he decided to publish a new paper. Although his primary goal was the "material and moral advancement of the race," his fourth point was about temperance: "we think a paper of a different tone upon the liquor issue still pending is in great demand." Turner's difference with Burnett over prohibition was a major reason for his leaving the *Defiance*. He said he could not "officially or conscientiously co-operate" any longer with the *Weekly Defiance* "while entertaining views so divergent upon the alcoholic question." Turner enthusiastically used the *Recorder*'s pages to editorialize on the temperance and prohibition movement locally and nationally. He reprinted several articles from *The Conflict*, a white temperance paper that had begun publishing just a few months before the *Recorder*. Turner included a regular temperance column as did many other newspapers, which was a potpourri of poetry and anecdotal prose gleaned from a variety of temperance-minded periodicals.[28]

When prohibition candidates and prohibition itself suffered defeat, Turner seized those opportunities to reiterate his principled position. Speaking with his characteristically sharp tongue, he conveyed the intense spiritual passion of many prohibitionists. Atlantans not only elected municipal leaders in the fall of 1886, but they also elected state legislators from their 35th congressional district. The leaders of the Young Men's Prohibition Club announced their endorsement of certain candidates for the election, but they did so without consulting their club members or members of the black prohibition clubs. Anti-prohibitionists were angry that prohibition had been dragged back into politics, but the move also created a backlash among those prohibitionists not consulted in the process. The *Weekly Defiance* chided Turner and the other ministers for cooperating with white Democratic prohibitionists who used blacks for their own purposes and then ignored them when convenient. Turner, never reticent when it came to criticism, quickly drew a distinction between the moral and the political to explain the clergy's position:

> We have only to say, the prohibition contest was a moral struggle, the other was political, the same thing white democrats did colored republicans could have done. . . . If the black men have no leaders politically, do not blame the colored ministers for trying to lead morally. The quiet of the Georgia negro, politically, is a disgrace. It shows he is weak in intellect, destitute of race patriotism, too big a

coward to take a position . . . the men who have capacity to be leaders are too busy fighting for liquor.[29]

In calling prohibition non-political Turner, a former politician himself, was consistent with his 1885 campaign speech in which he said the "question was not a political one, but one of humanity and divineness." Likewise, his assessment of the weakness of Georgia's Republican Party was painfully accurate.[30] The reference to effective black leaders supporting whiskey might have been a swipe at Burnett as much as at William Pledger. As it turned out, the candidates endorsed by the Young Men's Prohibition Club lost. With complete consistency Turner opined that, although some men may have been defeated, "prohibition was not defeated."[31]

When Texans rejected state prohibition after Turner's extensive speaking tour, he pronounced judgment and prophesied eventual victory with all the anger and passion of an ancient Hebrew prophet:

> Thousands of those who turned their backs on God, virtue, principle, honor and common sense, to extend the reign of liquor in Texas, will be cursed with premature deaths; will be stabbed, shot, hung, will die in jails, penitentiaries, in want, in disgrace, here and damnation in the everafter. . . . Liquor will as certainly go as heaven rules earth. The antis may rejoice and exult for a short time, but prohibition will come again and come ultimately to stay.[32]

Prohibitionists such as Turner willingly subjected themselves to charges of fanaticism and extremism, but their worldview prevented them from seeing things any other way.

In addition to the work of the clergy, the principled prohibitionist women continued their organizing. On March 10, 1887, some ladies gathered at Friendship Baptist Church to organize a second Colored WCTU for Atlanta. These ladies were not in competition with the older union because they organized on the west side of town and called their union the West Atlanta W.C.T.U. The Reverend E. R. Carter's wife was the first vice president, and Mrs. Ella Pitts became the first president. In the early months they took time to read literature and educate themselves on the temperance cause, as well as carry out visitations of the sick and hold regular prayer meetings.[33]

Turner and other principled prohibitionists entertained strong strains of perfectionism and millennialism, showing their continued rootedness in reform nexus theology. A high license fee on saloons, which many people in the 1880s considered part of a reasonable or "conservative" approach because it reduced the number of saloons, could never satisfy these purists because it still was permissive of sin. As one prohibitionist explained, "a barroom protected by high license and a barroom under low license, is a barroom all the same, and the evil influences radiating from it are just the same." A little evil sanctioned by the government was still evil in their eyes, but worse, because the government sanctioned it. As Turner said, "we can never boast of a perfect civilization while whisky saloons and grog-shops are counted by the hundreds and by the thousands all over this land." Principled prohibitionists could neither compromise their position one iota nor be discouraged by electoral defeats or the contradictions of prohibition, for they were on a divine mission.[34]

Prohibition in Atlanta was like prohibition elsewhere in the United States. The citizenry was divided, even hostile at times, and this provided fertile soil for all sorts of incriminations and recriminations to fly back and forth between leaders. Despite all the dissatisfaction among blacks, no group was more dissatisfied or anxious than white anti-prohibitionists. They could hardly wait for the next campaign to begin. They began organizing as soon as "real" prohibition began in July 1886. The 1887 campaign was just as heated as the 1885 one, but the momentum had shifted because the turbulent years of 1886 and 1887 had removed the most important reasons opportunistic blacks used for voting dry. This time the wets had the wind at their back, and they were determined to make the most of it.

> Prohibition is an awful flop.
> We like it.
> It can't stop what it's meant to stop.
> We like it.
>
> It's left a trail of graft and slime,
> It's filled our land with vice and crime,
> It don't prohibit worth a dime,
> Nevertheless, we're for it.
> —Franklin P. Adams

CHAPTER 7

Prohibition Revisited

Atlanta's 1887 Local Option Election

We will rally to the polls, boys,

We'll rally once again,

Shouting the battle-cry of freedom!

We will rally from the hillside,

We'll rally from the plain,

Shouting the battle-cry of freedom!

—"We Are Going to the Polls, Boys," third stanza

Eighteen hundred and eighty seven was not a good year for Southern prohibitionists. Much to their chagrin, on the fourth of August, Texas voters rejected a constitutional prohibition amendment, and the same scene was repeated in Tennessee on the twenty-ninth of September. The news was national, but above all, Southern. Prohibitionist speakers had come from throughout the nation, including the city of Atlanta, to rally the voters, and all for naught. White prohibitionists were "disappointed" at the lack of support they received from black voters, while mostly ignoring how few whites had voted dry.

The issue was so provocative that even Jefferson Davis, former president of the Confederacy, emerged from obscurity to speak his mind. During the Texas campaign Davis wrote an open letter condemning the prohibition movement, which was reprinted in newspapers throughout the South. According to Davis, personal liberty was a "cornerstone" of the government established by the nation's founding fathers, and prohibition was a sumptuary law that violated that principle. Tensions ran high, as an argument between friends over Davis's ideas erupted into a fistfight in the middle of a train ride in Tennessee. Davis's letter was reprinted in the *Atlanta Constitution*, producing many heated conversations just a few months before Atlanta's second local option vote.[1]

Less than one month after Atlanta's saloons closed, the city's anti-prohibitionists began organizing for prohibition's overthrow. They held their first meeting on July 23, displaying a feisty combative tone right from the beginning. One attendee declared, "We mean to begin the fight now, and we mean to keep it up until we have triumphed or been beaten past recovery. . . . The prohibitionists may as well understand once for all that they will not be allowed any rest." On July 30 they formalized their organization with the very politically astute moniker Conservative Citizens Club (CCC) and wrote a platform and elected officers. They committed themselves to high license fees for saloons, electing people of their persuasion, and fighting city council ordinances and policies that ostensibly were designed to offset the negative economic effects of prohibition. Many of the outspoken leaders in the October 1886 citizens' mass meeting and the nominating committee of 50 were CCC members. Bishop Turner, not exactly an objective voice, characterized them as being composed largely of ex-barkeepers, their landlords, and the employees of both groups. The CCC did not include African Americans.[2]

While the Conservative Citizens Club was public, printing its officers list, platform, members' names, and meeting times in various Atlanta newspapers, the Mutual Aid Brotherhoods, or MABs, were much more secretive. Their impetus for organizing a few months later appears to have been the dissatisfaction of some people with the "fusion ticket" created by the committee of 50 for city elections. In addition to anti-prohibitionists, they appealed to immigrants and labor. The MAB membership and platform were not reported in the press, although occasional references were made to the group, its influence, and individual members. It is possible that the secrecy of this organization permitted many saloon owners to join it and network in a way not likely if it were public. Following the fall 1886 municipal elections the Conservative Citizens Club seemed to decline and the Mutual Aid Brotherhood rose in prominence.[3]

The existence of an organized anti-prohibition movement and the differences of opinion among prohibitionists themselves made for turbulent and sometimes acrimonious politics until the November 1887 vote. With the founding of the CCC in July 1886, anti-prohibitionists openly declared their intention to take the fight into politics, but ironically, three months later they criticized the Young Men's Prohibition Club for endorsing prohibitionists for the state legislature. The incriminations and recriminations never stopped, for the prohibitionists accused antis of trying to undermine the will of the people and then complicated matters by fighting among themselves about how much trust to extend to the antis in the government. But for all the animosity between them, the groups had no difficulty agreeing to suppress black political involvement.[4]

In early September 1887 anti-prohibitionists began circulating petitions for another local option referendum, but they had one last obstacle to beginning the second campaign. Atlanta was scheduled to host the second of its three city-booster cotton expositions. These expos were the favorites of New South men intent on making Atlanta the regional center of trade and industry. The Piedmont Exposition was scheduled for October 10–22 in Piedmont Park. The highlight of the expo was a two-day presidential visit orchestrated by Henry Grady. President Grover Cleveland's visit was no small thing for Atlantans, and Southerners generally, since he was the first Democratic president since the Civil War. Both sides agreed to postpone the campaign until after the expo so as not to detract from its booster and economic potential for the city. Although the wets began collecting petition signatures in September for another vote and began publishing accusatory newspaper articles, they stopped with the articles once the prohibitionists complained.

In early October, shoe wholesaler R. D. Spalding and attorney Walter R. Brown turned in a petition with 2,500 names requesting a second local option vote, even though only 800 were needed. On October 28 the county ordinary certified the petition and scheduled the vote for Saturday, November 26, the earliest possible date according to General Local Option law. As in 1885, animated even vitriolic arguments, appeals, denunciations, speeches, and letters filled the local press daily, for weeks.[5]

Blacks and the "Antis" the Second Time

This time it was the antis who set the tone of the campaign, not the prohibitionists. The antis were on the offensive throughout, with a well-thought-out and powerfully articulated list of arguments. Convinced that the masses had tired of prohibition and were ready to bring back saloons, the antis became confident and aggressive, even militant at times. Anti-prohibitionists braided together a variety of rhetorical strategies and capitalized on serendipitous events like Jefferson Davis's letters and the momentum from the Texas and Tennessee votes to produce a definitive victory for their cause. Reform had been tried, and the antis simply had to point out its failure. They accurately gauged the "pulse" of the masses and employed arguments that made intuitive, practical sense to blacks and working-class whites. In addition, this time the antis were even able to claim the high moral ground.

A small group of white anti-prohibitionist leaders launched their campaign with a public address on October 25 that introduced their platform. After listing complaints about prohibitionist policies, they stated clearly their support for strict control of saloons. They argued that the high license approach would yield better morals than prohibition and that prior to prohibition Atlanta already was one of the most sober cities of its size in America. The antis claimed that prohibitionists wanted to keep liquor away from certain classes of people, especially Negroes, "contrary to the principles of popular government." Prohibitionists received all the blame for the strife and divisiveness that had characterized Atlanta's government for two years. They criticized Atlanta's growth as too slow for a city its size and promised that the overthrow of prohibition would bring back prosperity. Finally, the antis decried the use of blue badges by the prohis as too divisive. These themes appeared over and over in the arguments of anti speakers during the campaign.[6]

Anti-prohibitionists designed their campaign around eight major citywide rallies, multiple ward meetings, and several meetings in communities beyond the city limits. Probably all meetings were interracial. Giving no less than ten speeches, William Pledger was by far the most active black speaker. Among the most prominent local antis were Evan P. Howell and Clark Howell and P. J. Moran, all connected to the *Atlanta Constitution*. The most popular out-of-town speaker was Texas Republican A. M. Cochran, who arrived fresh from Texas's recent defeat of constitutional prohibition. Stealing a page from the drys' playbook, the newly organized Young Men's Anti-Prohibition Club organized black chapters in each ward. Aside from the ward clubs, there was no black attempt to organize on a citywide basis, as in the first election. Black concerns with prohibition so closely paralleled those of white antis that they saw no need to create their own organization, and while a strong spirit of interracial cooperation was evident, the antis did not gush over blacks as white prohibitionists had done in 1885.

One of the surprises of the 1887 campaign was the breakup of the solid black clergy support for prohibition. Baptist pastor C. O. Jones, previously a dry, announced that he would vote the "Liberty" ticket this time around. Bethel's J. S. Flipper, the pastor who replaced Wesley J. Gaines in January 1886, refused to speak publicly for prohibition during most of the campaign, much to the consternation of white prohibitionists. Senator Colquitt arrogantly took it upon himself to ask Flipper's bishop, Alexander Wayman, to place another man at Bethel who would be more supportive of prohibition. Colquitt's request betrayed the racial hubris harbored by so many white drys at the time. The North Georgia Annual Conference, where pastoral appointments were made, convened about ten days before the election. Having no reason to remove Flipper, Bishop Wayman reappointed him according to his congregation's request. The newspaper quoted Flipper as saying that he had never taken a drop of whiskey in his life, and the AME church was a temperance church, but that he was going to be his "own man" on the prohibition issue. These comments caused quite a stir because they implicitly called into question the integrity and independence of outspoken prohibitionist black clergy. Flipper said he did not have anything against other ministers who participated in the campaign, but since it was creating such "bad feeling" he personally preferred not to participate. "Strife is becoming great," he said, "and I shant make it greater by speaking either way." He promised to fight whiskey from his pulpit instead of the political stump. The next week, however, just before the election, he wrote a letter to the *Atlanta Constitution* and came out squarely for prohibition: "Put me down for time and eternity on the side of God and the right—PROHIBITION." Perhaps Flipper believed this statement and its timing was the safest way out of a tricky situation. He embraced the position of his church and his conscience and at the same time came across as not giving in to pressure from whites, thereby maintaining his "manhood" and retaining the respect of his parishioners. Although he had squandered his ability to influence the outcome of the election, he had retained something even more important.[7]

Anti-Prohibition Rhetoric Targeting Black Voters

The antis scored a major coup with blacks and working-class whites by successfully framing prohibition in the language of class warfare. They went to great lengths to point out its class-based inequities. They argued that rich people designed prohibition for their own benefit because they were the only ones who could still easily get liquor in their private clubs or import wholesale quantities, while "every man with a dime . . . can not do so openly but in such a manner as to make him feel like a thief." This reality "arrays one class of citizens against another, and thereby hurts all classes," complained another speaker. "If prohibition isn't a law to benefit the rich I'd like to know it," said Fulton Colville, president of the Young Men's Anti-Prohibition Club. "He can buy his whisky in quantity, and when a snake bites him he has it at hand. But the poor man can't do this, and when a snake bites him . . . he has to fall back on water." Antis also identified a shared victimization between blacks and working-class whites: "They say, Oh, yes, we drink, but then you know we don't want the working men to drink it, especially the colored people! They don't mean anything good for white or colored working men." The poor man "is as abundantly able to take care of himself as the rich man," asserted one speaker. Another announced that "The prohibitionists want to be the poor man's guardian. But you don't want such guardianship, do you?" Of course the audience responded with cries of "No we don't!" Attorney and former mayor John B. Goodwin surely said what was in the minds of his audience when he asserted, "We stand as freemen proclaiming that there is manhood enough within us to guard our appetites." The wets stood in a long tradition of working-class Americans who asserted their own (republican) virtuousness.[8]

Another element of the antis' defense of the working class attacked police officers' enforcement practices, especially the arrests of individuals who possessed liquor, just to hold them as witnesses. Undoubtedly this practice was more of a problem for the lower classes. Fulton Colville called this police behavior "an outrage on law and liberty." Another angry speaker, merchandise broker Eugene Mitchell, turned 1885 prohibitionists' rhetoric back on themselves:

> I'm going to steal an expression from Dr. Hawthorne. In one of his speeches two years ago Dr. Hawthorne concluded with this sentence: "Blot the era of oppression out and let a universal freedom in." Talk about oppression! Isn't it oppression for the police to rob the people on the public highways and fire upon people, merely because the officer suspects they have bought liquor. These are some of the damnable outrages that result from prohibition. Yes, blot the era of oppression out![9]

One of the most clever attacks against prohibitionists' promises came from the black porter Walter Landrum early in the campaign in a mostly black First Ward meeting. He attacked prohibitionists for being untrustworthy, betraying blacks, and using oppressive enforcement practices. "You can't place any dependence upon the promises of the prohibitionists. They may promise to place a policeman's club in your hand, but they will place it on your head," he declared. "Great applause" followed this comment from the mostly black audience, who obviously "got it." This line was so witty that a white speaker used it in a mostly colored third meeting a couple of days later. White prohibitionists fearful of the social and political implications of hiring black police learned that failure to hire them could just as easily backfire.[10]

Landrum's comments suggest a third way wets appealed to the concerns of their political base. They reminded black voters how little prohibitionists had done for them. William Pledger harped on this theme more than most. In the same First Ward meeting where Landrum spoke, Pledger asked, "When did these prohibitionists ever help you?" and received cries of "Never!" from the audience. Pledger then related a personal story in which he witnessed a confrontation that led to the arrest of an innocent black man. Pledger asked several prominent white prohibitionists to help raise bail money because the individual claimed to be a prohibitionist, but no one helped. He eventually found a white anti who "cheerfully" helped bail the man out of jail. In another speech Pledger predicted that the same white preachers who were now cozying up to their black colleagues would be the first to oppose sharing a railroad car with the same black clergy after the election.[11]

In addition to appealing to working-class blacks and whites, the anti-prohibitionists aggressively crafted a positive political image for themselves. They attacked arguably the two most influential groups of prohibitionists, preachers and women. Speakers openly proclaimed their high honor for women and respect for the clergy, in their *proper* roles, but they argued that their political involvement "debased their holy calling." Speakers usually linked their comments about women and preachers. In the 1885 campaign, Pledger complained about Reverend E. R. Carter and other preachers' involvement in politics, but no one had attacked women. In 1887 Livingston Mims, an employee of New York Life Insurance's Atlanta office, testified that "no man" had a "higher admiration for woman than" he, but that women's political involvement with prohibition had caused him to "hang my head in shame for them." Speakers claimed that when preachers entered politics they "descended" from their pulpits. "I believe in old fashioned forms, old fashioned church, which kept their preachers aloof from the mire of politics," Mims declared. "Those who prostitute their religion . . . I have no respect for." Preachers not only "descended" from their high calling but, according to William Pledger, caused women to do the same:

> The women had better stay home and attend to their domestic duties. I honor a woman. Around the fire-side she rules as undisputed queen. But so soon as she divests herself of her womanly nature, comes out into the world and takes her place with men, she at that moment deprives herself of man's homage. [Applause.] The preachers are responsible for this.[12]

Speakers admonished voters not to listen to the advice of either their pastors or their wives but to make their own independent decisions, which played on well-respected traditions. The wets' attack on the clergy appealed to many because it was based on the widely embraced "spirituality of the church" doctrine. This concept, as originally developed by antebellum Southern clergy, maintained that since the church was a spiritual entity it should not speak out on worldly or political matters such as slavery. Now that slavery had ended, prohibition appeared to be another appropriate application of this teaching. Also, middle-class Victorian values held that the home was the proper sphere for women, while politics and business were male arenas. By embracing strong Southern traditions and the cultural norms of middle-class America, wets attractively positioned themselves and their cause as moderate, even conservative, not radical and certainly not "evil."[13]

In addition to aligning themselves with traditional gender and clergy roles, wets further buttressed their image by contrasting their own integrity with the hypocrisy, lies, and immorality of the drys. Antis' characterization of prohibitionists ranged from "inconsistent" to the "party of fraud and deception." One speaker constructed an entire speech around a list of ten prohibitionist inconsistencies. His list earned him "vociferous applause and laughter" from the audience. Blacks charged prohibitionists with not fulfilling the promise of improved race relations. John Emory Bryant, the Republican prohibitionist, announced that just as in the last local option election the colored Young Men's Prohibition Clubs would receive monetary awards based on the number of voters they got to the polls. Antis jumped on this announcement, calling it vote buying and indicative of the hypocrisy of prohibitionists who talked incessantly in the first election about the immorality of the antis' vote-buying efforts. Attorney Carroll Payne condemned the prohibitionists in no uncertain terms:

> Let every man who wears the blue ribbon swear never to touch liquor more, and then we will either see the blue ribbons disappear or whisky one or the other. [Laughter and cheering.] The people have discovered the sham, the train of evils such as lying hypocrisy, deceit, violation of law, and a thousand contemptible vices . . . the people are tired of it. [Cheers.][14]

Whatever the accusation, audiences always seemed heartily to affirm speakers' charges of prohibitionist inconsistency and deception.[15]

In contrast to the deceitful wine-bibbing prohibitionists, the wets practically turned their rallies into temperance society meetings. They drew a clear distinction between advocating temperance and advocating prohibition. On one occasion William Pledger repeated his temperance position several times just to make it clear, something he rarely mentioned in the 1885 campaign. "Because I am an ardent opponent of prohibition, it does not follow that I am in favor of drunkenness. I emphatically announce my hostility to intemperance. I am opposed to the excessive use of liquor. It's a bad thing. I want everyone to avoid the abuse of whiskey." Former mayor John B. Goodwin asserted that antis were as much a "temperance party" as the drys, while another speaker proudly announced that he had never been in a barroom in his life. Some speakers, such as the one who bragged about his history in the Good Templars, stressed their support for moral suasion but not for the coerciveness of prohibition.[16]

But anti speakers went even farther, asserting their morality and religious devotion. One speaker asserted he had "more respect for pure undefiled religion" than any other man, while A. M. Cochrane of Texas declared he was proud of being a Methodist his whole life and planned on being one when he died. Evan P. Howell, president of the Atlanta Constitution Company, was among those speakers who employed Bible passages. Howell reminded his listeners that too much whiskey was harmful. He said he knew that because "God's book says so, and I believe every word in the Bible." This comment elicited "great applause." Pledger read Scripture verses and on one occasion taught on their meaning for 30 minutes. On another occasion, a minister offered up a prayer at an anti rally. Such things were unheard of in wet rallies in 1885. In openly identifying with temperance, religion, and the Bible, anti-prohibitionists brilliantly positioned themselves squarely in the middle of respectable Southern society.[17]

In addition to developing these new themes for 1887, anti-prohibitionists continued to harp on their favorite theme from 1885, the prosperity of the city. Antis marshaled a long list of economic statistics and anecdotal evidence to suggest that the city's population and economic growth had suffered under prohibition. Wets also complained that the thousands of dollars citizens spent on liquor imported from other cities could be going into the local economy. They complained that prohibition had caused many working-class men to go to other cities to look for work and that local capitalists were investing in business enterprises elsewhere. The return of saloons, the brewery, and wholesale liquor houses would also mean a return of workers and capital to Atlanta. Unlike in 1885, the economic arguments primarily targeted whites, but black voters in majority white meetings and rallies would have been exposed to them. Because antis' economic arguments focused so extensively on property, business ownership, and employer concerns, these arguments probably lacked saliency for most black voters.[18]

The final and maybe most powerful argument was that of personal liberty. In 1885 "Liberty" was the antis' motto; in 1887 it was their mantra. Everywhere that people voted on prohibition across the South, antis cried "Liberty!" No single concept received as much attention from wet speakers as this "foundation stone." Virtually every anti speaker made some mention of the fact that prohibition trampled on people's personal liberty to eat and drink what they wanted. Although this argument was framed in political and national terms, speakers also used religious and historical arguments. While one person referred to the "divine liberty" bequeathed by the "fathers of the revolution," others reminded their listeners that America was a nation of sovereign citizens, not monarchical subjects, and warned that a decline in the love of freedom was a "sure sign of national decay," a slip in some republican-sounding language. Depending on the speaker, personal liberty was a human trait, a right of citizenship, or a democratic principle. Jefferson, Washington, and Madison were often invoked. Speakers praised their black listeners for being such strong supporters of liberty. People for whom emancipation meant so much could certainly be counted on to defend their long-awaited liberty and not deny it to others. Just to make sure his assumptions were correct, A. M. Cochrane asked his black listeners, "Now my colored friend, will you stand firm and vote for liberty?" and "Can I say to the white man that if he won't vote your liberty away you won't vote his away?" As expected, he received shouts of "Yes!" to each question. Personal liberty received such prominence that it seemed to some prohibitionists the wets rarely mentioned anything else.[19]

Throughout the campaign, anti-prohibitionists effectively set its agenda and assumed the moral high ground. Anti-prohibitionists skillfully crafted their rhetoric to draw in blacks, the white working class, and Atlanta's civic-minded merchant class. At the same time, antis projected a respectable public image of themselves and their cause. All of this put the prohibitionists on the defensive this time.

Prohibitionists and Blacks the Second Time

The prohibitionists' campaign began in earnest following the Piedmont Exposition when they chose former mayor George Hillyer as their president. Many of the leaders from 1885 spearheaded this campaign also, but some new people joined. Although no blacks were members of the finance committee, the advisory board included E. R. Carter, Wesley Gaines, and Smith W. Easley. Wilbur P. Thirkield, the dean of the Gammon School of Theology, also served. The blacks who served on ward committees included the contractor Alexander Hamilton, the undertaker David T. Howard (whose wife was active in the Woman's Christian Temperance Union), Republican activist Jackson McHenry (dry again, after having briefly opposed prohibition in 1886), mail carrier C. C. Wimbish, shoemaker Nick Holmes, Smith W. Easley, the undertaker Mitchell Cargile, and Wesley J. Gaines, recently made presiding elder of the Atlanta district of the North Georgia Conference of the African Methodist Episcopal Church. Atlanta University professor H. M. Sessions also served on a ward committee. A. E. Buck, John Emory Bryant, and James G. Thrower stirred up black voters again. Unlike in 1885, Sam Small never preached, and Sam Jones did not raise his tent. The lack of Jones's tent did not prevent the drys from rallying their troops, however. More than 40 people addressed large audiences in 12 major rallies and numerous ward meetings. The Young Men's Prohibition Club and Colored Young Men's Prohibition Club reorganized themselves in each ward, proudly distributing blue "For Prohibition" badges. They usually met before the rallies and paraded through the streets with bands and banners. Black and white women organized separately, by ward. They prayed regularly and prepared and served lunches on Election Day, while antis criticized them for trying to influence the vote. Sam Jones opened the campaign with a sermon at the opera house on Sunday, October 23, but he left town after that to preach in the West for several weeks. As in 1885, the prohibitionists temporarily "withdrew" the color line so audiences practiced mixed seating, blacks and whites shared the same platform, and members of each race addressed mixed audiences.[20]

One of the main campaign strategies prohibitionists repeated in 1887 was canvassing the city. Workers went from door to door, polling residents on their

Fig. 25—Cartoonist's perspective on Atlanta's 1887 Local Option election. From *Macon Telegraph*, November 20, 1887. NewsBank, inc., a division of Readex

opinions regarding prohibition, reminding them to register, and urging them to vote for prohibition. These brief encounters could be unpleasant for both parties. Canvassers reported that antis cursed them and abused them in various ways. Sometimes drys met wet workers while they were out. While two Spelman Seminary teachers canvassed a part of the city on Sunday, November 13, they talked to unpersuadable wets they met along the way who rehearsed their personal liberty arguments. They called it a memorable experience but admitted it was "no easy task." One reason these encounters sometimes became contentious was often that the woman of the house was being addressed by a man in the absence of her husband, and it was not considered proper etiquette for a woman to speak on political issues, especially to a strange man. One man's wife was offended by the tone of a canvasser's comment, so she told her husband after he returned from work. A couple of days later when the husband met the canvasser he confronted him about his comments. The canvasser denied them, but the husband cursed him out anyway. Indignant, the canvasser turned in the husband for disorderly conduct and using profane language in public, and the husband paid a small fine. When asked about the situation, the mayor defended the husband's right to defend the "sanctity of his fireside." Although dry canvassers were not professionally trained to deal with the public, the anti-prohibitionists who called them "unprincipled roughs" were practicing electioneering hyperbole. These encounters stoked the tensions that pervaded the city.[21]

One pleasant surprise for prohibitionists was the conversion of two former black anti leaders: Moses Bently and Alonzo W. Burnett. During the election Bently worked on the prohibitionists' Sixth Ward committee. In late October Burnett surprised his readers with an editorial in his *Weekly Defiance* announcing that "now we have seen both sides and are certainly convinced that for the Negro at any rate, prohibition is best." In a subsequent editorial he explained the offense in the fall of 1886 when the wet citizens' committee did not consider appointing a black to the committee of 50 until they saw the drys had. Burnett decried the "treachery and deception" of the wets and concluded that they had "never shown the Negro any recognition except such as the prohibitionists have forced them to show him." Again, he pointed out, when the wets published their resolutions at the beginning of the 1887 campaign they included no black signatories. Beyond being angry at white antis, Burnett also believed prohibition had positive effects on his race despite the fact that "everything that could be done has been done to bring the law into contempt and to cast obloquy upon its advocates." The press did not indicate whether Burnett played an active role in campaign rallies, but the editorial column of the *Defiance* was his mouthpiece. The paper soon became known as "one of the prohibition organs of the city." As with Jackson McHenry and James B. Parker, Burnett and Bently evidently changed positions because of their own reassessment of the effects of prohibition and whatever other issues were important to them at the time. Newspaper reports of Young Men's Prohibition Club meetings mention other blacks who became drys in 1887, but Burnett and Bently were by far the most prominent.[22]

The prohibitionists failed to control the direction of the public debate as they had in 1885 and were constantly scrambling to keep up with wet tactics and rhetoric. A few months before the election some members of the city council introduced a bill that would have created, in case Atlantans overturned prohibition, strict limits on saloons. They would be restricted to a half-mile radius from the city center where they could be most easily policed, and there would be a $1,500 license fee. The council approved it, but since it wanted these provisions enshrined in the city's charter, the state legislature had to approve it also. In the legislature, a shrewd move by anti-prohibitionists put the drys in an impossible situation. A Fulton County representative submitted an amendment to the bill that earned it the support of anti-prohibitionist groups such as the secretive Mutual Aid Brotherhood. The amendment required a citywide referendum to implement the changes. This provision made the bill unacceptable to the prohibitionists.

The prohibitionists feared that the referendum requirement would make voters think that if they repealed prohibition they could turn around the next week and vote in strict saloon controls. Undoubtedly, some prohibition-leaning voters would have liked this alternative, and the drys feared losing their votes if the election appeared to be a choice between prohibition and high license. The prohis considered the bill little more than a tactic to help the antis win the election. They argued that the wets might say to one group they supported high license but turn around and promise another group saloons throughout the city. In legislative hearings prohibitionists argued that high license was by definition discriminatory "class" legislation because it prevented less-well-off businessmen from entering the business. It was unlikely that citizens would have ever voted for such legislation, and the antis knew it. For drys this further proved their contention that antis' "support" for high license had always been disingenuous. Prohibitionists' lobbying killed the bill, but their success enabled the antis to portray the prohis as uncompromising extremists. Throughout the campaign prohibitionists constantly reminded their audiences that "Our platform is: Keep the barrooms out. The platform of the antis is: Bring the barrooms in." It was a straight up or down vote, and the prohibitionists offered no nightmare scenarios about what would happen if the wets won.[23]

Prohibitionist Rhetoric Targeting Black Voters

The wets determined much of the rhetoric of the campaign by hurling accusations to which drys felt obliged to respond. Virtually every prohibitionist speaker had to devote a portion of his talk to "damage control" because of the wets' aggressive campaigning. Prohibitionists responded to seven charges: prohibition is a violation of personal liberty; prohibition does not prohibit; prohibition is hurting Atlanta's economy; preachers and women have no business in politics; prohibitionists have brought divisiveness to city politics; drys are really only concerned with keeping liquor from blacks and working-class whites; and prohis are really uncharitable people. Prohibitionists spent more time responding to the personal liberty charge than any other. They repeatedly argued that there was no such thing as absolute personal liberty as long as people lived outside a state of savagery and under the rule of law. Henry Grady, a teetotaler who was known to serve liquor to his guests, gave two extensive speeches in which, as far as the drys were concerned, he presented conclusive evidence of Atlanta's economic growth under prohibition. All drys asserted without qualification that there were fewer drunkards on the streets and fewer criminals being sent to the chain gang, and that streets previously the home of many saloons, like Peters and Decatur Streets, showed a much improved moral character. There was one charge prohis never tried to deny—police brutality in enforcing prohibition.[24]

Although these charges and rebuttals were of interest to blacks—especially the lack of response to charges of police brutality—it seems that blacks particularly wanted to know why they should vote for prohibition since white prohibitionists did not keep their promises the first time, specifically in the area of adding blacks to the police force. At least three black speakers addressed this issue, taking different positions. Sam Jones was the only white who dared to address it, and he simply asked blacks rhetorically what the current anti-prohibitionist mayor had done for them. E. R. Carter, however, argued that a vote for the wets would be analogous to what the blind Hebrew prophet Samson did when he knocked down the pillars of the temple, killing himself along with his Philistine enemies. Carter said he personally would rather make a choice so that all parties live and not die, meaning a vote for prohibition. One popular outside black speaker brought in for the campaign was Reverend C. N. Grandison from North Carolina. Grandison tried to get voters to see that the prejudice of the police commissioners was race-based, having nothing to do with prohibition. As proof of his point, he reminded his listeners that when the antis were a majority on the police board they never appointed blacks either. On another occasion Grandison echoed Carter's sentiment by saying, "You can't spite the white man without spiting your own race." Bishop Turner also opposed making an issue out of black policemen. Intra-communal friction, he argued, would result if some blacks got on the force and others did not. There would be jealousy and perhaps even worse. "We know one another so well that it is better that colored policemen were not on the force," he declared. "They would find out more than white men ever dreamed of." A black coping mechanism since slavery days had been to avoid, as much as possible, giving information to whites in authority. That mistrust had changed little in freedom and it frustrated criminal investigations done by white police. "There is no more comparison between the liquor traffic and a policeman's place than there is between hell and heaven," he said. Turner asked rhetorically, "When you vote against whisky do you vote for the white people?" When the crowd yelled back, "No, we vote for ourselves," Turner responded, "It is the foolishness of folly to say otherwise."[25]

Prohibitionists saved their sharpest and most caustic rhetoric for the antis' hypocritical discovery of religion and their crude attack on the clergy and women. Reverend Grandison criticized the antis for suddenly finding religion and then only using Scriptures before black audiences. Senator Colquitt once began his speech with compliments for the song and prayer that opened the meeting and then asked if anyone had ever heard of an anti-prohibitionist meeting opening with prayer. What sort of prayer could a liquor dealer offer, he asked? Colquitt then made up a mock prayer of a hypothetical liquor seller who asked God to give men and boys "unquenchable thirst" for whiskey. Of course, this elicited much laughter and applause. Given the central place of the clergy in Atlanta's prohibition movement, it is not surprising that some of the prohis' sharpest sarcasm was used to defend ministers, 77 of whom (all white) signed a public statement at the beginning of the campaign praising the benefits of prohibition in Atlanta. When opening his one major speech of the campaign, Bishop Turner sarcastically announced that he made no apology for his appearance despite the "exceedingly fastidious" concerns antis had recently raised about the "dignity of the ministry." Turner mockingly added that maybe the other camp would soon open a theological institute. Another speaker charged that those who presumed the right to tell preachers what they ought to do and not do "are the very men who know less about preachers and the duty of preachers than any other class of men." Then there was the witty approach of Dr. J. W. Lee, pastor of Trinity Methodist Episcopal Church, who accepted at face value the antis' characterization of politics and preachers but carried it to its logical conclusion: "If the politicians have brought politics so low that a minister cannot even speak of the subject . . . without staining his precious clerical robes, it is about time politics was taken out of the hands of those who have brought them so low and turned over to people who have conscience and taste enough to elevate them."[26]

Expending so much energy and resources defending themselves and their cause seemed to have kept prohibitionists from going on the offensive. As in 1885, prohis repeated their call for women to influence their husbands and sons, and they argued that crime had decreased just as they had predicted. One speaker claimed that Fulton County was even beginning to rent convicts from other counties because of a shortage on its chain gang. Given the prosperous economy and declining crime rates, prohis asked rhetorically how the liberty that bringing back the saloon represented could possibly improve life for whites or blacks. Despite their efforts, however, the prohibitionists remained back on their heels during the entire election campaign.[27]

Final Week of the Campaign

The hysteria of the campaign peaked in its final week. Nearly every evening each side sponsored some sort of parade or public display. Several fortuitous events for the wets occurred during the last week, not giving the drys enough time to respond. Apparently drawn to Atlanta during the Piedmont Expo, a black patent medicine salesman named Yellowstone Kit had been drawing crowds for weeks. Part showman, part doctor, and part stump speaker, Kit was very popular. During his nightly shows, which drew thousands, he sold a "Japanese Herb Pad" that promised to cure a variety of ailments. Four days before the election Kit announced his opposition to prohibition and urged his audience, "Don't sell your liberty. Why these people will buy your vote now and this winter they will turn you out of your house." Although he spoke against drunkenness, he cynically reminded drinkers' wives that one benefit of saloons is that they would at least know where to look for their husbands. His popularity among blacks probably made his opinion as important for blacks as Jefferson Davis's summertime endorsement was for whites. Even before Kit announced his position, wets had assumed from his rhetoric that he was on their side.[28]

Also during the last week of the campaign, an unidentified group of wet black voters drew up a list of resolutions that a minister read at a rally. They condemned Senator Colquitt's attempt to fire Big Bethel's J. S. Flipper, they honored Flipper and four other black pastors by name for the "manly course" they pursued in the campaign, and they listed the reasons why they were planning to vote wet. They planned to vote "for the sale" because in 1885 white prohibitionists intentionally deceived them with lies, procuring whiskey had been inconvenient for them compared to wealthy people, and because as a race they had been treated like criminals by the police because of the actions of a few lawbreakers. They also condemned as affronts to their manhood the attempts by prohis to buy their votes and by women to influence their vote by offering them free lunches on election day. They pledged themselves to support "all necessary" means to regulate the sale of intoxicants and declared they were as competent to "take care of ourselves as some of the prohibition leaders, who belong to clubs where drinking is as freely done as in a barroom." The reading of the resolutions was followed by "wild cheers and calls." Read publicly just three nights before the election, it seemed designed to make it appear as though Black Atlanta en masse had issued its definitive statement on the prohibition experiment and an explanation of its expected response. Its formulaic and summative qualities, combined with no public explanation of its origins or signatories, suggest that maybe it was written by one of the anti committees. It carefully rehearsed almost all of the antis' principal arguments. The antis—black and white—successfully portrayed themselves as traditional, moral, and peace- and prosperity-loving patriotic citizens. It has always been difficult to lose an American election with *that* image.[29]

Shortly before the election, William Pledger capitalized on Jefferson Davis's open letters. As a wet, Pledger was excited about Davis's endorsement and not the least bothered by his background, much to the horror of dry blacks. Pledger announced to a crowd that even though Davis led the government determined to keep his people in shackles, he could still honor him for his "high character, purity of life and great learning." In the same rally he and hundreds of other black men lifted three cheers for Jefferson Davis. Horrified at the thought of this, Smith W. Easley in his *Herald of United Churches* accused the men in the crowd of giving up their sense of honor for a few dollars. Alonzo Burnett also expressed his shock: "Whenever a man's zeal for a cause leads him into the indiscriminate eulogy of patriots and TRAITORS, it is time to abandon that cause. . . . If the negro is not to despise Jeff Davis, pray, whom or what is he to despise?" One can hardly imagine a more jarring scene than a crowd of blacks cheering Jefferson Davis. The prohibition campaign had created the strangest imaginable bedfellows![30]

Yet another significant last-minute occurrence was a slickly done flyer that appeared just a few days before the vote. It pictured Abraham Lincoln with a recently freed black family, with the man kneeling before him. Underneath the picture were the words: "Prohibition is slavery. I will cut the manacles from your hands." Further writing purported to be quoting Lincoln attacking prohibition as contrary to the freedom he had just fought for. This appropriation of Lincoln by the antis (there is no evidence Lincoln ever made the attributed statement) could have only helped their cause, especially among voters never privy to Lincoln's image in the Storrs School chapel or among those who had never been moved to sign the Lincoln Temperance Pledge.[31]

The campaign culminated with three mass rallies. Two nights before the election the prohibitionists began their rally with an "immense" torchlight parade containing hundreds of drummers. Hundreds, perhaps thousands, could not fit in the warehouse, so leaders quickly arranged for simultaneous outdoor meetings. Among the many who addressed the crowd were C. N. Grandison, E. R. Carter, Henry Grady, Senator Colquitt, and Dr. J. B. Hawthorne. On election eve the drys met for one last rally and an inspirational speech from Dr. William Felton, who reviewed all the prohibition arguments as if his audience were preparing for an exam the next day.

The wets held their election eve rally in DeGive's Opera House. As their faithful followers arrived they were greeted by brass bands and several bonfires in the streets. Because an overflow crowd filled the streets for several blocks, the leaders hastily arranged for several speakers to address the masses outside. Unlike in 1885, neither camp corralled and entertained voters all night, but that did not stop some from drinking anyway. One paper reported more drunks on the street on election eve than had been seen in a long time.[32]

Fig. 26—Anti-Prohibition Handbill, 1887. From *National Temperance Advocate*, January 1888. New York Public Library

Election Day and Its Aftermath

Election Day assumed a festive character throughout the city. The press reported that if a traveler had not known about the election and happened to arrive at the train station on November 26, he could not have missed the excitement. Blue and red badges were everywhere. Antis paraded through the streets with brass bands and red-and-white banners emblazoned with "Liberty!" Carriages were adorned with placards saying "Prohibition" or "Return Prosperity to the city and VOTE FOR THE SALE." WCTU women and anti women operated lunch counters next to each polling station for their respective voters. White and black ladies calling each other "sister" openly entreated men to "vote for Jesus," with some white women even speaking to unfamiliar black men, something normal etiquette frowned upon. One black man was so struck by whites' solicitation of his people that he reportedly exclaimed, "Bless de Lawd; I'se lived to see de cullud folks as good as de whites!" Young women in prayer bands walked from polling station to polling station.[33]

Underlying the festive mood, however, were some real logistical difficulties. Even though the city increased the number of voting precincts from two to six (one for each ward), all voters did not get a chance to cast their ballot, as they had in 1885. Each party sent black and white poll watchers who, among other things, tried to count how many voted for each side and challenged supposedly illegal voters for the other side. Despite the efforts of poll watchers, several prohibitionist leaders contended that there were many illegal votes, insinuating they were all on the wet side, although when pressed they admitted there might have been some on their side, too.

Table 7—Local Option Registration Compared, 1885 and 1887

	1885	*1887*
Atlanta	7,213	8,570
Fulton County outside of Atlanta	1,753	2,570
Total Registration	8,966	11,140

Data compiled by the author from "11,140: Fulton County's Registration for the Prohibition Election," *Atlanta Constitution*, November 16, 1887.

Rumors begun by each camp added to the tension and excitement of election day. Probably in an attempt to encourage their supporters, the drys began a rumor that the wet mayor had actually voted dry, which was a lie. When a policeman was heard shooting at someone and it became known that the person was black, a rumor began that the "prohibitionist policeman" (as of March all policemen were prohibitionists) had shot at a black man trying to vote wet. Blacks waiting in line to vote had to be urged by white wets to remain. The truth was that a policeman had shot at a black thief running away from the scene of a crime, but police-black relations were so poor that it seemed plausible that a police officer would shoot at a black voter.[34]

As in 1885, a record number of people registered to vote, making voting long and tedious. There were 8,570 registered city voters, an increase of 1,357 over 1885 (see table 7). About 35 percent of all registrants were black.[35] Early in the day the drys voted heavily and appeared to be in the lead, but by mid-afternoon the "For the Sale" ballots began to swamp the ballot box. Some voters went home rather than wait for hours to cast their ballot. Making matters even worse for the drys was Atlanta's policy that the only votes counted were the ones cast before the polling station closed. When the polling stations closed at six o'clock, most still had a line of people waiting to cast their ballot. The number of citizens who did not get to cast their ballot ran into the hundreds. At the end of the day the wets had a majority in every precinct except South Bend, the one containing Clark University. The wets won with 5,183 votes compared to 4,061 for the prohibition-ists. Probably a majority of both whites and blacks voted "For the Sale."[36]

Almost immediately prohibitionist leaders claimed they had lost because of illegal voting by wets. Their initial thoughts were that they should either challenge the election results because of ostensibly illegal votes or support the prosecution of illegal voters by supplying what information they had to the authorities. But they also admitted early on that neither approach would change the election re-sults and that even if they could, that manner of victory and the animosity it would generate would not be worth the effort. Others wanted to challenge all illegal votes from both sides simply because of the necessity of preserving the "purity" of the ballot box.[37] Henry Grady opposed taking any legal action, and by November 29 his opinion had won the day—the election results were not contested. Many also talked about remaining organized so that they would be prepared to conduct another campaign in two years. Most saw the end of prohibition in Atlanta as only a temporary setback, and they were anxious to move beyond the tensions created by the campaign. It is not clear whether blacks participated in these post-election meetings, but if they did they probably played a minor role.[38]

It seems clear that black voters took their stand against prohibition after the two-year experiment. Late on Election Day, based on reports from their poll

Table 8—Local Option Election Results, 1887

	"For the Sale"	*"Against the Sale"*	*Totals*
Atlanta	3,929	3,112	7,041
Fulton County outside of Atlanta	1,254	949	2,203
Totals	5,183 (56%)	4,061 (44%)	9,244

Data compiled by author from "It Is Wet," *Atlanta Constitution*, November 27, 1887.

watchers, W. T. Turnbull, chairman of the Young Men's Prohibition Club, esti-mated that only four hundred to six hundred blacks voted dry. "We had perhaps four hundred of the best negroes of Atlanta with us from first to last. They were ready to work all the time, but whenever we touched the negro ranks we found them wet. . . . We could never get enough negroes to make the fight a safe one." Turnbull went on to say that he was "sure" that the prohis did not get even 600 black votes out of an estimated 3,200 registered blacks. These estimates put the number of dry black votes at less than 20 percent, maybe one-third of what it was in 1885. It is suggestive of black sentiment that the ward with the largest black population, the Fourth Ward, also produced the largest margin of victory for the wets. In addition, some blacks were so turned off by the whole campaign that they simply refused to register; compared to 1885 the percentage of eligible blacks who registered dropped by about 10 percent. While approximately 1,500 more whites registered to vote than in 1885, only about 100 more blacks registered, if even that many. The nation's press reported that the black "stampede" to the anti camp overturned prohibition in Atlanta.[39]

Atlanta, Once Again "Torn Up from the Lowest Foundation of Her Emotions"

Accusations immediately began to fly within prohibitionist circles. While some claimed most blacks voted dry, many others immediately accused blacks of voting wet, revealing previously muted prejudices. One strident paper chas-tised blacks—"Atlanta's ignorance and depravity"—for exercising the "sovereign prerogative of free American citizens" to "fasten the teeth of the rum fiend in the hearts of fifty thousand people." Another paper viewed the black vote as harmful to the race and demonstrated both a paternalistic attitude and the typical white misunderstanding of the Southern black experience by asking, "Why is it that the colored people . . . are found acting against their own interests?" From the perspective of Atlanta's wet black voters, of course, they *were* acting in their own interests. Black prohibitionist opinions paralleled those of whites. The *Christian Recorder* said it was "extremely sorry" that the majority of the race voted wet and that the city as a whole lacked the "moral courage" to retain prohibition. To the consternation of white and black drys, Atlanta's local option elections demonstrated that its blacks had just as many divisions and interests as did its whites. Since whites were in the majority, however, a strong white dry vote could have easily passed prohibition over a strong black wet vote, but white prohis *again* chose to ignore this fact. Instead, they began a dangerous racialized finger-pointing.[40]

A tragic event that occurred on election night even further racialized the election results. Charnell Hightower, a white member of the Young Men's Prohibition Club, met a small group of drunken blacks on Ivy Street. They asked him how he voted; after some hesitance he finally admitted he was a dry. After he passed them, one of the black men threw a rock and hit him in the back of his head, causing severe bleeding and a concussion. Hightower died four days later. On December 1, the Young Men's Prohibition Club hosted his funeral, and Dr. J. B. Hawthorne was among the eulogizers. He said it would be "unjust" and "exceedingly foolish" to blame anti-prohibitionists for the murder, but he called the murder the "fruit" of the "iniquitous traffic" that the recent election had just returned to the city. The irony of the fact that drunkards had just committed murder under "double" prohibition[41] seemed to have escaped him. Hawthorne warned that the act was prophetic, saying that the high license men would prove "powerless before the savage fury of the black rabble howling for free liquor," violating his pledge not to blame the antis for Hightower's murder. Before saloons could be legally reopened, a certain few blacks had already created a negative racial image for frustrated white prohibitionists to use against all blacks in the name of progress. But it was not just white prohibitionists who were angry at black wets.[42]

The strong anti-prohibitionist black vote also exposed previously hidden divisions within the black community. The significant reduction in the black dry vote meant that some church members had voted wet despite their pastor's exhortations, and this fact created weeks of strife in several congregations. Big Bethel and Allen Temple's leadership were so exercised over the fact that some of their flock voted wet that they cancelled their first regularly scheduled prayer meeting following the election just to keep peace in the church. Other churches experienced worse repercussions. The pastor of Lloyd Street Methodist Episcopal Church, who repeatedly warned his members not to vote wet, removed a couple of deacons for insubordination and put so much pressure on a third one that he simply resigned. The pastor then appointed a committee to decide if the ousted deacons should be expelled. The black prohibitionist leader Nick Holmes, a member of E. R. Carter's Friendship Baptist Church, chaired a committee in his church that recommended the removal from office of "straight out anti" deacons and any other officeholder who had voted wet.[43]

Of all the post-election church tensions, however, the press provided the most detailed coverage about the troubles at First Congregational Church, which still had a white pastor. As discussed in chapter two, the church had a formal process for charging and removing members.[44] Prohibitionist members "preferred" charges against at least four fellow members for "violating your church covenant in working for the return of the rum traffic to the city." Micah Mitchell had given speeches for the wets, and Charlie Harper used his hack to transport wet voters to the polls. The disciplinary committee recommended their expulsion, but its decision had to be ratified by a majority vote of the membership. Many people arrived early for the trial meeting. Each member had his charges read publicly by an appointed "prosecutor" and had an opportunity to speak for himself. Since the first three men were unrepentant for their anti votes and campaign support, more than 75 percent of the voting members supported their expulsion. The fourth member was an old barber named Dougherty Hutchins, who was simply charged with being drunk and using abusive language. He challenged anyone to stand up and say in public they had seen him drunk. No one did, and by this and other "conciliatory" gestures he retained his membership. But several members were so disaffected by the whole process that even though they attended they refused to vote.[45]

Bishop Henry M. Turner, who did not pastor a church at this time, vented his anger through the pages of his *Southern Recorder*. He praised J. S. Flipper for his "bold stand" for prohibition but accused him of being too late. During the campaign, black wets had accused white drys of being disingenuous in their relationship to blacks; now was Turner's chance to retaliate in kind: "Can *we* go the Opera House and sit in the dress circle since you gained *your* 'personal liberty'?" "Since the Negro has succeeded in obtaining his 'personal liberty,' we want him to exercise a part of it by asking his white friends to grant him liberty enough to allow him to get a license and sell whiskey in his own name. YOU CAN'T GET IT!" The fact that neither a dry nor a wet vote could realistically enable a black man to anticipate improved race relations demonstrated the hegemony of white supremacy in 1880s Atlanta. The fact that black voters on both sides sought the same results suggests how deeply they longed for the equal treatment that would validate their independence and manhood. The internecine struggles of Black Atlanta that followed the vote revealed the pent-up frustrations created by white supremacy.[46]

But it was not just the losers who commented on the outcome of the election. *Atlanta's Experience*, an anonymously authored pamphlet published following the vote, used a barrage of statistics to demonstrate the economic harm done by prohibition and to implicitly predict prosperous days ahead. The author quoted a landlord saying that rental prices had plummeted 25 percent or more on his business properties in the central business district. Convictions in Fulton County Superior Court had increased during prohibition, as well as arrests for drunkenness. The amount of whiskey shipped into Atlanta did not decrease, and if one counted the wine rooms and clubs, there were nearly as many places to purchase liquor as before prohibition. The author made it clear that the 1887 vote was a choice to bring economic prosperity back to the city.[47]

Some observers continued to be bothered by the general disregard for racial etiquette demonstrated during the campaign. From a neighboring county, the *DeKalb Chronicle* editorialized about the efforts of white WCTU ladies to work with black women: "We desire temperance, but if our women must sacrifice their crowning jewel, womanly modesty, and associate themselves with people of questionable character, and with those in whom they can find no congeniality, we prefer less temperance." Blacks also criticized the relaxed etiquette. One black man was quoted in the paper as saying that the forwardness of white ladies with black voters was dangerous because, "if one of our young men . . . should speak to one of them the next day, he would stand a mighty good chance of getting lynched." Just as in 1885, Atlanta had once again been "torn up from the lowest foundation of her emotions."[48]

Why 1887 Was Not 1885

Atlanta went wet in 1887 because the black vote went wet. The fissures within the black community were not apparent during the 1885 vote, but prohibition and the 1887 vote exposed the growing divide between principled prohibitionists and opportunistic prohibitionists, or blacks who had been influenced by Northerners from the evangelical reform nexus and those who had not. African Americans with a stronger connection to the cultural and spiritual traditions of their African past than to the ideas of the reform nexus were predisposed toward a relatively more pragmatic approach to survival in a racist society. They were more inclined to evaluate prohibition based on whether it delivered on its promises, whether it "worked," analogous to the traditional African method of responding to priests, and even spirit beings. Judged against the needs of their community, personal temperance might be effective, hence "good," and even "virtuous," but prohibition proved to be none of these. With the ethical dexterity (ambiguity, to some) of Brer Rabbit, many black voters who supported prohibition in 1885 saw no contradiction in rejecting it in 1887 after it failed to produce the promised results. For principled prohibitionists, the minority of black voters who viewed temperance and prohibition in absolute moral terms, such thinking could only be interpreted as equivocation or compromise. But that was the cultural and ethical space in which most blacks lived, and in some ways being an opportunistic prohibitionist voter was a more authentically "African" position than that of the principled prohibitionists.

Yet Atlanta also went wet in 1887 because the white vote went wet. Too many Southern white prohibitionists turned the 1880s local option elections into referendums on the freed people's supposed "readiness" for citizenship and ignored the strong wet sentiment among rank-and-file white voters, even evangelical whites. Joe Coker has persuasively argued that, before prohibition could become successful in the "Land of the Lost Cause," evangelicals had to adapt it to Southern white culture. They did that by gradually co-opting the Southern sense of honor by redefining it from one that glorified drinking, fighting, and gambling to one that embraced abstinence, support for law and order, and morally upright behavior. Second, by their unflinching persistence they overturned the doctrine of the "spirituality of the church" by continuously arguing that Christians were obligated to "vote as you pray." The third area of which Coker speaks is race relations. On the issue of race, rather than co-opt or invert the cultural norm, evangelical prohibitionists surrendered to it. They refused to oppose lynchings ostensibly carried out to defend white women's purity from black male rapists and instead argued that the best defense for white women (and hence the best way to stop the lynching) was to stop the sale of liquor. In January 1908 Georgia became the first Southern state to adopt prohibition. Coker argues that prohibition did not and could not come to the South until all three of these cultural conversions occurred, and these changes were not complete until the late 1890s at the earliest. This explains Atlanta's large white wet votes in the 1880s.[49]

White Atlantans were unconvinced, and Black Atlanta had a sense of "twoness" that created competing and unequal sets of motivating factors. The lived experience of prohibition—broken promises, bickering, absence of increased political opportunities for blacks—effectively eliminated the opportunistic dry black vote. Beneath all the acrimony between dry and wet whites lay a solid substratum of commitment to white supremacy, which was not lost on black Atlantans. The interracialism displayed by white prohibitionists in 1885 was truly out of character for them. They could not maintain it. They were not ready to treat blacks as political equals, not to mention economic or social equals. In terms of race relations, the "relative balance of progressive and conservative political forces," which Rochon maintains is critical to the political acceptance of reform movement ideas, was clearly tilted the wrong way.[50]

Support for temperance and prohibition was maintained by the rising better class of blacks, and it grew among whites, but when prohibition finally came to Georgia 20 years later it was not done by plebiscite. By the time it arrived, the better class of blacks had solidified itself with social organizations, a modicum of assets, and sophisticated networking, and they retained their commitment to temperance rooted in the values of the evangelical reform nexus. But whites had become so distant from blacks that they did not notice, and besides, it did not matter because African Americans had been disfranchised.

> Defeat we never will confess,
> We shall win, yes, we shall win;
> Because we fight for righteousness.
> We shall win, yes, we shall win;
> Though enemies may all unite
> Our holy purposes to blight,
> They all shall flee before the light,
> We shall win, yes, we shall win.
> —"We Shall Win," second stanza

Afterword

Atlanta's 1885 vote was the apogee of an era; its 1887 vote was the finale of that era. It is tempting to view these votes as referenda on the effectiveness of 20 years of temperance work among the freed people, but they were much more than that. They offer us a window into the evanescent racial world of 1880s Atlanta. The African American temperance movement continued in both its political/legal suasion (only briefly) and its social/moral suasion dimensions, but they would never again merge with the white temperance movement, because everything changed.

Both the black and white communities emerged from the 1887 contest licking their wounds and prioritizing race-based unity. In January 1888, 350 black men from across the state convened in Macon to assess the state of African Americans in Georgia. Among those present were Bishop Henry M. Turner, William Pledger, Smith W. Easley, Alonzo Burnett, and Antoine Graves. When Easley called for a committee on temperance, he faced opposition from those who feared the issue would divide the convention. Although Easley finally got his committee, and Turner and Graves served on it, they produced a brief, innocuous statement that simply reiterated their support for personal abstinence, something on which all could agree. Publicly at least, black leaders had reached a truce. Racial unity had trumped prohibition activism. Although in Atlanta's 1888 municipal election the candidates presented themselves as prohibitionists and anti-prohibitionists, the issue only received sporadic attention in subsequent elections. White prohibitionists never called for another local option vote, fearing the city could not afford its divisiveness. In Atlanta politics, prohibition was dead.[1]

Undaunted, black principled prohibitionists continued their work, laboring on multiple fronts. Bishop Turner joined the newly organized Prohibition Party of Georgia and served as a delegate to its national convention in 1888, where he gave a brief address.[2] But most activity was apolitical. In 1890 Wesley J. Gaines, recently promoted to bishop, wrote a history of the AME Church in the South, and included a chapter on temperance, without which he said the book would be "incomplete." Gaines also addressed the World's Temperance Congress in

1893. Atlanta's Colored WCTUs kept up an active schedule for several years. New WCTUs were organized, and by February 1888 six colored unions operated in Atlanta. The West and East WCTUs each had more than 50 members and several departments. Alumni of Spelman Seminary and Atlanta University held offices in the city's unions and in the statewide union. In the nineties, reformer and activist Ida Wells-Barnett challenged the national WCTU to oppose lynching, to little effect. The nineties also witnessed the rise of three major national evangelical youth organizations—the Young People's Christian Endeavor Society, Baptist Young People's Union, and Epworth League—all of which promoted temperance instruction by the mid-1890s, and prohibition soon thereafter. Atlanta's black churches and schools sponsored chapters of these organizations, which remained active well into the twentieth century. The major African American Baptist and Methodist denominations continued to produce committee reports and publications endorsing personal abstinence and prohibition well into the twentieth century, in line with major white Protestant groups.

As long as they remained enfranchised, black principled prohibitionists remained active in city politics, but they pursued other, more attainable objectives. Moses Bently, Antoine Graves, and Smith Easley fought for an African American on the 1887 "Citizen's Ticket," but as usual they were unsuccessful. As blacks continued to jockey for influence they finally struck a deal with the prohibitionist candidate for mayor, John Glenn: if he received the black vote, he would build a school for blacks in the Fifth Ward. When one thousand black voters supported Glenn, the school board built the Gray Street School in 1888. Blacks made a similar agreement again in 1891, receiving the Roach Street School, which opened in 1892. Working-class whites eventually became frustrated with failed efforts to make political alliances with blacks and began pushing for the white primary for municipal elections.[3] By 1893, in line with practices throughout the South, so many black Atlanta voters had been disfranchised that the number of remaining voters had become inconsequential.

At the same time African Americans were being disfranchised, Black Atlanta was experiencing increased internal stratification, fueled in part by values introduced through Northern-run missionary schools. The strengthening of social boundary lines was reflected in increasingly consistent patterns of behavior in such areas as residential housing, social networks, church life, and alcohol consumption. By the turn of the century, Auburn Avenue and Decatur Street starkly illustrated this divide. Both streets were in the Old Fourth Ward, a historically black-majority neighborhood, but that was all they had in common. Auburn Avenue's growing nucleus of black-owned businesses, churches, and residences of the college-educated earned it the moniker "richest Negro street in the world"; black Atlantans called it "Sweet Auburn." Sweet Auburn's residents generally shunned

Decatur Street, however, known for its "sporting houses," "dives," cheap boarding houses, gambling, and vaudeville houses. No less than 34 saloons graced Decatur Street in 1900. The *Augusta Herald* described the street as having an "unsavory reputation" because almost the entire street was "given over to low dives, cheap hand-me-downs and other like establishments." Decatur Street was a neighborhood on the margins between three or four neighborhoods. Blacks, Jews, whites, and Chinese worked, shopped, and entertained themselves mixing on nearly equal terms. But it had not always been this way. Atlanta's zoning and policing practices had gradually pushed these less respectable activities out of other neighborhoods, turning the street into what Kevin Mumford calls an "interzone," a marginal area of interracial culture and vice.[4]

In addition to increasing internal stratification, de facto racial segregation spread to virtually every area of life. Wealthy residents on streets like West Peachtree stopped permitting their help to live in or to live in alleys near their houses. The quality of life in almost any black neighborhood was lower than in almost any white neighborhood. Black neighborhoods experienced "deplorable and inadequate" sanitation services, streetlighting, housing, roads, and sidewalks. In the Pittsburg neighborhood, the city so regularly dumped tin cans and other trash to fill the gullies that one section was nicknamed "Tin Can Alley." City planners designed streetcar lines, sewers, and the public water system to bypass black communities. Such characteristics coupled with police neglect, unschooled children, unemployment, underemployment, low incomes, and high illiteracy created not only high crime rates but also physically unhealthy neighborhoods. The African American mortality rate rose to about 150 percent that of whites, with consumption and pneumonia being the biggest culprits. Illegal liquor selling (selling without a license) became a problem even before state prohibition began. In sum, ghettoization was well underway years before the city created the state's first residential Jim Crow ordinance in 1913.[5]

Even entrepreneurial blacks withdrew from their white clientele. In the early years following emancipation, black professionals like dentist Roderick D. Badger and skilled workers like the merchant tailor William Finch had built their businesses and their wealth on white patronage. By the turn of the century, the growing black population, increasing racial segregation, newfound race pride, and popularity of self-help strategies led the rising black petit bourgeoisie to turn to the black masses for their customer base. Black Atlanta newspaper editor Benjamin Davis joined his peers across America in calling for readers to buy from blacks and to employ blacks. This was an integral part of becoming a proud twentieth-century "race man."

Each race turned inward, only increasing the distance between them. W. E. B. DuBois observed that "despite much physical contact and daily intermingling, there is almost no . . . point of transference where the thoughts and feelings of one race can come into direct contact and sympathy with the thoughts and feelings of the other."[6] One black editor put it this way:

> The Southern people know really very little about the Negro as he is. They see him on the streets, at railway stations, as porters at hotels, and on Pullman cars; but as a cultured lady and gentleman, in the church, at the fireside, in the school-room, on the platform, in the pulpit, and even in the editorial room, they know scarcely anything of us.[7]

The absence of lynchings and an active KKK did not accurately reflect Atlanta's increasing racial hostility. During the 1890s Atlanta's newspapers portrayed holiday binge drinking by blacks as an increasing problem. News stories increasingly exaggerated stories of drunken blacks being arrested for various crimes. Cartoonists began portraying blacks with ape-like features. This denigrating image coincided with the rise of Jim Crow laws throughout the South and scientific racism throughout the nation. The drunken "black beast" image stoked white fears, intensified white prejudices, and racialized the prohibitionists' message. The nadir had arrived.

Deteriorating race relations established the ideal social and political conditions for prohibition in Georgia. In 1906 Georgians experienced a gubernatorial campaign characterized by race-baiting and a sensational and irresponsible Atlanta press that stoked public hysteria with false stories of rape. This election became a match on the tinder of racial hostility that Atlanta had become. When the saloons closed one September night and men filled the streets in various degrees of inebriation, just a few sharp words and an assault were all that was needed to spark one of the worst race riots in the nation's history. In the wake of the riot many people, black and white, blamed the saloons. A year later, partly as a result of the riot and partly the result of many years of prohibition activism, the Hardeman-Covington prohibition law created statewide prohibition effective January 1, 1908. Georgia became the first former Confederate state to go dry years before national prohibition began.

Black Atlanta's story was not an isolated one; rather, it blended seamlessly into the larger narratives of Southern temperance and black enfranchisement and should be interpreted as such. In 1887 Atlanta's vote became the third horse in a trifecta of prohibition defeats, signaling the end to one era of Southern temperance. Between July and November 1887, Texas, Tennessee, and Atlanta had all rejected prohibition, and according to some white prohibitionists, it was the "fault" of black voters. This broader context makes it even easier to assess Black Atlanta's reception of temperance and response to prohibition.

From the perspective of 1887 it seems clear that most 1885 dry black voters did not base their vote on a principled commitment to teetotalism. While upwardly mobile blacks at least practiced temperate consumption of alcoholic beverages for the obvious non-religious reasons, little evidence exists that large numbers of blacks outside the orbit of the evangelical reform nexus organizations had been persuaded to adopt the teetotal lifestyle, accentuating its fundamentally evangelical Christian character in the African American experience. Twenty years after emancipation, the structural adolescence of Black Atlanta meant it lacked the necessary resources, channels, and institutions to enable teetotalism to "break out of the movement community" and become a widely held value comparable to what had occurred among antebellum Northern blacks and New Englanders. The 1885 call for a local option election prematurely converted Black Atlanta's social movement into a political movement, reducing temperance to prohibition, which, for many blacks, turned out to be little more than a pragmatic political tactic designed to improve race relations. Thus principled teetotalism was not the basis for the 1885 dry black vote.

It is now clear that the critical elements that created the dry victory in 1885 Atlanta were an exceptional degree of black clergy unity, the systematic and enticing blurring of racial etiquette, and most importantly, a black electorate unacquainted with life under prohibition. Each of these elements was absent from the 1887 votes in Atlanta, Texas, and Tennessee. With all due respect to W. E. B. DuBois's youthful observation that "Perhaps never before was the Negro as generally recognized . . . as a man" as during Tennessee's prohibition campaign, that campaign failed to bring together these three components. Although Tennessee's campaign practices yielded its own commentary about "blurred racial lines," its prohibition activists eschewed strong clergy alliances in the beginning, only joining forces with them as the campaign wore on. In Texas's vote, from the beginning, the main Prohibition leaders were professionals and businessmen who feared clergy involvement and made a conscious effort to downplay the clergy's role in the campaign. Texas drys exacerbated racial distrust by telling blacks that wets were "Negro haters" and then turning around and telling white audiences that wets were too cozy with blacks. This doublespeak only alienated black voters, removing any basis for hope that a vote for prohibition could improve race relations, their single most pressing concern. In 1887 some of Atlanta's black pastors broke rank, either opposing or failing to speak up for prohibition, thus sending a mixed message. Although some contemporary observers thought Atlanta's 1887 campaign witnessed a breakdown of racial etiquette comparable to that of 1885, Atlanta prohibitionist Wilbur P. Thirkield asserted that relatively poor race relations characterized their 1887 defeat: "There was no bond of moral union, no well-defined basis of cooperation, no fusion of the races, as before."[8]

Finally, the degree of experience with prohibition prior to voting on it undoubtedly was a major factor in these prohibition votes. The promises of 1885 were incredibly tantalizing to black voters who wanted to believe the dry campaign's seemingly new racial ethos could be made permanent by a dry vote. Nothing so gnawed at the sense of black manhood as their continued infantilization at the hands of white people. Whatever could make a white man call a black man "brother" and a white woman call a black woman "sister" demanded careful consideration, if not a vote. But the power of that argument was largely predicated on a lack of experience with prohibition, and presumably few Atlanta blacks had ever lived under prohibition because almost all of them had migrated to the city before the creation of dry counties throughout the state. Two years of prohibition thoroughly dispelled any notion that white prohibitionists sought a new racial paradigm. By the time Tennessee and Texas voted on state prohibition, many localities within those states had been dry for a while, so many black voters in those campaigns already knew how prohibition "worked," and as in 1887 Atlanta, no amount of campaigning rhetoric or tactics could persuade them otherwise. For Atlanta's black voters who had supported prohibition in 1885, the characteristically pragmatic African American worldview offered a ready-made ethical and existential framework with which to rationalize an opposite vote in 1887.

Prohibition voting was tricky at best for blacks, who often seemed to hold the balance of power in Southern elections. When blacks voted with prohibitionists they *frightened* the antis, who loathed the idea of having black voters settle divisive issues; and when blacks voted with the antis they *angered* the prohis, who charged them with being a force for unrestrained immorality. Since both sides were ultimately committed to white supremacy, neither could bear the thought of blacks comprising the swing vote on major public policy issues. When it was not yet certain whether black voters were responsible for making Atlanta dry in 1885, one wet editor opined, "wouldn't it be an unfortunate condition of things to have such a law forced upon white men by negro votes?"[9] But the trend among white voters was toward prohibition, and Bishop Turner accurately sensed this fact. Just prior to the 1887 vote he penned the following prescient, yet stern, prophecy:

> We venture to predict, that if the Negro vote continues to defeat prohibition with all of the concomitant blessings with which it is freighted, there will be an effort made to disfranchise him in less than five years, and whenever the attempt is inaugurated by the better class of whites, it will succeed, for the white liquor sots will join with them.[10]

Although all of the "better class" of whites were certainly not the prohibitionists that Turner implied and race relations were rapidly heading downhill regardless of blacks' prohibition voting practices, he correctly predicted that white wets and drys would lay aside their differences and unite to disfranchise blacks.[11] Atlanta's white primary began in 1892, and after that year black voter participation, although still permitted in general elections, became inconsequential.

But Black Atlanta's experience with the temperance movement does more than expose turning points in the trajectory of Southern prohibition and black enfranchisement. It also suggests nascent intra-communal cultural boundary lines, reveals the limitations of nineteenth-century reform movements, and reaffirms what we have come to know about the hostility of Southern race relations in the 1880s. Freed people exposed to the intense teetotal message of Northern evangelicalism could accept its logic with some ease because of the intersections between Northern nexus theology and certain African elements of their African American worldview. However, their inability to diffuse these values to the masses increasingly made attitudes toward alcohol use a marker of class differences within the black community. Resilient and pragmatic African–rooted cultural orientations combined with the exigencies of poverty nourished by a racist environment and likely kept many from a commitment to teetotalism as much as it encouraged them to oppose prohibition in 1887. Although they voted Republican, the "personal liberty" plank of the Democracts resonated deeply with a people recently emancipated from centuries of slavery. The divergent reactions of black voters to the contradictions and hypocrisies of two years of prohibition lifted the veil on this emerging divide.

My research into nineteenth-century temperance and prohibition has been somewhat of a bittersweet experience because of my admiration for the reformers' original vision, and because to this day I embrace key elements of their brand of Christianity. But no matter how noble the religious-inspired vision of nineteenth-century temperance reformers might have been, in the end their theology and praxis were held hostage by their culture (as all religious experience is), and the movement was a dismal failure as judged by its own criteria. When the Anti-Saloon League (ASL) pioneered twentieth-century political pressure tactics targeting elected officials, they achieved in a matter of years what moral suasion could not do in more than a century. But despite the approval of national prohibition by traditionally moral suasion–oriented organizations, the political tactics used by the ASL to secure prohibition differed substantially from the grueling face-to-face grassroots citizen work of organizations such as the American Missionary Association, American Baptist Home Mission Society, National Temperance Society, and AME Church. The nineteenth-century temperance movement makes it clear just how difficult it was to transform public sentiment from the bottom up before the late twentieth-century proliferation of mass communication technologies and institutions committed to generating and disseminating new knowledge and ideas. The most recent example of how rapidly social and political change can occur in the twenty-first century is the issue of same sex marriage. The subject went from virtual nonexistence in public discourse to affirmed legal status in several states in less than 25 years. Recent public opinion polls show a 26 percent swing in public opinion favoring same sex marriage within a decade. This is simply unprecedented in the history of social reform movements.[12]

The changing world of the postbellum South as revealed through the temperance movement also invites analysis in terms of the classic C. Vann Woodward thesis.[13] The 1885 vote initially appears to have been a clear example of Woodward's so-called missed opportunities in race relations. This study has argued that black voters did not reject prohibition on principle, but rather, the pragmatic worldview of African Americans predisposed most black voters—despite influences from principled prohibitionists—to assess it based on the degree to which it fulfilled its promise to ameliorate the strictures of white supremacy and undermine the practices that perpetuated it. White supremacy was so deeply engrained, and whites themselves were so divided, that those promises could never materialize; so in round number two, blacks rejected prohibition like their ancestors rejected priests offering ineffectual incantations. The reason contemporaries viewed the 1885 vote as a "most stirring and significant episode" was that race relations following Redemption were *not* the "unstable interlude" Woodward imagined. Instead, a discriminatory and demeaning racial etiquette were well-known and firmly established, and hence the behaviors and rhetoric of white prohibitionists were shocking to all concerned. The forces that converged on Atlanta were powerful enough to transcend that etiquette very briefly (for a few weeks), but the brevity of that moment only illustrates the hegemonic power of white supremacy in the period of supposedly "missed opportunities." While black Atlantans largely failed to adopt teetotalism because of structural issues internal to their community, both their historic cultural orientation and factors external to their community converged to lead them to reject prohibition.

Appendix I

Biographical Sketches of Key Personalities

John Alvord—Alumnus of Oberlin College; Congregational minister; agent for American Anti-Slavery Society; colporteur for American Tract Society-Boston; Superintendent of Schools for the Freedmen's Bureau

Frederick Ayer—Antebellum missionary to the Ojibwe; ordained by Charles Finney; first AMA missionary in Black Atlanta (1865–1867); founder of the Storrs School, First Congregational Church, and Atlanta's first temperance society for blacks

Dr. Roderick Dhu Badger—African American dentist opposed to prohibition

Lyman Beecher—Northern antebellum Congregational minister whose preaching and work spurred the creation of benevolent societies

John Emory Bryant—Northern migrant to Atlanta following the war; Republican; outspoken prohibitionist

Alonzo W. Burnett—Editor of *Weekly Defiance*; sometimes prohibitionist

E. R. Carter—A freedman; pastor of Friendship Baptist Church (1882–1944); graduate of Atlanta Baptist Seminary; outspoken prohibitionist

Alfred Colquitt—Member of Georgia's Bourbon Triumvirate; Georgia governor (1877–1882); U.S. senator from Georgia (1883–1894); outspoken prohibitionist; friend of William E. Dodge and Henry Grady; supporter of the New South movement

Theodore L. Cuyler—Founding pastor of Lafayette Avenue Presbyterian Church, Brooklyn, NY (1860–1890); a founder of the National Temperance Society, and its president (1885–1893)

William E. Dodge—Founding president of the National Temperance Society (1865–1883); major New York philanthropist for African American higher education, temperance, and other causes; visited Atlanta several times; spoke at Atlanta University; friend of Alfred Colquitt

John Dougall—Immigrant from Scotland and Canada; published and edited the *New York Weekly Witness*; for two years mailed the *Witness* free of charge to African American clergy, including some in Atlanta; ardent abolitionist and temperance reformer

Smith W. Easley—Alumnus of Storrs School; lodge organizer for Independent Order Good Samaritans in Georgia; Right Worthy grand chief of Georgia's Grand Lodge; editor of *Herald of United Churches*; active prohibitionist

Charles Finney—Most prominent antebellum evangelist; professor and president of Oberlin College; promoter of temperance; many of his converts involved in abolitionism, temperance, and other reforms

Wesley J. Gaines—A freedman from Georgia; second pastor of Bethel AME Church (1867–1869); active prohibitionist; a Good Templar; ordained bishop in 1888; a founder of Morris Brown College; author of *African Methodism in the South, or Twenty-Five Years of Freedom* (1890)

Henry Grady—Editor of the *Atlanta Constitution*; supporter of the New South movement; active prohibitionist

Dr. J. B. Hawthorne—Pastor of First Baptist Church; supporter of the New South movement; active prohibitionist

Sam Jones—Methodist evangelist from Cartersville, Georgia; active prohibitionist; the "Moody of the South"; supporter of the New South movement

Honorable Jefferson Franklin Long—A freedman from Georgia; a member of the Forty-First Congress (1870–1871), from Macon, Georgia; first African American elected to the U.S. House of Representatives from Georgia; an anti-prohibitionist

Jackson McHenry—Aspiring African American Republican politician who worked a variety of jobs; sometimes prohibitionist

Henry L. Morehouse—Baptist missionary and pastor from New York state who served as corresponding secretary of the American Baptist Home Mission Society (1879–1892, 1902–1917) and as its field secretary (1893–1902); Atlanta Baptist Seminary was renamed Morehouse College in his honor in 1912. He originated the phrase "talented tenth"

Daniel A. Payne—Born free in South Carolina; seminary-trained; president of Wilberforce College who organized the AME Church in South Carolina and Georgia following the war; advocate for educated clergy and temperance; ordained an AME bishop in 1852

William A. Pledger—Alumnus of Storrs School; grand worthy master of Georgia's Grand Fountain of the United Order of True Reformers in 1870s; editor, teacher, Republican Party leader; prohibitionist in Clarke County and anti-prohibitionist in Fulton County

Ebenezer Porter—Antebellum New England Congregational pastor and Andover Seminary professor; the idea to organize several benevolent societies, including the American Tract Society and the American Temperance Society, arose out of Bible studies he hosted

J. C. Price—Minister in the AME Zion Church; president of Livingstone College in North Carolina; a missionary for the National Temperance Society who spoke in Atlanta

Sam Small—Journalist and former-drinker-turned-evangelist; active prohibitionist; worked with evangelist Sam Jones

J. N. Stearns—A founder of the National Temperance Society and editor of *National Temperance Advocate* (1865–1893); a Good Templar; traveled regularly throughout the South on behalf of temperance; visited Atlanta's missionary schools several times

"Mother" Eliza Stewart—Organized the South's first colored chapter of the Woman's Christian Temperance Union in Atlanta in 1880 while on a trip through the South on behalf of the WCTU

Michael Strieby—Oberlin College alumnus; secretary of the American Missionary Association

Wilbur P. Thirkield—Methodist minister; founding dean of Clark University's Gammon School of Theology in 1883; active prohibitionist

James G. Thrower—Northern building contractor who moved to Atlanta following the war; he organized the city's first Good Templar Lodges (white) and True Reformer Fountains (black); introduced traveling temperance speakers to the black schools; worked closely with National Temperance Society missionaries; a prohibitionist

Henry McNeal Turner—Born free in South Carolina; converted in a Methodist revival meeting and licensed to preach in 1853; army chaplain during Civil War; organized Georgia congregations for the AME Church following the war; Georgia Republican politician during Reconstruction; ordained bishop in 1880; Atlanta resident during the 1880s and 1890s; editor of *Southern Recorder*; active prohibitionist

Frances E. Willard—President of the WCTU (1879–1898); visited Atlanta in 1881

Elder Joseph Wood—Brought Atlanta's oldest black congregation into the AME Church in 1865 and served as Bethel AME's first pastor (1865–1866); founded and pastored Wood's Chapel (later known as Allen Temple) (1866–1870, 1879–1883); worthy master of Atlanta's first True Reformer Fountain; leader of a Good Samaritan Lodge; president of the temperance society of the North Georgia Annual Conference of the AME Church

Appendix II

Regulating Atlanta's Liquor Industry, 1865–1907

As early as 1870 Atlanta's liquor industry included three breweries, several wholesale distributors, and a lively saloon scene. Atlanta was growing, and boosters excited about the city's potential sought ways to boost its liquor industry while simultaneously defending it against stereotypes of being a liquor-soaked city. The 1871 booklet *Atlanta As It Is* reported that there were more licensed saloons in the city than any other licensed enterprise except physicians and logically concluded that the liquor business was "very important" to Atlanta. After reviewing details about the sizes of the various wholesale liquor houses, it reminded readers that much of the liquor was shipped outside the city and that "a drunken man on our streets is rather a rare sight." Early in 1885 the *Atlanta Constitution* listed 150 licensed businesses where a citizen could "wet his whistle" with some form of alcohol. While the article noted that "A man don't have to walk much out of his way to get his toddy," it also tried to reduce any sense of alarm by noting that there were other cities in the state with far more barrooms than Atlanta.[1]

Atlanta's retail liquor industry may have been growing in absolute numbers, but relative to other factors it was actually in decline. Tables II.1 and II.2 show that according to the city directories, although the number of saloons steadily increased relative to the population and total city revenue, they did not keep pace with Atlanta's growth. Atlanta's citizen-to-saloon ratio was high relative to that of other cities of comparable size in the 1890s. An 1894 survey of 345 cities with more than 10,000 people showed an average of one saloon for every 250 persons, while in Atlanta there was one saloon for every 618 in 1890 and one for every 707 in 1900. Several forces were limiting Atlanta's liquor industry.[2]

While private temperance and prohibition groups did their best to curb the demand for alcoholic beverages, the various levels of government actively regulated their supply and distribution. Notwithstanding some colorful episodes of Atlanta police officers, and a fire chief and a mayor being charged with public drunkenness, Atlanta's government was on the front lines of liquor regulation. The city issued various annual licenses to regulate the liquor trade: licenses for breweries, distilleries, retailers of spirituous liquors, retailers of beer only, and beginning in 1889, liquor wholesalers. Brewery licenses fluctuated between $25 and $100,

Table II.1—Number of Saloons in Atlanta

Year	Number of Saloons	Number of Citizens per Saloon
1870	36	605
1880	82	456
1890	106	618
1900	127	707

Data compiled by author from the business and residential pages of the city directory.

while licenses for distilleries, beer-only retailers, and liquor wholesalers rose steadily from $25 to $250.[3]

But the license attracting the most attention in Atlanta, and in America, was the one allowing its owner to sell spirituous liquors by the drink to be consumed on the premises—the saloon license. Municipalities took three approaches toward these licenses: "low license," "high license," and "no license" (that is, prohibition). Contemporary literature was filled with arguments for and against these various approaches.[4]

Low-license advocates insisted that fees be kept low (less than $500) to allow the greatest number of people possible to enter the trade. Its supporters considered this the fairest and most democratic approach. They argued that requiring high licenses was "class legislation" because the high license priced out of the business the small businessmen, many of whom were likely to be nonwhite.

No-license advocates opposed a low license on the grounds that it could result in a saloon on practically every corner. They argued that since the saloons produced crime, any licensing was nothing more than government endorsement of and profiting from evil.

High-license advocates felt their approach had the triple benefit of increasing city revenue, reducing saloons to a manageable number, and ensuring that only men of high status and "good reputation" would own them, ostensibly guaranteeing the saloons' "respectable" character. They viewed themselves as conservative and reasonable because they freely admitted that the retail trade produced crime and other negative side effects, but they also argued that, realistically speaking, in large cities "prohibition does not prohibit," so high-license was the best alternative.

In 1867 Atlanta had an extremely high $500 license fee. High-license supporters advocated retaining a high fee, arguing that a low license would create an unmanageable proliferation of saloons. However, from 1868 to 1884 the city council

Table II.2—Average Annual Retail Liquor License Revenue by Decade

Decade	*Average Annual Retail Liquor License Revenue*	*Average Annual Retail License Revenue as a Percentage of Total City Revenue*
1871–1880	$17,626.43	6.0%
1881–1890	$37,492.07	5.4%
1891–1900	$80,132.49	5.1%

Data are missing for the following years: 1880, 1895, 1897, and 1900.

Data are compiled by author from annual and quarterly reports of the City Clerk as reported in the Atlanta City Council Minutes, Atlanta History Center.

reduced the fee to $300. Two changes occurred in 1885. In May the city council returned to the $500—"high license"—fee, which reduced the number of saloons by about a third, until November's local option election closed them all. After saloons were returned to Atlanta in 1887, the city moved to a $1,000 license fee. Atlanta was one of a very small group of cities with more than 50,000 people to have a fee $1,000 or higher in the 1880s, and the fee remained unchanged until state prohibition began in January 1908. During these years Atlanta had the highest license fee of any Southern city its size or larger.[5]

The liquor regulations of the Atlanta City Council were constantly changing. In 1879 the council raised the fee to $400 but rescinded the increase after one year. In 1882 the police commission chairman unsuccessfully argued for a $1,000 fee in order to close the many "low dives," a thinly veiled attack on saloons patronized primarily by blacks. No one on the police commission supported him. Prior to 1876 the council read and approved or disapproved a license application in a single council meeting, but beginning in 1876 it referred requests to the council's police committee, which reported back favorably or unfavorably one or two weeks later, presumably after some discussion and investigation. The council granted retail liquor licenses, and all other business licenses, for 12 months, but because the fee was so high for liquor, saloon keepers were permitted to pay it quarterly. Most retailers received a license in July for 12 months, although some were approved at other times at well. Between 1890 and 1892 the council tried another approach. All licenses expired on December 31 and June 30, no matter when they were approved. The vast majority of applicants submitted their applications from four to six weeks before the expiration, and they were considered as a group by the police committee.

This attempt to tighten up the process failed to impress the local press, which claimed licenses were still being issued "indiscriminately." In 1893 the council returned to annual licenses, although they continued to be reviewed as a group every June. Until 1898 the police committee had permitted applicants to begin conducting business while their license was still under consideration, but in 1899 they ended that practice. As one would expect, the council entertained complaints from neighbors about saloons and sometimes rejected licenses based on such petitions. A variety of council ordinances established saloon closing times and regulated sales and operations in various ways.[6]

In spite of all these changes, or perhaps because of them, the city fathers touted the effectiveness of their liquor regulation. The Annual Report of the Police Committee for 1881 claimed that every retail liquor license application received a "rigid and searching investigation." In 1894 they allegedly had the "best regulated liquor traffic of any city in the country," but in 1898 they more modestly claimed to possess a liquor traffic "better regulated than in any other city of the state." There is no way to know exactly how well the police enforced the laws, but even ardent prohibitionist evangelist Sam P. Jones thought in the 1890s that Atlanta's saloon owners were particularly careful about obeying regulations. If Atlanta's saloons were actually that well regulated, the credit must go to a police department assiduous about enforcement, because during these years the chief of police repeatedly requested funds to hire more officers and was repeatedly turned down.[7]

But the city government was not the only level of government regulating Atlanta's liquor industry. The state legislature's actions were ultimately more important. For example, in response to the longtime candidate practice of treating voters, in March 1869 it banned the sale of liquor within one mile of any town on Election Day. In 1873 lawmakers banned gaming in saloons, and beginning in 1875 it became a violation of state law to sell spirituous liquors to minors. But the most significant liquor-related legislation to come out of the state legislature was the General Local Option law of 1885, which paved the way for Atlanta's 1885 and 1887 local option elections. In 1906 Fulton was one of only 26 wet Georgia counties surrounded by a sea of 120 dry counties. Each year from 1893 to 1901 lawmakers introduced some form of state prohibition legislation, only to see it defeated. Finally, in August 1907, in the wake of Atlanta's horrible 1906 race riot, the legislature passed the Hardeman-Covington state prohibition bill, making the whole state dry as of January 1, 1908. Blacks had been effectively disenfranchised long before 1907. Atlanta and all of Georgia remained dry until 1938, five years after the end of national prohibition. Ultimately, prohibition in Atlanta was a result of state, not local, government.[8]

Notes

Introduction

1. Thomas R. Rochon, *Culture Moves: Ideas, Activism, and Changing Values* (Princeton, NJ: Princeton University Press, 1998), 22–32.

2. Donald Yacovone, "The Transformation of the Black Temperance Movement, 1827–1854: An Interpretation," *Journal of the Early Republic* 8 (Fall 1988): 281–97; Denise Herd, "Migration, Cultural Transformation and the Rise of Black Liver Cirrhosis Mortality," *British Journal of Addiction* 80 (1985): 397–410; Herd, "The Paradox of Temperance: Blacks and the Alcohol Question in Nineteenth-Century America," in *Drinking: Behavior and Belief in Modern History*, ed. Susanna Barrows and Robin Room, 354–75 (Berkeley and Los Angeles: University of California Press, 1991); Kenneth Christmon, "Historical Overview of Alcohol in the African American Community," *Journal of Black Studies* 25 (January 1995): 318–30; Shelley Block, "A Revolutionary Aim: The Rhetoric of Temperance in the *Anglo-African Magazine*," *American Periodicals* 12 (2002): 9–24; John Hammond Moore, "The Negro and Prohibition in Atlanta, 1885–1887," *South Atlantic Quarterly* 69 (1970): 38–57; Gregg Cantrell, "'Dark Tactics': Black Politics in the 1887 Texas Prohibition Campaign," *Journal of American Studies* 25 (1991): 85–93; James D. Ivy, *No Saloon in the Valley: The Southern Strategy of Texas Prohibitionists in the 1880s* (Waco: Baylor University Press, 2003).

3. John Allen Krout, *The Origins of Prohibition* (New York: Alfred A. Knopf, 1925); Gilbert Barnes, *The Antislavery Impulse, 1830–1844* (New York: D. Appleton-Century Company, 1933); Alice Felt Tyler, *Freedom's Ferment: Phases of American Social History from the Colonial Period to the Outbreak of the Civil War* (Minneapolis: University of Minnesota Press, 1944); Joseph R. Gusfield, *Symbolic Crusade: Status Politics and the American Temperance Movement* (Urbana: University of Illinois Press, 1963); Norman H. Clark, *Deliver Us from Evil: An Interpretation of American Prohibition* (New York: W. W. Norton & Company, 1976); William J. Rorabaugh, *The Alcoholic Republic: An American Tradition* (New York: Oxford University Press, 1979); David Montgomery, "The Shuttle and the Cross: Weavers and Artisans in the Kensington Riots of 1844," *Journal of Social History* 5 (1972): 411–46; Jack Blocker Jr. *"Give to the Wind thy Fears": The Women's Temperance Crusade, 1873–1874* (Westport, CT: Greenwood Press, 1985); Ruth Bordin, *Woman and Temperance: The Quest for Power and Liberty, 1873–1900* (New Brunswick: Rutgers University Press, 1990); Carol Mattingly, *Well-Tempered Women: Nineteenth-Century Temperance Rhetoric* (Carbondale: Southern Illinois University Press, 1998); Holly Berkley Fletcher, *Gender and the American Temperance Movement of the Nineteenth Century* (New York: Routledge, 2007); Scott C. Martin, *Devil of the Domestic Sphere: Temperance, Gender, and Middle-Class Ideology, 1800–1860* (DeKalb: Northern Illinois University Press, 2008).

4. James R. Rohrer, "The Origins of the Temperance Movement: A Reinterpretation," *Journal of American Studies* 24 (August 1990): 228–35; Robert Abzug, *Cosmos Crumbling: American Reform and the Religious Imagination* (New York: Oxford University Press, 1994); Douglas W. Carlson, "'Drinks He to His Own Undoing': Temperance Ideology in the Deep South," *Journal of the Early Republic* 18 (Winter 1998): 659–91; Michael P. Young, *Bearing Witness*

against Sin: The Evangelical Birth of the American Social Movement (Chicago: University of Chicago Press, 2006). See also Stephen Wills Murphy, "'It Is a Sacred Duty to Abstain': The Organizational, Biblical, Theological, and Practical Roots of the American Temperance Society, 1814–1830" (PhD diss., University of Virginia, 2008), and Steven Mintz, *Moralists and Modernizers: America's Pre–Civil War Reformers* (Baltimore: Johns Hopkins University Press, 1995).

5. Martin E. Marty, *Righteous Empire: The Protestant Experience in America* (New York: Dial Press, 1970).

6. Janette Thomas Greenwood, *Bittersweet Legacy: The Black and White "Better Classes" in Charlotte, 1850–1910* (Chapel Hill: University of North Carolina Press, 1994), 5.

1: "Our Enterprise Flows from the Gospel of Christ"

1. Wilbur Stone Deming, *The Church on the Green: The First Two Centuries of the First Congregational Church at Washington, Connecticut, 1741–1941* (Hartford: Brentano's, 1941), 3–76; Lyman Matthews, *Memoir of the Life and Character of Ebenezer Porter, D.D.* (Boston: Perkins & Marvin, 1837), 318–28; William A. Hallock, *Light and Love: A Sketch of the Life and Labors of the Rev. Justin Edwards, D.D.* (New York: American Tract Society, 1855), 43–44; Murphy, 29–30. I am borrowing the term "Andover Circle" from Stephen Wills Murphy.

2. Thomas S. Grimke, *Address on the Patriot Character of the Temperance Reformation* (Charleston, SC: Observer Office Press, 1833), 5; "Address of the Executive Committee," *Journal of the American Temperance Union* 1 (January 1837): 5; Lebbeus Armstrong, *The Temperance Reformation of this XIXth Century, the Fulfillment of Divine Prophecy* (New York: Pudney, Hooker & Russell, 1845), 3–15.

3. Benjamin Rush, *An Inquiry into the Effects of Spirituous Liquors upon the Human Body, and their Influence upon the Happiness of Society*, 3rd edition (Philadelphia: John McCulloch, 1791), Early American Imprints, Series I, Evans, 1639–1800, 2–4, 6–8; Lebbeus Armstrong, *The Temperance Reformation. Its History from the Organization of the First Temperance Society* (New York: Fowlers and Wells, Publishers, 1853), 18–27, 134–44; William Hay, *A History of Temperance in Saratoga County, N.Y.* (Saratoga Springs: G. M. Davison, 1855), 13–22. The first Southern temperance society was organized in 1822 in North Carolina.

4. Ebenezer Porter, *The Fatal Effects of Ardent Spirits: A Sermon* (Morris-Town: Henry P. Russell, 1812), 2; Charles Beecher, ed., *Autobiography, Correspondence, etc. of Lyman Beecher, D.D.* (New York: Harper & Brothers, Publishers, 1864), 1:245–52, 2:35–36; Allan M. Winkler, "Lyman Beecher and the Temperance Crusade," *Quarterly Journal of Studies on Alcohol* 33 (1972): 943–45, 954.

5. *Fourth Report of the American Temperance Society* in *Permanent Temperance Documents of the American Temperance Society*, vol. 1 (Boston: S. Bliss, 1835), 11, 69–70; Hallock, 43–44, 194–96; Murphy, 64–67; James R. Rohrer, "Battling the Master Vice: The Evangelical War against Intemperance in Ohio, 1800–1832" (Master's thesis, Ohio State University, 1985), 65–73.

For examples of contemporary criticism of temperance reformers' attitudes see "Let the Drunkard Alone," *Christian Watchman*, September 8, 1827, and Abraham Lincoln, "Address Before the Springfield Washingtonian Temperance Society, February 22, 1842," in *Complete Works of Abraham Lincoln*, vol. 1, new and enlarged edition, ed. John G. Nicolay and John Hay (New York: F. D. Tandy, 1905), 201.

6. *Seventh Annual Report of the American Temperance Union*, in *Permanent Temperance Documents of the American Temperance Society,* vol. 2 (New York: American Temperance Union, 1852), 1, 21.

7. Jack S. Blocker Jr., *American Temperance Movements: Cycles of Reform* (Boston: Twayne Publishers, 1989), 48–51.

8. J. James Ridge, *Band of Hope Catechism* (London: United Kingdom Band of Hope Union, n.d.); *Constitution and Minute Book,* March 4, 1876–October 20, 1879, of Band of Hope Miamisburg, Ohio, Ohio Historical Society; *Temperance Lesson Manual for the Band of Hope and Loyal Temperance Legion* 2 (January 1886): 1–4; Lillian Lewis Shiman, "The Band of Hope Movement: Respectable Recreation for Working Class Children," *Victorian Studies* 17 (September 1973): 49–74.

9. Tyler, 316; Paul E. Johnson, *A Shopkeeper's Millennium: Society and Revivals in Rochester, New York, 1815–1837,* 25th anniversary edition (New York: Hill and Wang, 2004), xviii; Othniel A. Pendleton, "Temperance and the Evangelical Churches," *Journal of the Presbyterian Historical Society* 25 (March 1947): 45.

10. David M. Ludlum, *Social Ferment in Vermont, 1791–1850* (Montpelier: Vermont Historical Society, 1948), 69.

11. E. N. Kirk, *The Temperance Reformation Connected with the Revival of Religion and the Introduction of the Millennium* (London: J. Pasco, 1838), 17.

12. My discussion of revival theology is based on the following works: Mark A. Noll, *America's God: From Jonathan Edwards to Abraham Lincoln* (New York: Oxford University Press, 2002); E. Brooks Holifield, *Theology in America: Christian Thought from the Age of the Puritans to the Civil War* (New Haven, CT: Yale University Press, 2003); Marie Caskey, *Chariot of Fire: Religion and the Beecher Family* (New Haven, CT: Yale University Press, 1977); William R. Sutton, "Benevolent Calvinism and the Moral Government of God: The Influence of Nathaniel W. Taylor on Revivalism in the Second Great Awakening," *Religion and American Culture* 2 (Winter 1992): 23–47; John L. Hammond, *The Politics of Benevolence: Revival Religion and American Voting Behavior* (Norwood, NJ: Ablex Publishing Corporation, 1979); James H. Moorhead, "Social Reform and the Divided Conscience of Antebellum Protestantism," *Church History* 48 (December 1979): 416–30; John Opie Jr., "Conversion and Revivalism: An Internal History from Jonathan Edwards through Charles Grandison Finney" (PhD diss., University of Chicago, 1963); Douglas M. Strong, *Perfectionist Politics: Abolitionism and the Religious Tensions of American Democracy* (Syracuse, NY: Syracuse University Press, 1999); Timothy L. Smith, *Revivalism and Social Reform: American Protestantism on the Eve of the Civil War* (1957; repr., New York: Harper & Row Publishers, 1965); Smith, "Righteousness and Hope: Christian Holiness and the Millennial Vision in America, 1800–1900," *American Quarterly* 31 (1979): 21–45.

13. "The Principles and Means of the Temperance Reformation," *The Oberlin Evangelist,* October 27, 1841; Whittier as quoted in Anne C. Loveland, "Evangelicalism and 'Immediate Emancipation' in American Antislavery Thought," *Journal of Southern History* 32 (May 1966): 172–88.

This connection between perfectionist theology, teetotalism, and abolitionism raises the question of why all teetotalers were not also abolitionists? The evangelical abolitionists (who were consistently teetotalers) were the more intellectually honest of the two groups. Any attempt to explicate the thinking of evangelical teetotalers who were not abolitionists must unpack: the nuances of nineteenth-century American racism; the individualism of evangelical theology; prevailing conceptions of federalism, constitutional law, and property law; and the realities of contemporary politics. Such a study is beyond the scope of this work. What is clear is this: temperance could be embraced without upending the body politic, but abolitionism required a radical reconceptualizing of fundamental American social, political, religious, and economic structures. Only the most radical and intrepid evangelicals dared to join the cause.

14. Theodore L. Cuyler, *Lafayette Avenue Presbyterian Church, Its History and Commemorative Services, 1860–1885* (New York: Robert Carter & Brothers, 1885), 207; *Scrapbook* 3:18, 112, 125, box 1, Theodore L. Cuyler Manuscript Collection, Princeton Theological Seminary Libraries, Department of Archives and Special Collections; John Marsh, *The Cause of Temperance as Connected with Home Evangelization* (New York: American Temperance Union, 1863), 19; E. H. Pratt, *The Church and Temperance* (New York: National Temperance Society and Publication House, n.d.), 3; Kirk, 4, 15–16; General Convention of Vermont as quoted in Ludlum, 69.

15. Justin Edwards, *On the Traffic in Ardent Spirits* (New York: American Tract Society, 187-), 17; *Temperance Manual of the American Temperance Society for the Young Men of the United States* (Boston: Seth Bliss et al., 1836), 9; *Seventh Annual Report of the American Temperance Union* (1843) in *Permanent Temperance Documents*, vol. 2 (New York: American Temperance Union, 1852), 21–22; Kirk, 12, 17–18; *Proceedings of the Pennsylvania State Temperance Convention, Harrisburg, PA* (1843) as quoted in Asa E. Martin, "The Temperance Movement in Pennsylvania prior to the Civil War," *Pennsylvania Magazine of History and Biography* 49 (1925): 206; "The Use of Ardent Spirits," *American Baptist Magazine* 10 (February 1830): 43–44.

This concern about negating one's free moral agency was shared by evangelical abolitionists. The absolute control a master had over his slave was the functional equivalent of the drunkard's insatiable appetite for alcohol. In both cases, an outside power effectively nullified the person's God-given ability to use reason and respond to God. This logic accounts for why Southerners feared that Northern temperance speakers would slip over into abolitionist analogies and appeals. This was a Southern concern as early as 1833. Southern temperance speakers were not given to this type of "slippage" between reforms because they generally opposed pro-revival Calvinist theology, embracing instead more traditional doctrines. See "Slavery and Intemperance," *The Liberator*, June 15, 1833; Daniel A. Payne, "Slavery Brutalizes Man," *Lutheran Herald and Journal of the Fort Plain, N.Y. Franckean Synod*, August 1, 1839, http://www.blackpast.org/?q=1839-daniel-payne-slavery-brutalizes-man (accessed December 16, 2010).

16. Lyman Beecher, *A Reformation of Morals Practicable and Indispensable* (Utica: Merrell and Camp, 1813), 9; Charles Finney, *Lectures on Revivals of Religion* (New York: Fleming H. Revell Company, 1868), 386–87; Garth M. Rosell, "Charles Grandison Finney and the Rise of the Benevolence Empire" (PhD diss., University of Minnesota, 1971), 130–43; Gerrit Smith to Edward C. Delavan, November 6, 1837, digital edition, Gerrit Smith Broadside and Pamphlet Collection, Special Collections Research Center, Syracuse University Library, http://library.syr.edu/digital/collections/g/GerritSmith/406.htm (accessed September 4, 2010).

17. *Proceedings of the First Ten Years of the American Tract Society, Instituted at Boston, 1814* (Andover: Flagg and Gould, 1824), 11–15; *First Annual Report of the Executive Committee of the American Society for the Promotion of Temperance, 1828* (Andover: Flagg and Gould, 1828), 4.

18. This dramatic act was arguably more theatrical than effective for organized temperance in Rochester. See Steve C. Bullock, "The Temperance Movement in Rochester, 1827–1835" (unpublished manuscript on file at the American Baptist Historical Society, Atlanta, Georgia).

19. Jarrett Burch, *Adiel Sherwood: Baptist Antebellum Pioneer in Georgia* (Macon, GA: Mercer University Press, 2003), 33–35; Charles G. Finney to Theodore Weld, 21 July 1836, in *Letters of Theodore Dwight Weld, Angelina Grimké Weld, and Sarah Grimké, 1822–1844*, ed. Gilbert H. Barnes and Dwight L. Dumond (Gloucester, MA: Peter Smith, 1965), 319; Asahel Nettleton, *Temperance and Revivals* (New York: National Temperance Society and Publication House, n.d.), 1–7; Kirk, 13; Pratt, 3.

20. Christian republicanism was also a grassroots political movement that was annoyingly influential to the Whigs and Democrats. See Paul Goodman, "Moral Purpose and

Republican Politics in Antebellum America, 1830–1860," *The Maryland Historian* 20 (Fall/Winter 1989): 5–39.

21. William Gribbin, "Republicanism, Reform, and the Sense of Sin in Ante Bellum America," *Cithara* 14 (1974): 25–41; "Moral Reform—Remarks to Young Men," *The Oberlin Evangelist*, September 25, 1839; Christopher Grasso, "Deist Monster: On Religious Common Sense in the Wake of the American Revolution," *Journal of American History* 95 (June 2008): 43–48; W. C. Brownlee, *An Appeal to the Patriot and Christian on the Importance of the Gospel: its Ministry, its Sabbath, and its Ordinances, to the Well-Being and Perpetuity of our Free Institutions* (New York: American Tract Society, n.d.); James Hutson, *Religion and the Founding of the American Republic* (Washington, DC: Library of Congress, 1998), 99–114.

22. Noll, 90–91; John G. West Jr., *The Politics of Revelation and Reason: Religion and Civic Life in the New Nation* (Lawrence: University Press of Kansas, 1996), 11–78.

23. *Annual Report of the Executive Committee of the American Society for the Promotion of Temperance* (Andover: Flagg and Gould, 1828), 4; *Journal of Humanity and Herald of the American Temperance Society*, May 27, 1829, 1; Heman Humphrey, *Parallel Between Intemperance and the Slave Trade* (Amherst: J. S. and C. Adams, Printers, 1828), 26; Heman Humphrey, *The Way to Bless and Save Our Country: A Sermon* (Philadelphia: American Sunday School Union, 1831), 16; Albert Barnes, *The Connexion of Temperance with Republican Freedom* (Philadelphia: Boyle and Benedict, 1835); Mark Edward Lender and James Kirby Martin, *Drinking in America: A History*, revised and expanded edition (New York: The Free Press, 1987), 35–40, 79–85.

These sentiments were not just Northern. In 1829, an Alabama newspaper warned that the habit of "treating" voters would eventually result in the "loss of political virtue and rise of total corruption, thus making Americans incapable of self-government and leading to the country's downfall." *Alabama State Intelligencer*, May 17, 1829, as quoted in John Quist, *Restless Visionaries: The Social Roots of Antebellum Reform in Alabama and Michigan* (Baton Rouge: Louisiana State University Press, 1998), 164.

24. Hammond, 63.

25. Horace Bushnell, *Barbarism, The First Danger* (New York: American Home Missionary Society, 1847), 4–5. See also Lyman Beecher, *A Plea for the West* (Cincinnati: Truman and Smith, 1835).

26. American Tract Society, *A Brief History of the American Tract Society, Instituted at Boston, 1814, and its Relations to the American Tract Society at New York, Instituted 1825* (Boston: T. R. Marvin, 1857), 22–39.

27. *Proceedings of the First Ten Years of the American Tract Society, Instituted at Boston, 1814* (Andover: Flagg and Gould, 1824), 11, 13, 35–36; *First Annual Report of the American Tract Society, Instituted at New York, 1825* (New York: American Tract Society, 1826), 30; Elizabeth Twaddell, "The American Tract Society, 1814–1860," *Church History* 15 (June 1946): 126–28.

28. *Reprint of the First Edition of the Discipline of the African Methodist Episcopal Church* (Atlanta: n.p., 1917), 58–59; Clarence E. Walker, *A Rock in a Weary Land: The African Methodist Episcopal Church during the Civil War and Reconstruction* (Baton Rouge: Louisiana State University Press, 1982), 10, 25–26; Monroe Fordham, *Major Themes in Northern Black Religious Thought, 1800–1860* (Hicksville, NY: Exposition Press, 1975), 12–17.

29. The *Christian Recorder* did not have a continuous run during these years, so these 14 issues represent a greater frequency than this range of years suggests. There were 19 issues between 1852 and 1854, then a new editor published 24 issues between 1854 and 1856, and it did not appear again regularly until after the Civil War. Through 1856, almost one-third of the issues addressed temperance.

30. Benjamin T. Tanner, "The Temperance Status of the A.M.E. Church: Historically," *AME Church Review* 2 (January 1886): 220–21; "African Methodist Episcopal Church Conference, 1840," in *A Documentary History of the Negro People in the United States*, vol. 1, ed. Herbert Aptheker (New York: Citadel Press, 1951), 205–6; June 21, 1860, Diary, reel 4, Benjamin Tucker Tanner Papers, 1827–1872, in the Carter G. Woodson Collection of Negro Papers and Related Documents, 1803–1936, microfilm, Schomburg Center for Research in Black Culture; *Catalogue of Wilberforce University, 1872–73,* 26.

31. *Proceedings of the Convention held in the City of New-York for the Formation of the American Baptist Home Mission Society* (New York: American Baptist Home Mission Society, 1832), 15; *The First Report of the Executive Committee of the American Baptist Home Mission Society* (New York: American Baptist Home Mission Society, 1833), 18–19; *Baptist Home Missions in North America, Jubilee Report 1832–1882* (New York: Baptist Home Mission Rooms, 1883), 291–322.

32. *Third Report of the Executive Committee of the American Baptist Home Mission Society* (New York: American Baptist Home Mission Society, 1835), 21, 27; *Ninth Report of the American Baptist Home Mission Society* (New York: American Baptist Home Mission Society, 1841), 51–52; *Fourth Report of the Executive Committee of the American Baptist Home Mission Society* (New York: American Baptist Home Mission Society, 1836), 14.

33. *Fifteenth Report of the American Baptist Home Mission Society* (New York: American Baptist Home Mission Rooms, 1847), 15; *Twenty-Fifth Report of the American Baptist Home Mission Society* (New York: American Baptist Home Mission Society, 1857), 32.

34. The American Missionary Association (AMA) created a doctrinal definition of "evangelical" that eliminated the Unitarians and Universalists: "By evangelical sentiments we understand, among others, a belief in the guilty and lost condition of all men without a Saviour; the Supreme Deity, incarnation and atoning sacrifice of Jesus Christ, the only Saviour of the world; the necessity of regeneration by the Holy Spirit; repentance, faith, and holy obedience, in order for salvation; the immortality of the soul; and the retributions of the judgment in the eternal punishment of the wicked, and salvation of the righteous." See Constitution of the American Missionary Association, *Third Annual Report of the AMA* (1849), 34–35.

What the AMA meant by "caste" discrimination was discrimination against all people of a particular group just because they were a member of that group, regardless of what made them different. All AMA churches and schools welcomed all people regardless of their race or ethnicity.

35. Clara Merritt DeBoer, "Congregationalism and Racism: The 19th-Century Challenge," *Bulletin of the Congregational Library* 48 (1997): 4–14; Lewis Tappan, *History of the American Missionary Association: Its Constitution and Principles* (New York: n.p., 1855), 3, 44–45.

36. Robert Samuel Fletcher, *A History of Oberlin College from Its Foundation through the Civil War*, vol. 1 (Oberlin, OH: Oberlin College, 1943), 88–110; Michael E. Strieby, *Oberlin and the American Missionary Association* (Oberlin, OH: Oberlin College, 1891), 1–6; E. H. Fairchild, *Historical Sketch of Oberlin College* (Springfield, OH: Republic Printing Co., 1868), 3–4.

C. W. Francis claimed that every year through the mid-1880s, Atlanta University experienced a "season of special religious interest," which was his way of saying "revival." See "Religious Work at Atlanta University," *American Missionary* (April 1886).

37. *Thirteenth Annual Report of the AMA* (1859), 6.

38. *Tenth Annual Report of the AMA* (1856), 73.

39. *Sixth Annual Report of the AMA* (1852), 11.

40. *Third Annual Report of the AMA* (1849), 7; *Seventh Annual Report of the AMA* (1853), 16; "Concert Exercise," *American Missionary* 37 (May 1883): 136–41.

41. *Proceedings of the Fifth National Temperance Convention held at Saratoga Springs, NY,*

August 1–3, 1865 (New York: J. N. Stearns Publisher, 1865).

42. My portrayal contrasts sharply with that of John Rumbarger who characterizes the National Temperance Society (NTS) as beholden to the will of conservative, elite, industrial capitalists whose support for two-party politics inspired less than collegial relations with the Prohibition Party. While in principle the NTS was non-partisan and Presidents Dodge and Theodore Cuyler spoke against the Prohibition Party, Rumbarger fails to address the fact that several NTS-affiliated people were simultaneously active in both organizations. James Black, who was instrumental in founding both organizations, was not a descendent of New England's mercantile elite, was raised on a Pennsylvania farm, and became a lawyer and railroad agent. After founding the Prohibition Party he remained connected with the NTS till his death in 1893. One of the NTS's original vice presidents, Clinton B. Fisk, ran on the Prohibition Party ticket for New Jersey governor in 1884 and for president in 1888 and in 1886 joined the NTS Board of Managers. The following NTS vice presidents were also involved with the Prohibition Party: Alonzo A. Miner (a founding member), Gerrit Smith (keynote speaker at the first convention), and Neal Dow (1880 presidential candidate). Rumbarger speaks of lawyer-turned-full-time temperance activist Samuel F. Cary as disliking the NTS's "aristocracy of wealth and fashion," suggesting that the "middle class concerns" of the Prohibition Party were more his style. Cary, however, did not mind having his name listed as vice president while Dodge was president. In the 1880s Theodore Cuyler and John N. Stearns reversed themselves and in an open letter endorsed the Prohibition Party. Whatever disagreements existed between temperance reformers, the NTS successfully positioned its policies to be acceptable to reformers of all "stripes." See John J. Rumbarger, *Profits, Power, and Prohibition: Alcohol Reform and the Industrializing of America, 1800–1930* (Albany: State University of New York Press, 1989).

43. Theodore L. Cuyler, *Recollections of a Long Life* (New York: American Tract Society, 1902), 55–56; *National Temperance Advocate* 1 (June 1866): 96; *Second Annual Report of the National Temperance Society and Publication House* (1867), 7.

2: The Message Trickles South

1. John Richard Dennett, *The South As It Is: 1865–1866*, ed. Henry M. Christman (1866; repr., New York: Viking Press, 1965), 267–68.

2. "Frederick Ayer, Teacher and Missionary to the Ojibway Indians, 1829–1850," *Collections of the Minnesota Historical Society* 6 (1894): 429–37; William E. Bigglestone, "Oberlin College and the Beginning of the Red Lake Mission," *Minnesota History* 45 (Spring 1976): 21–31; *American Missionary* (November 1867): 257–58.

I am indebted to Linda Bryan of Maplewood, Minnesota, for pointing me to the articles and providing information about Ayer's physical description and his temperance work among the Ojibwe. She conveyed this information in emails to the author on February 14, 2009, September 29, 2009, and June 20, 2011. Bryan has conducted extensive research on Frederic(k) and Elisabeth Ayer's missionary work among the Ojibwe for a manuscript titled "Servants of God and Man." This information is used with her permission.

3. Atlanta conducted two local censuses in 1867 and 1869 and counted 9,288 and 13,184 blacks, respectively, making the 1870 U.S. Census count of 9,929 appear to be a sudden decrease. Assuming the accuracy of these numbers, evidently many freed people quickly became disillusioned with city life. The immigration flooded the labor market, depressing already low wages, and on top of that, migrants had to deal with crowded, unsanitary living conditions that

increased incidents of disease, making city living very trying at best. If this is what happened, it was a common trend in postbellum cities. Of course it is also likely that transiency caused all of these numbers to be an undercount. See Howard N. Rabinowitz, *Race Relations in the Urban South* (1978; repr., Athens: University of Georgia Press, 1996), 18; Rabinowitz, "Continuity and Change: Southern Urban Development, 1860–1900," in *The City in Southern History: The Growth of Urban Civilization in the South*, ed. Blaine A. Brownell and David R. Goldfield (Port Washington, NY: Kennikat Press, 1977), 99.

4. Tera W. Hunter, *To 'Joy My Freedom: Southern Black Women's Lives and Labors after the Civil War* (Cambridge, MA: Harvard University Press, 1997), 2.

5. My description of Black Atlanta is drawn from Allison Dorsey, *To Build Our Lives Together: Community Formation in Black Atlanta, 1875–1906* (Athens: University of Georgia Press, 2004); Joseph O. Jewell, *Race, Social Reform, and the Making of a Middle Class: The American Missionary Association and Black Atlanta, 1870–1900* (Lanham, MD: Rowman & Littlefield Publishers, Inc., 2007); Jerry J. Thornbery, "The Development of Black Atlanta, 1865–1885" (PhD diss., University of Maryland, 1977); Dorothy Slade, "The Evolution of Negro Areas in the City of Atlanta" (Master's thesis, Atlanta University, 1946); Dana F. White, "The Black Sides of Atlanta: A Geography of Expansion and Containment, 1970–1870," *Atlanta Historical Journal* 26 (Summer/Fall 1982): 208–12; Alton Hornsby Jr., *A Short History of Black Atlanta, 1847–1990* (Atlanta: APEX Museum, 2003); James M. Russell, "Atlanta, Gate City of the South, 1847–1885" (PhD diss., Princeton University, 1971).

6. Frederick Ayer to Samuel Hunt, January 1, 1866; Harriet N. Phillips to Sam Hunt, January 15, 1866; Mrs. E. T. Ayer to Samuel Hunt, February 3, 1866; R. M. Craighead to Samuel Hunt, April 30, 1866, reel 1, American Missionary Association Archives, Georgia Series, microfilm edition (hereafter, AMA); John Kellogg, "Negro Urban Clusters in the Postbellum South," *Geographical Review* 67 (July 1977): 310–17.

7. This is $27.90 in 2009 US dollars. See http://www.measuringworth.com/ppowerus/.

8. Frederick Ayer to E. P. Smith, July 22, 1867, reel 3, AMA.

9. Eugene M. Mitchell, "Queer Place Names in Old Atlanta," *Atlanta History Bulletin* 1 (April 1931): 29. For examples of how the white press reported on black neighborhoods see "Shermantown," *Daily Intelligencer*, June 11, 1867; "The Battle of Jenningstown," *Atlanta Constitution*, July 7, 1869; "A Widow's Troubles," *Atlanta Constitution*, September 25, 1875; "Jenningstown Hari-Kari," *Atlanta Constitution*, July 9, 1876.

10. Charlie Bailey to Gov. Joseph M. Brown, March 7, 1912, box 182, Governor's Incoming Correspondence, Georgia Department of Archives and History (hereafter, GDAH).

11. Blake McKelvey, "Penal Slavery and Southern Reconstruction," *Journal of Negro History* 20 (April 1935): 153–55; Martha A. Myers, *Race, Labor & Punishment in the New South* (Columbus: Ohio State University Press, 1998), 7–21.

12. A. Elizabeth Taylor, "The Origin and Development of the Convict Lease System in Georgia," *Georgia Historical Quarterly* 26 (March 1942): 113–18; *Report of the Principal Keeper of the Penitentiary, 1868*, as quoted in Matthew J. Mancini, "Race, Economics, and the Abandonment of Convict Leasing," *Journal of Negro History* 63 (October 1978): 341; Ray Stannard Baker, *Following the Color Line: American Negro Citizenship in the Progressive Era* (1908; repr., New York: Harper and Row, 1964), 50; W. E. B. DuBois, ed., *Some Notes on Negro Crime*, Atlanta University Publication, no. 9 (1904; repr., New York: Octagon, 1968), 2–9; Alex Lichtenstein, *Twice the Work of Free Labor: The Political Economy of Convict Labor in the New South* (London: Verso, 1996), 58.

13. James C. Bonner, "The Georgia Penitentiary at Milledgeville, 1817–1874," *Georgia*

Historical Quarterly 55 (1971): 318; Matthew J. Mancini, *One Dies, Get Another: Convict Leasing in the American South, 1866–1928* (Columbia: University of South Carolina Press, 1996), 81–98; A. J. McKelway, "The Convict Lease System of Georgia," *Outlook* 90 (September 12, 1908): 67; Lichtenstein, xiv–xv, 3–5, 60.

14. Russell, 303–5; DuBois, *Some Notes*, 25; Eugene J. Watts, "The Police in Atlanta, 1890–1905," *Journal of Southern History* 39 (May 1973): 171–72; Barbara Collier Thomas, "Race Relations in Atlanta, from 1877 through 1890, as Seen in an Analysis of the Atlanta City Council Proceedings and Other Related Works" (Master's thesis, Atlanta University, 1966), 50–56; Howard N. Rabinowitz, "The Conflict between Blacks and the Police in the Urban South, 1865–1900," in *Race, Ethnicity, and Urbanization: Selected Essays,* ed. Howard N. Rabinowitz (Columbia: University of Missouri Press, 1994), 167–80.

For more on the treatment of blacks in Atlanta's police court see Howard Steven Goodson, "'South of the North, North of the South': Public Entertainment in Atlanta, 1880–1930 (PhD diss., Emory University, 1995), 282–88.

15. *Minutes of the Atlanta City Council,* 7:511, 534, 549, 629, Atlanta History Center; William J. Mathias and Stuart Anderson, *Horse to Helicopter: First Century of the Atlanta Police Department* (Decatur, GA: National Graphics, Inc., 1973), 181; Rabinowitz, "The Conflict between Blacks and the Police," 172–79; Russell, 310–11; "Scarborough's Trouble," *Atlanta Constitution,* August 1, 1883.

16. Although the evidence in the next three paragraphs of the negative effects of drunken white behavior on blacks is from the 1880s and later, there is no reason to believe that these examples were not also typical of the years 1865–1876.

17. "Scarborough's Trouble," *Atlanta Constitution,* August 1, 1883; "A Drunken Policeman," *The Vindicator,* August 4, 1883 in box 15, John Emory Bryant Papers, Rare Book, Manuscript, and Special Collections Library, Duke University Library.

18. The records in 1873 do not indicate who brought the charges or the situation out of which the charges of drunkenness arose.

19. *Weekly Defiance,* October 8, 22, 29, 1881, October 24, 1882, February 29, 1883, October 3, 1885; Russell, 307–10; Watts, "The Police in Atlanta," 175.

Police mistreatment of blacks was sometimes decried in the white press. See "To Our Atlanta Readers," *Macon Telegraph,* November 5, 1887.

20. *Atlanta Constitution,* May 12, 1883; Charlie Bailey to Gov. Joseph M. Brown, March 7, 1912, box 182, Governor's Incoming Correspondence, GDAH; *Atlanta Constitution,* April 15, 17, 1892; Eugene Genovese, *Roll, Jordan, Roll: The World the Slaves Made* (New York: Pantheon Books, 1974), 645–46. Atlanta also maintained a chain gang from early in the postwar period for those who could not pay the Recorder fines, and the gang remained either all black or mostly black. See *Atlanta Daily Herald,* January 10, 1873.

21. *Atlanta Constitution,* September 4, 1885.

22. A "hot toddy" is a hot drink, usually drunk before going to bed. It is made with an alcoholic beverage like whiskey, plus hot water, spices, maybe juice, and a sweetener. It does not have to include alcohol, as mulled cider is also considered a "hot toddy." "Dram drinking" refers to the practice of drinking a shot of a whiskey (or other hard liquor) several times during the day.

23. My discussion about African and slave alcohol use is drawn from Christmon, 326–27; Denise Herd, "Ambiguity in Black Drinking Norms: An Ethnohistorical Interpretation," in *The American Experience with Alcohol: Contrasting Cultural Perspectives,* ed. Linda A. Bennett and Genevieve M. Ames (New York: Plenum Press, 1985), 152–53; William B. Smith, "The Persimmon Tree and the Beer Dance," in *The Negro and His Folklore in Nineteenth-Century Periodicals,* ed. Bruce

Jackson (Austin: University of Texas Press, 1967), 3–9; Robin Room, "Alcohol, the Individual and Society: What History Teaches Us," *Addiction* 92 (1997 Supplement): s8; Emmanuel Akyeampong, *Drink, Power, and Cultural Change: A Social History of Alcohol in Ghana, c. 1800 to Recent Times* (Portsmouth, NH: Heinemann, 1996), 1–8; Charles Ambler, "Alcohol and Disorder in Precolonial Africa," Working Paper in African Studies, no. 126, African Studies Center, Boston University, 11–13, 1987.

24. Genovese, 577–78, 643–44; Booker T. Washington, *Up From Slavery* (1901; repr., New York: Lancer Books, Inc., 1968), 136–38; Shuana Bigham and Robert E. May, "The Time O' All Times? Masters, Slaves, and Christmas in the Old South," *Journal of the Early Republic* 18 (Summer 1998): 271; David W. Blight, ed. *Narrative of the Life of Frederick Douglass, an American Slave: With Related Documents* (Boston: Bedford/St. Martin's, 2003), 89–91, 106; Frederick Douglass, "Temperance and Anti-Slavery: An Address Delivered in Paisley, Scotland, on 30 March 1846," in *The Frederick Douglass Papers*, series one, vol. 1., ed. John W. Blassingame (New Haven, CT: Yale University Press, 1979), 207; Charles Stearns, *The Black Man of the South and the Rebels* (1872; repr., New York: Negro Universities Press, 1969), 334; William Wells Brown, *Narrative of William Wells Brown, a Fugitive Slave* (Boston: The Anti-Slavery Office, 1847), 21.

For alternative perspectives on slaves' drinking see Kenneth Stampp, *The Peculiar Institution: Slavery in the Ante-Bellum South* (New York: Knopf, 1956), 370–71; Stephanie M. H. Camp, *Closer to Freedom: Enslaved Women and Everyday Resistance in the Plantation South* (Chapel Hill: University of North Carolina, 2004), 66, 90–92, 166; Stanley K. Schultz, "Temperance Reform in the Antebellum South: Social Control and Urban Order," *South Atlantic Quarterly* 83 (Summer 1984): 323–39.

Others argue that laws prohibiting slaves from buying alcohol were poorly enforced. If so, Frederick Douglass's assertion that masters viewed drunken slaves as relatively benign might explain the lax enforcement. Antebellum urban slave drinking patterns would have had little effect on practices in post-emancipation Black Atlanta since the vast majority of its residents were rural slaves before migrating to Atlanta after the war. See William Monroe Geer, "The Temperance Movement in Georgia in the Middle Period" (Master's thesis, Emory University, 1937), 75–77; Richard C. Wade, *Slavery in the Cities: The South, 1820–1860* (New York: Oxford University Press, 1964), 149–51.

25. Sidney Andrews, *The South Since the War* (1866; repr., New York: Arno Press, 1969), 376–77; Robert Somers, *The Southern States Since the War, 1870–71* (London: Macmillan & Co., 1871), 245; George Campbell, *White & Black: The Outcome of a Visit to the United States* (1879; repr., New York: Negro Universities Press, 1969), 46; David Macrae, *The Americans at Home: Pen-and-ink Sketches of American Men, Manners, and Institutions* (Glasgow: Gowans & Gray, 1885), 418–19; Henry M. Field, *Blood is Thicker than Water: A Few Days Among Our Southern Brethren* (New York: George Munro, Publisher, 1886), 27–28; "Prospects of the Negro," *American Missionary* (March 1870): 59; E. A. Ware to E. P. Smith, February 28, 1867, reel 2, AMA.

AMA missionaries who reported excessive drinking were mostly in rural areas. See *American Missionary* (February 1866): 27, (February 1869): 25, (March 1870): 64–66, and (April 1870): 75.

26. *National Republican* as quoted in Charles Nordhoff, *The Cotton States in the Spring and Summer of 1875* (New York: D. Appleton & Co., 1876), 105.

The following travelers through the postbellum South omitted any reference to blacks and liquor: John Trowbridge, Henry Latham, John Kennaway, Linda Slaughter, W. Robbins Falkiner, Lady Duffus Hardy, Henry McElwin, Timothy Harley, and George Augustus Sala.

27. John W. Alvord, *Letters from the South, Relating to the Condition of the Freedmen, Addressed to Major General O. O. Howard* (Washington, DC: Howard University Press, 1870),

18–27; Alvord, *Fourth Semi-Annual Report, July 1, 1867,* in *Semi-Annual Report on Schools for Freedom* (Washington, DC: Government Printing Office, 1868), 71–72.

28. Until 1871 the mayor of Atlanta personally dispensed with misdemeanors such as public drunkenness and fighting. In 1871 the state established a Recorder's Court, or police court, for Atlanta that assumed the functions of the Mayor's Court. Because blacks were mostly arrested for petty crimes, this was an important element of the system used to control blacks' behavior and was the center of a lot of abuse. Watts, "The Police in Atlanta," 170–72.

My analysis in the following paragraphs is based on extensive reading in the following Atlanta newspapers: *Daily Intelligencer, Daily New Era, Atlanta Constitution, Weekly Sun, Atlanta Daily Herald, Atlanta Daily News, Daily Evening Commonwealth,* and *Atlanta Journal.*

29. Some newspapers gave the names of people brought before the court, while others just mentioned case numbers or mentioned what charges were brought against people that day, and the total number of each type of charge.

30. *Weekly Sun*, June 17, 1871; *Daily New Era*, July 6, 1870; *Atlanta Daily Herald*, July 6, 1873; Harriet Beecher Stowe, "The Education of Freedmen," *North American Review* 128 (June 1879): 613.

31. I searched the newspapers listed in note 28 for the dates immediately following Emancipation Day/New Year's Day, Independence Day, and Christmas. On several occasions there were either no extant papers or no reports about the holiday.

32. African American communities celebrated emancipation on various dates. Atlantans celebrated on January 1, the date the Emancipation Proclamation took effect, while other communities were known to celebrate it on the date it was issued (September 22), or on the date the Civil War ended (April 9).

33. Ted Ownby, *Subduing Satan: Religion, Recreation, and Manhood in the Rural South, 1865–1920* (Chapel Hill: University of North Carolina Press, 1990), 45–46, 54; "Negro Demonstration on the Glorious Fourth," *Atlanta Constitution*, July 5, 1868; *Daily New Era*, July 6, 1871; "African Odd Fellows," *Daily Sun*, January 3, 1872; *Atlanta Constitution*, July 5, 1885. Also, on July 4, 1882, the papers reported that "by noon the stationhouse was full of drunks and crooks." While the report does not indicate race, it is reasonable to assume most were whites. See "Independence Day," *Atlanta Constitution*, July 5, 1882.

34. *Atlanta Constitution*, December 28, 1875; December 27, 1876; December 27, 1877; December 27, 1878.

35. *Daily Intelligencer*, July 6, 1866.

36. *Daily Intelligencer*, July 6, 1867; "Negro Demonstration on the Glorious Fourth," *Atlanta Constitution*, July 5, 1868; *Daily New Era*, July 6, 1871.

37. *Daily Intelligencer*, July 6, 1866; "Closing of Bar-Rooms," *Daily Intelligencer*, July 3, 1867.

38. *Atlanta Constitution*, September 4, 1885; M. L. Wells, "Southern Awakenings," *Union Signal*, June 4, 1885. According to the Tenth U.S. Census (1880), black people died from alcoholism at less than half the rate of native-born whites or people of Irish or German parentage. John S. Billins, *Department of the Interior, Tenth Census, Report on the Mortality and Vital Statistics of the United States* (Washington, DC: Government Printing Office, 1885), xxxviii.

39. "The Freed People and Temperance," *National Temperance Advocate* 8 (January 1873): 10; *Twenty-Third Annual Report of the AMA* (1869), 87; *Twenty-Sixth Annual Report of the AMA* (1872), 116.

40. H. Shelton Smith, *In His Image, But . . . Racism in Southern Religion, 1780–1910* (Durham, NC: Duke University Press, 1972), 216–17; James McPherson, *The Abolitionist Legacy: From Reconstruction to the NAACP* (Princeton, NJ: Princeton University Press, 1975), 201.

41. George Fredrickson, *The Black Image in the White Mind: The Debate on Afro-American Character and Destiny, 1817–1914* (1971; repr., Middletown, CT: Wesleyan University Press, 1987), 101–2; "The Necessity of Great Enlargement in the Work among the Freedmen," *American Missionary* 11 (February 1867): 34.

42. "Colored Pupils Compared with White," *Home Mission Echo* 7 (June 1891): 5; H. L. Morehouse, "The Negro Problem," *Home Mission Echo* 7 (February 1891): 9; "Culture is Colorless," *Home Mission Monthly* 15 (November 1894): 436; George A. Towns, "The Sources of the Tradition of Atlanta University," *Phylon* 3 (Second Quarter 1942); Molly Oshatz, *Slavery and Sin: The Fight against Slavery and the Rise of Liberal Protestantism* (New York: Oxford University Press, 2012).

43. *The Southern Advance Association of Atlanta, Georgia*, box 16, John Emory Bryant Papers, Rare Book, Manuscript, and Special Collections Library, Duke University, Durham, North Carolina; *Thirteenth Annual Report of the Woman's American Baptist Home Missions Society* (1891), 4; *Minutes of the Fifth Annual Meeting of the National Council of Congregational Churches, 1883* (Boston: Congregational Publishing Society, 1883), 128.

I do not mean to suggest that everyone in the AMA shared Strieby's thinking, only that it was accepted and embraced by the organization's leadership. Michael Strieby's speeches and writings provide an excellent example of the ability of AMA leadership to discern institutional racism and systemic or structural injustices. See Strieby's entire speech, titled "History of Congregationalism in the Southern States," given at the Fifth Annual National Council Meeting cited above, and his report, "The Religious Aspects of the Work of the American Missionary Association," included in the *Minutes of the National Council of the Congregational Churches of the United States at their Third Session, 1877* (Boston: Congregational Publishing Society, 1877), 105–13, especially page 107.

44. Tate and Daniels remained to assist Ayer after he arrived. See Dorsey, 193n5.

45. Frederick Ayer to Samuel Hunt, January 1, 1866; Rose Kinney to Samuel Hunt, January 27, 1866; R. M Craighead to Samuel Hunt, February 1, 1866; Mrs. E. T. Ayer to Sam Hunt, February 3, 1866; Frederick Ayer to George Whipple, February 15, 1866, reel 1, AMA; *American Missionary* 10 (March 1866): 63; *American Missionary* 10 (May 1866): 98. A classic example of romantic racialist and culturalist thought is the AMA report *The Nation Still in Danger; or Ten Years after the War* (New York: American Missionary Association, 1875).

46. "Teachers: Their Qualifications and Support," *American Missionary* 10 (July 1866): 151–52; Sandra E. Small, "The Yankee Schoolmarm in Freedmen's Schools: An Analysis of Attitudes," *Journal of Southern History* 45 (August 1979): 394.

47. Ruth Miller Elson, *Guardians of Tradition: American Schoolbooks of the Nineteenth Century* (Lincoln: University of Nebraska Press, 1964), 8–9; Robert C. Morris, *Reading, 'Riting, and Reconstruction: The Education of the Freedmen in the South, 1861–1870* (Chicago: University of Chicago Press, 1981), 185–91, 198–99. Non-religious freedmen's organizations did not like ATrS literature.

48. Paul A. Cimbala, *Under the Guardianship of the Nation: The Freedmen's Bureau and the Reconstruction of Georgia, 1865–1870* (Athens: University of Georgia Press, 1997), 124; G. S. Eberhart to Samuel Hunt, December 2, 1865, Frederick Ayer to George Whipple, February 15, 1866, G. S. Eberhart to Samuel Hunt, February 8, 1866, AMA; *Report of G. S. Eberhart, State Superintendent of Schools for the State of Georgia, October 1, 1865–October 1, 1866*, Records of the Assistant Commissioner for the State of Georgia, Bureau of Refugees, Freedmen, and Abandoned Lands, 1865–1869, microfilm edition; "Storrs School, Atlanta, GA," *American Missionary* 11 (May 1867): 98; Ebem Shute to Frederick Ayer, April 28, 1866, folder 6, box 8, Atlanta University

Presidential Records, 1856–1984, Archives and Special Collections, Robert W. Woodruff Library, Atlanta University Center (hereafter, AUC).

49. "The Cure of the Drunkard," *The Freedman* 3 (January 1866): 4.

50. See *The Freedman*, January 1866, May 1866, July 1866, March 1867, August 1867, March 1868, June 1868, October 1868, March 1869 and *Freedman's Journal*, April 1866, June 1866, July 1866, August 1866, September 1866, October 1866.

51. Each "class" had several lessons. Students were not necessarily taught either one class per day or one lesson per day.

52. American Tract Society, *The Freedman's Spelling-Book*; *The Freedman's Second Reader; The Freedman's Third Reader* (1865–1866; repr., New York: AMS Press, 1980), 13, 44, 46, 48, 62, 79 (New York: AMS Press, Inc., 1980).

53. American Tract Society, *The Freedman's Spelling-Book ; The Freedman's Second Reader; the Freedman's Third Reader*, 52–55, 57–58; *Tenth Annual Report of the New England Branch of the American Tract Society* (1869), 16.

54. *Report of G. S. Eberhart, State Superintendent of Schools for the State of Georgia, October 1, 1865–October 1, 1866*, Records of the Assistant Commissioner for the State of Georgia, Bureau of Refugees, Freedmen, and Abandoned Lands, 1865–1869, microfilm edition; "The American Tract Society's Work among the Freedmen," *Freedman's Journal* 2 (November 1866): 42; "Our Papers in Georgia," *The Freedman's Journal* 2 (August 1866): 30–31; *Forty-Third Annual Report of the American Tract Society—New York* (1868), 31, 36; *Fifty-Fourth Annual Report of the American Tract Society for the Year Ending April 30, 1868—Boston*, 83–84.

55. "Advice to Freedmen" and "A Warning to Freedmen against Intoxicating Drinks," box 1, group 1484, Isaac W. Brinckerhoff Papers, American Baptist Historical Society, Atlanta, Georgia; Rev. G. S. F. Savage to Frederick Ayer, August 7, 1866, folder 5, box 8, Atlanta University Presidential Records, 1856–1984, AUC.

56. Herbert Gutman, "Schools for Freedom: The Post-Emancipation Origins of Afro-American Education," in *Power and Culture: Essays on the American Working Class*, ed. Ira Berlin (New York: Pantheon Books, 1987), 260–97; Heather Andrea Williams, *Self-Taught: African American Education in Slavery and Freedom* (Chapel Hill: University of North Carolina Press, 2005), 72–79.

57. Stories of Lincoln's abstinence circulated in temperance/prohibition circles into the twentieth century. See Richard F. Hamm, "The Prohibitionists' Lincoln," *Illinois Historical Journal* 86 (Summer 1993): 93–118.

58. "President Lincoln's Treat," *The Freedman* 3 (May 1866): 20; "President Lincoln a Temperate Man," *Freedman's Journal* 2 (August 1866): 31; June 30, 1866, *Minute Book—Publication Committee of the National Temperance Society and Publication House, June 30, 1866–December 26, 1882*, item 3, box 3, series 2, Record Group 54, National Temperance Society and Publication House Records, Presbyterian Historical Society (hereafter, NTS-PHS); *Twenty-First Annual Report of the AMA, 1867* (New York: American Missionary Association, 1867), 17; "Temperance," *American Missionary* 11 (July 1867): 155–56.

59. E. A. Ware to E. P. Smith, February 28, 1867, AMA.

60. "Temperance," *American Missionary* 11 (July 1867): 155–56; John W. Alvord to M. E. Strieby, July 31, 1867, District of Columbia series, AMA Archives, Amistad Research Center; Alvord, *Fourth Semi-Annual Report, July 1, 1867*, in *Semi-Annual Report on Schools for Freedom*, Bureau of Refugees, Freedmen, and Abandoned Lands (Washington, DC: Government Printing Office, 1868), 71–72; "Intemperance Among the Freedmen," *The American Freedman* 2 (June 1867): 226; A. E. Newton, *Manual of the Vanguard of Freedom* (New York: National Temperance

Society and Publication House, 1867); *Fourth Annual Report of the National Temperance Society and Publication Society* (1869), 18.

61. C. W. Francis to E. P. Smith, October 7, 1867, reel 3, AMA; *American Missionary* (May 1868): 108, (November 1868): 244, (September 1881): 268.

62. *Records of the First Congregational Church of Atlanta, Georgia, 1867–1882*, box 1, folder 12, Records of the First Congregational Church, U.C.C., Atlanta, Georgia Collection, Atlanta University Center, Archives and Special Collections, Robert W. Woodruff Library, AUC. The excommunication steps as I determined them from First Congregational's records were as follows: Those brought up on charges underwent a process modeled on the teachings of Jesus and the Apostle Paul in Matthew 18:15–18 and I Corinthian 5:1–6:2, and apparently without any significant gender discrimination. After charges were brought to the pastor or deacons, a committee was appointed to meet with the person to verify the truthfulness of the charges, and if they were correct, to admonish them and to seek a confession. Sometimes individuals were asked to come to a church meeting to answer charges. If the person refused to confess, or even talk to the church or the committee, they would be excommunicated by a formal statement that would be read during the next Sunday morning service so all would understand why the action was taken. The statements invariably claimed that their evidence was solid because they had several witnesses to the charges and ended by saying they had prayed about their decision, regretted having to do it, and were praying for the person to be restored at some point. Occasionally they went on at length about their opposition to the particular sin and then added that this action should be a warning to those in the church. In each case, however, there were multiple charges, the first being that the person had ignored attendance at God's house for an extended period of time. The process seemed to apply to people who had already been absenting themselves for an extended period of time, and about whom news had had plenty of time to spread. The formal statements also lamented the damage the person had done to the cause of Christ, and/or their church.

63. Dougherty went on to become Atlanta's first black lawyer.

64. *Records of the First Congregational Church of Atlanta, Georgia, 1867–1882*, AUC.

65. *Records of the First Congregational Church of Atlanta, Georgia, 1867–1882*, AUC. No reasons are given for excommunication after March 1877.

66. Minutes of the Annual Meeting of the Central South Congregational Conference, 1873–1877; Minutes of the Annual Meeting of the Georgia Congregational Conference, 1878–1888. One study of black Baptists showed that they excommunicated only about 60 percent of those charged, compared to First Congregational's 95 percent. See Gregory Wills, *Democratic Religion: Freedom, Authority, and Church Discipline in the Baptist South, 1785–1900* (New York: Oxford University Press, 1997), chapter 5.

67. Daniel Alexander Payne, *The African M. E. Church in its Relations to the Freedmen* (Xenia, OH: Torchlight Co., 1868), 4–7; Payne, *Recollections of Seventy Years* (Nashville: AME Sunday School Union, 1888), 162; Walker, 21–24.

68. Thornbery, 138–43. Gaines's education consisted of studying theology privately under various white clergymen.

69. Wesley J. Gaines, *African Methodism in the South, or Twenty-Five Years of Freedom* (Atlanta: Franklin Publishing House, 1890), 34; *Minutes of the 5th Session of the Georgia Annual Conference of the AME Church* (1871), 13–14, Benjamin Arnett Papers, Stokes Library, Archives, Wilberforce University (hereafter, BAP); *Minutes of the 6th Session of the Georgia Annual Conference of the AME Church* (1872), 51–52, 70–71, BAP.

70. *Minutes of the 1st Session of the North Georgia Annual Conference of the AME Church* (1874), 19, 25, BAP; *Minutes of the 2nd Session of the North Georgia Annual Conference of the AME*

Church (January 1875), 11, BAP; *Minutes of the 3rd Session of the North Georgia Annual Conference of the AME Church* (December 1875), 12, BAP; *Minutes of the 4th Session of North Georgia Annual Conference of the AME Church* (1876), 26, BAP.

71. *Minutes of the 5th Session of the Georgia Annual Conference of the AME Church* (1871), Church Table, BAP; *Minutes of the 6th Session of the Georgia Annual Conference of the AME Church* (1872), Church Table, BAP.

72. *Minutes of the 18th Annual Session of the North Georgia Annual Conference of the AME Church* (1890), Church Table, BAP.

73. "Extract from Report of 1867," reel 3, AMA; Mrs. F. Ayer to Samuel Hunt, September 1, 1866, reel 2, AMA.

74. *Fourth Annual Report of the National Temperance Society and Publication House* (1869), 18.

75. *Christian Recorder*, February 2, 1867.

3: The Trickle Becomes a Flood

1. David Leigh Colvin, *Prohibition in the United States: A History of the Prohibition Party and of the Prohibition Movement* (New York: George H. Doran Company, 1926).

2. Packard and Giles had taught, in the 1860s, at Oread Institute, in Worcester, MA. Oread was a school for girls founded by abolitionist Eli Thayer.

3. Florence Read, *The Story of Spelman* (Princeton, NJ: Princeton University Press, 1961), 176; Harold Lynn McManus, "The American Baptist Home Mission Society and Freedmen Education in the South, with Special Reference to Georgia, 1862–1897" (PhD diss., Yale University, 1953), 142, 368. Giles as quoted in Beverly Guy-Sheftall, *Daughters of Sorrow: Attitudes toward Black Women, 1880–1920* (Brooklyn: Carlson Publishing, Inc., 1990), 136.

4. See W. E. B. DuBois, "The Talented Tenth," in *The Negro Problem: A Series of Articles by Representative American Negroes of To-day*, ed. Booker T. Washington et al. (1903; repr., New York: Arno Press and the *New York Times*, 1969), 31–76; Benjamin Brawley, *History of Morehouse College* (Atlanta: Morehouse College, 1917), 9.

5. Atlanta University and Spelman Seminary have the best-preserved records from the 1880s, so they receive the most attention in this book. The limited records available for this period for Clark University, Atlanta Baptist Seminary, Morris Brown (founded in 1881 by the AME Church but did not open its doors until 1885), and Gammon Theological Seminary (a department within Clark University until it became independent in 1883) strongly suggest that their cultures and practices were no different.

6. Blocker, *American Temperance Movements*, 80–85; Bordin, 76–78.

7. Rev. D. Jones's description of the *New York Weekly Witness*. Jones was a black minister in Clarksville, TN. *New York Weekly Witness*, April 25, 1878.

8. "The Colored Preachers' Fund," *New York Weekly Witness*, May 3, 1877; Jan Noel, *Canada Dry: Temperance Crusades before Confederation* (Toronto: University of Toronto Press, 1995), 75–88; Lorraine Vander Hoef, "John Dougall (1808–1886): Portrait of an Early Social Reformer and Evangelical Witness in Canada," *Journal of the Canadian Church Historical Society* 43 (2001): 115–45; J. I. Cooper, "The Early Editorial Policy of the *Montreal Witness*," *Report of the Annual Meeting of the Canadian Historical Society* (1947): 53–62.

For the intensity of Dougall's faith and its effects on his family, see Joanna Dean, *Religious Experience and the New Woman: The Life of Lily Dougall* (Bloomington: Indiana University Press, 2007), 18–33.

9. "A Unique Weekly," *Christian Recorder*, December 16, 1880.

10. *New York Weekly Witness*, May 29, July 31, 1879. Dougall's strident tone riled some Southern readers, and they wrote in to complain. See September 14, 1876.

11. Some examples of articles on temperance and prohibition are April 19, September 20, October 4, 1877; October 10, 1878; March 20, 1879; July 27, August 17, 1882; April 11, 1888.

12. "Southern Missionaries and Teachers," *New York Weekly Witness*, March 9, 1872; "How are the Freedmen to Be Educated?" *New York Weekly Witness*, March 8, 1877.

13. "To the Two Thousand Colored Pastors who Receive the Witness," *New York Weekly Witness*, April 4, 1878; "Colored Preachers," *New York Weekly Witness*, April 17, 1879; "Colored Pastors," *New York Weekly Witness*, April 13, 1882; *Catalog of Spelman Seminary, 1885–1886*, 32; *New York Weekly Witness*, July 18, 1878; *Minutes of the 16th Quadrennial Session of the General Conference of the AME Church* (1880), 77, BAP.

Although all *Witness* recipients were clergy, not all were pastors. The 17 Atlanta clergy who received the *Witness* in 1877–1878 were: Baptists—Jerry M. Jones, W. H. Tilman, Charles O. Jones, and M. Mitchell; AME—F. J. Peck, J. L. Smith, Allen Frazier, A. Gonickey, William Finch, George Washington, J. A. Woods, D. T. Howard; Religious affiliation unidentifiable—T. J. Peck, William Maddox, H. Bunt, Thomas Belsaws, B. Scott. Also listed among the black clergy was Clark University's white president, R. E. Bisbee. The 1878–1879 recipients were W. H. Tillman, Charles O. Jones, R. A. Hall, W. S. Covington, and B. Scott. *Witness* subscriptions also did not go exclusively to Southern blacks. Some black clergy in Pennsylvania and New York also received free subscriptions.

During the 1885–1886 school year Spelman received 12 free subscriptions to religious publications. Undoubtedly other black schools in Atlanta also received free subscriptions, but the records are not available.

14. *New York Weekly Witness*, May 3, July 26, October 4, 1877; April 25, June 6, July 18, 1878; June 19, 1879.

15. "Colored Preachers," *New York Weekly Witness*, April 17, 1879.

16. Theodore L. Cuyler to John D. Rockefeller, April, 10, 1886, reel 9, part 3, Office Correspondence, Papers of John D. Rockefeller, Sr., microfilm edition, Rockefeller Family ArchivesRockefeller Archive Center (hereafter RAC).

17. This statement appeared in the annually published *National Temperance Almanac and Teetotaler's Yearbook*, beginning in 1886 and continuing through the 1890s.

18. "Temperance Reform among the Negroes," *American Missionary* (June 1875); "Editorial Correspondence," *National Temperance Advocate* 18 (May 1883): 73–74.

19. William E. Dodge, *The Church and Temperance* (New York: National Temperance Society and Publication House, 1880), 9–13; D. Stuart Dodge, compiler,. *Memorials of William E. Dodge* (New York: Anson D. F. Randolph and Company, 1887), 149–66, 208–20; Carlos Martyn, *William E. Dodge: The Christian Merchant* (New York: Funk & Wagnalls, 1890), 88–95; November 19, 1872, March 25, 1881, *Minute Book of the Board of Managers of the National Temperance Society, November 14, 1865—December 26, 1882*, item 6, box 2, RG 54, NTS-PHS; Mrs. T. N. Chase, "Hon. William E. Dodge and Atlanta University," *American Missionary* (May 1882): 141; "National Prohibition Alliance," *Atlanta Constitution*, February 26, 1882; "Intemperance in the South," *New York Times*, April 10, 1882; *Seventh Annual Report of the National Temperance Society and Publication House* (1872), 43; "From Macon: The Temperance Question Agitating the Central City," *Atlanta Constitution*, January 24, 1885.

20. Peter Carter, *Peter Carter, 1825–1900* (New York: De Vinne Press, 1901), 68–78, 100–101; Grace Goulder, *John D. Rockefeller: The Cleveland Years* (Cleveland: Western Reserve

Historical Society, 1972), 63–64; Joshua L. Baily to Wistar Morris, July 4, 1880, Miscellaneous letters from 1880–1905 folder, box 1, Joshua L. Baily Collection, 1818–1917, Haverford College Library Special Collections; Josiah Forster to Joshua L. Baily, June 17, 1847, and Josiah Forster to Joshua L. Baily, September 18, 1848, Letters to F–G folder, box 2, Joshua L. Baily Collection, 1818–1917, Haverford College Library Special Collections.

Many former abolitionists made temperance their new priority, as indicated by the1873 merger of the *National Standard* (formerly the *Anti-Slavery Standard*) with the *National Temperance Advocate*. See "The National Standard," *National Temperance Advocate* 7 (December 1872): 185.

21. Michael E. Strieby, *Work of Half a Generation* (New York: American Missionary Association, 1878), 13.

22. American Missionary Association, *The Nation Still in Danger; or Ten Years After the War* (New York: American Missionary Association, 1875), 8–9; *Minutes of the Third Annual Session of the North Georgia Conference of the AME Church* (1875), 12, BAP; *People's Advisor* as quoted in "Whiskey and the Colored People," *National Temperance Advocate* 17 (March 1882): 42; *Minutes of the Missionary Baptist Convention of Georgia* (1875), 26; *Minutes of the Ebenezer Baptist Association* (1877), 17, Special Collections, Mercer University, Jack Tarver Library, Macon, Georgia; "Among the Freedmen," *National Temperance Advocate* 16 (January 1881): 5. The minutes of all black Baptist associations and conventions cited are held by the same library (hereafter SCMU).

23. "Temperance for the Freedmen," *New York Times*, April 14, 1881; "Home News," *New York Tribune*, April 14, 1881; "Whiskey and the Colored People," *National Temperance Advocate* 17 (March 1882): 42; "Intemperance in the South," *New York Times*, April 10, 1882; "Temperance Among the Freedmen," *National Temperance Advocate* 20 (April 1885): 51; *Eighteenth Annual Report of the National Temperance Society and Publication House* (1883), 20.

24. *Sixteenth Annual Report of the National Temperance Society and Publication House* (1881), 20–21, 31; "Appeal for the Freedmen," *National Temperance Advocate* 16 (July 1881): 126; minutes for September 30, 1881, February 13, April 25, 1882, *Minutes of the Missionary Committee of the National Temperance Society, September 30, 1881–December 16, 1897*, file 6, box 3, RG 54, NTS-PH; minutes for April 8, 1884, *Minute Book: Board of Managers of the National Temperance Society and Publication House,* item 7, box 2, series 2, RG 54, NTS-PH; *Seventeenth Annual Report of the National Temperance Society and Publication House* (1882), 16–18; "National Prohibition Alliance," *Atlanta Constitution*, February 26, 1882; "The National Temperance Society and Publication House," *National Temperance Advocate* 19 (December 1884): 198–99.

25. Minutes for June 12, December 18, 1882, February 19, April 23, December 27, 1883, April 8, June 10, 1884, January 17, 1885, *Minutes of the Missionary Committee of the National Temperance Society, September 30, 1881–December 16, 1897*, file 6, box 3, RG 54, NTS-PHS; "A Returned Missionary," *The Voice*, April 23, 1885; *Eighteenth Annual Report of the National Temperance Society* (1883), 18–19; *Nineteenth Annual Report of the National Temperance Society* (1884), 15–17; *National Temperance Advocate* 19 (March 1884): 41; *National Temperance Advocate* 19 (July 1884): 126; "The African Methodist Episcopal Zion Church," *National Temperance Advocate* 20 (December 1885): 198–99; *Home Mission Echo* 2 (April 1886): 3; "Temperance Talk," *Atlanta Constitution*, March 11, 1889.

26. Minutes for September 22, 1886, *Minutes of the Missionary Committee of the National Temperance Society, September 30, 1881–December 16, 1897*, file 6, box 3, RG 54, NTS-PHS; *Seventeenth Annual Report of the National Temperance Society and Publication House* (1882), 18.

27. Minutes for November 16, 1885, September 22, 1886, January 29, April 23, November 19, 1887, January 24, September 25, November 26, 1888, September 23, November 19, 1889,

January 28, April 8, September 22, 1890, January 12, 1891, September 19, November 22, 1892, November 28, 1893, *Minutes of the Missionary Committee of the National Temperance Society, September 30, 1881–December 16, 1897,* file 6, box 3, RG 54, NTS-PHS.

28. "Temperance among the Freedmen," *National Temperance Advocate* 22 (February 1887): 19; *Conflict,* as quoted in "Professor Price in Atlanta," *National Temperance Advocate* 22 (February 1887): 27; "Georgia," *National Temperance Advocate* 22 (February 1887): 29–30; William Jacob Walls, *Joseph Charles Price, Educator and Race Leader* (Boston: Christopher Publishing House, 1943), 52, 306, 327–29, 385–86.

29. Minutes for June 13, September 21, 1882, June 25, December 1883, January 14, February 8, 1884, April 9, 1888, *Minutes of the Missionary Committee of the National Temperance Society, September 30, 1881–December 16, 1897,* file 6, box 3, RG 54, NTS-PHS; "Temperance Work in the South," *The Voice,* November 13, 1884.

30. Minutes for December 27, 1883, May 18, 1885, September 22, 1886, April 23, 1887, September 19, 1892, *Minutes of the Missionary Committee of the National Temperance Society, September 30, 1881–December 16, 1897,* file 6, box 3, RG 54, NTS-PHS; "Our Eleventh Anniversary," *National Temperance Advocate* 11 (June 1876): 90; *Eighteenth Annual Report of the National Temperance Society and Publication House* (1883), 23; *Nineteenth Annual Report of the National Temperance Society and Publication House* (1884), 17–18; donations for April 21, 1879, vol. 28, Donation Ledger 1876–1880, series 3, NTS-PHS; *Twentieth Annual Report of the National Temperance Society and Publication House* (1885), 14; "Georgia," *American Missionary* 33 (June 1879): 172; *National Temperance Advocate* 16 (June 1881): 99.

31. *Twentieth Annual Report of the National Temperance Society and Publication House* (1885), 15; *Twenty-Fourth Annual Report of the National Temperance Society and Publication House* (1889), 19; June 19, 1879, vol. 28, Donation Ledger 1876–1880, series 3, NTS-PHS; "Atlanta University—An Encouraging Precedent," *American Missionary* 34 (October 1880): 305; "Religious Work," *Bulletin of Atlanta University,* November 1885, 4; minutes for September 22, 1884, September 16, 1885, September 19, 1892, *Minutes of the Missionary Committee of the National Temperance Society, September 30, 1881–December 16, 1897,* file 6, box 3, RG 54, NTS-PHS.

32. *Home Mission Echo* 2 (April 1886): 3; *Spelman Messenger* 2 (December 1885): 5; *Spelman Messenger* 4 (December 1889): 4; *Sixth Annual Report of the Woman's American Baptist Home Mission Society* (1884), 14; *Catalog of Spelman Seminary, 1885–1886,* 32; "Spelman Seminary," *National Temperance Advocate* 20 (October 1885): 170.

33. *Temperance Tracts Issued by the National Temperance Society and Publication House* (New York: J. N. Stearns, Publishing agent, n.d.); "The Blacks at the South," *National Temperance Advocate* 18 (February 1883): 20; "Our Work in the South," *National Temperance Advocate* 18 (March 1883): 42; "A Call for Help," *National Temperance Advocate* 18 (May 1883): 68; "Temperance among the Colored People," *National Temperance Advocate* 18 (November 1883): 182; "Temperance Work among the Freedmen," *National Temperance Advocate* 20 (February 1885): 20.

34. W. E. B. DuBois, *Souls of Black Folk* (1903; repr., New York: Bantam Classics, 1989), 70.

35. James McPherson, "The New Puritanism: Values and Goals of Freedmen's Education in America," in *The University in Society,* vol. 2, ed. Lawrence Stone (Princeton: Princeton University Press, 1974), 626–31; *Baptist Home Missions in North America, Jubilee Report 1832–1882* (New York: Baptist Home Mission Rooms, 1883), 415; *Fifty-Fourth Annual Report of the American Baptist Home Mission Society* (1886), 22; "Make Haste Slowly," *American Missionary* 34 (July 1880): 205; McManus, 145, 167–69, 333.

36. Sandy Dwayne Martin, "The American Baptist Home Mission Society and Black Higher Education in the South, 1865–1920," *Foundations* 24 (1981): 318; *Fifty-Second Annual Report of the American Baptist Home Mission Society* (1884), 23; *Fifty-Fourth Annual Report of the American Baptist Home Mission Society* (1886), 22; *Fourth Annual Report of the Woman's American Baptist Home Mission Society* (1882), 5; *Eighth Annual Report of the Woman's American Baptist Home Mission Society* (1886), 23; "The Freed People," *Home Mission Echo* 7 (February 1891): 2; Lynn D. Gordon, "Race, Class and the Bonds of Womanhood at Spelman Seminary, 1881–1923," *History of Higher Education Annual* 9 (1989): 13.

37. "Intemperance in the South," *American Missionary* 35 (July 1881): 195; "Concert Exercise," *American Missionary* (May 1883): 140; "Temperance Text-books in Our Schools," *American Missionary* 36 (August 1882): 230; "Temperance Work in Churches," *American Missionary* 37 (May 1883): 141; *Fifty-First Annual Report of the American Baptist Home Mission Society* (1883), 45; *Fifty-Fifth Annual Report of the American Baptist Home Mission Society* (1887), 33; "The Race Problem," *Atlanta Constitution*, June 21, 1887; Sister Hancock to Missouri Stokes, July 9, 1887, in Missouri H. Stokes Papers, Rare Book, Manuscript, and Special Collections Library, Duke University, Durham, North Carolina.

38. In the years following the Civil War if Southern rural black children received any education at all, it was only for about three months in the summer, after the crops had been "laid by." County officials regularly hired black students on vacation from high school or college-level studies as teachers. Storrs School sent out students in 1868, even before Atlanta University began holding classes. Even then, the students tried to organize temperance societies. See Caroline Gordon, "The Beginnings of Negro Education in Atlanta," *Bulletin of Atlanta University*, February 1909, 4.

39. *Catalog of the Normal and Preparatory Departments of Atlanta University, 1870–1871*, 24; minutes for June 12, 1886, *Minutes of the Missionary Committee of the National Temperance Society, September 30, 1881–December 16, 1897*, file 6, box 3, RG 54, NTS-PHS. Some of the sources that speak of the summer student work and the literature disseminated are "Georgia: Atlanta University," *American Missionary* 35 (January 1881): 20; "Our Southern Work," *National Temperance Advocate* 18 (July 1883): 118; *Spelman Messenger* 2 (December 1885): 5; "Spelman Seminary," *Home Mission Monthly* 9 (March 1887): 66; *Twelfth Annual Report of the Woman's American Baptist Home Mission Society* (1890), 21.

40. *Bulletin of Atlanta University*, June 1883, 4; *Home Mission Echo* 2 (August 1886): 3; *Home Mission Echo* 5 (August 1889): 3–4.

41. *Catalog of Spelman Seminary, 1883–1884*, 24; *Sixth Annual Report of the Woman's American Baptist Home Mission Society* (1884), 14; *Seventh Annual Report of the Woman's American Baptist Home Mission Society* (1885), 15; "Temperance Work at Spelman," *Spelman Messenger* 5 (June 1889): 6; *Spelman Messenger* 4 (April 1888): 5; Brawley, 120–21.

42. "Woman's Temperance Work in the South," *American Missionary* 42 (July 1888): 198–200; Mrs. J. J. Ansley, *History of the Georgia W. C. T. U., 1883–1907* (Columbus, GA: Gilbert Printing Co., 1914), 77–78. The white chapters of the city and state WCTU never recognized the black ones as coequals.

43. Vermont was the first state (1882) persuaded to implement mandatory Scientific Temperance Instruction, and Georgia was the last (1901).

44. Elson, 1; Alexander M. Gow, *Good Morals and Gentle Manners for Schools and Families* (New York: Van Antwerp, Bragg & Co., 1873), iii–iv, 73–77; "Let's Take a Look at Our History," folder 2, box 1, First Congregational Church, U.C.C. Atlanta, Georgia Collection, AUC; *Catalog of Atlanta University*, 1873–1895; *Catalog of Spelman Seminary*, 1890–1891; "In Memoriam—

Mrs. Mary Tuttle Chase," *The Scroll*, November 1900, 12.

For this and other textbooks discussed below, my dates of implementation are approximate because I have used college catalogs to determine them, and the catalogs were very irregular in indicating which texts were used each year. In addition, hardly any school has a complete run of catalogs. The dates I give are simply the ones that appear in the existing catalogs.

45. "In Memoriam—Mrs. Mary Tuttle Chase," *The Scroll*, November 1900, 14; Benjamin Ward Richardson, *Temperance Lesson Book* (New York: National Temperance Society and Publication House, 1880), 5–6.

46. "Women as Public Speakers," *National Temperance Advocate* 7 (March 1872): 36; Julia Colman, *Alcohol and Hygiene: An Elementary Lesson Book for Schools* (New York: National Temperance Society and Publication House, 1880); *Spelman Messenger* 6 (December 1890): 6.

47. "Spelman Seminary," *National Temperance Advocate* 20 (October 1885): 170; Julia Colman, *The Primary Temperance Catechism* (New York: published by the National Temperance Society and Publication House for the WCTU, 1885).

48. "Temperance Work at Spelman," *Spelman Messenger* 5 (June 1889): 6; James Weldon Johnson, *Along This Way* (1933; repr., New York: Da Capo Press, 2000), 82–84; "The Colored People of Athens," *Atlanta Constitution*, November 11, 1885; "Hon. J. D. Finch," *Spelman Messenger* 3 (February 1887): 1; *Spelman Messenger* 7 (December 1890): 5; Darlene Rebecca Roth, *Matronage: Patterns in Women's Organizations, Atlanta, Georgia, 1890–1940* (Brooklyn: Carlson Publishing, Inc., 1994), 30; "Annual Report of the Secretary of the YWCA," *Spelman Messenger* 6 (June 1890): 7.

49. "Spelman Seminary," *Home Mission Monthly* 9 (March 1887): 66; *Tenth Annual Report of the Woman's American Baptist Home Mission Society* (1888), 18–19; "Echoes from the Field," *Home Mission Echo* 3 (December 1887): 3; "Clark University," *Atlanta Journal*, June 9, 1886; "Our Students' Summer Work," *Bulletin of Atlanta University*, October 1889, 3.

50. Rochon, 24.

51. To increase the Christian pressure on unconverted students, Spelman purposely paired Christian and non-Christian students in dorm rooms. See "Echoes from the Field," *Home Mission Echo* 5 (April 1889): 3.

52. Social purity pledges referred to sexual purity. For a discussion of Spelman's Social Purity Club see Dorsey, 105–6. This type of moral training found support among Northern black clergy. See Alexander Crummell, "The Need of New Ideas and New Aims for a New Era," *AME Church Review* 2 (October 1885): 124–26.

53. George Sale, *Atlanta Baptist Seminary: A Statement and a Plea* (New York: American Baptist Home Mission Society, 1895), folder 5, box 4, American Baptist Home Mission Society Archives, American Baptist Historical Society; Norman Calvin Rothman, "Curriculum Formation in Black Colleges, 1881–1980" (PhD diss., Georgia State University, 1981), 12; *Fifty-First Annual Report of the American Baptist Home Mission Society* (1883), 21; *Fifty-Second Annual Report of the American Baptist Home Mission Society* (1884), 61; *Fifty-Third Annual Report of the American Baptist Home Mission Society* (1885), 62; Towns, 121; *Seventh Annual Report of the Woman's American Baptist Home Mission Society* (1885), 12; "The Freedmen," *American Missionary* 32 (March 1878): 75–77; "Atlanta and Fisk Universities," *American Missionary* 32 (June 1878): 166–67; "The American Missionary Association—Its Place and Work," *American Missionary* 43 (December 1889): 346; *Baptist Home Missions in North America, Jubilee Report*, 416–17; Willard B. Gatewood, *Aristocrats of Color: The Black Elite, 1880–1920* (Bloomington: Indiana University Press, 1990), 256–57.

When Clark University requested its state charter in 1890, it also asked the state legislature to prohibit the sale of intoxicating beverages within one mile of campus. Although Clark was chartered, the legislature rejected the prohibition bill. See *Journal of the House of Representatives of the State of Georgia* 1890, 396, 557.

54. DuBois, *Souls*, 70.

55. "Letters from Graduates," *Bulletin of Atlanta University*, November 1895; *Fifty-Second Annual Report of the American Baptist Home Mission Society* (1884), 61; *Eighth Annual Report of the Woman's American Baptist Home Mission Society* (1886), 18; *Twelfth Annual Report of the Woman's American Baptist Home Mission Society* (1890), 20–21; Henry L. Morehouse, "The Worth of Spelman Seminary to the World," *Spelman Messenger* 12 (June 1896): 1–3, 5–6.

56. W. E. B. DuBois, "The Cultural Missions of Atlanta University," *Phylon* 3 (Second Quarter, 1942): 105–15; Henry L. Morehouse, "The Talented Tenth," *Home Mission Monthly* 18 (August 1896): 277; Evelyn Brooks Higginbotham, *Righteous Discontent: The Women's Movement in the Black Baptist Church, 1880–1920* (Cambridge, MA: Harvard University Press, 1993), 28.

57. Jonathan Zimmerman, *Distilling Democracy: Alcohol Education in America's Public Schools, 1880–1925* (Lawrence: University Press of Kansas, 1999), 15–114; Norton Mezvinsky, "Scientific Temperance Instruction in the Schools," *History of Education Quarterly* 1 (March 1961): 48–54; Ivan H. Light, *Ethnic Enterprise in America: Business and Welfare among Chinese, Japanese, and Blacks* (Berkeley and Los Angeles: University of California Press, 1972), 131–32; Jack S. Blocker Jr., "Did Prohibition Really Work? Alcohol Prohibition as a Public Health Innovation," *American Journal of Public Health* 96 (February 2006): 235.

58. Hunter, 147–49; Jewell, 57–58, 87–134. Joseph O. Jewell's description—from a sociological perspective—of how AMA missionaries and their cultural perspective came to dominate freed people's education is very helpful. He argues that the desire of the freed people for access to education was a movement for self-empowerment—upward social mobility—but because blacks did not have the resources needed to fulfill their goals, they turned to AMA missionaries, whose philosophy was to uplift the freed people from without, using Northern Protestant cultural values. I would argue that this process applies broadly toward all evangelical antebellum nexus groups operating schools for the freed people.

4: Taking Ownership

1. Two prominent Africanists have argued that slaves arriving from Central Africa had actually begun their creolization process in Africa. See Linda M. Heywood and John K. Thornton, *Central Africans, Atlantic Creoles, and the Foundation of the Americas, 1585–1660* (New York: Cambridge University Press, 2007).

2. Dianne M. Stewart, *Three Eyes for the Journey: African Dimensions of the Jamaican Religious Experience* (New York: Oxford University Press, 2004), 23.

3. My understanding of the African elements of the African American worldview is based on the following works: Henry H. Mitchell, *Black Belief: Folk Beliefs of Blacks in America and West Africa* (New York: Harper & Row Publishers, 1975); Albert J. Raboteau, *Slave Religion: The "Invisible Institution" in the Antebellum South* (New York: Oxford University Press, 1978); Mechal Sobel, *Trabelin' On: The Slave Journey to an Afro-Baptist Faith* (Princeton, NJ: Princeton University Press, 1979); Karin Barber, "How Man Makes God in West Africa: Yoruba Attitudes towards the 'Orisa,'" *Africa: Journal of the International African Institute* 51 (1981): 724–45; Sterling Stuckey, *Slave Culture: Nationalist Theory and the Foundations of Black America* (New

York: Oxford University Press, 1987); John Thornton, *Africa and Africans in the Making of the Atlantic World, 1400–1800,* 2nd edition (New York: Cambridge University Press, 1998); Peter J. Paris, *The Spirituality of African Peoples: The Search for a Common Moral Discourse* (Minneapolis: Fortress Press, 1995); Samuel K. Roberts, *In the Path of Virtue: The African American Moral Tradition* (Cleveland: The Pilgrim Press, 1999).

4. Robert H. Nassau, *Where Animals Talk: West African Folk Lore Tales* (Boston: The Gorham Press, 1912), 126–28; Newbell Niles Puckett, *Folk Beliefs of the Southern Negro* (Chapel Hill: University of North Carolina Press, 1926), 525.

5. Holifield, 377–94; Jason R. Young, "Spirituality and Socialization in the Slave Community," in *A Companion to African American History,* ed. Alton Hornsby Jr. (Malden, MA: Blackwell Publishing, 2005), 183.

6. "Means of Elevation—No. III," *The Colored American,* July 20, 1839.

7. Roberts, 15–17.

8. Patricia Bradley, *Slavery, Propaganda, and the American Revolution* (Jackson: University Press of Mississippi, 1998), 1–24; Ronald Takaki, *Iron Cages: Race and Culture in Nineteenth-Century America* (1979; repr., New York: Oxford University Press, 1990), 3–15.

9. "A Pioneer Negro Society, 1787," in Aptheker, 18; "Rules of an Early Negro Society, 1796," in Aptheker, 39; Roberts, 15, 34; Robert L. Harris Jr., "Early Black Benevolent Societies, 1780–1830," *Massachusetts Review* 20 (1979): 603–25.

10. "Speech by William Whipper," in *The Black Abolitionist Papers,* vol. 3, ed. C. Peter Ripley (Chapel Hill: University of North Carolina Press, 1991), 125; *Proceedings of the National Convention of Colored People, and Their Friends, 1847,* in *Minutes of the Proceedings of the National Negro Conventions, 1830–1864,* ed. Howard H. Bell (New York: Arno Press and the New York Times, 1969), 17.

11. "To the People of Color throughout New England," *The Liberator,* September 17, 1836; "Temperance," *The Colored American,* August 31, 1839.

12. "Colored Temperance Convention," *The Liberator,* July 30, 1836; "A Call to the Colored Citizens of Maine and New-Hampshire," *The Colored American,* September 4, 1841.

13. "Rumselling and Pro-Slavery," *The Colored American,* March 20, 1841; "Temperance Address," *Palladium of Liberty,* June 12, 1844; *Minutes of the Fifth Annual Convention for the Improvement of the Free People of Colour in the United States, 1835,* in *Minutes of the Proceedings of the National Negro Conventions, 1830–1864,* 8; Carlson, 685–86.

14. Block, 9–24.

15. *Minutes of the Third Annual Session of the North Georgia Conference of the AME Church* (1875), 12, BAP; *Minutes of the Ebenezer Baptist Association* (1875), 12, (1877), 17, (1882), 21, SCMU; *Minutes of the Missionary Baptist Convention of Georgia* (1876), 29, SCMU; *Minutes of the New Hope Baptist Association* (1887), 6, SCMU; "Temperance Committees," *Christian Recorder,* November 19, 1885.

16. *Minutes of the Eleventh Annual Session of the North Georgia Conference of the AME Church* (1884), 25, BAP; *Minutes of the Seventeenth Annual Session of the North Georgia Conference of the AME Church* (1889), 47, BAP.

17. *Minutes of the Ebenezer Baptist Association* (1875), 12, (1880), 11, (1891), 16, SCMU; *Minutes of the New Hope Baptist Association* (1887), 17, SCMU; Wills, 52–54.

White evangelical clergy spoke of intemperance as a threat to the Church and state just like black clerics. See Larry Jerome Watson, "Evangelical Protestants and the Prohibition Movement in Texas, 1887–1919" (PhD diss., Texas A & M University, 1993), 25–27.

18. Although since the 1830s the AME Church had defined intemperance as drinking any

intoxicating beverage, it is not clear from the reports that black Baptists held this position as late as the 1870s. In the earlier years after the war the language of some Baptist reports suggests that they only opposed the use of distilled spirits.

19. For some examples of the use of Scriptural arguments, see *Minutes of the Ebenezer Baptist Association* (1867), 11, SCMU; *Minutes of the New Hope Baptist Association* (1882), 13, SCMU; *Minutes of the Friendship Baptist Association* (1889), 5, SCMU.

20. *Minutes of the Ebenezer Baptist Association* (1887), 14, SCMU.

21. *Minutes of the Eleventh Annual Session of the North Georgia Conference of the AME Church* (1884), 25, BAP. For another similar account see *Minutes of the New Hope Baptist Association* (1887), 6, SCMU.

22. *Minutes of the Ebenezer Baptist Association* (1884), 16, SCMU. For other similar arguments see *Minutes of the Ebenezer Baptist Association* (1882), 15, (1886), 26, SCMU.

23. *Minutes of the Missionary Baptist Convention of Georgia* (1875), 27, SCMU.

24. *Minutes of the Ebenezer Baptist Association* (1885), 22, SCMU.

25. *Minutes of the Second Annual Session of the North Georgia Conference of the AME Church* (1875), 12, BAP; *Minutes of the New Hope Baptist Association* (1873), 8, (1876), 11, (1877), 12, (1887), 6, (1889), 14, SCMU; *Minutes of the Ebenezer Baptist Association* (1882), 21, (1886), 10, (1887), 14, (1889), 15, SCMU. This rhetoric can also be understood as the African American version of the white jeremiad tradition. See Matthew James Zacharias Harper, "Living in God's Time: African-American Faith and Politics in Post-Emancipation North Carolina" (PhD diss., University of North Carolina, 2009), 172–209.

26. *Minutes of the Missionary Baptist Convention of Georgia* (1875), 12, (1877), 17, (1880), 11, (1885), 21, SCMU; *Minutes of the Eleventh Annual Session of the North Georgia Conference of the AME Church* (1884), 25, BAP; *Minutes of the Ebenezer Baptist Association* (1875), 12, (1887), 14, (1889), 15, SCMU; *Minutes of the New Hope Baptist Association* (1876), 11, (1884), 14, (1887), 6, SCMU.

27. David Wood Wills, "Aspects of Social Thought in the African Methodist Episcopal Church, 1884–1910" (PhD diss., Harvard University, 1975).

28. Rufus B. Spain, *At Ease in Zion: A Social History of Southern Baptists, 1865–1900* (1967; repr., Tuscaloosa: University of Alabama Press, 2003), 5–9; Foy Valentine, "Baptist Polity and Social Pronouncements," *Baptist History and Heritage* 14 (July 1979): 52–61; Paul Harvey, *Redeeming the South: Religious Cultures and Racial Identities among Southern Baptists, 1865–1925* (Chapel Hill: University of North Carolina Press, 1997), 168–80; Leroy Fitts, *A History of Black Baptists* (Nashville, TN: Broadman Press, 1985), 243.

Not only did the associations and conventions have little coercive authority, but Harvey argues that they also received little support from congregations, financially or otherwise, because of their commitment to localism, further weakening their ability to exercise "control." Harvey, 62–63.

29. *Reprint of the First Edition of the Discipline of the African Methodist Episcopal Church* (Atlanta: n.p., 1917), 58–59; Edward L. Wheeler, *Uplifting the Race: The Black Minister in the New South, 1865–1902* (Lanham, MD: University Press of America, Inc., 1982), 11; *Minutes of the Sixteenth Session and Fifteenth Quadrennial Session of the General Conference of the AME Church* (1876), 129, BAP.

30. Those with voting authority at an annual conference included all the traveling elders, deacons, licentiates, and local preachers (who had been so for at least four years).

31. *The Doctrine and Discipline of the African Methodist Episcopal Church* (Philadelphia: AME Book Concern, 1885), 137–39, 148–52; "That's the Way to Reform," *Christian Recorder*,

July 2, 1885; "Temperance Committees," *Christian Recorder*, November 19, 1885; Larry Murphy, "Education and the Preparation for the Ministry in the African Methodist Episcopal Church, 1787 to 1900 (Conclusion)," *AME Church Review* 101 (July–September 1986): 25–34; *Fifteenth Quadrennial Session of the General Conference of the AME Church* (1872), 85, BAP.

32. Harvey, 170–71; Wheeler, 7–8, 81; C. Eric Lincoln and Lawrence H. Mamiya, *The Black Church in the African American Experience* (Durham, NC: Duke University Press, 1990), 13–16; *Journal of the American National Baptist Convention* (Louisville: The Bradley & Gilbert Company, Printers, 1892), 57, SCMU.

33. I found one case where, because of family connections, members of a western AME conference voted into the ministry a man whom several of them had personally seen drunk on multiple occasions. See "A Conference Temperance Report," *Christian Recorder*, December 25, 1890.

34. "The Christian's Bible vs. The Methodist Book of Discipline," *Christian Index and South-Western Baptist*, September 12, 1878.

35. *Minutes of the Fifth Annual Session of the Georgia Conference of the AME Church* (1871), 13, BAP; *Minutes of the First Annual Session of the North Georgia Conference of the AME Church* (1874), 19, BAP; *Minutes of the Thirteenth Annual Session of the North Georgia Conference of the AME Church* (1885), 26, BAP. The Baptist polity quote comes from the white Baptist Convention of Georgia, but the polity issues were essentially the same for black Baptists. See *Minutes of the Baptist Convention of Georgia* (1887), 24, SCMU.

Various people have weighed in on the matter of the moral and intellectual "fitness" of late nineteenth-century black clergy and the effectiveness of black churches in addressing the matter. Bishop Daniel Payne and Booker T. Washington saw little difference between black Baptist and Methodist clergy, thinking very little of both groups. Payne believed only one-third of all black clergy were mentally and morally qualified, while Washington thought only one-fourth were. See Dennis C. Dickerson, *Religion, Race and Region: Research Notes on A.M.E. Church History* (Nashville: AMEC Sunday School Union/Legacy Pub, 1995), 40. Gregory Wills argues for the rigor of the black Baptist credentialing process, but the ongoing problem with drinking among the Baptist clergy undermines Wills's view. See Wills, 79. William Montgomery believes that Baptist associations and conventions did exercise meaningful control over their members, contrary to how the Baptist polity was supposed to work. See William E. Montgomery, *Under Their Own Vine and Fig Tree: The African-American Church in the South, 1865–1900* (Baton Rouge: Louisiana State University Press, 1993), 116–17. I have discussed this issue with Robert Gardner, a leading scholar of Georgia Baptist history. Gardner is perhaps the only person who has read through the extant records of every black Baptist association and convention in Georgia during the late nineteenth century, and his conclusion is that "My impression is that there was little 'control' exercised, real or otherwise, over churches by associations and denominations." Robert Gardner, e-mail message to author, March 21, 2005.

36. *Minutes of the Sixth Annual Session of the Georgia Conference of the AME Church* (1872), 71, BAP; *Minutes of the Third Annual Session of the North Georgia Conference of the AME Church* (1875), 21, BAP; *Minutes of the Missionary Baptist Convention of Georgia* (1876), 29, (1881), 19, (1882), 35, BAP; *Minutes of the Ebenezer Baptist Association* (1875), 12, SCMU.

37. "Antis Grand Rally," *Atlanta Constitution*, November 21, 1885; Spain, 182; *Minutes of the Baptist Convention of Georgia [White]* (1879), 22, (1880), 25, (1882), 21, (1887), 24, SCMU.

38. W. S. Harwood, "Secret Societies in America," *North America Review* 164 (May 1897): 617–24. Harwood's statistics only include black Odd Fellows and Masons, omitting many other black fraternities. See also David T. Beito, "To Advance the 'Practice of Thrift and Economy':

Fraternal Societies and Social Capital, 1890–1920," *Journal of Interdisciplinary History* 29 (Spring 1999): 585–612.

39. Edward Aiken, *The Claims of the Order of Good Templars upon Temperance Men, Women and Youth* (New Brighton, PA: D. R. Johnson, n.d.), 3.

40. David M. Fahey, *Temperance and Racism: John Bull, Johnny Reb, and the Good Templars* (Lexington: University Press of Kentucky, 1996), 11–13; Fahey, "How the Good Templars Began: Fraternal Temperance in New York State," *The Social History of Alcohol Review* nos. 38–39 (1999): 17–27.

41. In fraternal orders each local lodge must receive a charter to be considered legitimate. There were different sources from which to receive a charter, depending on the rules of the order and its stage of development. Generally, when a new order was created the first lodge to organize assumed the right to issue charters to other lodges. If there were enough lodges to form a statewide lodge, then that body issued charters. The state lodge was often called the "Grand Lodge." When a national lodge was organized it was also called a "Grand Lodge," and it also had authority to grant charters. In this case it appears that Browne applied to the national Grand Lodge.

42. D. Webster Davis, *The Life and Public Services of William W. Browne* (Philadelphia: AME Book Concern, 1910), 51–56; David M. Fahey, *The Black Lodge in White America: "True Reformer" Browne and His Economic Strategy* (Dayton, OH: Wright State University Press, 1994), 13–15; James D. Watkinson, "William Washington Browne and the True Reformers of Richmond, Virginia," *Virginia Magazine of History and Biography* 97 (1989): 376–78; Henry A. Scomp, *King Alcohol in the Realm of King Cotton* (Blakely, GA: Blakely Printing Company, 1888), 722–23.

43. The other three were John W. Drew of New Hampshire, and Mother Eliza Stewart and Frances Willard representing the WCTU. They will be discussed in the next chapter.

44. Thrower spoke at Spelman, and probably other black schools. See *Spelman Messenger* 6 (December 1890): 5.

45. "True Reformers," *Atlanta Constitution*, November 29, 1873; "U.O. of T. R.," *Atlanta Constitution*, October 29, 1874; "U. O. T. R.," *Atlanta Constitution*, September 4, 1875; "United Order of True Reformers," *Savannah Tribune*, February 5, 1876.

46. "United Order of True Reformers of Georgia, Office Grand Worthy Master of the State," box 9, William A. Pledger Scrapbook, John E. Bryant Papers, Rare Book, Manuscript, and Special Collections Library, Duke University, Durham, North Carolina.

47. "Colonel William Anderson Pledger—Race Leader, Editor, Lawyer, Politician and Patriot," *Atlanta Age* (1904), clipping in William A. Pledger Biographical Vertical File, Robert W. Woodruff Library, Archives and Special Collections, AUC; Cyrus F. Adams, "Colonel William A. Pledger, The Forceful Orator and Fearless Editor," *Colored American Magazine* 5 (1902): 146–48; "Letter Book of W. A. Pledger," box 9, John E. Bryant Papers, Rare Book, Manuscript, and Special Collections Library, Duke University, Durham, North Carolina.

48. *Minutes of the Missionary Baptist Convention of Georgia* (1876), 29.

49. "True Reformers," *Atlanta Constitution*, September 3, 1875; "U. O. T. R.," *Atlanta Constitution*, September 4, 1875.

50. For some reason the Right Worthy Grand Lodge of the World did not have much success in signing up Georgia's True Reformer lodges. Although in 1881 they appointed an Atlanta schoolteacher and Methodist minister, Charles P. Wellman, to recruit True Reformers, he seems to have spent most of his time in Tennessee and Alabama. "Good Templary," *Christian Recorder*, October 6, 1881.

51. Fahey, *Black Lodge*, 14; International Order of Good Templars, Georgia Grand Lodge, *An Appeal from the Temperance Workers of Georgia to the Officers and Members of the Right Worthy*

Grand Lodge I.O.G.T. in behalf of the Colored People of the South (Atlanta, 1882), 1–3. For a full discussion of the impact of the IOGT schism on black Templars see Fahey, *Temperance and Racism*, 105–25.

The AME's *Christian Recorder* became the official organ of the U.S. lodges of the RWGL of the World. Pledger's resignation was not based on some animus toward temperance fraternities per se, for in the *Athens Blade* he promoted temperance fraternity-related causes. See *Athens Blade*, February 6, 1880.

52. Fahey, *Temperance and Racism*, 110–11; "Atlanta's Colored People," *American Missionary* 34 (October 1880): 292; "Town Topics," *Atlanta Constitution*, June 13, 1877; "Colored Good Templars," *Atlanta Constitution* (October 1878); "Georgia," *National Temperance Advocate*, April 1882, 61; "Dual Grand Lodge of Good Templars," *Southern Recorder*, October 2, 1886.

53. Scomp, 721–22; Howard H. Turner, *Turner's History of the Independent Order of Good Samaritans and Daughters of Samaria* (Washington, DC: R. A. Waters, 1881), 18–27, 63–64.

54. Scomp, 721–22; E. R. Carter, *Biographical Sketches of Our Pulpit* (1888; repr., Chicago: Afro-Am Press, 1969), 161–63.

55. Scomp, 721; "Good Samaritans," *Atlanta Constitution*, March 18, 1876; Turner, 155; E. R. Carter, *The Black Side: A Partial History of the Business, Religious, and Educational Side of the Negro in Atlanta, Georgia* (Atlanta, 1894), 26; "The Good Samaritans," *Atlanta Constitution*, September 8, September 11, 1891; "Their Convention Over," *Atlanta Constitution*, September 12, 1891.

56. Carter, *Black Side*, 27; "Benevolent Association," *Atlanta Constitution*, September 22, 1876; "Good Samaritans Dedicate Their New Hall," *Atlanta Times*, June 28, 1890; "The Good Samaritans," *Atlanta Constitution*, June 23, 1890; Dorsey, 109.

57. David T. Beito, *From Mutual Aid to the Welfare State: Fraternal Societies and Social Services, 1890–1967* (Chapel Hill: University of North Carolina Press, 2000), 20–21.

58. Carter, *Black Side*, 41; "The Temperance Mutual Benefit Association of Philadelphia," *Southern Recorder*, October 29, 1886; *Southern Recorder*, September 30, 1887; "Colored Benevolence," *Atlanta Constitution*, November 13, 1883; Hunter, 70–73.

59. "Atlanta's Colored People," *American Missionary* 34 (October 1880): 292; Harris, 611.

60. "Colored Odd Fellows," *Atlanta Constitution*, April 30, 1872; Charles B. Wilson, *Official Manual and History of the Grand United Order of Odd Fellows in America* (Philadelphia: George F. Lasher, 1894), 313, 320; "Atlanta's Colored People," *American Missionary* 34 (October 1880): 292; "The Odd Fellows," *Southern Recorder*, March 9, 1888.

61. William A. Muraskin, *Middle Class Blacks in a White Society: Prince Hall Freemasonry in America* (Berkeley and Los Angeles: University of California Press, 1975), 43–74; Mark C. Carnes, "Middle-Class Men and the Solace of Fraternal Ritual," in *Meanings for Manhood: Constructions of Masculinity in Victorian America*, ed. Mark C. Carnes and Clyde Griffen (Chicago: University of Chicago Press, 1990), 37–66; "Colored Odd Fellows," *Atlanta Constitution*, April 30, 1872; "Colored Odd Fellows Anniversary," *Atlanta Daily Herald*, May 13, 1873; "G. U. O. F." *Daily Evening Commonwealth*, February 2, 1875; "A Colored Gathering," *Atlanta Constitution*, February 11, 1879; "The Colored Odd Fellows," *Atlanta Constitution*, October 7, 1880.

62. In the late 1800s there was a move among the white Masons to get their whole organization to take a strong prohibitionist stand and ban saloon keepers from membership, but many members objected. Many white Masons defined temperance as not drinking to excess rather than total abstinence. Most probably drank but "wouldn't be caught dead, drunk." Lynn Dumenil, *Freemasonry and American Culture, 1880–1930* (Princeton, NJ: Princeton University Press, 1984), 75–80.

63. "G.U.O.F." *Daily Evening Commonwealth*, February 2, 1875; "Atlanta's Colored People,"

American Missionary 34 (October 1880): 292; "Police Court," *Atlanta Daily Herald*, March 11, 1873.

64. "What Atlanta University has done for Georgia," *Bulletin of Atlanta University*, January 1888, 5; *Bulletin of Atlanta University*, January 1896, 4; "From Mr. Hershaw's Address," *Bulletin of Atlanta University*, May 1897, 3; Jennifer Lund Smith, "The Ties that Bind: Educated African-American Women in Post-Emancipation Atlanta," in *Georgia in Black and White: Explorations in the Race Relations of a Southern State, 1865–1950*, ed. John C. Inscoe (Athens: University of Georgia Press, 1994), 91–105.

65. DuBois, *Souls*, 3; Lawrence W. Levine, *Black Culture, Black Consciousness: Afro-American Folk Thought from Slavery to Freedom* (New York: Oxford University Press, 1977), 33.

5: "The Most Enthusiastic Election Ever Held in This Country"

1. *Springfield Globe-Republic* (Springfield, OH), November 27, 1885, Chronicling America,http://chroniclingamerica.loc.gov/lccn/sn87076916/1885-11-27/ed-1/seq-2/;words=Atlanta+prohibition (accessed February 16, 2011).

2. Gaines M. Foster, *Moral Reconstruction: Christian Lobbyists and the Federal Legislation of Morality, 1865–1920* (Chapel Hill: University of North Carolina Press, 2002).

3. Eighteen states held referenda on constitutional prohibition in the 1880s: Connecticut, Iowa, Kansas, Maine, Massachusetts, Michigan, Nebraska, New Hampshire, North Dakota, Ohio, Oregon, Pennsylvania, Rhode Island, South Dakota, Tennessee, Texas, Washington, and West Virginia. North Carolina held a referendum on a statewide law, not a constitutional amendment. Ann-Marie E. Szymanski, *Pathways to Prohibition: Radicals, Moderates, and Social Movement Outcomes* (Durham, NC: Duke University Press, 2003), 2, 219n5.

4. "E. P. Howell's Speech," *Atlanta Constitution*, November 20, 1887.

5. "The Georgia Press Association and Temperance," *Atlanta Constitution*, May 24, 1881; John M. Dobson, *Politics in the Gilded Age* (New York: Praeger Publishers, 1972), 25–42.

Even the idea of endorsing a popular vote on prohibition was feared by national party leaders. At the state level, however, attitudes varied. State Democratic parties rarely called for popular votes on prohibition, but during the 1880s ten state Republican Party platforms did: Arkansas, Massachusetts, Michigan, Missouri, Nebraska, New Jersey, Oregon, Pennsylvania, Tennessee, and Texas. In addition, the Connecticut, Indiana, Ohio, and Wisconsin Republican Party platforms included "indefinite expressions favoring the eradication of the evils of intemperance and the restraint of the traffic." A party's call for local option votes did not mean the rank-and-file supported prohibition. For example, in Texas, where the Republican Party called for a plebiscite, when the vote was finally held in 1887, probably the majority of Republicans opposed prohibition. Ivy, 97–98; Colvin, 175–76.

6. Rochon, 31; "Temperance," *New York Evangelist*, July 28, 1887. See also "Some Plain Words on Prohibition," *The Advance*, November 10, 1887. What it meant to "politicize" temperance had evolved over time. Bills with far less political significance than local option could not pass in 1850. For example, in 1850 Georgia's Sons of Temperance sought incorporation under state law, but Joseph Brown, the state senator who chaired the special committee assigned to consider the issue, reported that even though most committee members were temperance men, they opposed the request because there was considerable public prejudice against the organization, and legislating on it would "inflame the public mind." Joseph H. Parks, *Joseph E. Brown of Georgia* (Baton Rouge: Louisiana State University Press, 1977), 10.

7. "The Georgia Plan," *Atlanta Journal*, November 23, 1885.

8. Sam Small was a heavy drinker for years. At several points in his life it threatened his ability to earn a living. The same month Drew arrived in Atlanta, Small received an appointment to a temporary job in New Orleans and lapsed back into heavy drinking. Small did not finally give up alcohol until August 1885, during a Sam Jones revival. See Samuel W. Small, *White Angel of the World* (Philadelphia: Peerless Publishing Co., 1891), 16–21.

9. According to Drew he calculated correctly about Atlanta's significance. From Atlanta he received invitations to many places throughout the South, including cities in Arkansas, Florida, and South Carolina.

10. "Mr. John W. Drew," *Atlanta Constitution*, January 17, 1880; *Our Union*, January 15, 1880.

11. "Woman's Christian Temperance Union," *Atlanta Constitution*, April 15, 1880; "Woman's Christian Temperance Union," *Atlanta Constitution*, April 23, 1880; Mother Stewart, *Memories of the Crusade* (Columbus, OH: William G. Hubbard & Co., 1888), 510–17; Bordin, 78–79.

12. Ansley, 38–49, 61, 90–91.

13. "'Dry' Atlanta," *Richmond Dispatch*, November 27, 1885.

14. Theodore L. Cuyler to John D. Rockefeller, April 4, 1886, reel 9, Office Correspondence, Papers of John D. Rockefeller, Sr., microfilm edition, RAC; *National Temperance Advocate* 20 (November 1885): 188; "The Good Templars," *Atlanta Constitution*, January 31, 1886; "Templars at Work," *Atlanta Constitution*, February 2, 1886; "The Colored Vote," *Atlanta Journal*, October 1, 1885; "Whisky or No Whisky," *Atlanta Constitution*, September 20, 1885.

15. James M. Wright, *The License System of the City of Atlanta* (Atlanta: Harper Publishing Co., 1964), 186–88; "Drinks for 1885," *Atlanta Constitution*, January 3, 1885.

16. Raymond B. Nixon, *Henry W. Grady: Spokesman of the New South* (New York: Alfred A. Knopf, 1943), 271. Although Nixon's reference to "communicated" articles is about 1887, the *Constitution* followed the same policy in the 1885 election. For descriptions of the campaigns see John Hammond Moore. Even more thorough is W. Dennis Mason, "Protestants, Politics, and Prohibition: The Prohibition Elections of Fulton County in 1885 and 1887" (Master's thesis, University of Georgia, 1986).

17. "Whisky or No Whisky," *Atlanta Constitution*, September 20, 1885; "Our Atlanta Letter," *The Weekly Sentinel*, October 3, 1885.

18. Eugene J. Watts, "Black Political Progress in Atlanta, 1868–1895," *Journal of Negro History* 59 (July 1974): 268–75; Watts, *The Social Bases of City Politics, Atlanta, 1865–1903* (Westport, CT: Greenwood Press, 1978), 23–25.

19. "Prohibition in the South," *Atlanta Constitution*, December 31, 1885; "A Joyful City," *Atlanta Journal*, November 27, 1885.

20. "Fifth Ward Temperance," *Atlanta Constitution*, October 14, 1885; "Munhall and Small," *Atlanta Constitution*, October 15, 1885; "Fighting Whisky," *Atlanta Constitution*, October 16, 1885; "Prohibition," *Spelman Messenger* 2 (December 1885): 1; "Black and White," *Atlanta Constitution*, November 13, 1885; "Spelman Seminary," *Atlanta Journal*, November 13, 1885.

21. Mary Jane Smith, "Constructing Womanhood in Public: Progressive White Women in a New South" (PhD diss., Louisiana State University, 2002), 123–31.

22. Scomp, 814.

23. "Prohibition Points," *Atlanta Journal*, October 21, 1885; "Colored Prohibitionists," *Atlanta Constitution*, November 6, 1885; "Still Booming," *Atlanta Journal*, November 18, 1885; "The Cold Water Wave," *Atlanta Journal*, November 13, 1885.

A letter to the editor of the *Atlanta Journal* openly questioned whether Julius L. Brown's opposition to prohibition—expressed in several lengthy letters to the editor between November 3 and 8—constituted a conflict of interest because so much of his family's wealth was derived from leasing convicts from the state to work coal mines the family owned. (Brown was the son of Georgia Senator Joseph E. Brown.) See "A Father's Opinion," *Atlanta Journal*, November 6, 1885.

24. "Bishop Turner's Reply to Gov. Bullock," *Atlanta Constitution*, November 24, 1885; "Bryant's Battalions," *Atlanta Constitution*, December 10, 1879; "Prohibition Meetings," *Macon Telegraph*, October 20, 1885; "Prohibition Points," *Atlanta Journal*, October 21, 1885; "Still Booming," *Atlanta Journal*, November 18, 1885; "Increased Enthusiasm," *Atlanta Journal*, November, 20, 1885; "Down with Whisky," *Atlanta Constitution*, November 21, 1885; "For Prohibition," *Atlanta Constitution*, November 24, 1885; "The Cold Water Wave," *Atlanta Journal*, November 13, 1885.

25. "Prohibition in Atlanta," *Sunny South*, November 4, 1885. I only found two examples of wets urging blacks not to sell their votes to the drys.

26. Watts, *Social Bases*, 32–34; "The Republican Vote in Georgia," *Atlanta Constitution*, September 28, 1887; "Distributing Whiskey to Control the Colored Vote," *National Temperance Advocate* 22 (August 1887): 135. See also Atticus G. Haygood, *Save Our Homes: A Prohibition Sermon* (Macon, GA: J. W. Burke & Co., 1884), 19–20.

27. *Atlanta Journal*, November 14, 1885; "Black and White," *Atlanta Constitution*, November 13, 1885; "The Inside of Atlanta," *Macon Telegraph*, October 24, 1885.

28. "Fighting Whisky," *Atlanta Constitution*, October 16, 1885; "At the Atlanta University," *Atlanta Constitution*, November 12, 1885; "The Cold Water Wave," *Atlanta Journal*, November 13, 1885.

29. "Colored Prohibitionists," *Atlanta Constitution*, November 6, 1885; "Prohibition Meetings," *Atlanta Constitution*, November 20, 1885.

30. "Manhood," *Weekly Defiance*, February 24, 1883; "Wet or Dry," *Atlanta Constitution*, November 25, 1885. See also Matt J. Harper, "The Ballot or the Bottle: Temperance, Black Manliness, and the Struggle for Citizenship in North Carolina, 1881–1901" (Master's thesis, University of North Carolina, 2003); William H. Becker, "The Black Church: Manhood and Mission," in *African-American Religion: Interpretive Essays in History and Culture*, ed. Timothy E. Fulop and Albert J. Raboteau (New York: Routledge, 1997), 180–99.

31. "The Anti-Prohibition Meeting," *Atlanta Constitution*, October 28, 1885; "Opposing Prohibition," *Atlanta Constitution*, October 29, 1885.

32. It is not clear if this committee was assembled solely for the purpose of fighting prohibition or if it was a standing organization designed to facilitate employee-management relations, but it was probably the former.

33. "The Colored Citizens," *Atlanta Constitution*, October 30, 1885; "Anti-Prohibition," *Atlanta Journal*, November 3, 1885.

34. In 1880 Badger's taxable assets totaled $5,850, and in 1885 they were $8,000. See Dorsey, 172–73.

35. Although Bullock's term in office ended in disgrace when he fled the state in 1871 to avoid prosecution on corruption charges, and he was arrested and returned to Atlanta for trial in 1876, he was acquitted on all charges and by the 1880s had become respected once again in Atlanta society.

36. "The Anti-Prohibition Committee," *Atlanta Constitution*, October 31, 1885.

37. "Prohibition in Georgia," *New York Tribune*, November 25, 1885; "Clark Goes Dry," *Atlanta Constitution*, February 26, 1885; "Pledger on Trial," *Macon Telegraph*, October 27, 1885; "Pledger Convicted," *Atlanta Constitution*, October 28, 1885; "Pledger Sentenced," *Atlanta Constitution*, October 29, 1885; "The Colored Citizens," *Atlanta Constitution*, October 30, 1885; "Antis Grand Rally," *Atlanta Constitution*, November 21, 1885.

38. "The Colored Citizens," *Atlanta Constitution*, October 30, 1885; "Taking it Straight," *Atlanta Constitution*, November 3, 1885; "The Anti-Prohibitionists," *Atlanta Constitution*, November 12, 1885; "Antis Grand Rally," *Atlanta Constitution*, November 21, 1885; "Anti-Prohibition," *Atlanta Journal*, November 3, 1885; "W. A. Pledger to the Colored People," *Atlanta Constitution*, November 24, 1885.

39. Committee of Twenty-Five, *An Appeal to the Voters of Atlanta* (Atlanta: Atlanta Constitution Job Print, 1885).

40. Atlanta grew up around a railroad juncture, consequently logistics (trade, transportation, warehousing) was, and has remained, its economic raison d'être. A major regional distribution center, the city has historically employed more people in logistics than in manufacturing. In 1880, 29 percent of all Atlantans worked in manufacturing, while 35 percent worked in trade and transportation. See Richard Hopkins, "Status, Mobility, and the Dimensions of Change in a Southern City: Atlanta, 1870–1910," in *Cities in American History*, ed. Kenneth T. Jackson and Stanley K. Schultz (New York: Knopf, 1972), 230n8; "For the Sale," *Atlanta Constitution*, November 20, 1885; Charles Davidson, "Moving Things Along," *Georgia Trend*, March 2004, 13–18. 41. "An Anti-Prohibition Meeting," *Atlanta Constitution*, November 6, 1885; "Jeff Long Speaks a Piece," *Macon Telegraph*, November 21, 1885; "W. A. Pledger to the Colored People," *Atlanta Constitution*, November 24, 1885.

42. Wright, 186; "Drinks for 1885," *Atlanta Constitution*, January 3, 1885; *Weekly Defiance*, October 8, 1881; "When Liquor Licenses Expire," *Atlanta Journal*, November 27, 1885.

43. "The Cold Water Wave," *Atlanta Journal*, November 13, 1885.

44. This is an intriguing charge, but I found no evidence to support the idea that liquor dealers contributed to black schools.

45. "Antis Grand Rally," *Atlanta Constitution*, November 21, 1885; "An Anti-Prohibition Meeting," *Atlanta Constitution*, November 6, 1885; "The Inside of Atlanta," *Macon Telegraph*, November 20, 1885; "For the Sale of Whiskey," *Atlanta Journal*, November 20, 1885.

46. "Antis Grand Rally," *Atlanta Constitution*, November 21, 1885.

47. Ibid.

48. "An Anti-Prohibition Meeting," *Atlanta Constitution*, November 6, 1885; "W. A. Pledger to the Colored People," *Atlanta Constitution*, November 24, 1885.

49. "Antis Grand Rally," *Atlanta Constitution*, November 21, 1885.

50. *Perrysburg Journal* (Perrysburg, OH), November 27, 1885, Chronicling America, http://chroniclingamerica.loc.gov/lccn/sn87076843/1885–11–27/ed-1/seq-2/;words=Atlanta+Prohibition (accessed February 16, 2011).

51. It would not take much for Atlanta's police to fear that a fight was about to break out when several blacks got together and showed any excitement about anything. While I question how close their conversation was to an actual fight, I cite this to illustrate the passions the campaign aroused in African Americans.

52. It was important to a woman to be able to influence her husband and/or son to vote for prohibition. One lady said she would have a "very poor" opinion of herself as a woman "if she could not persuade him to vote on any question of right so plainly indicated as that in the prohibition movement." "A Woman's Opinion," *Atlanta Journal*, November 17, 1885. The *Atlanta Journal* specifically called on women to influence the men in their lives to wear the blue badge. "The Ladies and the Blue Badge," *Atlanta Journal*, November 16, 1885. The press rarely ever mentioned women persuading their men to vote wet.

53. According to Ebenezer's own history, the church was not organized until November 1886. Rev. John Parker, its founding pastor, came out of Wheat Street Baptist. According to

the *Atlanta Journal*, however, Parker was pastor of Ebenezer in November 1885. While it is not surprising that a white paper could record incorrect information about Black Atlanta, it is odd that it would accidentally identify a pastor with a church name that did not exist at the time but which did come into existence the following year. All the records on W. H. Tillman say he pastored Wheat Street from 1875 to 1897. While the following chronology is purely speculative, the general scenario is not improbable: Perhaps Tillman voluntarily or involuntarily stepped down from the pulpit for a time, and Parker replaced him; and while in charge, he changed the church's name to Ebenezer. After a period of several months (in 1886) Tillman returned, and Parker withdrew with several members, keeping the Ebenezer name for his congregation, while the remainder of the church retained the original Wheat Street Baptist name and their pastor Tillman. See Tommy Jones, "Historical Background and Context," *Structure Report on Ebenezer Baptist Church*, prepared for the National Park Service on file at the Martin Luther King Jr. National Historic Site, Atlanta, Georgia (2000), 2; "Prohibition," *Atlanta Journal*, November 11, 1885.

54. "The Grand Battle, and the Whiskey Defeat," *Christian Index*, December 3, 1885; "Dry It Is," *Atlanta Constitution*, November 26, 1885; "Prohibition in Georgia," *New York Times*, November 12, 1885; "Prohibition in Atlanta," *Wesleyan Christian Advocate*, November 25, 1885; "Atlanta's Experiment," *Augusta Chronicle*, November 29, 1885; "An Incipient Row Prevented," *Macon Telegraph*, November 24, 1885; "An Anti-Prohibition Meeting," *Atlanta Constitution*, November 6, 1885; "Black and White," *Atlanta Constitution*, November 13, 1885; "Inside of Atlanta," *Macon Telegraph*, November 18, 1885; "Prohibition," *Atlanta Journal*, November 11, 1885.

For examples of how prohibition mania affected students and employees, see "Girls and Prohibition," *Atlanta Constitution*, November 12, 1885, and "High Pressure of Prohibition," *Atlanta Constitution*, November 23, 1885.

55. "Wet or Dry?" *Atlanta Constitution*, November 25, 1885.

56. "Wet or Dry?" *Atlanta Constitution*, November 25, 1885; "Corralling the Voters," *New York Times*, November 25, 1885; "Inside of Atlanta," *Macon Telegraph*, November 25, 1885; "The Battle On," *Atlanta Journal*, November 25, 1885; Scomp, 811–12.

57. "Wet or Dry?" *Atlanta Constitution*, November 25, 1885; "Corralling the Voters," *New York Times*, November 25, 1885; "Inside of Atlanta," *Macon Telegraph*, November 25, 1885; "The Battle On," *Atlanta Journal*, November 25, 1885; Scomp, 811–12; "A Fight Over Prohibition," *New York Times*, November 27, 1885.

58. "Dry It Is," *Atlanta Constitution*, November 26, 1885.

59. "An Army of Voters," *Atlanta Constitution*, November 15, 1885; "Wet or Dry?" *Atlanta Constitution*, November 25, 1885; Ansley, 87–88; "Free Lunch," *Atlanta Constitution*, November 19, 1885; "Food for the Voters," *Atlanta Constitution*, November 25, 1885.

60. "An Army of Voters," *Atlanta Constitution*, November 15, 1885; "How Can They Vote?" *Atlanta Constitution*, November 17, 1885; "Threats of Violence," *Atlanta Constitution*, November 17, 1885; "The Great Election," *Atlanta Constitution*, November 22, 1885; "Tomorrow's Contest," *Atlanta Constitution*, November 24, 1885; "The Voting Hours," *Atlanta Constitution*, November 25, 1885; "Police Laconics," *Atlanta Journal*, November 26, 1885; "Prohibition," *Spelman Messenger* 2 (December 1885): 1; "Dry It Is," *Atlanta Constitution*, November 26, 1885.

61. Georgia's 1877 constitution established a cumulative poll tax that required voters to be up to date on all their back taxes prior to the previous year.

62. "Inside of Atlanta," *Macon Telegraph*, October 24, 1885; "Negroes Registered in Atlanta," *New York Times*, November 2, 1885; "Inside of Atlanta," *Macon Telegraph*, November 12, 1885; "Working the Prohibitionists," *New York Times*, November 14, 1885; "How Can They Vote?" *Atlanta Constitution*, November 17, 1885; "The Cold Water Wave," *Atlanta Journal*,

November 13, 1885; "To the Colored Voters," _Atlanta Constitution_, November 22, 1885; Levine, 102–21; Riggins R. Earl Jr., _Dark Symbols, Obscure Signs: God, Self, & Community in the Slave Mind_ (Maryknoll, NY: Orbis Books, 1993), 131–58. Wesley Gaines gave the same advice as Carter when asked if it was all right to vote the dry ticket after the wets had paid their back taxes.

63. "An Army of Voters, _Atlanta Constitution_, November 15, 1885; "Dry It Is," _Atlanta Constitution_, November 26, 1885; Wright, 199; "The Inside of Atlanta," _Macon Telegraph_, November 27, 1885; "Tomorrow's Contest," _Atlanta Constitution_, November 24, 1885; "Prohibition Prizes," _Atlanta Constitution_, December 3, 1885.

64. "Prohibition Prizes," _Atlanta Constitution_, December 3, 1885; "The Banner," _Atlanta Constitution_, January 14, 1886; "The Banner," _Atlanta Constitution_, January 15, 1886; "Banner Presentation," _Spelman Messenger_ 2 (December 1885): 5; _Augusta Chronicle_, November 29, 1885.

65. "A Remarkable Event in Georgia," _The Sun_ (New York, NY), November 27, 1885, Chronicling America, http://chroniclingamerica.loc.gov/lccn/sn83030272/1885-11-27/ed-1/seq-2/ (accessed February 16, 2011).

66. _Springfield Globe-Republic_ (Springfield, OH), November 25, 1885, Chronicling America, http://chroniclingamerica.loc.gov/lccn/sn87076916/1885–11–25/ed-1/seq-2/;words=Atlanta+prohibition (accessed February 16, 2011);"Badly Cut," _Atlanta Journal_, November 26, 1885; "Pelting Prohibitionists," _Atlanta Constitution_, November 28, 1885; "Pedestrianism and Prohibition," _Atlanta Constitution_, December 1, 1885; "Two Atlanta Prohibitionists," _The Washington Post_, December 2, 1885; "Crazy on Prohibition," _Atlanta Constitution_, November 28, 1885; "The Inside of Atlanta," _Macon Telegraph_, November 29, 1885; "The Inside of Atlanta," _Macon Telegraph_, November 27, 1885; "A Temperance Orator Crazed," _New York Times_, June 21, 1886; "Hosannas Being Sung," _Fort Worth Daily Gazette_, November 26, 1885, The Portal to Texas History, http://texashistory.unt.edu/ark:/67531/metapth86650/m1/8/ (accessed May 21, 2012).

67. "Battle Between Badgers," _Atlanta Journal_, October 18, 1886.

68. "Remarkable Contest," _St. Paul Daily Globe_, November 23, 1885, Chronicling America, http://chroniclingamerica.loc.gov/lccn/sn90059522/1885-11-23/ed-1/seq-2/(accessed February 16, 2011).

69. A small sampling of articles expressing this view: "Let it Stay out of Politics," _Atlanta Constitution_, December 1, 1885; "Prohibition in Atlanta," _New York Tribune_, November 28, 1885; "Prohibition in Atlanta," _Wesleyan Christian Advocate_, December 2, 1885.

70. A small sampling of articles expressing this view: "The New South—A Triumph," _New York Weekly Witness_, December 3, 1885; "Press Comments," _Atlanta Journal_, December 1, 1885; "Prohibition in Atlanta," _Wesleyan Christian Advocate_, November 25, 1885.

71. "Hail Ye Freemen!" _Atlanta Journal_, November 26, 1885; "Press Comments," _Atlanta Journal_, December 1, 1885; "What Georgia Editors Say," _Atlanta Journal_, December 4, 1885; _Christian Recorder_, December 10, 1885; "North Georgia A.M.E. Conference," _Atlanta Constitution_, December 5, 1885; "Was It a Mistake?" _Atlanta Constitution_, December 3, 1885.

Whites also acknowledged that victory would have been impossible without the black vote. See "Prohibition in Georgia," _New York Weekly Witness_, December 3, 1885; _Twenty-First Annual Report of the National Temperance Society_ (1886), 19. One man specifically noted the influence of black graduates of Atlanta University: "Progress at the South," _Atlanta Constitution_, April 16, 1886.

72. "The Afterclap," _Augusta Chronicle_, December 2, 1885; "Colored Men Want Recognition," _New York Times_, March 26, 1887; "Was It a Mistake?" _Atlanta Constitution_, December 3, 1885.

73. "Atlanta's Agitation," *Columbus Sunday Enquirer*, November 22, 1885; Lewis L. Gould, "The Republican Search for a National Majority," in *The Gilded Age*, revised and enlarged edition, ed. H. Wayne Morgan (Syracuse, NY: Syracuse University Press, 1970), 171–87; "Boston Letter," *Atlanta Journal*, December 3, 1885; Olive Hall Shadgett, *The Republican Party in Georgia: From Reconstruction through 1900* (Athens: University of Georgia Press, 1964), vii–viii, 1–89; HanesWalton, *Black Republicans: The Politics of the Black and Tans* (Metuchen, NJ: Scarecrow Press, Inc., 1975), 47–61; Vincent P. DeSantis, *Republicans Face the Southern Question—The New Departure Years, 1877–1897* (Baltimore: Johns Hopkins University Press, 1959), 9–13; *Augusta Chronicle*, November 29, 1885; "Prohibition in Georgia," *New York Weekly Witness*, December 3, 1885; "Prohibition and Crankyism," *New York Freeman*, December 12, 1885.

74. "The Southern People," *The National Liberator, and Illustrated Weekly*, Frances E. Willard Scrapbook Number 5, Frances E. Willard Memorial Library and Archives; "Miss Willard's Eloquence," *The Voice*, October 23, 1884; "Why Firm for St. John," *The Voice*, November 6, 1884.

75. "Atlanta's Agitation," *Columbus Sunday Enquirer*, November 22, 1885; *Augusta Chronicle*, November 29, 1885; "Prohibition in the South," *Atlanta Constitution*, December 31, 1885; "Prohibition in Georgia," *New York Weekly Witness*, December 3, 1885; "Prohibition and Crankyism," *New York Freeman*, December 12, 1885.

76. "Mr. Blaine Talks Again," *New York Times*, August 26, 1886; "Angry with Blaine," *New York Times*, August 28, 1886.

77. "Blaine for Prohibition," *Atlanta Constitution*, August 13, 1886; "Blaine's Fondest Hope," *Boston Daily Globe*, August 11, 1886; "Republicanism in the South," *Atlanta Constitution*, September 20, 1886; Cantrell, 89; "The Republican Danger," *Washington Post*, November 26, 1887; "Prohibition Queries," *Southern Recorder*, September 25, 1886.

These same issues appeared in the 1887 Texas and Tennessee state prohibition campaigns. See Cantrell, 87; Paul E. Isaac, *Prohibition and Politics: Turbulent Decades in Tennessee, 1885–1920* (Knoxville: University of Tennessee Press, 1965), 45–46.

In June of 1887 the *New York Times* correctly predicted that despite all the talk, the Republican Party would never officially endorse prohibition. See "The Temperance Issue," *New York Times*, June 18, 1887.

78. Albert Griffin to John D. Rockefeller, Sr., May 4, 1887, August 22, 1888; "Anti-Saloon Republicanism" and "The Only Certain Route from Defeat to Victory," reel 15, Office Correspondence, Papers of John D. Rockefeller, Sr., Rockefeller Family Archives, microfilm edition, RAC; Gould, 175–78, 187.

79. "Prohibition in Politics," *Macon Telegraph*, November 12, 1885; "What Georgia Editors Say," *Atlanta Journal*, December 4, 1885; "Very Bad Policy," *Atlanta Constitution*, July 9, 1886; "Prohibition in the South," *Atlanta Constitution*, December 31, 1885; "Prohibition and Crankyism," *New York Freeman*, December 12, 1885; "Press Comments," *Atlanta Journal*, December 1, 1885; "Prohibition in Georgia," *New York Weekly Witness*, December 3, 1885; "High License and Prohibition," *Macon Telegraph*, November 30, 1885; *Augusta Chronicle*, November 27, 1885.

80. "Prohibition in Atlanta," *New York Tribune*, December 28, 1885; "Standing Firm," *Atlanta Journal*, November 28, 1885; "The Inside of Atlanta," *Macon Telegraph*, December 3, 1885; "The Atlanta Election," *Augusta Chronicle*, December 3, 1885.

81. "Our Atlanta Letter," *Weekly Sentinel*, October 3, 1885; "Inside of Atlanta," *Macon Telegraph*, November 18, 1885; "Inside of Atlanta," *Macon Telegraph*, November 27, 1885.

6: The "Dry" Years, 1885–1887

1. "Prohibition at the South," *New York Tribune*, August 23, 1885.

2. *Southern Recorder*, December 2, 1887.

3. "They Are Excited," *Atlanta Constitution*, July 12, 1886.

4. "The Result Declared," *Atlanta Constitution*, December 25, 1885; "Status of Prohibition," *Atlanta Journal*, December 26, 1885; "Atlanta's Wine Rooms," *Atlanta Constitution*, July 1, 1886; "Atlanta's Wine Rooms," "What 'Native Wines' Mean," and "Winking for a Drink," *Atlanta Constitution*, July 2, 1886.

5. "Will Not Close," *Atlanta Constitution*, June 23, 1886; "Prohibition in Atlanta," *Atlanta Constitution*, June 28, 1886; "On the Verge," *Atlanta Constitution*, June 29, 1886; "Willing to Obey the Law," *Atlanta Constitution*, July 2, 1886.

6. "Everything Goes," *Atlanta Journal*, November 22, 1886. Soft drinks (ginger ale and root beer) had just been created in the 1870s and were being sold at pharmacy soda fountains. In May 1886, Atlanta pharmacist John Pemberton invented Coca-Cola and sold it in Jacob's Pharmacy. However, it did not sell particularly well in its first year, despite prohibition.

7. "The Day on the Streets," and "The Last Drink," *Atlanta Constitution*, July 1, 1886; "Atlanta's Jollifications," *Augusta Chronicle*, July 1, 1886; "How They Look" and "After the Battle," *Atlanta Constitution*, July 2, 1886.

8. "No Bar'l at Home," *Atlanta Constitution*, July 7, 1886.

9. "Beer and Whisky," *Atlanta Constitution*, July 7, 1886; "Not Altogether Dry," *Atlanta Constitution*, July 17, 1886; "Prohibition in Atlanta," *New York Times*, July 15, 1887; "Making More Liquor Cases," *Atlanta Constitution*, July 16, 1886; "The First Big Gun," *Atlanta Constitution*, July 20, 1886; "Prohibition in Atlanta," *Atlanta Constitution*, October 10, 1886.

10. "A Demand for Nerve Tonic," *Atlanta Constitution*, November 28, 1887; "The People's Forum—The Wine Room Nuisance," *Atlanta Journal*, November 19, 1886; "The Wine Rooms," *Atlanta Constitution*, November 20, 1886; "After the Wine Rooms," *Atlanta Constitution*, December 14, 1886; "The Wine Room Tax," *Atlanta Constitution*, December 18, 1886; "Atlanta Wine Rooms," *Atlanta Journal*, February 15, 1887; "The Wine Room Men," *Atlanta Constitution*, February 23, 1887; "They Will Close," *Atlanta Constitution*, September 14, 1887; "The Wine Room Bill," *Wesleyan Christian Advocate*, September 21, 1887.

11. "Prohibition in Atlanta," *New York Times*, October 10, 1886; "Only One More," *Atlanta Constitution,* October 10, 1886; "Hawthorne on Atlanta," *Atlanta Constitution*, June 5, 1887; "A 'Black Sheep,'" *Atlanta Constitution*, November 4, 1887.

12. In other parts of the nation illegal sellers were known as "blind pigs."

13. "Those Who Drank Yesterday," *Atlanta Constitution*, July 3, 1886; "Moonshiners in Georgia," *New York Times*, February 7, 1887; "Breaking the Law," *Atlanta Constitution*, July 20, 1886; "The Blind Tiger," *Atlanta Constitution*, August 21, 1886.

14. "They Are Excited," *Atlanta Constitution*, July 12, 1886; "Prohibition in Atlanta," *New York Times*, October 10, 1886; "Colored Candidates Out," *Atlanta Constitution*, October 6, 1886.

15. Atlanta Police Court Docket, MSS 787, Atlanta History Center; "Temperance," *New York Evangelist*, July 28, 1887; "The Negro Vote in the South," *New York Evangelist*, December 8, 1887.

16. "Vox Populi: The People to be Consulted as to Their Choice," *Atlanta Journal*, October 23, 1886.

17. Gaines apparently did not serve, because the press reported that Smith W. Easley replaced him during the deliberations of the committee. See "Compromise Effected," *Atlanta*

Journal, October 30, 1886.

18. "The Meeting Upstairs," *Atlanta Constitution*, October 27, 1886; "What the Anti-Prohibitionists Did," *Atlanta Constitution*, October 27, 1886; "'Come Ye Out From Among Them' 'And the Sheep Were Separated From the Goats,'" *Southern Recorder*, October 29, 1886.

19. "Compromise Effected," *Atlanta Journal*, October 30, 1886; "The Mass Meeting Tonight," November 4, 1886; "Ratified" and "The Fusion Ticket Endorsed," November 5, 1886; "A Story about Atlanta that the Telegraph Correspondents Do Not Make Much of," *The Voice*, December 16, 1886.

20. Atlanta's system of election was designed to control who got elected by limiting voter participation. Voters had to register separately for each election. Between 1884 and 1891 blacks comprised between 16 percent (1886) and 32 percent (1888) of all registered voters. See Clarence A. Bacote, "The Negro in Atlanta Politics" *Phylon* 16 (Fourth Quarter, 1955): 334.

21. "The Committee's Actions," *Atlanta Journal*, October 30, 1887.

22. *Southern Recorder*, April 1, 1887; "They All Left the Tent," *Atlanta Constitution*, March 14, 1887; "The Gospel Tent filled with People to Hear Evangelist Tillman," *Atlanta Constitution*, March 2, 1887.

23. "Negro Policemen for Atlanta," *Daily Intelligencer*, September 8, 1867; "The New Captains," *Atlanta Constitution*, April 2, 1885; Rabinowitz, *Race Relations*, 41–43; "Colored Men Want Recognition," *New York Times*, March 26, 1887; "Inside of Atlanta," *Macon Telegraph*, April 5, 1887.

24. Rabinowitz, *Race Relations*, 41–50; "Inside of Atlanta," *Macon Telegraph*, April 7, 1887; "The Darky's Story," *Atlanta Constitution*, April 8, 1887; "Detectives Arrested on the Charge of Unlawful Trespass," *Atlanta Journal*, April 7, 1887; "The Officers Exonerated," *Atlanta Constitution*, April 24, 1887.

25. "Is This Prohibition?" *Atlanta Constitution*, October 23, 1887; "A 'Black Sheep,'" *Atlanta Constitution*, November 4, 1887.

26. "Atlanta Liars," *Southern Recorder*, September 16, 1887.

27. "The Killing of Mr. Haygood," *New York Times*, March 3, 1886; "Fighting Whisky," *Atlanta Constitution*, February 23, 1886; "Prohibition in Hall," *Atlanta Constitution*, February 27, 1886; *Southern Recorder*, April 1, June 10, and August 12, 1887.

28. *Southern Recorder*, September 18, 1886.

29. *Southern Recorder*, October 8, 1886.

30. I say "painfully" accurate because Turner was one of the founders of Georgia's Republican Party and had served as a Republican state representative during Reconstruction, until he and all other blacks were kicked out of the House by white lawmakers, on account of their color.

31. "Colored Prohibitionists," *Atlanta Constitution*, November 6, 1885; *Southern Recorder*, October 2, 1886.

Stephen Angell found that the moral argument was only one of five prohibition arguments Turner used throughout his career. The others were (1) alcohol was harmful to the body, (2) alcohol was socially degrading, (3) temperance was an "appropriate" successor to abolitionism and was endorsed by Abraham Lincoln, and (4) the "best men" of white society were abstainers, and therefore adopting the practices of the "best men" was a sure way for blacks to ensure their survival. See Stephen W. Angell, *Bishop Henry McNeal Turner and African-American Religion in the South* (Knoxville: University of Tennessee Press, 1992), 185–87.

32. "Prohibition Defeated in Texas," *Southern Recorder*, August 12, 1887.

33. Carter, *Black Side*, 43.

34. "Items Paragraphically Noted," *Christian Recorder*, January 3, 1889; "The Proceedings in Detail," Fifth National Prohibition Convention, reel 1, series II, Temperance and Prohibition Papers, microfilm edition, Ohio Historical Society; "The Anti-Platform," *Atlanta Constitution*, November 1, 1887.

7: Prohibition Revisited

1. *Open Letters on Prohibition: A Controversy between Hon. Jefferson Davis and Bishop Charles B. Galloway* (Nashville: Publishing House of the Methodist Episcopal Church, South, 1893).

2. "The Liberal Club," *Atlanta Constitution*, July 24, 1886; "The Liberal Club," *Atlanta Constitution*, July 31, 1886; "Conservative Citizens," *Atlanta Constitution*, August 15, 1886; "What Shall Be Done?" *Atlanta Constitution*, August 18, 1886; "The Correct List," *Atlanta Constitution*, August 19, 1886; "The Conservative Citizens," *Atlanta Constitution*, August 25, 1886; "The Elevation of Labor," *Southern Recorder*, September 25, 1886.

3. "The M.A.B.'s," *Atlanta Constitution*, November 27, 1887.

4. "The Right View," *Atlanta Constitution*, October 29, 1887; "The Anti-Platform," *Atlanta Constitution*, November 1, 1887; "Judge Anderson Takes an Outing," *Atlanta Constitution*, September 7, 1887.

5. "Prohibition and the Exposition," *Atlanta Constitution*, September 1, 1887; "It Will Be Held," *Atlanta Constitution*, September 20, 1887; "Inside of Atlanta," *Macon Telegraph*, October 21, 1887; "The Official Order," *Atlanta Constitution*, October 28, 1887; "Wet or Dry," *Atlanta Constitution*, October 22, 1887; "The Wets in the Wet," *Atlanta Constitution*, November 8, 1887.

6. "An Anti Meeting," *Atlanta Constitution*, October 25, 1887.

7. "Prohi and Anti," *Atlanta Constitution*, November 6, 1887; "A Letter for Flipper," *Atlanta Constitution*, November 16, 1887; "Flipper's Return," *Atlanta Constitution*, November 17, 1887; "Rev. J. S. Flipper," *Atlanta Constitution*, November 25, 1887.

8. "In the Courthouse Basement," *Atlanta Constitution*, November 16, 1887; "A Black Sheep," *Atlanta Constitution*, November 4, 1887; "Third Ward Wets," *Atlanta Constitution*, November 5, 1887; "An Anti Night," *Atlanta Constitution*, November 9, 1887; "The Wets in the Wet," *Atlanta Constitution*, November 8, 1887; "Thousands Massed," *Atlanta Constitution*, November 17, 1887.

9. "A Black Sheep," *Atlanta Constitution*, November 4, 1887.

10. "A Black Sheep," *Atlanta Constitution*, November 4, 1887; "The First Ward," *Atlanta Constitution*, November 3, 1887.

11. "The Wets in the Wet," *Atlanta Constitution*, November 8, 1887; "The First Ward," *Atlanta Constitution*, November 3, 1887.

12. "The First Ward," *Atlanta Constitution*, November 3, 1887.

13. "In the Courthouse Basement," *Atlanta Constitution*, November 16, 1887; "An Anti Night," *Atlanta Constitution*, November 9, 1887; "The Wets in the Wet," *Atlanta Constitution*, November 8, 1887.

14. "The Fifth Ward," *Atlanta Constitution*, November 13, 1887.

15. "Third Ward Wets," *Atlanta Constitution*, November 5, 1887; "A Black Sheep," *Atlanta Constitution*, November 4, 1887; "The Wets in the Wet," *Atlanta Constitution*, November 8, 1887; "An Anti Night," *Atlanta Constitution*, November 9, 1887; "An Outdoor Meeting," *Atlanta Constitution*, November 12, 1887; "Thousands Massed," *Atlanta Constitution*, November 17,

1887; "Earnest East Pointers," *Atlanta Constitution*, November 19, 1887; "E. P. Howell's Speech," *Atlanta Constitution*, November 20, 1887; "Prohibition and Its Evils," *Atlanta Constitution*, November 12, 1887.

16. "The First Ward," *Atlanta Constitution*, November 3, 1887; "In the Courthouse Basement," *Atlanta Constitution*, November 16, 1887; "A Tremendous Crowd," *Atlanta Constitution*, November 2, 1887; "An Anti Night," *Atlanta Constitution*, November 9, 1887; "The First Ward," *Atlanta Constitution*, November 3, 1887.

17. "An Outdoor Meeting," *Atlanta Constitution*, November 12, 1887; "Thousands Massed," *Atlanta Constitution*, November 17, 1887; "A Grand Gathering," *Atlanta Constitution*, November 18, 1887; "Dripping Wet," *Atlanta Constitution*, November 24, 1887.

18. "A Tremendous Crowd," *Atlanta Constitution*, November 2, 1887; "Third Ward Wets," *Atlanta Constitution*, November 5, 1887; "The Wets in the Wet," *Atlanta Constitution*, November 8, 1887; "Against Prohibition," *Atlanta Constitution*, November 8, 1887; "An Anti Night," *Atlanta Constitution*, November 9, 1887; "Thousands Massed," *Atlanta Constitution*, November 17, 1887; "A Grand Gathering," *Atlanta Constitution*, November 18, 1887; "Stubborn Facts!" *Atlanta Constitution*, November 13, 1887.

19. "Speech of the Hon. John L. Hopkins before the Young Men's Prohibition Club, October 27, 1887," *Atlanta Constitution*, October 30, 1887; "What They Are Doing," *Atlanta Constitution*, October 25, 1887; "A Tremendous Crowd," *Atlanta Constitution*, November 2, 1887; "The Wet Meetings" and "The First Ward," *Atlanta Constitution*, November 3, 1887; "A Black Sheep," *Atlanta Constitution*, November 4, 1887; "Third Ward Wets," *Atlanta Constitution*, November 5, 1887; "The Wets in the Wet," *Atlanta Constitution*, November 8, 1887; "An Anti Night," *Atlanta Constitution*, November 9, 1887; "An Outdoor Meeting," *Atlanta Constitution*, November 12, 1887; "Thousands Massed," *Atlanta Constitution*, November 17, 1887; "A Grand Gathering," *Atlanta Constitution*, November 18, 1887; "Earnest East Pointers," *Atlanta Constitution*, November 19, 1887; "Dripping Wet," *Atlanta Constitution*, November 24, 1887; "The Campaign in Atlanta," *Wesleyan Christian Advocate*, November 9, 1887.

20. "Wet or Dry," *Atlanta Constitution*, October 22, 1887; "Sunday Services," *Atlanta Constitution*, October, 24, 1887; "For the Campaign," *Atlanta Constitution*, October 26, 1887; "The Women," *Atlanta Constitution*, November 1, 1887; "Woman's Work for Prohibition," *Atlanta Constitution*, November 19, 1887; "Atlanta All Aglow," *Macon Telegraph*, November 2, 1887.

21. *Spelman Messenger* 4 (December 1887): 4–5; "The Prohibitionists," *Atlanta Constitution*, November 5, 1887; "On the Warpath," *Atlanta Constitution*, November 22, 1887; "Insulting Women," *Atlanta Constitution*, November 23, 1887.

22. *Weekly Defiance*, as quoted in *Southern Recorder*, November 4, 1887; *Weekly Defiance*, as quoted in *Southern Recorder*, November 11, 1887; "Jefferson Davis," *Atlanta Constitution*, November 23, 1887.

23. "A Popular Vote," *Atlanta Constitution*, September 21, 1887; "The Square Issue," *Atlanta Constitution*, October 8, 1887; "In Every Ward," *Atlanta Constitution*, November 2, 1887; "The Young Men's Club," *Atlanta Constitution*, November 20, 1887; "Still Fighting," *Atlanta Constitution*, November 22, 1887; "Smith Speaks," *Atlanta Constitution*, November 23, 1887; "The Grand Climax," *Atlanta Constitution*, November 25, 1887.

During the hearings on the bill, prohibitionists claimed they had spoken to citizens and that they found no support for the bill and that the city council therefore did not represent the will of the people. If they did speak with citizens they must have only spoken with fellow prohibitionists.

24. The following is a sample of articles containing speeches that include prohibitionists

defending themselves: "Prohibition Rally," *Atlanta Constitution,* October 28, 1887; "In Every Ward," *Atlanta Constitution,* November 2, 1887; "Dr. J. W. Lee," *Atlanta Constitution,* November 24, 1887.

25. "Sunday Services," *Atlanta Constitution,* October 24, 1887; "Speech of Mr. Carter before the Young Men's Prohibition Club," *Atlanta Constitution,* October 30, 1887; "The Warehouse," *Atlanta Constitution,* November 8, 1887; "The Prohibitionists," *Atlanta Constitution,* November 12, 1887; "The Warehouse," *Atlanta Constitution,* November 15, 1887.

26. "The Prohibitionists," *Atlanta Constitution,* November 12, 1887; "Ministers for Prohibition," *Atlanta Constitution,* October 5, 1887; "A Glorious Meeting," *Atlanta Constitution,* November 4, 1887; "The Warehouse," *Atlanta Constitution,* November 15, 1887; "The Dry Side," *Atlanta Constitution,* November 11, 1887; "Dr. J. W. Lee," *Atlanta Constitution,* November 24, 1887.

27. "In Every Ward," *Atlanta Constitution,* November 2, 1887; "The Meeting of the Drys," *Atlanta Constitution,* November 9, 1887; "At the Warehouse," *Atlanta Constitution,* November 19, 1887; "Dr. J. W. Lee," *Atlanta Constitution,* November 24, 1887.

28. "Prohibition in Atlanta," *Columbus Enquirer-Sun,* November 22, 1887; "He Is an Anti," *Atlanta Constitution,* November 23, 1887; "A Day of Triumph," *Atlanta Constitution,* November 26, 1887.

29. "Dripping Wet," *Atlanta Constitution,* November 24, 1887.

30. "Jeff Davis vs. Prohibition," *Atlanta Constitution,* July 30, 1887; Ivy, 98–99; quotes come from the *Herald of United Churches* and *Weekly Defiance,* as cited in "Jefferson Davis Denounced as a Man Who Should Be Despised," *Atlanta Constitution,* November 23, 1887.

31. "The Atlanta Election," *Atlanta Constitution,* December 12, 1887; Hamm, 114–16. This flyer continued to be used by anti-prohibitionists in other campaigns.

32. "Routed and Demoralized: The Antis Lines Are Broken" and "Seen from the Streets," *Atlanta Constitution,* November 25, 1887; "The Lists Corrected," *Macon Telegraph,* November 25, 1887; "In the Opera House," "The Last," and "15,000 People," *Atlanta Constitution,* November 26, 1887; "The Atlanta Prohibition Campaign," *Washington Post,* November 26, 1887; "The Prohibition Contest," *Columbus Enquirer-Sun,* November 26, 1887.

33. *Western Appeal* (St. Paul & Minneapolis), December 3, 1887; "Atlanta Is Wet," and "It Is Wet," *Atlanta Constitution,* November 27, 1887; "Rum Win at Atlanta," *Savannah Morning News,* November 27, 1887; *Southern Recorder,* December 2, 1887; "Done with Prohibition," *New York Tribune,* November 27, 1887.

34. "It Is Wet," *Atlanta Constitution,* November 27, 1887; "Local and Personal," *Southern Recorder,* December 2, 1887; "A Talk with Judge Hillyer," *Atlanta Constitution,* November 27, 1887; "The Wets Have Won," *Columbus Enquirer-Sun,* November 27, 1887; "Done with Prohibition," *New York Tribune,* November 27, 1887.

35. The only available statistics on black registration come from the chairman of the Young Men's Prohibition Club, W. T. Turnbull. His numbers—3,285 blacks and 5,695 whites—yield a total of 8,980, which is 410 more than the total city registration reported by the county ordinary. "A Talk with Judge Hillyer," *Atlanta Constitution,* November 27, 1887; "11,140: Fulton County's Registration for the Prohibition Election," *Atlanta Constitution,* November 16, 1887.

36. "It Is Wet," *Atlanta Constitution,* November 27, 1887; "11,140: Fulton County's Registration for the Prohibition Election," *Atlanta Constitution,* November 16, 1887; "About Town," *Atlanta Constitution,* November 28, 1887.

37. A member of Fulton's grand jury did approach the leaders of both camps with instructions to gather evidence on illegal voting, with an eye toward prosecuting. See letter to the

editor by J. Henly Smith in *Atlanta Constitution*, November 30, 1887.

38. "A Talk with Judge Hillyer," *Atlanta Constitution*, November 27, 1887; "After the Battle," *Atlanta Constitution*, November 28, 1887; "A Minister's Views," "Receiving the Returns," and "The City Ministry," *Atlanta Constitution*, November 29, 1887; "No Contest," *Atlanta Constitution*, November 30, 1887; "The Final Decision," *Atlanta Constitution*, December 1, 1887; "Defeat in Atlanta," *Christian Index*, December 1, 1887; *Southern Recorder*, December 2, 1887; "The Atlanta Election," *Atlanta Constitution*, December 12, 1887.

39. "A Talk with Judge Hillyer," *Atlanta Constitution*, November, 27, 1887; "Whiskey Back in Atlanta," *Southern Christian Advocate*, December 15, 1887; "The Colored Vote at Atlanta," *Savannah Morning News*, November 30, 1887; "Atlanta Is Wet," *New York Times*, November 27, 1887; "Echoes of the Election," *Atlanta Constitution*, December 1, 1887.

40. "Whiskey Back in Atlanta," *Southern Christian Advocate*, December 15, 1887; "The Colored Vote at Atlanta," *Savannah Morning News*, November 30, 1887; *Western Appeal* (St. Paul/ Minneapolis), December 3, 1887; *Christian Recorder*, December 1, 1887.

41. Not only was Atlanta still dry on Election Day, but state law forbade alcohol sales anywhere near polling stations on election days.

42. "He Is Dead," *Atlanta Constitution*, December 1, 1887; "With Honors," and "The Prohibitionists and the Colored People," *Atlanta Constitution*, December 2, 1887.

43. "More Church Trials," *Atlanta Constitution*, December 25, 1887.

44. See chapter 2, n62.

45. "They Were Wet," *Atlanta Constitution*, December 9, 1887; "They Were Fired," *Atlanta Constitution*, December 14, 1887; "More Church Trials," *Atlanta Constitution*, December 25, 1887.

The idea of black pastors so strictly disciplining members for refusing to support prohibition was not unique to Atlanta. See "Baptists, Presbyterians, and Liquor," *Wesleyan Christian Advocate*, November 18, 1885.

46. "Local and Personal," *Southern Recorder*, December 2, 1887.

47. *Atlanta's Experience*, folder 2, box 4, Hunnicutt Family Papers, Manuscript, Archives, and Rare Book Library, Robert W. Woodruff Library, Emory University.

48. *DeKalb Chronicle*, November 3, 1887; "Prohibition in Atlanta," *Western Kansas World*, December 3, 1887, Chronicling America, http://chroniclingamerica.loc.gov/lccn/ sn82015485/1887–12–03/ed-1/seq-6 (accessed April 27, 2011); *Wichita Eagle*, November 27, 1887, Chronicling America, http://chroniclingamerica.loc.gov/lccn/sn85032490/1887–11– 27/ed-1/seq-2 (accessed April 27, 2011).

49. Joe L. Coker, *Liquor in the Land of the Lost Cause: Southern White Evangelicals and the Prohibition Movement* (Lexington: University Press of Kentucky, 2007).

50. Rochon, 200.

Afterword

1. *Proceedings of Consultation Convention of 350 Leading Colored Men of Georgia, held in Macon, Georgia, January 25th and 26th, 1888* (Augusta: Georgia Baptist Book and Job Print, 1888): 5–6, 17.

2. Several articles in the *AME Church Review* and *Christian Recorder* entertained the idea that the Prohibition Party was the best party for African Americans. See J. P. Sampson, "The Prohibition Party," *AME Church Review* 4 (July 1887): 506–7; John M. Palmer, "An Apology for Party Prohibition," *AME Church Review* 4 (October 1887): 136–53; "Rum, Politics and Human

Morals," *Christian Recorder*, May 8, 1890; "A Conference Temperance Report," *Christian Recorder*, December 25, 1890.

3. In 1892 the city reinstituted a rule which had been abandoned in the 1870s that permitted only whites registered as Democrats to vote in the city's primary elections. Since blacks consistently registered as Republicans, the nominee represented white voters, and black voters were limited to simply ratifying their selection in the general election (as usually happened), persuading whites to vote for one of their own (which never happened), or being a swing voting block when an independent Democrat ran for office (which occasionally happened). In the latter case they usually voted with the "establishment" Democratic candidate against the outsider, hence maintaining the political status quo. Bacote, 338–39.

4. Harvey K. Newman, "Decatur Street: Atlanta's African American Paradise Lost," *Atlanta History* 44 (Summer 2000): 5–13; "Atlanta and Her Decatur Street," *Augusta Herald*, December 24, 1909; John Merrill Spencer, "'Decatur Street': A Natural Area" (Master's thesis, Atlanta University, 1952), 23–29; Kevin J. Mumford, *Interzones: Black/White Sex Districts in Chicago and New York in the Early Twentieth Century* (New York: Columbia University Press, 1977), 19–20.

5. Thomas M. Deaton, "Atlanta during the Progressive Era" (PhD diss., University of Georgia, 1969); Hunter, 45–48.

6. DuBois, *Souls,* 128.

7. "Progressive Thought," *AME Zion Quarterly Review* 4 (January 1894): 185.

8. "An Open Letter to the Southern People," reel 81, The Papers of W. E. B. DuBois, microfilm edition; Ivy, 48, 52; Isaac, 35; Wilbur P. Thirkield, "A Cathedral of Cooperation," in *The Human Way: Addresses on Race Problems at the Southern Sociological Congress, Atlanta, 1913*, ed. James E. McCulloch (Nashville: Southern Sociological Congress, 1913), 135.

9. *Richmond Dispatch*, December 1, 1885.

10. "The Negro in the Test," *Southern Recorder*, November 11, 1887.

11. Hanes Walton "Another Force for Disfranchisement: Blacks and the Prohibitionists in Tennessee," *Journal of Human Relations* 18 (1970): 728–38; Denise Herd, "Prohibition, Racism and Class Politics in the Post-Reconstruction South," *Journal of Drug Issues* 13 (1983) 77–94; Charles Crowe, "Racial Violence and Social Reform: Origins of the Atlanta Riot of 1906," *Journal of Negro History* 53 (July 1968): 234–56.

12. "Same Sex Marriage Support Shows Pace of Social Change Accelerating," *New York Times,* May 11, 2012.

13. C. Vann Woodward, *The Strange Career of Jim Crow*, 2nd rev. ed. (New York: Oxford University Press, 1966), 32.

Appendix II

1. *Atlanta History Bulletin* 6 (January–April 1941): 17, 101–3; "The Liquor Trade of Atlanta," *Daily New Era*, September 6, 1871; "Drinks for 1885," *Atlanta Constitution*, January 3, 1885.

2. "Saloon Statistics," *Quarterly Journal of Inebriety* 16 (1894): 272.

3. My license data are compiled from the annual tax ordinances of Atlanta that are recorded in the Minutes of the Atlanta City Council (MACC), held by the Atlanta History Center (AHC).

4. For a sample of this literature see D. B. Lady, "The Drinking Habit and Prohibition," *The Reformed Quarterly Review* (1896): 468–80; "The Moral Side of the Question," *Atlanta Independent*, January 12, 1907; George Kibbe Turner, "Beer and the City Liquor Problem,"

McClure's 33 (1909): 528–43; John Koren, "Some Aspects of the Liquor Problem," *National Municipal Review* 3 (1914): 505–16.

5. In 1881 Nebraska's state legislature required all towns with more than 10,000 people to charge $1,000 for a retail liquor license. Aside from Lincoln and Omaha, the only two other major cities with a $1,000 license were in Minnesota, Minneapolis and St. Paul. Within Georgia, Savannah charged $200, and Columbus charged $500. Beginning in 1885, Fulton County outside of Atlanta charged $2,500 for a retail liquor license, as an indirect way to close all saloons. Many Georgia counties had been using this approach for years.

6. "The City Council," *Atlanta Constitution*, May 9, 1879, and June 8, 1882; MACC 5:1, 8:219, 10:582, 12:38, 14:613, 633, 18:312, 330, 663, AHC; "Council Minutes," *Daily New Era*, June 14, 1868, "Liquor Licenses," *Atlanta Journal*, June 17, 1891.

7. MACC 9:664, 15:670, 17:689, AHC; "Sam Jones on Saloons," Oversized Bound Volume, Sam P. Jones Papers, Special Collections, Robert W. Woodruff Library, Emory University, Atlanta, Georgia.

8. Scomp, 642–60. For a listing of the various state laws in effect as of 1889 see *The Cyclopaedia of Temperance and Prohibition* (NY: Funk & Wagnalls, 1891), s.v. "Legislation—Georgia."

Works Cited

Archival and Manuscript Collections

American Baptist Historical Society, Atlanta, GA
 American Baptist Home Mission Society Archives
 American Baptist Magazine
 Home Mission Echo (Women's American Baptist Home Mission Society)
 Home Mission Monthly (American Baptist Home Mission Society)
 Isaac W. Brinckerhoff Papers
 Proceedings of the Convention held in the City of New-York for the Formation of the American Baptist Home Mission Society
 Reports of the American Baptist Home Mission Society, 1839–1900
 Reports of the Executive Committee of the American Baptist Home Mission Society, 1833–1839
 Reports of the Women's American Baptist Home Mission Society, 1882–1900

Amistad Research Center, Tulane University, New Orleans, LA
 American Missionary Association Archives, District of Columbia series
 Annual Reports of the American Missionary Association, 1848–1859

Atlanta History Center, Atlanta, GA
 Atlanta Police Court Docket, 1886–1887
 Minutes of the Atlanta City Council, 1866–1900

Atlanta University Center, Robert W. Woodruff Library, Archives and Special Collections, Atlanta, GA
 Atlanta University Presidential Records, 1856–1984
 Bulletin of Atlanta University
 Catalog of Atlanta University
 Catalog of Spelman Seminary
 Records of the First Congregational Church, U.C.C., Atlanta, Georgia
 The Scroll
 Spelman Messenger
 William A. Pledger Biographical Vertical File

Congregational Library, Boston, MA
 The Advance
 Annual Reports of the American Missionary Association, 1860–1888
 The Helping Hand (Macon, GA)
 Minutes of the Annual Meeting of the Central South Congregational Conference, 1871–1877
 Minutes of the Annual Meeting of the Georgia Congregational Conference, 1878–1888
 Minutes of the National Council of the Congregational Churches of the United States, 1871–1886

Duke University, Rare Book, Manuscript, and Special Collections Library, Durham, NC
   John Emory Bryant Papers
   Missouri H. Stokes Papers

Emory University, Pitts Theology Library, Atlanta, GA
   Annual Report of the National Temperance Society and Publication House, 1867–1893

Emory University, Robert W. Woodruff Library, Atlanta, GA
   American Missionary Association Archives, Georgia series, microfilm edition
   The Papers of W. E. B. DuBois, microfilm edition
   Records of the Assistant Commissioner for the State of Georgia, Bureau of Refugees, Freed-
      men, and Abandoned Lands, 1865–1869, microfilm edition

Emory University, Robert W. Woodruff Library, Manuscript, Archives, and Rare Book Library,
      Atlanta, GA
   Hunnicutt Family Papers
   Sam P. Jones Papers

Frances E. Willard Memorial Library and Archives, Evanston, IL
   African American Women in the WCTU File
   Frances E. Willard Scrapbook Number 5

Georgia Department of Archives and History, Morrow, GA
   Governors' Incoming Correspondence

Haverford College Library, Special Collections, Haverford, PA
   Joshua L. Baily Collection, 1818–1917

Mercer University, Jack Tarver Library, Special Collections, Macon, GA
   Journal of the American National Baptist Convention, 1889–1891
   Minutes of the Baptist Convention of Georgia, 1869–1895
   Minutes of the Ebenezer Baptist Association, 1867–1891
   Minutes of the Friendship Baptist Association, 1882–1892
   Minutes of the New Hope Baptist Association, 1873–1891
   Minutes of the New Hope Sunday School Convention, 1888, 1890
   *Proceedings of Consultation Convention of 350 Leading Colored Men of Georgia, held in Macon,
      Georgia, January 25th and 26th, 1888.*
   Proceedings of the Missionary Baptist Convention of the State of Georgia, 1870–1892

National Park Service, Martin Luther King Jr. National Historic Site, Atlanta, GA
   Structure Report on Ebenezer Baptist Church

New York Public Library, Humanities and Social Sciences Library, New York, NY
   Annual Report of the American Tract Society, Boston, 1868
   Annual Report of the American Tract Society–New York, 1866–1875

New York Public Library, Schomburg Center for Research in Black Culture, New York, NY
    Benjamin Tucker Tanner Papers
    Carter G. Woodson Collection of Negro Papers and Related Documents, 1830–1936

Ohio Historical Society, Columbus, OH
    Constitution and Minute Book, Band of Hope, Miamisburg, OH
    Temperance and Prohibition Papers, microfilm edition

Presbyterian Historical Society, Philadelphia, PA
    National Temperance Society and Publication House Records

Princeton Theological Seminary, Princeton, NJ
    Theodore L. Cuyler Manuscript Collection

Rockefeller Archive Center, Tarrytown, NY
    The Papers of John D. Rockefeller, Sr., microfilm edition
    Rockefeller Family Archives

Syracuse University Library, Special Collections Research Center
    Gerrit Smith Broadside and Pamphlet Collection, digital edition

Wilberforce University, Stokes Library, Archives, Wilberforce, OH
    Benjamin Arnett Papers
    Catalogue of Wilberforce University, 1872–1873

Newspapers and Periodicals

American Freedman (American Freedman's Union Commission)
American Missionary (AMA)
Athens Blade (Georgia)
Atlanta Constitution
Atlanta Daily Herald
Atlanta Daily News
Atlanta Independent
Atlanta Journal
Atlanta Times
Augusta Chronicle (Georgia)
Boston Globe
Christian Index (Atlanta, Baptist)
Christian Index and Southwestern Baptist
Christian Recorder (AME Church)
Christian Watchman (Boston, Baptist)
Colored American (New York City)
Colored American Magazine
Columbus Enquirer-Sun (Georgia)
Columbus Sunday Enquirer (Georgia)

Daily Evening Commonwealth (Atlanta)
Daily Intelligencer (Atlanta)
Daily New Era (Atlanta)
Daily Sun (Atlanta)
DeKalb Chronicle (Georgia)
Fort Worth Daily Gazette (Texas)
The Freedman (ATrS-Boston)
Freedman's Journal (ATrS-Boston)
Journal of Humanity and Herald of the American Temperance Society
Journal of the American Temperance Union The Liberator
Lutheran Herald and Journal of the Fort Plain, N.Y. Franckean Synod
Macon Telegraph (Georgia)
National Temperance Advocate (National Temperance Society)
New York Evangelist
New York Freeman
New York Times
New York Tribune
New York Weekly Witness
Oberlin Evangelist
Our Union (WCTU)
Palladium of Liberty (Columbus, OH)
Perrysburg Journal (Perrysburg, OH)
Richmond Dispatch (Virginia)
Savannah Morning News
Savannah Tribune
Southern Christian Advocate (Charleston, SC)
Southern Recorder (Atlanta)
Springfield Globe-Republic (Springfield, OH)
St. Paul Daily Globe (Minnesota)
The Sun (New York)
Sunny South (Atlanta)
Temperance Lesson Manual for the Band of Hope and Loyal Temperance Legion
Union Signal (WCTU)
The Voice (New York City)
Washington Post (Washington, DC)
Weekly Defiance (Atlanta)
Weekly Sentinel (Augusta, GA)
Weekly Sun (Atlanta)
Wesleyan Christian Advocate (Methodist Episcopal Church, South, in Georgia)
Western Appeal (Minneapolis/St. Paul)
Western Kansas World (WaKeeney, KS)
Wichita Eagle (Kansas)

Published Sources

Abzug, Robert. *Cosmos Crumbling: American Reform and the Religious Imagination*. New York: Oxford University Press, 1994.

Aiken, Edward. *The Claims of the Order of Good Templars upon Temperance Men, Women and Youth.* New Brighton, PA: D. R. Johnson, 187–.

Akyeampong, Emmanuel. *Drink, Power, and Cultural Change: A Social History of Alcohol in Ghana, c. 1800 to Recent Times.* Portsmouth, NH: Heinemann, 1996.

Alvord, John W. *Letters from the South, Relating to the Condition of the Freedmen, Addressed to Major General O. O. Howard.* Washington, DC: Howard University Press, 1870.

———. *Semi-Annual Report on Schools for Freedom.* Washington, DC: Government Printing Office, 1866–1870.

Ambler, Charles. "Alcohol and Disorder in Precolonial Africa." Working Paper in African Studies, No. 126, African Studies Center, Boston University, 1987.

American Missionary Association. *The Nation Still in Danger; or Ten Years After the War.* New York: American Missionary Association, 1875.

American Tract Society. *A Brief History of the American Tract Society, Instituted at Boston, 1814, and its Relations to the American Tract Society at New York, Instituted 1825.* Boston: T. R. Marvin, 1857.

———. *The Freedman's Spelling-Book; The Freedman's Second Reader; The Freedman's Third Reader.* 1865–1866. Reprint. New York: AMS Press Inc., 1980.

Andrews, Sidney. *The South Since the War.* 1866. Reprint. New York: Arno Press, 1969.

Angell, Stephen W. *Bishop Henry McNeal Turner and African-American Religion in the South.* Knoxville: University of Tennessee Press, 1992.

Annual Report of the Executive Committee of the American Society for the Promotion of Temperance. Andover: Flagg and Gould, 1828.

Ansley, Lula Barnes (Mrs. J. J.). *History of the Georgia W. C. T. U., 1883–1907.* Columbus, GA: Gilbert Printing Co., 1914.

Aptheker, Herbert, ed. *A Documentary History of the Negro People in the United States.* Vol. 1. New York:The Citadel Press,1951.

Armstrong, Lebbeus. *The Temperance Reformation. Its History, from the Organization of the First Temperance Society.* New York: Fowlers and Wells, 1853.

———. *The Temperance Reformation of this XIXth Century, the Fulfillment of Divine Prophecy.* New York: Pudney, Hooker & Russell, 1845.

Arthur, William. *The Tongue of Fire, or the True Power of Christianity.* Nashville: published by E. Stevenson & F. A. Owen for the Methodist Episcopal Church, South, 1856.

Bacote, Clarence A. "The Negro in Atlanta Politics." *Phylon* 16 (Fourth Quarter, 1955): 333–50.

Baker, Ray Stannard. *Following the Color Line: American Negro Citizenship in the Progressive Era.* 1908. Reprint. New York: Harper & Row, 1964.

Baptist Home Missions in North America, Jubilee Report 1832–1882. New York: Baptist Home Mission Rooms, 1883.

Barber, Karin. "How Man Makes God in West Africa: Yoruba Attitudes towards the 'Orisa.'" *Africa: Journal of the International African Institute* 51 (1981): 724–45.

Barnes, Albert. *The Connexion of Temperance with Republican Freedom.* Philadelphia: Boyle and Benedict, 1835.

Barnes, Gilbert H. *The Antislavery Impulse, 1830–1844.* New York: D. Appleton-Century Company, 1933.

——— and Dwight L. Dumond, eds. *Letters of Theodore Dwight Weld, Angelina Grimké Weld, and Sarah Grimké, 1822–1844.* Gloucester, MA: Peter Smith, 1965.

Becker, William H. "The Black Church: Manhood and Mission." In *African-American Religion: Interpretive Essays in History and Culture,* edited by Timothy E. Fulop and Albert J. Raboteau, 190–99. New York: Routledge, 1997.

Beecher, Charles, ed. *Autobiography, Correspondence, etc. of Lyman Beecher, D. D.* New York: Harper & Brothers, Publishers, 1864.

Beecher, Lyman. *A Plea for the West.* Cincinnati: Truman and Smith, 1835.

———. *A Reformation of Morals Practicable and Indispensable.* Utica, NY: Merrell and Camp, 1813.

Beito, David T. *From Mutual Aid to the Welfare State: Fraternal Societies and Social Services, 1890–1967.* Chapel Hill: University of North Carolina Press, 2000.

———. "To Advance the 'Practice of Thrift and Economy': Fraternal Societies and Social Capital, 1890–1920." *Journal of Interdisciplinary History* 29 (Spring 1999): 585–612.

Bell, Howard H., ed. *Minutes of the Proceedings of the National Negro Conventions, 1830–1864.* New York: Arno Press and the *New York Times,* 1969.

Bigglestone, William E. "Oberlin College and the Beginning of the Red Lake Mission." *Minnesota History* 45 (Spring 1976): 21–31.

Bigham, Shuana, and Robert E. May. "The Time O' All Times? Master, Slaves, and Christmas in the Old South." *Journal of the Early Republic* 18 (Summer 1998): 263–88.

Billins, John S. *Department of the Interior, Tenth Census, Report on the Mortality and Vital Statistics of the United States.* Washington, DC: Government Printing Office, 1885.

Blassingame, John W., ed. *The Frederick Douglass Papers.* Series one, vol. 1. New Haven, CT: Yale University Press, 1979.

Blight, David W., ed. *Narrative of the Life of Frederick Douglass, an American Slave: With Related Documents. Written by Himself.* Boston: Bedford/St. Martin's, 2003.

Block, Shelley. "A Revolutionary Aim: The Rhetoric of Temperance in the *Anglo-African Magazine.*" *American Periodicals* 12 (2002): 9–24.

Blocker, Jack S., Jr. *American Temperance Movements: Cycles of Reform.* Boston: Twayne Publishers, 1989.

———. "Did Prohibition Really Work? Alcohol Prohibition as a Public Health Innovation." *American Journal of Public Health* 96 (February 2006): 233–43.

———. *"Give to the Wind Thy Fears": The Women's Temperance Crusade, 1873–1874.* Westport: Greenwood Press, 1985.

Bonner, James C. "The Georgia Penitentiary at Milledgeville, 1817–1874." *Georgia Historical Quarterly* 55 (Fall 1971): 303–28.

Bordin, Ruth. *Woman and Temperance: The Quest for Power and Liberty, 1873–1900.* Philadelphia: Temple University Press, 1981.

Bradley, Patricia. *Slavery, Propaganda, and the American Revolution.* Jackson: University Press of Mississippi, 1998.

Brawley, Benjamin. *History of Morehouse College.* Atlanta: Morehouse College, 1917.

Brown, William Wells. *Narrative of William Wells Brown, a Fugitive Slave.* Boston: The Anti-Slavery Office, 1847.

Brownlee, W. C. *An Appeal to the Patriot and Christian on the Importance of the Gospel: Its Ministry, its Sabbath, and its Ordinances, to the Well-Being and Perpetuity of our Free Institutions.* New York: American Tract Society, n.d.

Burch, Jarrett. *Adiel Sherwood: Baptist Antebellum Pioneer in Georgia.* Macon, GA: Mercer University Press, 2003.

Bushnell, Horace. *Barbarism: The First Danger.* New York: American Home Missionary Society, 1847.

Camp, Stephanie M. H. *Closer to Freedom: Enslaved Women and Everyday Resistance in the Plantation South.* Chapel Hill: University of North Carolina Press, 2004.

Campbell, George. *White & Black: The Outcome of a Visit to the United States.* 1879. Reprint. New York: Negro Universities Press, 1969.

Cantrell, Gregg. "'Dark Tactics': Black Politics in the 1887 Texas Prohibition Campaign." *Journal of American Studies* 25 (1991): 85–93.

Carlson, Douglas W. "'Drinks He to His Own Undoing': Temperance Ideology in the Deep South." *Journal of the Early Republic* 18 (Winter 1998): 659–91.

Carnes, Mark C. "Middle-Class Men and the Solace of Fraternal Ritual." In *Meanings for Manhood: Constructions of Masculinity in Victorian America*, edited by Mark C. Carnes and Clyde Griffen, 37–66. Chicago: University of Chicago Press, 1990.

Carter, E. R. *Biographical Sketches of Our Pulpit.* 1888. Reprint. Chicago: Afro-Am Press, 1969.

———. *The Black Side: A Partial History of the Business, Religious, and Educational Side of the Negro in Atlanta, Georgia.* Atlanta: n.p., 1894.

Carter, Peter. *Peter Carter, 1825–1900.* New York: De Vinne Press, 1901.

Caskey, Marie. *Chariot of Fire: Religion and the Beecher Family.* New Haven, CT: Yale University Press, 1978

Christmon, Kenneth. "Historical Overview of Alcohol in the African American Community." *Journal of Black Studies* 25 (January 1885): 318–30.

Cimbala, Paul A. *Under the Guardianship of the Nation: The Freedmen's Bureau and the Reconstruction of Georgia, 1865–1870.* Athens: University of Georgia Press, 1997.

Clark, Norman. *Deliver Us from Evil: An Interpretation of American Prohibition.* New York: W. W. Norton & Company, Inc., 1976.

Coker, Joe L. *Liquor in the Land of the Lost Cause: Southern White Evangelicals and the Prohibition Movement.* Lexington: University Press of Kentucky, 2007.

Colman, Julia. *Alcohol and Hygiene: An Elementary Lesson Book for Schools.* New York: National Temperance Society and Publication House, 1880.

———. *The Primary Temperance Catechism.* New York: National Temperance Society and Publication House, 1885.

Colvin, David Leigh. *Prohibition in the United States: A History of the Prohibition Party and of the Prohibition Movement.* New York: George H. Doran Company, 1926.

Committee of Twenty-Five. *An Appeal to the Voters of Atlanta.* Atlanta: Atlanta Constitution Job Print, 1885.

Cooper, J. I. "The Early Editorial Policy of the *Montreal Witness*." *Report of the Annual Meeting of the Canadian Historical Society* (1947): 53–62.

Crowe, Charles. "Racial Violence and Social Reform: Origins of the Atlanta Riot of 1906." *Journal of Negro History* 53 (July 1968): 234–56.

Cullen, Jim. "'I's a Man Now': Gender and African American Men." In *Divided Houses: Gender and the Civil War*, edited by Catherine Clinton and Nina Silber, 76–91. New York: Oxford University Press, 1992.

Cuyler, Theodore L. *Lafayette Avenue Presbyterian Church, Its History and Commemorative Services, 1860–1885.* New York: Robert Carter & Brothers, 1885.

———. *Recollections of a Long Life.* New York: American Tract Society, 1902.

The Cyclopaedia of Temperance and Prohibition. New York: Funk & Wagnalls, 1891.

Davidson, Charles. "Moving Things Along." *Georgia Trend* (March 2004): 13–18.

Davis, D. Webster. *The Life and Public Services of William W. Browne.* Philadelphia: AME Book Concern, 1910.

Dean, Joanna. *Religious Experience and the New Woman: The Life of Lily Dougall.* Bloomington: Indiana University Press, 2007.

DeBoer, Clara Merritt. "Congregationalism and Racism: The 19th Century Challenge." *Bulletin of the Congregational Library* 48 (1997): 4–14.

Deming, Wilbur Stone. *The Church on the Green: The First Two Centuries of the First Congregational Church at Washington, Connecticut, 1741–1941.* Hartford, CT: Bretano's 1941.

Dennett, John Richard. *The South As It Is: 1865–1866.* Edited by Henry M. Christman. 1866. Reprint. New York: Viking Press, 1965.

DeSantis, Vincent P. *Republicans Face the Southern Question—The New Departure Years, 1877–1897.* Baltimore: Johns Hopkins University Press, 1959.

Dickerson, Dennis C. *Religion, Race and Region: Research Notes on AME Church History.* Nashville: AMEC Sunday School Union/Legacy Pub., 1995.

Dobson, John M. *Politics in the Gilded Age: A New Perspective on Reform.* New York: Praeger Publishers, 1972.

The Doctrine and Discipline of the African Methodist Episcopal Church. Philadelphia: AME Book Concern, 1885.

Dodge, D. Stuart, comp. *Memorials of William E. Dodge.* New York: Anson D. F. Randolph and Company, 1887.

Dodge, William E. *The Church and Temperance.* New York: National Temperance Society and Publication House, 1880.

Dorsey, Allison. *To Build Our Lives Together: Community Formation in Black Atlanta, 1875–1906.* Athens: University of Georgia Press, 2004.

DuBois, W. E. B. "The Cultural Missions of Atlanta University." *Phylon* (Second Quarter 1942): 105–15.

———. *Some Notes on Negro Crime.* Atlanta University Publications, No. 9. 1904. Reprint. New York: Octagon, 1968.

———. *The Souls of Black Folk.* 1903. Reprint. New York: Bantam Classics, 1989.

———. "The Talented Tenth." In *The Negro Problem: A Series of Articles by Representative American Negroes of To-day,* edited by Booker T. Washington, W. E. B. DuBois, Paul Lawrence Dunbar, 31–76. 1903. Reprint. New York: Arno Press & the *New York Times,* 1969.

Dumenil, Lynn. *Freemasonry and American Culture, 1880–1930.* Princeton, NJ: Princeton University Press, 1984.

Earl, Riggins R., Jr. *Dark Symbols, Obscure Signs: God, Self, & Community in the Slave Mind.* Maryknoll, NY: Orbis Books, 1993.

Edwards, Justin. *On the Traffic in Ardent Spirits.* New York: American Tract Society, 187–.

Elson, Ruth Miller. *Guardians of Tradition: American Schoolbooks of the Nineteenth Century.* Lincoln: University of Nebraska Press, 1964.

Ewing, George W. *The Well-Tempered Lyre: Songs & Verse of the Temperance Movement.* Dallas: Southern Methodist University Press, 1977.

Fahey, David M. *The Black Lodge in White America: "True Reformer" Browne and His Economic Strategy.* Dayton, OH: Wright State University Press 1994.

———. "How the Good Templars Began: Fraternal Temperance in New York State." *The Social History of Alcohol Review* 38–39 (1999): 17–27.

———. *Temperance and Racism: John Bull, Johnny Reb, and the Good Templars.* Lexington: University Press of Kentucky, 1996.

Fairchild, E. H. *Historical Sketch of Oberlin College.* Springfield, OH: Republic Printing Co., 1868.

Field, Henry M. *Blood Is Thicker than Water: A Few Days among Our Southern Brethren.* New York: George Munro, Publisher, 1886.

Finney, Charles. *Lectures on Revivals of Religion.* Oberlin: E. J. Goodrich, 1868.

First Annual Report of the American Tract Society, Instituted at New York, 1825, 30. New York: American Tract Society, 1826.

The First Report of the Executive Committee of the American Baptist Home Mission Society, 18–19. New York: American Baptist Home Mission Society, 1833.

Fitts, Leroy. *A History of Black Baptists*. Nashville: Broadman Press, 1985.

Fletcher, Holly Berkley. *Gender and the American Temperance Movement of the Nineteenth-Century*. New York: Routledge, 2007.

Fletcher, Robert Samuel. *A History of Oberlin College from its Foundation through the Civil War*, vol. 1. Oberlin, OH: Oberlin College, 1943.

Fordham, Monroe. *Major Themes in Northern Black Religious Thought, 1800–1860*. Hicksville, NY: Exposition Press, 1975.

Foster, Gaines M. *Moral Reconstruction: Christian Lobbyists and the Federal Legislation of Morality, 1865–1920*. Chapel Hill: University of North Carolina Press, 2002.

Fourth Report of the American Temperance Society in *Permanent Temperance Documents of the American Temperance Society*. Vol. 1. Boston: S. Bliss, 1835.

Fourth Report of the Executive Committee of the American Baptist Home Mission Society, 14. New York: American Baptist Home Mission Society, 1836.

"Frederick Ayer, Teacher and Missionary to the Ojibway Indians, 1829–1850." *Collections of the Minnesota Historical Society* 6 (1894): 429–37.

Fredrickson, George. *The Black Image in the White Mind: The Debate on Afro-American Character and Destiny, 1817–1914*. 1971. Reprint. Middletown, CT: Wesleyan University Press, 1987.

Gaines, Wesley J. *African Methodism in the South or Twenty-Five Years of Freedom*. Atlanta: Franklin Publishing House, 1890.

Gatewood, Willard B. *Aristocrats of Color: The Black Elite, 1880–1920*. Bloomington: Indiana University Press, 1990.

Genovese, Eugene. *Roll, Jordan, Roll: The World the Slaves Made*. New York: Pantheon Books, 1974.

Goodman, Paul. "Moral Purpose and Republican Politics in Antebellum America, 1830–1860." *The Maryland Historian* 20 (Fall/Winter 1989): 5–39.

Gordon, Caroline. "The Beginnings of Negro Education in Atlanta." *Bulletin of Atlanta University* (February 1909): 4.

Gordon, Lynn D. "Race, Class, and the Bonds of Womanhood at Spelman Seminary, 1881–1923." *History of Higher Education Annual* 9 (1989): 7–32.

Gould, Lewis L. "The Republican Search for a National Majority." In *The Gilded Age*. Revised and enlarged edition, edited by H. Wayne Morgan, 171–87. Syracuse, NY: Syracuse University Press, 1970.

Goulder, Grace. *John D. Rockefeller: The Cleveland Years*. Cleveland: Western Reserve Historical Society, 1972.

Gow, Alexander M. *Good Morals and Gentle Manners for Schools and Families*. New York: Van Antwerp, Bragg & Co., 1873.

Grasso, Christopher. "Deist Monster: On Religious Common Sense in the Wake of the American Revolution." *Journal of American History* 95 (June 2008): 43–68.

Greenwood, Janette Thomas. *Bittersweet Legacy: The Black and White "Better Classes" in Charlotte, 1850–1910*. Chapel Hill: University of North Carolina, 1994.

Gribbin, William. "Republicanism, Reform, and the Sense of Sin in Ante Bellum America." *Cithara* 14 (1974): 25–41.

Grimké, Thomas S. *Address on the Patriot Character of the Temperance Reformation*. Charleston: Observer Office Press, 1833.

Gusfield, Joseph R. *Symbolic Crusade: Status Politics and the American Temperance Movement*. Urbana: University of Illinois Press, 1970.

Gutman, Herbert G. *Power and Culture: Essays on the American Working Class*. Edited by Ira Berlin. New York: Pantheon Books, 1987.

Guy-Sheftall, Beverly. *Daughters of Sorrow: Attitudes toward Black Women, 1880–1920*. Brooklyn: Carlson Publishing, Inc., 1990.

Hallock, William A. *"Light and Love": A Sketch of the Life and Labors of the Rev. Justin Edwards, D. D*. New York: American Tract Society, 1855.

Hamm, Richard F. "The Prohibitionists' Lincoln." *Illinois Historical Journal* 86 (Summer 1993): 93–118.

Hammond, John L. *The Politics of Benevolence: Revival Religion and American Voting Behavior*. Norwood, NJ: Ablex Publishing Corporation, 1979.

Hardesty, Nancy A. "'The Best Temperance Organization in the Land': Southern Methodists and the W.C.T.U. in Georgia." *Methodist History* 28 (April 1990):187–94.

Harris, Robert L., Jr. "Early Black Benevolent Societies, 1780–1830." *Massachusetts Review* 20 (1979): 603–25.

Harvey, Paul. *Redeeming the South: Religious Cultures and Racial Identities among Southern Baptists, 1865–1925*. Chapel Hill: University of North Carolina Press, 1997.

Harwood, W. S. "Secret Societies in America." *North American Review* 164 (May 1897): 617–24.

Hay, William, Jr. *A History of Temperance in Saratoga County, N.Y.* Saratoga Springs, NY: G. M. Davison, 1855.

Haygood, Atticus G. *Save Our Homes: A Prohibition Sermon*. Macon, GA: J. W. Burke & Co., 1884.

Herd, Denise. "Ambiguity in Black Drinking Norms: An Ethnohistorical Interpretation." In *The American Experience with Alcohol: Contrasting Cultural Perspectives*, edited by Linda A. Bennett and Genevieve M. Ames, 149–70. New York: Plenum Press, 1985.

———. "Migration, Cultural Transformation and the Rise of Black Liver Cirrhosis Mortality." *British Journal of Addiction* 80 (1985): 397–410.

———. "The Paradox of Temperance: Blacks and the Alcohol Question in Nineteenth-Century America." In *Drinking: Behavior and Beliefs in Modern History*, edited by Susanna Barrows and Robin Room, 354–75. Berkeley and Los Angeles: University of California Press, 1991.

———. "Prohibition, Racism and Class Politics in the Post-Reconstruction South." *Journal of Drug Issues* 13 (1983): 77–94.

Heywood, Linda M., and John K. Thornton. *Central Africans, Atlantic Creoles, and the Foundation of the Americas, 1585–1660*. New York: Cambridge University Press, 2007.

Higginbotham, Evelyn Brooks. *Righteous Discontent: The Women's Movement in the Black Baptist Church, 1880–1920*. Cambridge, MA: Harvard University Press, 1993.

Holifield, E. Brooks. *Theology in America: Christian Thought from the Age of the Puritans to the Civil War*. New Haven, CT: Yale University Press, 2003.

Hopkins, Richard. "Status, Mobility, and the Dimensions of Change in a Southern City: Atlanta, 1870–1910." In *Cities in American History*, edited by Kenneth T. Jackson and Stanley K. Schultz, 216–31. New York: Knopf, 1972.

Hornsby, Alton, Jr. *A Short History of Black Atlanta, 1847–1990*. Atlanta: APEX Museum, 2003.

Humphrey, Heman. *Parallel between Intemperance and the Slave Trade*. Amherst: J. S. and C. Adams, Printers, 1828.

———. *The Way to Bless and Save Our Country: A Sermon*. Philadelphia: American Sunday School Union, 1831.

Hunter, Tera W. *To 'Joy My Freedom: Southern Black Women's Lives and Labors after the Civil War.* Cambridge, MA: Harvard University Press, 1997.

Hutson, James. *Religion and the Founding of the American Republic.* Washington, DC: Library of Congress, 1998.

International Order of Good Templars, Georgia Grand Lodge. *An Appeal from the Temperance Workers of Georgia to the Officers and Members of the Right Worthy Grand Lodge I.O.G.T in behalf of the Colored People of the South.* Atlanta: 1882.

Isaac, Paul E. *Prohibition and Politics: Turbulent Decades in Tennessee, 1885–1920.* Knoxville: University of Tennessee Press, 1965.

Ivy, James D. *No Saloon in the Valley: The Southern Strategy of Texas Prohibitionists in the 1880s.* Waco, TX: Baylor University Press, 2003.

Jewell, Joseph O. *Race, Social Reform, and the Making of a Middle Class: The American Missionary Association and Black Atlanta, 1870–1900.* Lanham, MD: Rowman & Littlefield Publishers, Inc., 2007.

Johnson, James Weldon. *Along This Way.* 1933. Reprint. New York: Da Capo Press, 2000.

Johnson, Paul E. *A Shopkeeper's Millennium: Society and Revivals in Rochester, N.Y., 1815–1837,* 25th anniversary edition. New York: Hill and Wang, 2004.

Kellogg, John. "Negro Urban Clusters in the Postbellum South." *Geographical Review* 67 (July 1977): 310–17.

Kirk, E. N. *The Temperance Reformation Connected with the Revival of Religion and the Introduction of the Millennium.* London: J. Pasco, 1838.

Koren, John. "Some Aspects of the Liquor Problem." *National Municipal Review* 3 (1914): 505–516.

Krout, John Allen. *The Origins of Prohibition.* New York: Alfred A. Knopf, 1925.

Lady, D. B. "The Drinking Habit and Prohibition." *The Reformed Quarterly Review* (1896): 468–80.

Lender, Mark E., and James K. Martin. *Drinking in America: A History.* Revised and expanded edition. New York: The Free Press, 1987.

Levine, Lawrence W. *Black Culture, Black Consciousness: Afro-American Folk Thought from Slavery to Freedom.* New York: Oxford University Press, 1977.

Lichtenstein, Alex. *Twice the Work of Free Labor: The Political Economy of Convict Labor in the New South.* London: Verso, 1996.

Light, Ivan H. *Ethnic Enterprise in America: Business and Welfare among Chinese, Japanese and Blacks.* Berkeley and Los Angeles: University of California Press, 1972.

Lincoln, C. Eric, and Lawrence H. Mamiya. *The Black Church in the African American Experience.* Durham, NC: Duke University Press, 1990.

Loveland, Anne C. "Evangelicalism and 'Immediate Emancipation' in American Antislavery Thought." *Journal of Southern History* 32 (May 1966) 172–88.

Ludlum, David M. *Social Ferment in Vermont, 1791–1850.* Montpelier: The Vermont Historical Society, 1948.

Macrae, David. *The Americans at Home: Pen-and-ink Sketches of American Men, Manners, and Institutions.* Glasgow: Gowans & Gray, 1885.

Mancini, Matthew J. *One Dies, Get Another: Convict Leasing in the American South, 1866–1928.* Columbia: University of South Carolina Press, 1996.

———. "Race, Economics, and the Abandonment of Convict Leasing." *Journal of Negro History* 63 (October 1978): 339–52.

Marsh, John. *The Cause of Temperance as Connected with Home Evangelization.* New York: American Temperance Union, 1863.

Martin, Asa E. "The Temperance Movement in Pennsylvania prior to the Civil War." *Pennsylvania Magazine of History and Biography* 49 (1925): 195–230.

Martin, Sandy Dwayne. "The American Baptist Home Mission Society and Black Higher Education in the South, 1865–1920." *Foundations* 24 (1981): 310–27.

Martin, Scott C. *Devil of the Domestic Sphere: Temperance, Gender, and Middle-Class Ideology, 1800–1860.* DeKalb: Northern Illinois University Press, 2008.

Marty, Martin E. *Righteous Empire: The Protestant Experience in America.* New York: Dial Press, 1970.

Martyn, Carlos. *William E. Dodge: The Christian Merchant.* New York: Funk & Wagnalls, 1890.

Mathias, William J., and Stuart Anderson. *Horse to Helicopter: First Century of the Atlanta Police Department.* Decatur, GA: National Graphics, Inc., 1973.

Matthews, Lyman. *Memoir of the Life and Character of Ebenezer Porter, D. D.* Boston: Perkins & Marvin, 1837.

Mattingly, Carol. *Well-Tempered Women: Nineteenth-Century Temperance Rhetoric.* Carbondale: Southern Illinois University Press, 1998.

McKelvey, Blake. "Penal Slavery and Southern Reconstruction." *Journal of Negro History* 20 (April 1935): 153–79.

McKelway, A. J. "The Convict Lease System of Georgia." *Outlook* 90 (September 12, 1908): 67–72.

McPherson, James. *The Abolitionist Legacy: From Reconstruction to the NAACP.* Princeton, NJ: Princeton University Press, 1975.

———. "The New Puritanism: Values and Goals of Freedmen's Education in America." In *The University in Society,* vol. 2, edited by Lawrence Stone, 611–39. Princeton, NJ: Princeton University Press, 1974.

Meier, August, and David Lewis. "History of the Negro Upper Class in Atlanta, Georgia, 1890–1958." *Journal of Negro Education* 28 (Spring 1959): 128–39.

Mezvinsky, Norton. "Scientific Temperance Instruction in the Schools." *History of Education Quarterly* 1 (March 1961): 48–54.

Mintz, Steven. *Moralists and Modernizers: America's Pre–Civil War Reformers.* Baltimore: Johns Hopkins University Press, 1995.

Mitchell, Eugene M. "Queer Place Names in Old Atlanta." *Atlanta History Bulletin* 1 (April): 22–31.

Mitchell, Henry H. *Black Belief: Folk Beliefs of Blacks in America and West Africa.* New York: Harper & Row Publishers, 1975.

Montgomery, David. "The Shuttle and the Cross: Weavers and Artisans in the Kensington Riots of 1844." *Journal of Social History* 5 (1972): 411–46.

Montgomery, William E. *Under Their Own Vine and Fig Tree: The African American Church in the South, 1865–1900.* Baton Rouge: Louisiana State University Press, 1993.

Moore, John Hammond. "The Negro and Prohibition in Atlanta, 1885–1887." *South Atlantic Quarterly* 69 (1970): 38–57.

Moorhead, James H. "Social Reform and the Divided Conscience of Antebellum Protestantism." *Church History* 48 (December 1979): 416–30.

Morris, Robert C. *Reading, 'Riting, and Reconstruction: The Education of the Freedmen in the South, 1861–1870.* Chicago: University of Chicago Press, 1981.

Mumford, Kevin J. *Interzones: Black/White Sex Districts in Chicago and New York in the Early Twentieth Century.* New York: Columbia University Press, 1977.

Muraskin, William A. *Middle Class Blacks in a White Society: Prince Hall Freemasonry in America.* Berkeley and Los Angeles: University of California Press, 1975.

Murphy, Larry. "Education and the Preparation for the Ministry in the African Methodist Episcopal Church, 1787–1900 (Conclusion)." *AME Church Review* 101 (July–September 1986): 25–34.

Myers, Martha A. *Race, Labor & Punishment in the New South*. Columbus: Ohio State University Press, 1998.

Nassau, Robert H. *Where Animals Talk: West African Folk Lore Tales*. Boston: The Gorham Press and Richard G. Badger, 1912.

Nettleton, Asahel. *Temperance and Revivals*. New York: National Temperance Society and House, n.d.

Newman, Harvey K. "Decatur Street: Atlanta's African American Paradise Lost." *Atlanta History* 44 (Summer 2000): 5–13.

Newton, A. E. *Manual of the Vanguard of Freedom*. New York: National Temperance Society and Publication House, 1867.

Nicolay, John G., and John Hay, eds. *Complete Works of Abraham Lincoln*. Vol. 1. New and enlarged edition. New York: F. D. Tandy, 1905.

Ninth Report of the American Baptist Home Mission Society, 51–52. New York: American Baptist Home Mission Society, 1841.

Nixon, Raymond B. *Henry W. Grady: Spokesman of the New South*. New York: Alfred A. Knopf, 1943.

Noel, Jan. *Canada Dry: Temperance Crusades before Confederation*. Toronto: University of Toronto Press, 1995.

Noll, Mark A. *America's God: From Jonathan Edwards to Abraham Lincoln*. New York: Oxford University Press, 2002.

Nordhoff, Charles. *The Cotton States in the Spring and Summer of 1875*. New York: D. Appleton & Company, 1876.

Open Letters on Prohibition: A Controversy between Hon. Jefferson Davis and Bishop Charles B. Galloway. Nashville: Publishing House of the Methodist Episcopal Church, South, 1893.

Oshatz, Molly. *Slavery and Sin: The Fight against Slavery and the Rise of Liberal Protestantism*. New York: Oxford University Press, 2012

Ownby, Ted. *Subduing Satan: Religion, Recreation, and Manhood in the Rural South, 1865–1920*. Chapel Hill: University of North Carolina Press, 1990.

Palmer, John M. "An Apology for Party Prohibition." *AME Church Review* 4 (October 1887): 136–53.

Paris, Peter J. *The Spirituality of African Peoples: The Search for a Common Moral Discourse*. Minneapolis: Fortress Press, 1995.

Parks, Joseph H. *Joseph E. Brown of Georgia*. Baton Rouge: Louisiana State University Press, 1977.

Payne, Daniel Alexander. *The African M. E. Church in Its Relations to the Freedmen*. Xenia, OH: Torchlight Co., 1868.

———. *Recollections of Seventy Years*. Nashville: AME Sunday School Union, 1888.

———. "Slavery Brutalizes Man." *Lutheran Herald and Journal of the Fort Plain, N.Y. Franckean Synod*, August 1, 1839. http://www.blackpast.org/?q=1839-daniel-payne-slavery-brutalizes-man (accessed December 16, 2010).

Pendleton, Othniel A. "Temperance and the Evangelical Churches." *Journal of the Presbyterian Historical Society* 25 (March 1947): 14–45.

Permanent Temperance Documents of the American Temperance Society. Vols. 1, 2, and 3. Boston: S. Bliss, 1835.

Porter, Ebenezer. *The Fatal Effects of Ardent Spirits: A Sermon*. Morris-Town: Henry P. Russell, 1812.

Pratt, E. H. *The Church and Temperance*. New York: National Temperance Society and Publication House, n.d.

Proceedings of the Fifth National Temperance Convention held at Saratoga Springs, NY, August 1–3, 1865. New York: J. N. Stearns Publisher, 1865.

Proceedings of the First Ten Years of the American Tract Society, Instituted at Boston, 1814. Andover: Flagg and Gould, 1824.

"Progressive Thought." *AME Zion Quarterly Review* 4 (January 1894): 185.

Puckett, Newbell Niles. *Folk Beliefs of the Southern Negro*. Chapel Hill: University of North Carolina Press, 1926.

Quist, John. *Restless Visionaries: The Social Roots of Antebellum Reform in Alabama and Michigan*. Baton Rouge: Louisiana State University Press, 1998.

Rabinowitz, Howard N. "The Conflict between Blacks and the Police in the Urban South, 1865–1900." In *Race, Ethnicity, and Urbanization: Selected Essays*, edited by Howard N. Rabinowitz, 167–80. Columbia: University of Missouri Press, 1994.

———. "Continuity and Change: Southern Urban Development, 1860–1900." In *The City in Southern History: The Growth of Urban Civilization in the South*, edited by Blaine A. Brownell and David R. Goldfield, 92–122. Port Washington, NY: Kennikat Press, 1977.

———. *Race Relations in the Urban South*. 1978. Reprint. Athens: University of Georgia Press, 1996.

Raboteau, Albert J. *Slave Religion: The "Invisible Institution" in the Antebellum South*. New York: Oxford University Press, 1978.

Read, Florence. *The Story of Spelman College*. Atlanta, 1961.

Reprint of the First Edition of the Discipline of the African Methodist Episcopal Church. Atlanta: n.p., 1917.

Richardson, Benjamin Ward. *Temperance Lesson Book*. New York: National Temperance Society and Publication House, 1880.

Ridge, J. James. *Band of Hope Catechism*. London: United Kingdom Band of Hope Union, 188–.

Ripley, C. Peter, ed. *The Black Abolitionist Papers*. Vol. 3. Chapel Hill: University of North Carolina Press, 1991.

Roberts, Samuel K. *In the Path of Virtue: The African American Moral Tradition*. Cleveland: The Pilgrim Press, 1999.

Rochon, Thomas R. *Culture Moves: Ideas, Activism, and Changing Values*. Princeton, NJ: Princeton University Press, 1998.

Rohrer, James R. "The Origins of the Temperance Movement: A Reinterpretation." *Journal of American Studies* 24 (August 1990): 228–335.

Room, Robin. "Alcohol, the Individual and Society: What History Teaches Us." *Addiction* 92 (1997 Supplement): s7–s11.

Rorabaugh, W. J. *The Alcoholic Republic*. New York: Oxford University Press, 1979.

Roth, Darlene Rebecca. *Matronage: Patterns in Women's Organizations, Atlanta, Georgia, 1890–1940*. Brooklyn: Carlson Publishing Inc., 1994.

Rumbarger, John J. *Profits, Power, and Prohibition: Alcohol Reform and the Industrializing of America, 1800–1930*. Albany: State University of New York Press, 1989.

Rush, Benjamin. *An Inquiry into the Effects of Spirituous Liquors upon the Human Body, and Their Influence upon the Happiness of Society*. 3rd ed. Philadelphia: John McCulloch, 1791. Early American Imprints, Series I, Evans, 1639–1800.

Sale, George. *Atlanta Baptist Seminary: A Statement and a Plea*. New York: American Baptist Home Mission Society, 1895.

"Saloon Statistics." *Quarterly Journal of Inebriety* 16 (1894): 272.

Sampson, J. "The Prohibition Party." *AME Church Review* 4 (July 1887): 506–7.

Sanders, Paul D., ed. *Lyrics and Borrowed Tunes of the American Temperance Movement.* Columbia: University of Missouri Press, 2006.

Schultz, Stanly K. "Temperance Reform in the Antebellum South: Social Control and Urban Order." *South Atlantic Quarterly* 83 (Summer 1984): 323–39.

Scomp, Henry A. *King Alcohol in the Realm of King Cotton.* Chicago Blakely Printing Company, 1888.

Seventh Annual Report of the American Temperance Union, in *Permanent Temperance Documents of the American Temperance Society.* Vol. 2. New York: American Temperance Union, 1852.

Shadgett, Olive Hall. *The Republican Party in Georgia: From Reconstruction through 1900.* Athens: University of Georgia Press, 1964.

Shiman, Lilian Lewis. "The Band of Hope Movement: Respectable Recreation for Working Class Children." *Victorian Studies* 17 (September 1973): 49–74.

Small, Samuel W. *White Angel of the World.* Philadelphia: Peerless Publishing Co., 1891.

Small, Sandra E. "The Yankee Schoolmarm in Freedmen's Schools: An Analysis of Attitudes." *Journal of Southern History* 45 (August 1979): 381–402.

Smith, H. Shelton. *In His Image, but . . . Racism in Southern Religion, 1780–1910.* Durham, NC: Duke University Press, 1972.

Smith, Jennifer Lund. "The Ties That Bind: Educated African-American Women in Post-Emancipation Atlanta." In *Georgia in Black and White: Explorations in the Race Relations of a Southern State, 1865–1950,* edited by John C. Inscoe, 91–105. Athens: University of Georgia Press, 1994.

Smith, Timothy L. *Revivalism and Social Reform: American Protestantism on the Eve of the Civil War.* 1957. Reprint. New York: Harper & Row, Publishers, 1965.

———. "Righteousness and Hope: Christian Holiness and the Millennial Vision in America, 1800–1900." *American Quarterly* 31 (1979): 21–45.

Smith, William B. "The Persimmon Tree and the Beer Dance." In *The Negro and His Folklore in Nineteenth-Century Periodicals,* edited by Bruce Jackson, 3–9. Austin: University of Texas Press, 1967.

Sobel, Mechal. *Trabelin' On: The Slave Journey to an Afro-Baptist Faith.* Princeton, NJ: Princeton University Press, 1979.

Somers, Robert. *The Southern States since the War, 1870–71.* London: Macmillan & Co., 1871.

Spain, Rufus B. *At Ease in Zion: A Social History of Southern Baptists, 1865–1900.* 1967. Reprint. Tuscaloosa: University of Alabama Press, 2003.

Stampp, Kenneth. *The Peculiar Institution: Slavery in the Ante-Bellum South.* New York: Knopf, 1956.

Stearns, Charles. *The Black Man of the South and the Rebels.* 1872. Reprint. New York: Negro Universities Press, 1969.

Stewart, Dianne M. *Three Eyes for the Journey: African Dimensions of the Jamaican Religious Experience.* New York: Oxford University Press, 2004.

Stewart, Mother. *Memories of the Crusade.* Columbus, OH: William G. Hubbard & Co., 1888.

Storms, Roger C. *Partisan Prophets: A History of the Prohibition Party, 1854–1972.* Denver: National Prohibition Foundation, Inc., 1972.

Stowe, Harriet Beecher. "The Education of the Freedmen." *North American Review* 128 (June 1879): 605–15.

Strieby, Michael E. *Oberlin and the American Missionary Association.* Oberlin, OH: Oberlin College, 1891.

———. *Work of Half a Generation*. New York: American Missionary Association, 1878.

Strong, Douglas M. *Perfectionist Politics: Abolitionism and the Religious Tensions of American Democracy*. Syracuse, NY: Syracuse University Press, 1999.

Stuckey, Sterling. *Slave Culture: Nationalist Theory and the Foundations of Black America*. New York: Oxford University Press, 1987.

Sutton, William R. "Benevolent Calvinism and the Moral Government of God: The Influence of Nathaniel W. Taylor on Revivalism in the Second Great Awakening." *Religion and American Culture* 2 (Winter 1992) 23–47.

Szymanski, Ann-Marie E. *Pathways to Prohibition: Radicals, Moderates, and Social Movement Outcomes*. Durham, NC: Duke University Press, 2003.

Takaki, Ronald. *Iron Cages: Race and Culture in Nineteenth-Century America*. 1979. Reprint. New York: Oxford University Press, 1990.

Tanner, Benjamin T. "The Temperance Status of the AME Church: Historically." *AME Church Review* 2 (January 1886): 220–21.

Tappan, Lewis. *History of the American Missionary Association: Its Constitution and Principles*. New York: 1855.

Taylor, A. Elizabeth. "The Origin and Development of the Convict Lease System in Georgia." *Georgia Historical Quarterly* 26 (March 1942): 113–29.

Temperance Manual of the American Temperance Society for the Young Men of the United States. Boston: Seth Bliss et al., 1836.

Temperance Tracts Issued by the National Temperance Society and Publication House. New York: J. N. Stearns, Publishing agent, 1870.

Third Report of the Executive Committee of the American Baptist Home Mission Society, 21, 27. New York: American Baptist Home Mission Society, 1835.

Thirkield, Wilbur P. "A Cathedral of Cooperation." In *The Human Way: Addresses on Race Problems at the Southern Sociological Congress, Atlanta, 1913*, 134–44. Nashville: Southern Sociological Congress, 1913.

Thornton, John K. *Africa and Africans in the Making of the Atlantic World, 1400–1800*. 2nd ed. New York: Cambridge University Press, 1998.

Towns, George A. "The Sources of Tradition of Atlanta University." *Phylon* 3 (Second Quarter 1942): 117–18, 121–22, 125–26, 129–30, 133–34.

Turner, George Kibbe. "Beer and the City Liquor Problem." *McClure's* 33 (1909): 528–43.

Turner, Howard H. *Turner's History of the Independent Order of Good Samaritans and Daughters of Samaria*. Washington: R. A. Waters, 1881.

Twaddell, Elizabeth. "The American Tract Society, 1814–1860." *Church History* 15 (June 1946): 116–32.

Twenty-Fifth Report of the American Baptist Home Mission Society, 32. New York: American Baptist Home Mission Society, 1857.

Tyler, Alice Felt. *Freedom's Ferment: Phases of American Social History to 1860*. Minneapolis: University of Minnesota Press, 1944.

Valentine, Foy. "Baptist Polity and Social Pronouncements." *Baptist History and Heritage* 14 (July 1979): 52–61.

Vander Hoef, Lorraine. "John Dougall (1808–1886): Portrait of an Early Social Reformer and Evangelical Witness in Canada." *Journal of the Canadian Church Historical Society* 43 (2001): 115–45.

Wade, Richard C. *Slavery in the Cities: The South, 1820–1860*. New York: Oxford University Press, 1964.

Walker, Clarence E. *A Rock in a Weary Land: The African Methodist Episcopal Church during the Civil War and Reconstruction*. Baton Rouge: Louisiana State University Press, 1982.

Walker, Jerome. *Anatomy, Physiology and Hygiene: A Manual for the Use of Colleges, Schools, and General Readers*. Boston: Allyn & Bacon, 1883.

Walls, William Jacob. *Joseph Charles Price, Educator and Race Leader*. Boston: Christopher Publishing House, 1943.

Walton, Hanes Jr. "Another Force for Disfranchisement: Blacks and the Prohibitionists in Tennessee." *Journal of Human Relations* 18 (1970): 728–38.

———. *Black Republicans: The Politics of the Black and Tans*. Metuchen, NJ: Scarecrow Press, Inc., 1975.

Washington, Booker T. *Up From Slavery*. 1901. Reprint. New York: Lancer Books, Inc., 1968.

Watkinson, James D. "William Washington Browne and the True Reformers of Richmond, Virginia." *Virginia Magazine of History and Biography* 97 (1989): 375–90.

Watts, Eugene J. "Black Political Progress in Atlanta, 1868–1895." *Journal of Negro History* 59 (July 1974): 268–86.

———. "The Police in Atlanta, 1890–1905." *Journal of Southern History* 39 (May 1973): 165–82.

———. *The Social Bases of City Politics, Atlanta, 1865–1903*. Westport, CT: Greenwood Press, 1978.

West, John G., Jr. *The Politics of Revelation and Reason: Religion and Civic Life in the New Nation*. Lawrence: University Press of Kansas, 1996.

Wheeler, Edward L. *Uplifting the Race: The Black Minister in the New South, 1865–1902*. Lanham, MD: University Press of America, Inc., 1986.

White, Dana F. "The Black Sides of Atlanta: A Geography of Expansion and Containment, 1970–1870." *Atlanta Historical Journal* 26 (Summer/Fall1989): 199–225.

Whittier, John Greenleaf. *Anti-Slavery Poems: Songs of Labor and Reform*. 1888. Reprint. New York: Arno Press & the *New York Times*, 1969.

Williams, Heather Andrea. *Self-Taught: African American Education in Slavery and Freedom*. Chapel Hill: University of North Carolina Press, 2005.

Wills, Gregory. *Democratic Religion: Freedom, Authority, and Church Discipline in the Baptist South, 1785–1900*. New York: Oxford University Press, 1997.

Wilson, Charles B. *Official Manual and History of the Grand United Order of Odd Fellows in America*. Philadelphia: George F. Lasher, 1894.

Winkler, Allan M. "Lyman Beecher and the Temperance Crusade." *Quarterly Journal of Studies on Alcohol* 33 (1972): 939–57.

Woodward, C. Vann. *The Strange Career of Jim Crow*. 2nd revised edition. New York: Oxford University Press, 1966.

Wright, James M. *The License System of the City of Atlanta*. Atlanta: Harper Publishing Co., 1964.

Yacovone, Donald. "The Transformation of the Black Temperance Movement, 1827–1854: An Interpretation." *Journal of the Early Republic* 8 (Fall 1988): 281–97.

Young, Jason R. "Spirituality and Socialization in the Slave Community." In *A Companion to African American History*, edited by Alton Hornsby Jr. Malden, MA: Blackwell Publishing, 2005.

Young, Michael P. *Bearing Witness against Sin: The Evangelical Birth of the American Social Movement*. Chicago: University of Chicago Press, 2006.

Zimmerman, Jonathan. *Distilling Democracy: Alcohol Education in America's Public Schools, 1880–1925*. Lawrence: University Press of Kansas, 1999.

Unpublished Sources

Bullock, Steve C. "The Temperance Movement in Rochester, 1827–1835." Unpublished paper on file at the American Baptist Historical Society, Atlanta, Georgia.

Deaton, Thomas M. "Atlanta during the Progressive Era." PhD diss., University of Georgia, 1969.

Geer, William Monroe. "The Temperance Movement in Georgia in the Middle Period." Master's thesis, Emory University, 1936.

Goodson, Howard Steven. "'South of the North, North of the South': Public Entertainment in Atlanta, 1880–1930." PhD diss., Emory University, 1995.

Harper, Matthew James Zacharias. "Living in God's Time: African-American Faith and Politics in Post-Emancipation North Carolina." PhD diss., University of North Carolina, 2009.

Harper, Matt J. "The Ballot or the Bottle: Temperance, Black Manliness, and the Struggle for Citizenship in North Carolina, 1881–1901." Master's thesis, University of North Carolina, 2003.

Mason, W. Dennis. "Protestants, Politics, and Prohibition: The Prohibition Elections of Fulton County in 1885 and 1887." Master's thesis, University of Georgia, 1986.

McManus, Harold Lynn. "The American Baptist Home Mission Society and Freedmen Education in the South, with Special Reference to Georgia, 1862–1897." PhD diss., Yale University, 1953.

Murphy, Stephen Wills. "'It Is a Sacred Duty to Abstain': The Organizational, Biblical, Theological, and Practical Roots of the American Temperance Society, 1814–1830." PhD diss., University of Virginia, 2008.

Opie, John, Jr. "Conversion and Revivalism: An Internal History from Jonathan Edwards through Charles Grandison Finney." PhD diss., University of Chicago, 1963.

Rohrer, James Russell. "Battling the Master Vice: The Evangelical War against Intemperance in Ohio, 1800–1832." Master's thesis, Ohio State University, 1985.

Rosell, Garth M. "Charles Grandison Finney and the Rise of the Benevolence Empire." PhD diss., University of Minnesota, 1971.

Rothman, Norman Calvin. "Curriculum Formation in Black Colleges, 1881–1980." PhD diss., Georgia State University, 1981.

Russell, James M. "Atlanta, Gate City of the South, 1847 to 1885." PhD diss., Princeton University, 1971.

Slade, Dorothy. "The Evolution of Negro Areas in the City of Atlanta." Master's thesis, Atlanta University, 1946.

Smith, Mary Jane. "Constructing Womanhood in Public: Progressive White Women in a New South." PhD diss., Louisiana State University, 2002.

Spencer, John Merrill. "'Decatur Street': A Natural Area." Master's thesis, Atlanta University, 1952.

Thomas, Barbara Collier. "Race Relations in Atlanta, from 1877 through 1890, as Seen in an Analysis of the Atlanta City Council Proceedings." Master's thesis, Atlanta University, 1966.

Thornbery, Jerry J. "The Development of Black Atlanta, 1865–1885." PhD diss., University of Maryland, 1977.

Watson, Larry Jerome. "Evangelical Protestants and the Prohibition Movement in Texas, 1887–1919." PhD diss., Texas A & M University, 1993.

Wills, David Wood. "Aspects of Social Thought in the African Methodist Episcopal Church, 1884–1910." PhD diss., Harvard University, 1975.

Index

Bold pages indicate illustrations.

Abbot, John (character in *The Freedman*), 68
Abolitionism, 91; connection between perfectionist theology, teetotalism and, 259n13
Absolute abstinence, 136
Abstinence: absolute, 136; African Methodist Episcopal Church commitment to, 35; of Carter, E. R., 211; of Gaines, Wesley J., 80, 211; Lincoln's stories of, 269n57; socioeconomic functions of, 98–99; of Turner, Henry McNeal, 80, 211; voter support for, 156
Abstinence pledges: at Atlanta University, 108; Drew, John W., signing of, 159; enforcement of, at Atlanta Baptist Seminary, 114; Giles, Harriet R., signing of, 114–15; Packard, Sophia, signing of, 114–15
Abzug, Robert, 5
Adair, A. D., as prohibitionist, 163
Adair, George W., libel suit against Pledger, 176
Adams, Franklin P., poem by, 214
Ad hominem attacks, 182
Advice to Freedmen, 71
African Americans: assessment of state of, in 1888, 241; development of cosmology, 121; disfranchisement of, 242–43; pragmatic syncretism of spirituality of, 121–24; pragmatic worldview of, 133–34, 248; publications of, 155; reform nexus theology and spirituality and, 123–124; temperance conventions of, 9. *See also* Blacks
African cosmology, basic assumptions of, 121–23
African Exposition, endorsement of temperance in, 155

African Methodist Episcopal (AME) Church: adoption of "General Rules of the United Societies of 1739" (Wesley), 134; under Allen, Richard, as leader, 35; centralized governance under, 134; commitment to abstinence of, 35; conferences of, 35–36, 80–81, 130, 131, 136, 218, 224; face-to-face grassroots work of, 247; focus of, 6; history of, in the South, 241–42; Morris Brown College of, 112; ordination process of, 135–136; origin of, 7, 34–36; purchase of Wilberforce University by, 36; temperance and, 32, 79–81, 120
African Methodist Episcopal (AME) Church Review, Tanner, Benjamin, as editor of, 166
Africans: adaptations of trickster tales of, 185–86; pragmatic syncretism of spirituality of, 121–24
Alcohol: abuse as problem in Black Atlanta, 63–64; crime and consumption of, 168–69; racialized use of, 63; use of, in Black Atlanta, 5, 47–50, **51**, **52**, 57–64. *See also* Liquor
Alcohol and Hygiene: An Elementary Lesson Book for Schools (Colman), 106, 111–12
Alexander, Archibald, attacks on New England revivalist doctrines by, 124
Allen, Ethan, marriage of, 15
Allen, Richard, 149; as leader of African Methodist Episcopal (AME) Church, 35; as leader of walkout from St. George's Church, 126; organization of Free African Society of Philadelphia by, 126
Allen Temple, 79, 81; Chapin, Sallie's, speeches at, 164–65; leadership at, 236
Alvord, John W., 249; antebellum reform nexus credentials of, 60; appointment to executive committee of Lincoln Temperance Society, 74–75; as colporteur, 73; Lincoln Temperance Pledge and,

74; as superintendent of schools of the
Freedmen's Bureau, 60
American Baptist Home Mission Society
(ABHMS): Christian republican
language in reports of, 37; creation of
denomination-specific groups and, 28;
face-to-face grassroots work and, 247;
leadership under, 36, 88; missionaries of,
in Black Atlanta, 124; origin of, 7, 36–38,
65; temperance policy of, 32, 37–38, 108
American Bible Society, 28
American Board of Commissioners for
Foreign Missions (ABCFM), 22, 28, 46
American Home Missionary Society, 28, 33;
preaching of temperance, 41
American Missionary, 39
American Missionary Association (AMA):
commitment to temperance, 32, 66,
108; constitution of, 41; creation of,
38; cultural uplift effort of, 66; doctrinal
definition of evangelical, 262n34; dubbing
of students as temperance propagandists,
109; face-to-face grassroots work of, 247;
hostility toward intemperance, 40–41;
influence of perfectionism on, 39–40;
Kirk as president of, 22; missionary
work of, 119, 124, 266n25; offering of
elementary-level education to Black
Atlanta, 107; origins of, 7, 38–41; policy
of founding schools and churches in
tandem, 78; regarding oppressed races,
91; shift of efforts to secondary education,
107; Smith, E. P., as field secretary of,
59; Strieby, Michael E., as corresponding
secretary of, 66; use of Lincoln
Temperance Pledge cards, 73, 74
American National Baptist Convention, 135
American Revolution (1775–1783), 33
American Society for the Promotion of
Temperance. *See* American Temperance
Society (ATS)
American Sunday School Union, 28
American temperance movement, origin of,
17, 18
American Temperance Society (ATS), 6;
constitution of, 19, 31; grassroots nature
of, 19; launch of *Journal of Humanity and*

Herald of the American Temperance Society
by, 19; origin of, 16, 28, 33
American Temperance Union (ATU):
issued call for fifth national temperance
convention, 42; Marsh, John, as leader of,
25–26; organization of, 19; publication of
Temperance Tract for the Freedmen, 71–72
American Tract Society (ATrS): adoption
of colporteur system, 34; classroom
readers produced by, 69–70; context of
revivalism and, 28; distribution of tracts
by, 33; literature from, 82; origins of, 7,
16, 33–34; spread of temperance message
and, 19, 32
American Tract Society (ATrS)-Boston
Branch, 33–34; Alvord, John W., as
colporteur for, 60; books sent to Atlanta
by, 67–68; publication of "Educational
Series" by, 67
American Tract Society (ATrS)-New York
Branch, 33
American white supremacy, 124–25
Amistad Committee, creation of American
Missionary Association and, 38
Anatomy, Physiology, and Hygiene (Walker),
111
Anderson, James A., as prohibitionist,
163–64, 169
Andover, Massachusetts, South Church in, 16
Andover Circle, 16, 33; discussion of
temperance reform by, 19; money raised
by, 34
Andover Seminary, 29, 158; Porter, Ebenezer,
as professor of, 16
Andover South Parish Society for the
Reformation of Morals, 16
Andrews, Sidney, 59
Anglo-African Magazine, 128
Annual Report of the Police Committee
(1881), 256
Antebellum United States: evolution of black
temperance discourse and activism,
124–25; reform nexus language in, 173;
urban slave drinking patterns in, 266n24
Anti-prohibitionists: arguments of, 157;
circulation of petition for local option
referendum in 1887, 217; design of 1887

campaign, 218–19; goal of, 172; handbill of, **232**; image problem of, 172; "Liberty" as motto of, 181, 183, 223; meetings held by, 173; organizing campaign of, 172–76, 216; rhetoric targeting black voters, 157, 176–81, 219–24; themes used by, 223

Anti-Saloon League (ASL), 10, 247

Anti-Saloon Republican National Committee (1887), 192

Appomattox Court House, Lee, Robert E., surrender of, at, 42

Armstrong, Lebbeus: on organization of Temperate Society of Moreau and Northumberland, 17–18; sermon of, in juxtaposing temperance movement and organized church, 17

Arthur, William, 15

Ashmun Institute, 95

Athens Blade, 145

Atlanta: Atlanta City Brewery in, 199; battle line in, 161–62; black population in, 47, **48**; black temperance reformers in, 10–11; breaking up of party and color lines in, 189–93; citizens' mass meeting in October 1886 in, 207–8; citizen-to-saloon ratio in, 253, **254, 255**; cotton expositions in, 217; Decatur Street in, 243; as "dry" city from 1885 to 1887, 196; East Side Colored Women's Christian Temperance Union in, 164; 1884 election reform in, 206; in 1880s, 45–46, **46**; 1888 municipal election in, 193, 208, 241; election system in, 291*n*20, 295*n*3; establishment of prohibition in, by plebiscite, 3–4; image problem of anti-prohibitionists, 172; impact of prohibition in, 176–77; increased racial hostility in, 244; Independence Day celebrations in 1866 in, 62–63; in-migration and labor market in, 263*n*3; involvement of blacks in politics in, 162–63; involvement of women in prohibition campaign in, 164–65; jug trade in, 202–3; license fee in, 254–55; liquor industry in, 172, 178, 253–56; local censuses in 1867 and 1869, 263*n*3; missionary schools in, 10–11; municipal elections in 1886 in, 208; 1906 race riot in, 256; organization of white temperance movement in, 156–57; police brutality toward blacks in, 55–57; population growth of, 47; postbellum demographic revolution in, 47; purchase of alcohol at pharmacies in, 199, 202; race relations in dry, 204, 206–11; rebuilding of, during Reconstruction, 53; retail liquor sales in, 161; saloons in, 161, 171, **179, 180,** 198, **254;** Sherman's burning of, 53; trade as economic raison d'être in, 286*n*40; voter registration in, 185; Women's Christian Temperance Union project in, 160; zoning and policing practices in, 243. *See also* Black Atlanta

Atlanta As It Is (1871 booklet), 253

Atlanta Baptist Seminary (Morehouse College), 88, 105; Carter, E. R., as graduate of, 137; education at, 115; enforcement of abstinence pledges at, 114; formation of YWCA at, 110; lack of dorms at, 114

Atlanta Brewing and Ice Company, **200,** 201

Atlanta City Brewery, 199; interracial workforce at, **201**

Atlanta City Council, constant changes in liquor regulations of, 255–57

Atlanta Constitution: "Christmas Crimes" column in, 61–62; on disposition of Atlanta on eve of election, 181; local option vote and, 182; Pledger, William's open letter to blacks published in, 176, 177; prediction on local option election, 160; prohibition and, 162, 201; on saloon industry in Atlanta, 161; "Was it a Mistake?" editorial in, 190

Atlanta Constitution Company, Howell, Evan P., as president of, 222

Atlanta Female Baptist Seminary, opening of, in basement of Friendship Baptist Church, 87–88

Atlanta Journal: as partisan, 182; support for prohibition, 162

Atlanta newspapers: reports on black drinking in, 60–61; spotlight on black decorum in, 61

Atlanta's Experience (pamphlet), 237–38

Atlanta University, 88, 89–90; abstinence pledge of, 108; adoption of National Temperance Society and Publication House *Temperance Lesson Book,* 110–11; chapel at, **114**; cultural mission of, 115; dorms at, 113–14; education at, 115; off-campus life at, 114; prohibition meeting held by, 164; season of special religious interest at, 262n36; shipments of National Temperance Society and Publication House literature to, 109; sponsorship of extracurricular temperance organizations, 110; Stearns, J. (John) N., visit to, 94

Augusta, Georgia, as "wet" town, 202

Augusta Chronicle, on beginning of prohibition in Atlanta, 199

Augusta Institute, relocation to Atlanta, 88

Ayer, Elizabeth, 87; arrival in Atlanta, 45–46; home visitations by, 82; missionary work among Ojibwe, 263n2

Ayer, Frederick, 46–47, 87, 249; on alcohol abuse, 57; arrival in Atlanta, 50; early life of, 45; founding of American Missionary Association school by, 68; founding of Ojibwe mission schools, 46; illness and death of, 47, 75; as missionary, 71, 263n2; organization of First Congregational Church by, 75; power of Lincoln's image and, 73; receipts of free shipments of American Tract Society literature, 71; teaching of Sunday school, 73; textbooks used by, 68, 72; as vanguard of American Missionary Association cultural uplift effort, 66

Badger, Robert, local option vote and, 188–89

Badger, Roderick Dhu, 243, 249; as anti-prohibitionist, 173, **175**; local option vote and, 188–89; as proponent of personal liberty argument, 181

Bailey, Charlie, 57

Baily, Joshua L., 96

Band of Hope, 109; organization of, 20; Spelman, Harvey Buel, establishment of, 113; Spelman Seminary efforts in forming, 105–6, 110; as temperance societies for children, 20

Band of Hope Catechism, 20, 75

Band of Hope Manuals, 75, 106

Baptist democracy, 134

Baptists: complaint on intemperance by Baptist Convention of Georgia, 137; editorial in *Home Mission Monthly,* 65; formation of missionary societies by women, 87; ordaining of men through ad hoc ministerial councils, 135

Baptist Young People's Union, 242

Barbarism, The First Danger, 33

Barber, Karin, on Yoruba culture, 122

Barnes, A. S., & Co. reader series, 67, 71

Barnes, Albert, 25; temperance sermon of, 31

Barnes, Gilbert, 5

Barnum, Jennie, as missionary, 67

Barry, A., 101

Beecher, Lyman, 27, 249; as antebellum revivalist, 22; Dwight, Timothy, as mentor of, 22; publication of temperance sermons by, 18

Beer-only retailers, licenses for, 253

Beman, Amos G., as active in temperance societies, 127

Benevolence, theology of, 127

Benevolent Empire, 27–28; societies of, 29

Bently, Moses, 208; as anti-prohibitionist, 173, 183; black-white prohibitionist alliance and, 180–81; at citizens' mass meeting, Oct. 1886, 207–8; conversion of, 226; fighting for African Americans on Citizen's Ticket by, 242; as opportunistic prohibitionist, 197; racial uplift and, 179

Berea College, establishment of, 40

"Bertie Rand's Temperance Pledge," 70–71

"Best class" of white men, 157

Bethel African Methodist Episcopal (AME) Church, 62–63, 66, 145; Chapin, Sallie's speeches at, 165; citywide rally for blacks at, 164; excommunication of members at, 81; leadership at, 236; Mead, Charles H., visits to, 100; prohibition meeting held by, 164

"Better class" of whites, 8, 120, 169, 247

Bible study in defining in temperance, 16

Biblical morality, 30

Big Bonanza saloon, sale of alcohol to whites at, 203

Black, James, 86, 87, 263*n*42

Black Atlanta: academic use of, as term, 7–8; alcohol abuse as problem in, 47–50, **51, 52,** 55–64, 63–64; "better classes" in, 8, 120, 247; blacks in, 47, 49–50, **51, 52;** convicts in, 53–55; educational opportunities in, 47; efforts to institutionalize temperance-based moral community, 119–53; housing shortage in, 48; intemperance as threat to, 132; internal stratification of, 242–43; lack of self-conscious entrepreneurial class in, 194; life in, 47; middle class in, 8, 115; national convention of Independent Order of Good Samaritans in, 11; northern missionaries and roots of temperance sentiment in, 64–84; population growth of, 80, 81; school-age children in, 82; smallpox epidemic in, 66; social reform efforts of lodges in, 139–51; temperance movement in, 4, 82–83, 129–37; urban cluster residential pattern in, 48–49. *See also* Atlanta

Black beast rhetoric, 204

Blackburn, Samuel, implication of local option vote, 188

Black clergy: breakup of solid support for prohibition, 218; dual heritage of critical community of, 129–34; moral and intellectual fitness of late nineteenth-century, 280*n*35

Black principled prohibitionists as active in city politics, 242

Blacks: anti-prohibitionists the second time and, 217–24; Black Atlanta and, 47; importance of race relations to, 170; interest in education, 72, 275*n*38; interest in joining police force, 210–11; involvement of, in politics in Atlanta, 162–63; police brutality toward, 56; priority of, on land ownership, 69; in Prohibition Party, 155; social reform in public schools of, 151; support for prohibition by, 193–94, 204, 206; types of prohibitionist voters, 196–97; use of alcohol by, 5, 47–50, **51, 52,** 57–64. *See also* African Americans

Black voters: anti-prohibition rhetoric targeting, 157, 176–81, 219–24; prohibitionist rhetoric targeting, 166, 168–72, 227–29

Blaine, James G., 191

Blake, Henry, 129

Blake: Or, The Huts of America (Delany), 128–29

Blind pigs, 290*n*12

Blind tigers, 210; as crime, 211; obtaining alcohol from, 202

Block, Shelley, 5

Boston: American Tract Society in, 33–34, 60, 67–68; constitution of African Society in, 126

Bourbon Triumvirate, 95, 163

Bourgeois work ethic, 59

Brer Rabbit: ethical dexterity of, 238–39; tales of, 185

Brewery licenses, cost of, 253

Brinckerhoff, Isaac, 71–72

Brooks, Preston, caning of Sumner, Charles, by, 62

Brothers of Love and Charity, 149

Brown, John, 91

Brown, John M., 152; as bishop of Georgia Annual Conference, 80

Brown, Joseph, 163, 175, 283*n*6

Brown, Julius L., opposition to prohibition, 175, 284*n*23

Brown, Walter R., 217

Brown, William Wells, 58

Brown & Dwyer's Saloon, **46**

Browne, William Washington, spread of Good Templary by, 141

Bryant, Alonzo W., 249

Bryant, John Emory, 222, 224; addressing black voters by, 165; as product of antebellum reform nexus, 169; as prohibitionist, 163; on race relations, 169; speech of, 182–83

Buck, A. E., 224; addressing black voters, 165; as prohibitionist, 163

Bullock, Rufus, as anti-prohibitionist speaker for blacks, 175

Burned-over district, 141

Burnett, Alonzo W., 208; call for committee

on temperance, 241; at citizens' mass meeting, Oct. 1886, 207–8; conversion of, 226; non-accommodationist stance of, on race relations, 175; as opportunistic prohibitionist, 197; as speaker at anti-prohibitionist rallies, 173; *Weekly Defiance* of, 212

Call-and-response spirituals, 152
Calvinism, 24; Five Point, 123; as pro-revival, 24
Campbell, Jabez P.: *Macon Telegraph* attack on, 182; as prohibitionist, 166
Cantrell, Gregg, 5
Carey, Alice D., as principal of Morris Brown College, 146
Cargile, Mitchell, 224
Carlson, Douglas, 5
Carswell, Edward, as National Temperance Society and Publication House vice president, 100
Carter, E. R., **140,** 147, 149, 228, 249; abstinence of, 211; as advisory board member, 224; at citizens' mass meeting, Oct. 1886, 207–8; claim that blacks needed whites for securing retail liquor licenses, 178; 1885 campaign complaints and, 221; encouragement of black drys, 185–86; of Friendship Baptist church, 162; at Jones, Sam's revival, 171; as outspoken temperance clergy, 137; as pastor of Friendship Baptist Church, 145, 237; personal attacks against, 176; as principled prohibitionist, 198; on prohibition, 168, 169–70, 187, 231; prohibition club led to polls by, 184; role of, in Pledger's conviction, 176
Carter, Mrs. R., as vice president of Colored Women's Christian Temperance Union, 213
Carter, Peter, 96, 99
Cary, Samuel F., 263n42
Caste discrimination, 38, 262n34
Chamberlin, E. P., as prohibitionist, 163
Chapin, Sallie, speeches of, in organizing black women, 164
Charleston, South Carolina Temperance

Society, 17
Chase, Mary, 111
Chase, Thomas N., 142
Chattahoochie Brick Company, 163
Christian Recorder: call for absolute abstinence in, 136; on 1887 election, 236; on local option election, 189; as not having continuous run, 261n29; as official organ of the Right Worthy Grand Lodge of the World, 281n50; as stridently pro-temperance, 81; suggestions to expose drinking problem within clergy, 130
Christian republicanism, 130; combination of, with pro-revival theology, 32–33; framework for, 43; as grassroots political movement, 260n20; language of, 106; as social-political-religious worldview, 29–31; temperance as element of, 29–32
Christmon, Kenneth, 5
Church polity, temperance and, 134–37
Citizen's Ticket, 242
Civic nationalism, 157
Civil War, North's victory in, 64
Clark, Billy J., on organization of Temperate Society of Moreau and Northumberland and, 17–18
Clark, George V., 132; as anti-prohibitionist speaker for blacks, 175, 177; conversion experience of, 119; education of, 119; as member of First Congregational, 119; as pastor, 120; planting of Congregational church in Athens, Georgia, 119–20; as prohibitionist, 166; as saloon porter, 178; as success story, 120
Clark College: Class of 1889 at, **166;** founding of, 49
Clarke County's February 1885 prohibition campaign, 176
Clark University, 88, 89–90; Chapin, Sallie's speeches as, 165; education at, 115; prohibition meeting held by, 164; prohibition of sale of intoxicating beverages within mile of campus and, 276n53; Thirkield, Wilbur P., as dean of Gammon School of Theology at, 108, 171
Classical republicanism, 125
Classroom temperance instruction, 110–13

Class warfare, framing prohibition in language of, 219

Clergy, central place of, in Atlanta's prohibition movement, 229

Cleveland, Grover, visit of, to Piedmont Exposition, 217

Coca-Cola, invention of, by Jacob's Pharmacy, 290*n*6

Cochran, A. M., 218; personal liberty and, 223; pride as Methodist, 222

Coker, Joe, 194, 239

Cold Water Templars, 10

Colgate, William, as treasurer of American Baptist Home Mission Society, 37

Colman, Julia, 111–12; books by, 111–12; as prohibition speaker, 113; as temperance activist, 92

Colored, 9

The Colored American (Beman), 127

Colored Men's Protective Association, 149

Colored Methodist Episcopal Church, 102

Colored Women's Christian Temperance Union (WCTU), organization of, for Atlanta, 213

Colored Young Men's Prohibition Clubs, 222, 224

Colporteurs, 34; Alvord, John W., as, 60, 73

Colquitt, Alfred, 218, 249; attempt to fire Big Bethel's Flipper, J. S., 218, 230; criticism of, for using religion at anti-prohibitionist meeting, 229; friendship of Dodge, William E. and, 163; as governor of Georgia, 145; as member of Bourbon Triumvirate, 95; National Temperance Society and Publication House literature and, 160; organization of temperance movement and, 157; prohibitionist address by, 231; questioning abstinence of, 211

Colquitt, Governor's wife, Women's Christian Temperance Union (WCTU) and, 159

Colville, Fulton: on police behavior as an outrage, 220; as president of Young Men's Anti-Prohibition Club, 219

Committee for West India Missions, creation of American Missionary Association and, 38

Committee of Twenty-Five, 161; pamphlet published by, 173

Community, relationship between individual and, 122–23

Compromise of 1877, 190

The Conflict: starting of, 211; as white temperance paper, 10, 102, 212

"The Conflict Is Past," 196

Congregationalists, 24; dominance of, 27–28

Connecticut Society for the Suppression of Vice and Promotion of Good Morals, 27

The Connexion of Temperance with Republican Freedom (Barnes), 31

Conservative Citizens Club (CCC), 216

Consolidated American Baptist Convention, 136

Constitutional prohibition, referenda on, 283*n*3

Convict lease systems, treatment of convicts, 53–55

Creolization process, 121

Crime: alcohol consumption and, 168–69; Blind tigers as, 211; prohibition and, 203–4. *See also* Law enforcement

Critical community as first element of reform movement, 4

Cromwell, Oliver, 142

Crummell, Alexander, 108

Crystal Fount Lodge, No. 1, 146; membership of, 147

Cult of domesticity, Spelman Seminary's embracement of, by founders, 107

Cummings, William, saloon ownership by, 178

Cuyler, Theodore L., 249; ending of opposition to Prohibition Party by, 190; endorsement of Prohibition Party by, 263*n*42; influence of temperance society and, 26; as National Temperance Society and Publication House leader, 91, 106, 156, 204; nomination of Baily, Joshua L., for board of managers, 96; prejudices and ignorances of, 204

Dade Coal Company, 57

Daniels, Granithan, 66; school operated by, 72

Dart, William M., 119

Daughters of Bethel, 149

Davis, Benjamin, 243

Davis, Jefferson: condemnation of prohibition movement by, 215–16, 217; endorsement of, 230; Pledger, William, capitalization on open letters of, 230–31

De facto racial segregation, spread of, 243–44

DeGives Opera House, 56, 160; election eve rally in, 231; operating at loss, during campaign meetings, 181

DeKalb Chronicle, 238

Delany, Martin R., 128–29

Democratic Party: collapse of, 163, 206; personal liberty plank of, 155, 247

Dennett, John, on Atlanta, 45

Discrimination, caste, 38, 262n34

Disinterested benevolence, doctrine of, 123–24

Distilleries, licenses for, 253

"Dixie Land for Temperance," 153

Doctrines and Discipline of the Methodist Episcopal Church, 35, 134, 136

Dodge, William Earl, 22, 249; "The" Church and Temperance" (paper) of, 106; Colquitt, Alfred, and, 163; creation of county bearing name, 95; death of, 94; interest in black education, 95; as leader of National Temperance Society and Publication House, 43, 73, 94–96, 99, 145; as New York City businessman and philanthropist, 94–95; Price, Joseph C. and, 102; as prohibition speaker, 113; statue of, in Bryant Park, **97**; as trustee of Ashmun Institute, 95

Dorsey, Allison, 7–8

Dougall, John, 42, 249; as abolitionist, 96; as founding publisher and editor of *New York Weekly Witness,* 90–93; as radical reformer, 23

Dougherty, Styles, excommunication of, for drinking, 76

Douglass, Frederick, 58; assertion on masters' views of drunken slaves, 266n24

Dow, Neal, as temperance activist, 92

Dram drinking, 265n22

Drew, John W.: crusade of, 163; organization of Atlanta's white temperance movement by, 156–57; signing of abstinence pledge and, 159; temperance meetings held by, 159

Dry years (1885–1887), 196–214; beginning of, 199–203; black prohibitionists in, 196–97; contradictions of prohibition and, 198–204; crime and, 203–4; principled black prohibitionists and, 211–14; race relations in Atlanta, 204, 206–11

Dual Grand Lodge, Thrower's efforts to reorganize lodges into state, 145

DuBois, W. E. B., 88; on convict leasing, 54; on race relations, 243–44; religious influences of, 115; youthful observations of, 245

Due process, 199

Duncan, William: excommunication of, 76–77; suspension of, 76

Durham Coal Company, 57

Dwight, Timothy, 18, 27; as antebellum revivalist, 22

Easley, Smith W., Jr., 250; as advisory board member of prohibitionists' campaign, 224; appointment of, to district deputy for organizing Good Samaritan lodges in Georgia, 146; call for committee on temperance, 241; fighting for African Americans on Citizen's Ticket by, 242; as Good Samaritan leader, 211; *Herald of United Churches* by, 231; as opportunistic prohibitionist, 198; *Southern Recorder* and, 212

East Side Colored Women's Christian Temperance Union (WCTU), 164, 165

Eatonton Baptist Church (Eatonton, GA), 29

Ebenezer Baptist Association, 98, 130, 132

Ebenezer Baptist Church, 182

Eberhart, Gilbert S., 67, 71

Economy, prohibition and, 177

Edwards, Justin, 16, 26, 34; American Temperance Society and, 19, 28–29, 33

Edwards, Lena, 151

Emancipation, 42

Emigration, 33

English, James W., as prohibitionist, 163

Enquiry into the Effects of Spirituous Liquors (Rush), 31

Epworth League, 242

Essays on Intemperance (Barnes), 25

Ethic of reciprocity, 121–22

Evangelical abolitionists, 9–10, 259n13; concern over negating one's free moral agency and, 260n15

Evangelical missionaries, racial attitudes of, 65

Evangelical missionary organizations: blurring of lines between Freedmen's Bureau and, 73; as influential temperance organization, 6

Evangelical reform nexus, origins of temperance movement in, 16, 21–32

Evangelical temperance reformers, commitment to reforms, 20–21

Evangelical theology, individualism of, 259n13

Evans, C. A., 142

Excommunication, 76–78, 81, 270n62

Exodusters, migration to Kansas, 91

Fee, John G., establishment of Berea College by, 40

Felton, Latimer, 202

Felton, William H.: as anti-prohibitionist speaker for blacks, 174; inspirational speech by, 231

Fifth Baptist Church, 187

Fifth National Colored Convention, 128

Fifth Ward committee, 164

Finch, John B., as prohibition speaker, 113

Finch, William, 208, 243; competing for prohibition votes and, 184; election of, 162–63

Finney, Charles G., 250; claim to make temperance "appendage" of revivals, **23**; founding of Oberlin College, 39; influence of, on Ayer, Frederick, 22–23; intemperance cause for stop of revival, 25; as revivalist, 22, 29, 46, 95; teachings of, 27; theology of benevolence of, 127

First Baptist Church, 142

First Congregational Church: Chapin, Sallie, speaking at, 165; Clark, George, joining of, 119–20; Duncan, William, excommunication from, 76–77; founding of, by Ayer, Frederick, **77**; organization of, 15–16; temperance and, 75–79; troubles at, 237

First Ward colored club, prohibition vote and, 187

Fisk, Clinton B., 68, 69, 263n42

Fisk University, 93, 115

Five Point Calvinism, 123

Flipper, J. S.: Colquitt's attempt to fire Big Bethel's, 218, 230; praise for bold stand for prohibition, 237; replacement of Gaines, Wesley J., by, 218–19

"For Home and the Red, White, and Blue," 195

Fourteenth Amendment, 199

Francis, Cyrus W., 78, 115; as missionary, 71; as pastor at First Congregational Church, 75–76; receipts of free shipments of American Tract Society literature, 71; as reverend at Storrs School, 119

Fraternal orders, need for charters for local lodges, 281n41

Fraternal temperance lodges, rise of, 19–20

Free African Society of Philadelphia, 126, 149

The Freedman, 68–69, 72

Freedman's Journal, 68–69, 72

Freedman's Spelling Book, 69–70

Freedmen: early temperance literature for, 67–72; pursuit of literacy following emancipation, 72; temperance societies in schools of, 72–75; use of alcohol by, 58

Freedmen's aid societies, 8, 107; origin of, 32

Freedmen's Bureau, 60; Alvord, John S., as superintendent of schools, in Georgia, 60; blurring of lines between evangelical missionary organizations and, 73; Eberhart, Gilbert S., as superintendent of schools, in Georgia, 67–68

Freemen, or Slaves (tract), 106

Free-Will Baptists, adoption of American Missionary Association, 38

Friendship Baptist Church, **89**, 137; Carter, E. R. and, 237; effort to sabotage efforts, 183; Mead, Charles H., visits to, 100; opening of Atlanta Female Baptist Seminary in basement of, 87–88; organization of second Colored Women's Christian Temperance Union for Atlanta by, 213;

prohibition meeting held by, 164
Fulton County, Georgia: local option
    elections in, 9, 120; as "wet" county, 256
"Fusion" Citizen's Ticket in 1886, 208

Gaines, Wesley J., 250; abstinence of, 80,
    211; on advisory board of prohibitionists'
    campaign, 224; as author of history of
    African Methodist Episcopal Church in
    the South, 241–42; as black prohibitionist,
    139; as brother of Gaines, William, 79; at
    citizens' mass meeting, Oct. 1886, 207–8;
    confidence of dry vote from blacks,
    160–61; as Good Samaritans' member,
    147; as opportunistic prohibitionist, 198;
    as outspoken temperance clergy, 137;
    as pastor of Bethel African Methodist
    Episcopal (AME) Church, 145, 162;
    replacement of, by Flipper, J. S., 218–19;
    as representative to national Grand Lodge,
    145; speech of, 182–83; vote buying and,
    171
Gaines, William, 79–80; arrival in Atlanta, 79;
    ordaining Bethel AME's pastor, 79–80;
    saloon ownership by, 178
Gainesville, Georgia, as "wet" town, 202
Gammon Theological Seminary, 105, 224
Gardner, Robert, 280*n*35
Garner, Bradford, excommunication of,
    77–78
Garrison, William Lloyd, 91
Gatewood, Willard B., 144
General Convention of Congregational
    Churches of Vermont, 26
General Local Option Law (Georgia, 1885),
    87, 158, 198
Genovese, Eugene, 57
Gentility, planters conception of, 58–59
Georgia: convict lease system in, 53–55;
    1868 constitution of, 54; establishment of
    temperance society in, 29; organization
    of True Reformer fountains, 142; penal
    system of, 54; Reconstruction-era
    government in, 8, 53; Republican Central
    Committee in, 143; Scientific Temperance
    Instruction in, 275*n*43; wine producers
    in, 198

Georgia and Alabama Railroad, contracting
    for convicts, 54
Georgia Baptist, endorsement of temperance
    in, 155
Georgia Baptist Convention, 29; temperance
    and, 158
Georgia Congregational Conference (1880),
    78
Georgia Press Association, endorsement of
    prohibition, 155
Georgia Prohibition Association, 10;
    organization of temperance movement
    and, 157
Giles, Harriet E.: opening of school for black
    girls, 87–88; signing of total abstinence
    and social purity pledges and, 114–15
Glenn, John, 242
Going, Jonathan, as leader of American
    Baptist Home Mission Society, 36
Goode, Captain, 57
*Good Morals and Gentle Manners for Schools
    and Families* (Gow), 111
Good Samaritans. *See* Independent Order
    of Good Samaritans and Daughters of
    Samaria
Good Templars' Grand Lodge, 141–42, 145,
    281*n*41; Thrower, James G., and, 142, 159;
    True Reformers reorganization of, into, 145
Goodwin, John B., 219; as anti-prohibitionist
    speaker for blacks, 175; assertion of anti-
    prohibitionists as temperance party, 222
Gordon, John B., 147; as member of Bourbon
    Triumvirate, 163
Gospel Aid Society, 149
Gospel Temperance, 99, 105
Gough, John B., 10; as temperance activist, 92
Gow, Alexander M., 111; books by, 111
Grady, Henry, 208, 250; "New South" speech
    of, 157; orchestration to have Cleveland,
    Grover, at Piedmont Exposition, 217;
    prejudices and ignorances of, 204;
    preserving purity of ballot box, 234;
    prohibition and, 162, 231; serving of
    liquor to guests, 227–28
Graham, George, election of, 163
Grandison, C. N., 228; prohibitionist address
    by, 231

Grand United Order of Odd Fellows, 61, 149, 150

Graves, Antoine, 101, **103**; fighting for African Americans on Citizen's Ticket by, 242; as member of committee on temperance, 241

Gray Street School, 242

Great Revival (Georgia), 29, 158

Greenwood, Janette Thomas, 8

Griffin, Georgia, as "wet" town, 202

Grimke, Thomas, 17

Gutman, Herbert, 72

Hagan & Co., **46**

Half Way Covenant, 15

Hallock, William, 16; position in American Tract Society, 33

Hamilton, Alexander, 224; vote buying and, 170–71

Hammock, Major, 61

Hammond, John, 31

Hammond, W. A., as prohibitionist, 164

Hankerson, Joseph, 147

Hardeman-Covington state prohibition bill (1907), 244, 256

Harper, Charlie, transporting of "wet" voters by, 237

Harper, Frances E. W., as prohibition speaker, 113

Hawthorne, J. B., 169, 211, 250; aggressive stand of, 171; as eulogizer at Young Men's Prohibition Club, 236; as prohibitionist, 164, 231

Hayden, Robert: exposure of prohibitionist chronic racism and, 180; involvement in anti-prohibitionist campaign, 179–80

Haygood, Atticus G., 157

The Helping Hand (Dart), 119

Hemphill, W. A., as prohibitionist, 163

Henry, R. J., 162

Herald of United Churches (Easley), 11, 211, 231

Herd, Denise, 5

Hewitt, Nathaniel, as traveling agent of American Temperance Society (ATS), 19

Higgins, Malvina: as missionary, 71; receipt of free shipments of American Tract Society literature by, 71

Higher-status blacks, 8

High license, 254, 255; impact on morals, 218

Hightower, Charnell, white member of Young Men's Prohibition Club, 236

Hillyer, George: as president of Piedmont Exposition, 224; as prohibitionist, 163–64

Hillyer, Henry, as prohibitionist, 199

Hodge, Charles, attacks on New England revivalist doctrines by, 124

Holifield, E. Brooks, 124

Holiness movement, 25

Holmes, Nick, 162, 224; as member of Friendship Baptist Church, 237

Hot toddy, 265*n*22

Houston Street School, 151

Howard, David T., 224

Howard, Oliver O. (General), 60; as commissioner of Freedmen's Bureau, 73–75; creation of Lincoln National Temperance Association and, 83

"Howard at Atlanta" (Whittier), 84

Howell, Clark: as anti-prohibitionist speaker for blacks, 175, 218; prohibition and, 162

Howell, Evan P.: as anti-prohibitionist, 218; as president of Atlanta Constitution Company, 222

Humphrey, Heman, temperance sermon of, 31

Hunt, Mary H., 112; temperance instruction and, 88, 89

Hunt, Thomas, 25

Hutchins, Dougherty, 237

Independent Order of Good Samaritans and Daughters of Samaria: arrival in Black Atlanta, 141; Black Atlanta's enduring temperance order, 146–47; Easley, Smith W. Jr., as leader in, 211; establishment of, 20; Gaines, Wesley J., as member of, 211; lodge of, 10, **148**; national convention of, 11; pledges of, 146–47; prohibition campaign and, 162

Independent Order of Good Templars (IOGT), 10, 94, 141; call for new reform party, 86; cooperation between Women's Christian Temperance Union and, 160; establishment of, 20; inviting of Stewart,

Eliza, to Atlanta, 159; prohibition campaign and, 162; schism destroying True Reformer fountains, 145; spread of, by Browne, William Washington, 141; support for national prohibition, 141

Individual, relationship between community and, 122–23

Inebriation, 57

Inman, Samuel, 171; addressing black voters, 165; as prohibitionist, 163

In-migration, 263n3

An Inquiry into the Effects of Spirituous Liquors on the Human Body and Mind (Rush), 17, 18

Intemperance, 25; American Missionary Association on, 40–41, 278n18; framing of arguments against, 30–31; slave ownership and, 128–29; as threat to Black Atlanta, 132; white evangelical clergy on, 278n17

Interracial cooperation, 189–90

Ivy, James, 5

Jackson, Andrew, 142

Jacob's Pharmacy, sale of Coca-Cola by, 290n6

Jennings, William, 49–50

Jenningstown, 49, 50

Jewell, Joseph O., 115; of American Missionary Association missionaries and their cultural perspective, 277n58

Jim Crow laws, 56, 243

Johnson, Edward A., as prohibitionist, 166

Johnson, James Weldon, 112, 115

Jones, Absalom, organization of Free African Society of Philadelphia by, 126

Jones, Alexander S.: class argument of, 181; racism and, 179; as speaker at anti-prohibitionist rallies, 173–74

Jones, Charles O., 93; voting of "Liberty" ticket by, 218

Jones, Jerry M., 162; meeting hosted by, 164; as pastor of Macedonia Baptist Church, 164

Jones, Sam, 224, 250; addressing issue of police brutality among blacks, 228; organization of temperance movement and, 157; as prohibitionist evangelist, 256; revival of, 161; speech of, 211; as

temperance speaker, 10; at Tillman's revival, 209

Jones, W. L., pastor of Mount Zion Baptist Church, 133

Jones (local drunk), 63

Journal of Humanity and Herald of the American Temperance Society, launch of, 19

Jug trade, 202–3

Juvenile temperance societies, rise of, 19–20

Kansas, Exoduster migration to, 91

Kansas-Nebraska Act (1854), 67

Kennedy, S. C., as missionary, 102

Kieth, Perry, charge against, for selling liquor, 78

Kimball, H. I., addressing black voters, 165

Kimball House, 165, 173; Employees Committee at, 173; wagering on election results at, 182

Kimball House Boys, 184

Kimball House saloon, 200; sale of alcohol to whites at, 203

King, James, excommunication of, 77

Kinney, Lucy, as missionary, 67

Kinney, Rose: as missionary, 67; as teacher at Storrs School, 119

Kirk, Edward Norris: as revivalist, 22, 23, 26, 90; on temperance, 29

Knights of Jericho, 10

Knights of Labor, 207

Knights of Pythias, 150

Knights of Temperance, 10

Krout, John Allen, 5

Ku Klux Klan (KKK), 244; blacks fear of violence from, 56

Lafayette Avenue Presbyterian Church (Brooklyn, NY), 91; 1866 revival at, 26

Landrum, Walter, attack on prohibitionists, 220

Lane Theological Seminary, 22

Law enforcement: abuse from, 211; resistance to change, 209–10. *See also* Crime; Police

Lay, Sarah, organization of Band of Hope by, 109–10

Lectures on Revivals of Religion (Finney), 25

Lee, J. W., pastor of Trinity Methodist Episcopal Church, 229

Lee, Robert E., surrender at Appomattox Court House, 42, 44

Levine, Lawrence, 152

"Liberty," as motto of anti-prohibitionists, 181, 183, 223

Liberty ticket, 218

Light, Ivan, 116

"The Light House," 44

Lincoln, Abraham: appropriation of, for temperance cause, 72–73; flyer with recently freed black family and, 231; reference in speech to, 183; stories of abstinence of, 269n57

Lincoln, Heman, 37

Lincoln National Temperance Association, 74; creation of, by Howard, O. O., 83

Lincoln Temperance Pledge, 146, 231; cards for, 74

Lincoln Temperance Society: appointment of Alvord, John W. to executive committee of, 74–75

Lincoln University, 95

Liquor: buying of votes and, 170–71; licenses for wholesalers of, 253; obtaining during prohibition, 202–3; regulating Atlanta's industry involving, 253–56. *See also* Alcohol

Livingstone College, 95

Lloyd Street Methodist Episcopal Church, 236

Local option election in Atlanta (1885), 3–4, 154–95; anti-prohibitionist campaign in, 172–81; Atlanta white temperance movement and, 158–60; climax of campaign, 181–88; election results, **187**; implications of vote, 188–95; prohibitionist campaign in, 162–66, 168–72

Local option election in Atlanta (1887), 3–4, 215–40; anti-prohibition rhetoric targeting black voters, 219–24; blacks and anti-prohibitionists in, 217–24; cartoonist's perspective on, **225**; election of 1887, 233–38; final week of the campaign, 229–31; prohibitionists and blacks in, 224–29; results of, **235**

Lodges, social reform efforts of, in Black

Atlanta, 139–51

Long, Jefferson Franklin, 250; as anti-prohibitionist speaker, **174**; prohibition and, 177–78; racial uplift and, 179

"Look Away, Look Away," 154

Louisiana Baptist Convention, 98

Low license, 254

Lynchings: absence of, 244; Wells-Barnett's, Ida challenge to Women's Christian Temperance Union (WCTU) to oppose, 242

Mabry, Miles J., quart license of, 200–201

Macedonia Baptist Church: Jones, Jerry M., as pastor of, 164; prohibition meeting held by, 164

Macon, Georgia, as "wet" town, 202

Macon Telegraph, 176; anti-prohibitionist campaign and, 179–80; on enforcement of prohibition, 201; opposition to prohibition, 162, 193; as partisan, 182

Mahan, Asa, as president of Oberlin College, 39

Manual of the Vanguard of Freedom, 75

Marion and Stafford saloon, 179

Marsh, John, 43; as leader of American Temperance Union, 25–26, 41

Marty, Martin, 7

"Mary and the Drunkard's Children," 70

Mayor's Court, 267n28

McCall, Lucy, 202–3

McDaniel, Henry, signing of temperance bill, 160

McHenry, Jackson, 224, 250; conversion of, 226; as prohibitionist leader, **167**, 197, 203; rhetoric of, 166, 168–69; running for office by, 163

McMoran, Tim, 69

McPherson, James, 64–65

Mead, Charles H., 142; on African Methodist Episcopal Church ordination process, 135–36; as missionary, 102; as speaker in Black Atlanta, 100–101; travel of, for society, 100–101

Memphis, growth of, 47

Methodism, embrace of revivalist practices, 24

Methodist Freedmen's Aid Society, 73; enforcement of temperance position for schools of, 108; founding of Clark College, 49; shift of efforts to secondary education, 107; Summer Hill School of, 75

Michigan Territory, 46

Middle class, 8, 115

Mims, Livingston, as employee of New York Life Insurance Atlanta office, 221

Miner, Alonzo A., 263n42

Misdemeanors, 267n28

Missed opportunities in race relations, 248

Missionary Baptist Convention of Georgia (1875), 98, 132, 133, 144

Missionary schools: in Atlanta, 10–11; controlled environments at, 113; temperance societies and students of, 108–10

Mitchell, Eliza, as missionary, 67

Mitchell, Eugene, 220

Mitchell, Micah, giving of speech for the "wets," 237

Montreal Temperance Society, Dougall as founding member of, 91

Montreal Witness, founding of, 91

Moody, Dwight L., 22; revivals of, 88, 95

Moore, Giles, accusation of being a blind tiger, 210

Moore, John Hammond, 5

Moral agency, concern about negating one's free, 260n15

Moral government of God theology, 24–25

Moral suasion, 9, 156; prohibitionist endorsement of, 168

Moral training, support for, among Northern black clergy, 276n52

Moran, P. J., as local anti-prohibitionist, 218

Morehouse, Henry L., 99, 250; as secretary of American Baptist Home Mission Society, 65, 88

Morehouse College. *See* Atlanta Baptist Seminary (Morehouse College)

Morgan, Charles H., 147

Morning Star Lodge, No. 4., membership of, 147

Morristown, New Jersey, revival in, 25

Mount Pleasant Baptist Church, prohibition

meeting held by, 164

Mount Zion Baptist Church (Atlanta), 133; prohibition meeting held by, 164

Mumford, Kevin, 243

Mutual Aid Brotherhoods (MABs), 227; membership of, 216; platform of, 216

Mutual aid societies, temperance and, 147, 149

Nashville, growth of, 47

National Association of Evangelicals, 10

National Council of Congregational churches, adoption of American Missionary Association (AMA), 38

National Temperance Advocate: biblical argument for total abstinence and, 136; *The Conflict* quoted in, 102; editing of, 94; as published without interruption into the 1900s, 44; publishing of Colman, Julia, in, 112; student's library access to, 112; subscriptions to, 85, 100, 105, 106

National Temperance Society and Publication House (NTS), 94–107; adoption of cutting-edge Scientific Temperance Instruction and, 85; "balance-wheel" of temperance movement and, 94–96; characterization of, 263n42; Christian republican framework of, 43; commitment to revivalism, 43; constitution of, 44; creation and role of Missionary Committee, 99, 100; Cuyler as president of, 156, 204; Dodge as president of, 73; Dougall as vice president of, 91; face-to-face grassroots work of, 247; "great work" of, among freed people, 99–102, 105–7; Howard as president of, 73; as last organization to form out of evangelical reform nexus, 41–44; literature from, 82, 160; organization of, 43; as passionate about mission, 106–7; postbellum work of, 6, 7; primary mission of, 102; sending of tracts to Ayer, Frederick, 72; spread of temperance by, 22, 32, 95–96; Stearns as secretary of, 190; support of Spelman Seminary and first temperance textbook, 88–89

Negrophilia, charges of, 187–88

Negro problem, true solution of, 191

Neo-religious school, views of temperance, 5–6

Nettleton, Asahel: Dwight, Timothy as mentor of, 22; as revivalist, 22, 29

New England revivalist doctrines, attacks on, 124

New England Temperance Society, creation of, 127

New England Tract Society, 33; organization of, 34; origin of, 16

New Hope Baptist Association, 130; on intemperance, 131, 132; Sunday School Convention of, 133

New Hope Presbyterian Church, prohibition meeting held by, 164

New Orleans, growth of, 47

"New South" ideology, rise of, 157

Newton, A. E., 75

New York Evangelist, 26

New York Good Templars, 42

New York Life Insurance Atlanta office, 221

New York Times, on possible effects of prohibition, 192

New York Weekly Witness, 85, 133, 136; distribution of, 23, 94, 113; Dougall, John, as founding publisher and editor of, 90–93; student's library access to, 112

Nexus organizations, 28

Nokes, John, 69

No-license advocates, arguments of, 254

Noll, Mark, 30

Norcross, Virgil, prohibition vote and, 187

Nordhoff, Charles, writings of, after tour of South, 59–60

North Carolina: State Colored Normal School in, 101; statewide temperance referendum in, 155

Northern antebellum black temperance, 124–29

Northern evangelical culture, relative influence of, 194

Northern free blacks, immersion in antebellum reform nexus, 120

Northern Missionary schools, temperance and, 107–16

North Georgia Conference of the African Methodist Episcopal Church, 218, 224;

intemperance of, 130; organization of temperance committee at first meeting of, 80–81

Oakland Cemetery, Independence Day celebrations in, 62–63

Oberlin College, 22, 39

Oberlin perfectionism, 39

Ojibwe Indians, 46; alcohol abuse among, 46; missionary work among, 39, 263n2; mission schools for, 46

On Temperance, 34

Opportunistic prohibitionists, 196–97; growing divide between principled prohibitionists and, 238

Order of the Eastern Star, 150

Order of the Golden Rod and Rising Generation, 62

Order of the Hickory Rod and Fallen Generation, 62

Our Union, publishing extensively of Colman, Julia, in, 112

Packard, Sophia, 113; as founder of Woman's American Baptist Home Mission Society, 87; opening of school for black girls, 87–88; signing of total abstinence and social purity pledges and, 114–15

Palmer, Jim, interest in being on police force, 209–10

Parallel fraternal societies, temperance and, 149–51

Parker, James B.: as anti-prohibitionist speaker for blacks, 174; class argument of, 181; conversion to prohibition, 170–71, 226; interest in being on police force, 209–10; as opportunistic prohibitionist, 197; on prohibition, 177, 211; *Southern Recorder* and, 212; switch to dry side, 182; vote buying and, 170–71

Parker, John, 286n53

Payne, Carroll, condemnation of prohibitionists by, 222

Payne, Daniel A., 79, 135, 250; as African Methodist Episcopal Church Bishop, 79; organization of South Carolina Conference by, 79; as president of

Wilberforce University, 79; temperance
message of, 152

Payne, George, suspension of, 76

Peck, F. Jesse, 80, 136; as founder of
Daughters of Bethel, 149; as Prince Hall
Mason, 150

Peck, John M., as leader of American Baptist
Home Mission Society, 36

People's Advisor, 98

Perfectionism, 25; connection between
teetotalism, abolitionism and, 259*n*13;
influence of, on American Missionary
Association, 39–40

Personal liberty: as argument used by anti-
prohibitionists, 181, 223; as plank of
Democrats, 155, 247

Pharmacies, Atlanta's purchase of alcohol at,
199, 202

Phelps, Dodge, & Company, 43

Piedmont Exposition, 217, 224, 230

Pierce, Franklin, 67

Pioneer Fountain No. 1, 142

Pitts, Ella, as president of Colored Women's
Christian Temperance Union (WCTU),
213

Planters, conception of gentility and, 58–59

Pledger, William, 250; as alumnus of Storrs
School, 142; as anti-prohibitionist
speaker for blacks, 174, 175, 177;
attack on prohibitionists, 220–21; call
for committee on temperance, 241;
capitalization on Davis, Jefferson's open
letters, 230–31; class argument of, 181;
as coeditor of *Weekly Defiance*, 162;
endorsement of Young Men's Prohibition
Club, 213; as Grand Worthy Master of
Georgia's Grand Fountain, **143**; as ignored
speaker at public meeting, 208; interest
in being on police force, 209–10; as
leader in Republican Atlanta politics and
temperance, 142–44; libel suit against,
176; open letter to blacks published
in *Atlanta Constitution*, 176, 177; on
prohibition, 211; public opinion and, 176;
reading of Bible passages at temperance
society meetings, 222–23; speeches at
campaigns by, 218; on temperance, 222;

women's political involvement and, 221

Police: brutality toward blacks, 56;
enforcement practices of, 220; interest of
blacks in joining, 209–11; ongoing abuses
of, 210–11. *See also* Law enforcement

Police commissioners, prejudice of, as race-
based, 228

Porter, Ebenezer, 250; Andover Circle and,
33; origin of American Temperance
Society (ATS) and, 33; as pastor of First
Congregational Church (Washington,
CT), 15–16; as professor at Andover
Seminary, 16; temperance sermons of, 18,
31; weekly meetings of, 28

Postbellum, 8

Post-emancipation Black Atlanta, 8;
temperance and nexus/missionary
organizations of, 32–44

*The Practicality of Suppressing Vice by Means
of Societies Instituted for that Purpose*
(Beecher), 27

Pragmatic syncretism, 121–24, 133–34

Presbyterians, dominance of, 27–28

Price, Joseph C., 251; announcement of
speech by, **104**; Dodge, William E.,
and, 102; as missionary for the National
Temperance Society, 102

The Primary Temperance Catechisms (Colman)
textbook, 111, 112; Spelman, Harvey
Buel, donation of, 105–6

Prince Hall Masons, 150

Principled prohibitionists, 197–98; black,
211–14; growing divide between
opportunistic prohibitionists and, 238

Progressives, 172

Prohibition: arguments for, 154–55; beginning
of real, 199–203; black support for, 193–94,
204, 206; contradictions of, 198–204;
crime and, 203–4; delay of until July 1,
1886, 198; distinction between temperance
and, 9; economy and, 177; establishment
of, in Atlanta, 3–4; as political expression
of temperance movement, 154; as talked
about public policy issue, 155; Tennessee's
rejection of, 155, 215, 246; Texas' rejection
of, 155, 215, 246; women's political
involvement with, 221

"Prohibition Battle Cry" (Shacklock), 45
Prohibitionists: campaign of, 162–66;
    campaign strategies of, 224–25; Davis,
    Jefferson, condemnation of, 215–16, 217;
    failure to control public debate, 226–27;
    opportunistic, 196–97; principled, 197–
    98, 211–14; Republicans as, 155; rhetoric
    targeting black voters, 166, 168–72,
    227–29; second time and, 224–29; Young
    Men's Prohibition Club endorsement of,
    216
Prohibition Party, 86–87, 94, 241; abolitionist
    heritage of, 155; blacks in, 155; in 1884
    presidential election, 191; encouraging
    black support for, 192; founding of,
    155; nomination of Black, James, to, 87;
    organization of, 44, 141; prohibitionists
    as, 155; woman's suffrage and, 156
Pro-revival theology, 7; Christian republican
    ideology combination of, with, 32–33;
    explanation for temperance-as-prelude-
    to-revival phenomenon, 26; teachings of,
    28–29
Proverbs 14:34, 19
Public drunkenness: charges of, by race, 204,
    205; fighting and, 267*n*28
Public-private split, 7

Quart licenses, 200–201

Rabinowitz, Howard, 55, 210
Race relations: in dry Atlanta, 204,
    206–11; effect of prohibition vote on,
    191; evangelical prohibitionists and,
    239; importance of, to blacks, 170;
    improvement in, and prohibition, 169;
    resistance to change, 208–10
Racial unity, 241
Racial uplift, as prohibition theme, 168
Raines, Thomas, 57
Randolph, J. W., 80
Reciprocity, ethic of, 121–22
Reconstruction, 8; emergence of prohibition
    and, 155
Recorder's Court, 267*n*28
*A Reformation of Morals Practicable and
    Indispensable* (Beecher), 27

Reform clubs, organization of abstinence
    pledgers into, 159
Reformist revivalism, 21
Reform nexus theology, African American
    spirituality and, 123–24
Registration, comparison of 1885 and 1887,
    233
Religion, rise of organized temperance and,
    16–21
Republican Party: Bryant, John Emory,
    as activist in, 169; call for wet/dry
    reconciliation and, 189; collapse of, in
    Atlanta, 163, 206; election of Finch,
    William, and Graham, George, 162–63;
    internal weakness of Georgia's, 190; plank
    on temperance in, 191, 192; split of state
    along party lines, 170; as unwilling to fully
    back temperance Prohibition movement,
    86; weakness of Georgia's, 213
Revivalism: as motive and method of
    antebellum reform, 31–32; reformist, 21;
    temperance and, 6, 24
Revivalists: Finney, Charles G., as, 22, 29,
    46, 95; Moody, Dwight L., as, 88, 95;
    Nettleton, Asahel, as, 22, 29; Tillman, J.
    L., as, 209
Revivals: in Morristown, New Jersey, 25;
    temperance as postlude to, 21–23, 27–29
Reynoldstown, 50
Richardson, Benjamin, 111
Richardson, Eliza, 56
Richmond, growth of, 47
Right Worthy Grand Lodge of the World, 145,
    282*n*50–51
Roach Street School, 242
Roberts, Samuel K., 126
Robinson, N. C., as officer of Kimball House
    Employees Committee, 173
Rochon, Thomas R., 4, 113
Rockefeller, John D., Sr., 88, 102
Rockefeller, Laura Spellman, 96
Rohrer, James, 5
Romantic racialism, 65, 67, 106
Rorabaugh, W. J., 153
Rucker, H. A., purchase of bakery by, 176
Rumbarger, John, 263*n*42
Rush, Benjamin, 17, 18, 31

Rutherford, L. A., as missionary, 101
Ryan, Jackson M., saloon ownership by, 178

St. George's Methodist Episcopal Church, 35;
    walkout from, 126
St. James Lodge, 150
St. Philips African Methodist Episcopal
    (AME) Church, prohibition meeting held
    by, 164
Savannah Tribune, endorsement of
    temperance in, 155
Scarborough, Holcomb, 56
Scientific Temperance Instruction (STI), 11,
    85; adoption of, by Woman's Christian
    Temperance Union, 85–86; in America's
    public schools, 116; Department of,
    headed by Hunt, Mary H., 88; in Georgia,
    275n43; students enrollment in, 110; in
    Vermont, 275n43
Scott, B., 93
Scott, Willie, 56
Second Baptist Church (Atlanta), 142
Second Great Awakening, 16, 39
Selma, Rome, and Dalton Railroad,
    contracting for convicts, 54
Sessions, H. M., 224
Shacklock, C. L., 45
"We Shall Win," 240
Sherman, William T., 50
Shermantown, 49, **49,** 50, 79–80; housing
    in, 48
Sherwood, Adiel, 29, 158; as founder of
    temperance society in Georgia, 37
Shiloh African Methodist Episcopal Church
    (Atlanta), 85; founding of, 80
Shipherd, John J., 39
*Six Sermons on the Nature, Occasions, Signs,
    Evils, and Remedy of Intemperance*
    (Beecher), 18
Sixth National Convention of Colored People
    (1847), 127
Slater, John, establishment of Slater Fund, 95
Slater Fund, 95
Slaves: intemperance association with,
    128–29; use of alcohol and, 58
Small, Sam, 251; addressing black voters, 165;
    as Atlanta journalist, 159; drinking by,

283n8; on prohibition, 169; speech by,
    164; at Tillman's revival, 209
Smith, E. E., 101
Smith, J. L., subscription to *New York Weekly
    Witness* and *National Temperance Advocate,* 85
Social Gospel movement, 65
Social purity pledges, 276n52
Social reform: in Black Atlanta's lodges,
    139–51; in black public schools, 151
Social sin, concept of, 66
Somers, Robert, 59
Sons of Temperance, 74, 94; call for new
    reform party, 86; establishment of, 20,
    283n6
South Atlanta, demonstration in, on election
    day, 183
South Carolina Conference, Payne, Daniel A.,
    organization of, 79
South Carolina Temperance Society,: Grinke,
    Thomas, as president of, 17
South Church in Andover, 16
Southern Good Templars, 10
The Southern Recorder, 11, 211, 212;
    endorsement of temperance in, 155; of
    Turner, Henry M., 192, 237
The Southern Temperance Magazine, 10
South-View Cemetery, 147
Spalding, R. D., 217
Spelman, Harvey Buel, 88, 96; donation
    of *Primary Temperance Catechisms* and
    Alcohol and Hygiene textbooks *by,* 105–6
Spelman, James J.: distribution of literature by,
    102, 105; as missionary, 101
Spelman, Lucy, 88
Spelman Seminary, 50, 88, 93; adoption of
    first temperance textbook, 88; dorms
    at, 113–14; education at, 115; efforts in
    forming a Band of Hope, 105–6; embrace
    of cult of domesticity by founders, 107;
    establishment of Bands of Hope, 113;
    High School Class of 1888, **165;** Mead,
    Charles H., visits to, 100; motto of, 113;
    prohibition meeting held by, 164
Spirituality of church doctrine, 221, 239
Spirituous liquors, selling of, by drink, 254
Springfield, Massachusetts, prohibition in,
    177

Springfield Baptist Church (Augusta), 135

Stafford, Thomas: saloon ownership by, 178–79; work as porter, 178

Star of the South Lodge, 150

Staunton, Virginia, local option campaign in, 211

Stearns, Charles, 58

Stearns, John N., 251; discussion of intemperance among freed people at special meeting and, 99; editorials of, 106; endorsement of Prohibition Party by, 263*n*42; Independent Order of Good Templars hosting of, 142; as leader of National Temperance Society and Publication House, 43, 94, 96, 190; as organizer of Chicago convention, 86; prohibition and, 112, 199–200

Stephens, Robert, saloon ownership by, 178

Stevens, Lizzie, as president of Women's Christian Temperance Union (WCTU), 159

Stevenson, Lizzie: as missionary, 71; receipt of free shipments of American Tract Society literature by, 71

Stevenson, Robert, saloon ownership by, 178

Stewart, Dianne, 121

Stewart, Eliza "Mother," 251; invitation to Atlanta, 159; organization of Atlanta's white temperance movement by, 156–57; organization of Women's Christian Temperance Union (WCTU) in Georgia, 159

Storrs, Henry M., 73

Storrs School: Mead, Charles H., visits to, 100; opening of, 73, **74,** 107; pushing of Vanguard chapters by, 75; sponsorship of extracurricular temperance organizations, 110; Stearns, J. (John) N., visit to, 94; taking of Stewart, Eliza, to, 159; temperance meeting at, 82–83, 119; Young Woman's Christian Temperance Union and, 110

Strieby, Michael E., 99, 251; as American Missionary Association Corresponding Secretary, 39, 66, 96, 98; speeches and writings of, 268*n*43

Summer Hill School, 49, 73

Sumner, Charles, 62; caning of, by Brooks, Preston, 62

Sunday School Advocate, publishing extensively of Colman, Julia, in, 112

Sunday School Convention of New Hope Baptist Association (1889), 133

Sunday school literature, temperance stories in, 28

Sweet Auburn, 242–43

Talented tenth principle, 107, 151

Tanner, Benjamin T.: as editor of *African Methodist Episcopal (AME) Church Review,* 166; as editor of *Christian Recorder,* 36; as prohibitionist, 166

Tanyard Bottom, 50

Tappan, Lewis, as abolitionist, 38

Tate, James, 66; school operated by, 72

Taxes, rejection of state prohibition, 213

Teetotalism, 9, 36, 127; connection between abolitionism, perfectionist theology, and, 259*n*13

Temperance, 9; African Methodist Episcopal Church and, 32, 79–81, 120; American Missionary Association commitment to, 66; Bible study in defining, 16; in Black Atlanta, 4, 129–37; church polity and, 134–37; distinction between prohibition and, 9; as element of Christian republicanism, 29–32; evangelical reform nexus roots of, 15–44; fifth national convention, at Saratoga Springs, New York, 42–43; First Congregational Church and, 75–79; in freed people's schools, 72–75; as long lasting reform movement, 4; meetings on, 21–22; methodological and personal connections between revivalism and, 24; mutual aid societies and, 147, 149; nexus/missionary organizations of post-emancipation Black Atlanta and, 32–44; Northern Missionary schools and, 107–16; parallel fraternal societies and, 149–51; preaching of first sermon, 15; prohibition as political expression of, 154; publications on, 18, 26, 67–72; religion and rise of organized, 16–21; revivalism and, 6, 21–23, 27–29; white Masons in defining, 282*n*62

The Temperance Advocate, 10

Temperance-as-prelude-to-revival
  phenomenon, 26

Temperance-based moral community, Black
  Atlanta's efforts to institutionalize, 119–53

Temperance Lesson Book (Richardson),
  110–11

Temperance lodges, 10

Temperance Mutual Benefit Association of
  Philadelphia, 149

Temperance newspapers, call for political
  party committed to national prohibition,
  86

*The Temperance Reformation Connected with
  the Revival of Religion and the Introduction
  of the Millennium* (Kirk), 26

Temperance Tract for the Freedmen
  (publication), 71–72

Temperance Watchman, 157

Temperate Society of Moreau and
  Northumberland, organization of, 17–18

Templars, 141

Tennessee: statewide temperance referendum
  in, 155, 215, 246

Texas: vote on state prohibition in, 155, 215,
  246

Third Baptist Church, 132–33

Third Ward Prohibition Club, 184

Thirkield, Wilbur P., 108, 251; as advisory board
  member, 224; assertions that race relations
  characterized 1887 defeat in Atlanta, 245–
  46; as dean of Clark University's Gammon
  School of Theology, 171

Thompson, W. E., as officer of Kimball House
  Employees Committee, 173

Thornbery, Jerry J., 7

Thornton, John, 123

Thornwell, James Henley, attacks on New
  England revivalist doctrines by, 124

"Three-mile law," temperance and, 158

Thrower, James G., 224, 251; appointment of,
  to superintendent of all True Reformer
  fountains, 142; efforts to reorganize
  lodges into a state Dual Grand Lodge,
  145; establishment of Georgia's first Good
  Templars' lodge by, 145, 159; inviting of
  Stewart, Eliza to Atlanta, 159; organization

of Atlanta's white temperance movement
  by, 156–57; as prohibitionist, 164,
  199–200; wife of, as officer of Women's
  Christian Temperance Union, 159

Tillman, J. L., tent revival of, 209

Tillman, W. H., 93, 136, 287*n*53; attack
  on character of, 182; as pastor of Third
  Baptist, 132–33

Tillory, Julie, 47

Tin Can Alley, 243

Trinity Methodist Episcopal Church, 142,
  159; Lee, J. W., as pastor of, 229

True Reformers: ethical standards of, 144;
  Independent Order of Good Templars
  schism destroying, 145; lodges of, 10, 145,
  282*n*51; organization of, 141, 142

Turnbull, W. T., chairman of Young Men's
  Prohibition Club, 235

Turner, Henry M., 251; abstinence of, 80, 211;
  address from, at building dedication, 147;
  as anti-prohibitionist speaker, 174; belief
  on prohibition and public drunkenness,
  169; call for committee on temperance,
  241; characterization of Conservative
  Citizens Club (CCC) members by, 216;
  as committed teetotaler, 80; as member
  of committee on temperance, 241; as
  member of Prohibition Party of Georgia,
  241; opposition to making issue of black
  policemen, 228; as outspoken temperance
  clergy, 137; praise for McHenry, Jackson,
  197; as preacher of temperance message,
  152; as principled prohibitionist, **138,**
  198, 211–14; on prohibition, 169, 291*n*31;
  prophecy of, 246–47; race relations in
  Atlanta and, 209; *Southern Recorder* of,
  192; speech of, 182–83; on temperance
  vote, 172; vented anger in pages of *Southern
  Recorder,* 237; vote buying and, 171

Tyler, Alice Felt, 5, 21

Uncle Tom's Cabin (Stowe), 18

Underground Railroad, 96; Oberlin as stop
  on, 39

Union Missionary Society, creation of
  American Missionary Association (AMA)
  and, 38

United Kingdom Band of Hope Union, 20
United Order of True Reformers, 133, 141, 142, 144

Van Buren, J. M., 105
Vanguards of Freedom, 74
Vermont, Scientific Temperance Instruction in, 275*n*43
Vigilant law enforcement, educating citizens about need for, 156
The Vindicator (black weekly), 56
Virtue: African Americans assertion of, 127; concept of, 29–32, 125, 126–27, 143; whites' denial of African Americans', 126
Voter registration, temperance and, 185
Votes, buying of, and liquor, 170–71
Vote selling, culturally powerful attacks on, 170–71

Walker, Jerome, 111
Walworth, Reuben, 42
Ware, Edmund A.: as American Missionary Association missionary, 59, 73; as superintendent of schools for Georgia, 73
A Warning to Freedmen against Intoxicating Drinks (Brinckerhoff), 72
Warren, E. W., 142
Washington, George, farewell address of, 30
Washington Post, editorials on prohibition in, 191–92
Wassom, George, 101
Water Lily (publication), 105
Wayman, Alexander, 218; reappointment of Flipper, J. S. by, 218–19
The Way to Bless and Save our Country (Humphrey), 31
"We Are Going to the Polls, Boys," 215
The Weekly Defiance (black newspaper): Burnett, Alonzo, and, 175, 212; "Manhood" editorial in, 172; Pledger, William, as coeditor of, 162
Weekly Sentinel (Augusta): support for prohibition, 193; Wright, Richard, as editor of, 166
Weld, Theodore, temperance sermon of, 29
Wellman, Charles P., recruitment of True Reformers, 282*n*51

Wells-Barnett, Ida, challenge to Women's Christian Temperance Union (WCTU) to oppose lynching, 242
Wesley, John: American Missionary Association adoption of "General Rules of the United Societies of 1739," 134; writings of, 35
Wesleyan Methodist Connection, adoption of American Missionary Association, 38
Western Evangelical Missionary Society, 39, 46; creation of American Missionary Association and, 38
West Point Railroad, 182
Wheat Street Baptist Church, 142; pastors of, 286*n*53
Whipper, William, 127
White Masons, definition of temperance by, 282*n*62
Whittier, John Greenleaf, 84; as abolitionist poet, 25
Wilberforce University, 112; African Methodist Episcopal Church purchase of, 36; Payne, Daniel A., as president of, 79
Willard, Frances, 10, 251; color-line speech of, 190; 1881 tour of the South, 190; organization of Atlanta's white temperance movement by, 156–57; as president of Women's Christian Temperance Union, 88–90; as prohibition speaker, 113; visit to Atlanta by, 160
Williams, Heather Andrea, 72
Wills, David, 134
Wimbish, C. C., 208, 224
Wine producers in Georgia, 198
Wine rooms, 201–2; critics calling for outlawing of, 202; as legal, 198; licenses for, 200; products sold in, 198
Winship, George, as prohibitionist, 163
Witchcraft, charges of, 122
Woman's American Baptist Home Mission Society (WABHMS), 7, 50; educational efforts of, 108; enforcement of temperance position for schools of, 108; New England organization of, 87
Woman's suffrage, Prohibition Party and, 156
Women: 1885 prohibition campaign and, 164–65, 184; 1887 political involvement

with prohibition, 221; influence on husband and/or son to vote for prohibition, 286n52

Women's Christian Temperance Union (WCTU): adoption of Scientific Temperance Instruction (STI) by, 85–86; calling for "colored" temperance conventions, 9; cooperation between Good Templars and, 160; Department of Scientific Temperance Instruction and, 88; Department of Southern Work of, 159, 164; desire for general local option bill, 156; efforts of white women to work with black women, 238; focus of, 6, 7; Howard, David T's wife as active in, 224; organization of, 88, 133, 157; project in Atlanta, 160; rise of, 83; South's first colored, 10; Stevens, Lizzie as president of, 159; Wells-Barnett's, Ida, challenge to, on lynching, 242; as white temperance lodge existence, 10; Willard, Frances E., as president of, 88–90

Women's Crusade (1873–1874, Ohio), 88, 159

Wood, Joseph A., 251; as committed teetotaler, 80; election as worthy master of Pioneer Fountain No. 1, 142; as leader of third temperance society, 147; ordained as elder in 1866, 79; as outspoken temperance clergy, 137; as pastor of Bethel African Methodist Episcopal Church, 62–63; as temperance society president, 81

Wood's Chapel, 79; lending library of, 81

Woodward, C. Vann, thesis, 248

Working-class, anti-prohibitionists appeal to, 219–21

Working-class whites, 242

Working synthesis, 134

World's Temperance Congress, Gaines, Wesley J., address of, 241–42

Wright, Richard R.: as editor of Augusta's *Weekly Sentinel,* 166; on interracial cooperation, 189; at Jones, Sam's revival, 171; "leveling" remark of, 189–90; as prohibitionist, 166

Yacovone, Donald, 5

Yeiser, J. G., 162; attack on character of, 182; campaign for prohibition, 193–94; as pastor of Allen Temple, 145; position of, 182; on vote buying, 171

Yellowstone Kit, 230

Young, Michael P., 5

Young Men's Anti-Prohibition Club: Colville, Fulton, as president of, 219; organization of black chapters, 218

Young Men's Prohibition Club, 161, 168, 226; endorsement of candidates in 1886 election, 212–13; endorsement of prohibitionists for state legislature, 216; Hawthorne, J. B., as eulogizer at, 236; Hightower, Charnell, as white member of, 236; organization of, 224; Pledger, William, endorsement of, 213; Turnbull, W. T., as chairman of, 235

Young People's Christian Endeavor Society, 242

Young Women's Christian Association (YWCA), 110; formation of, at Atlanta Baptist Seminary, 110

Young Women's Christian Temperance Union (WCTU), 165; circulation of *Youth's Temperance Banner,* 110

Youth's Temperance Banner, 94; publishing extensively of Colman, Julia, in, 112; student's library access to, 112

Zion Wesley Institute, establishment of, 95